ルーズ戦記 オールド ボーイ

OLDBOY

publisher
MIKE RICHARDSON

editor
CHRIS WARNER

collection designer
DARIN FABRICK

art director
LIA RIBACCHI

English-language version produced by DARK HORSE MANGA.

OLD BOY Vol. 5

Dark Horse Manga
A division of Dark Horse Comics, Inc.
10956 SE Main Street
Milwaukie OR 97222

darkhorse.com

To find a comics shop in your area, call the Comic Shop Locator Service toll-free at 1-888-266-4226

First edition: April 2007
ISBN-10: 1-59307-714-9
ISBN-13: 978-1-59307-714-3

1 3 5 7 9 10 8 6 4 2
Printed in Canada

OLDBOY

volume 5

story by
GARON TSUCHIYA

art by
NOBUAKI MINEGISHI

translation
KUMAR SIVASUBRAMANIAN

lettering and retouch
MICHAEL DAVID THOMAS

®

DARK HORSE MANGA™

CONTENTS

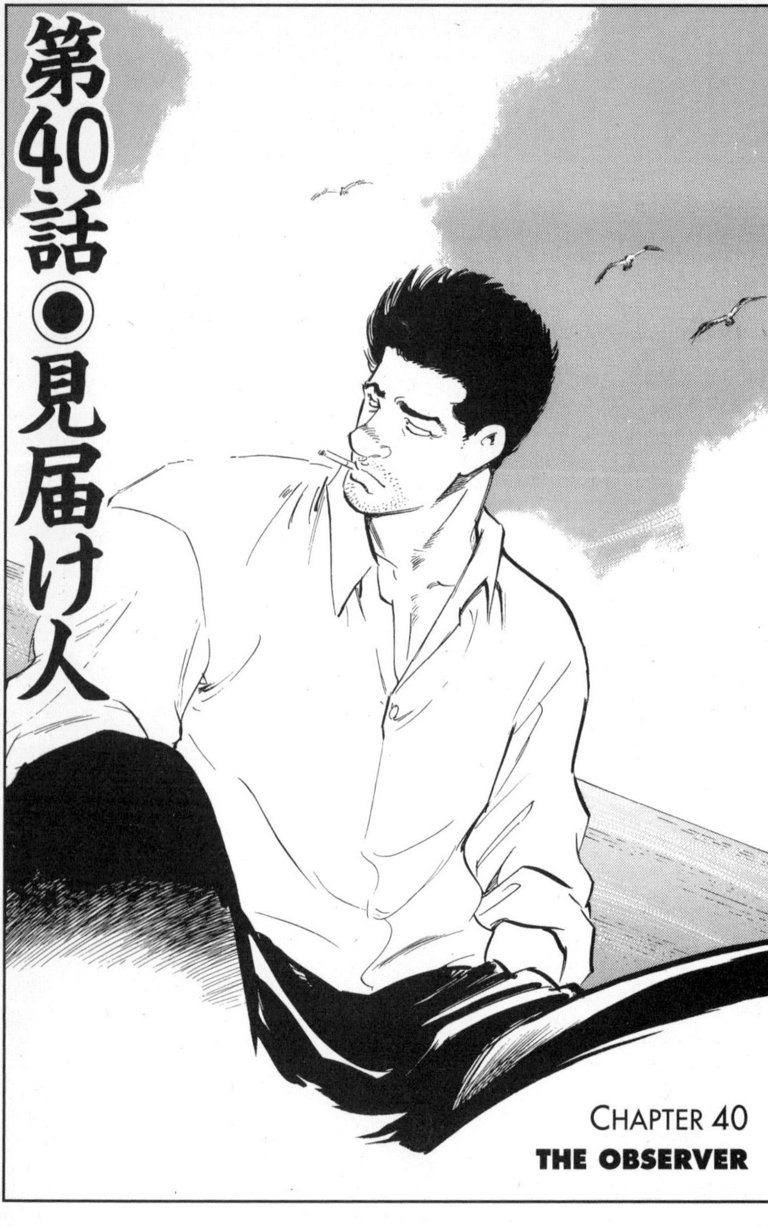
第40話●見届け人
CHAPTER 40
THE OBSERVER

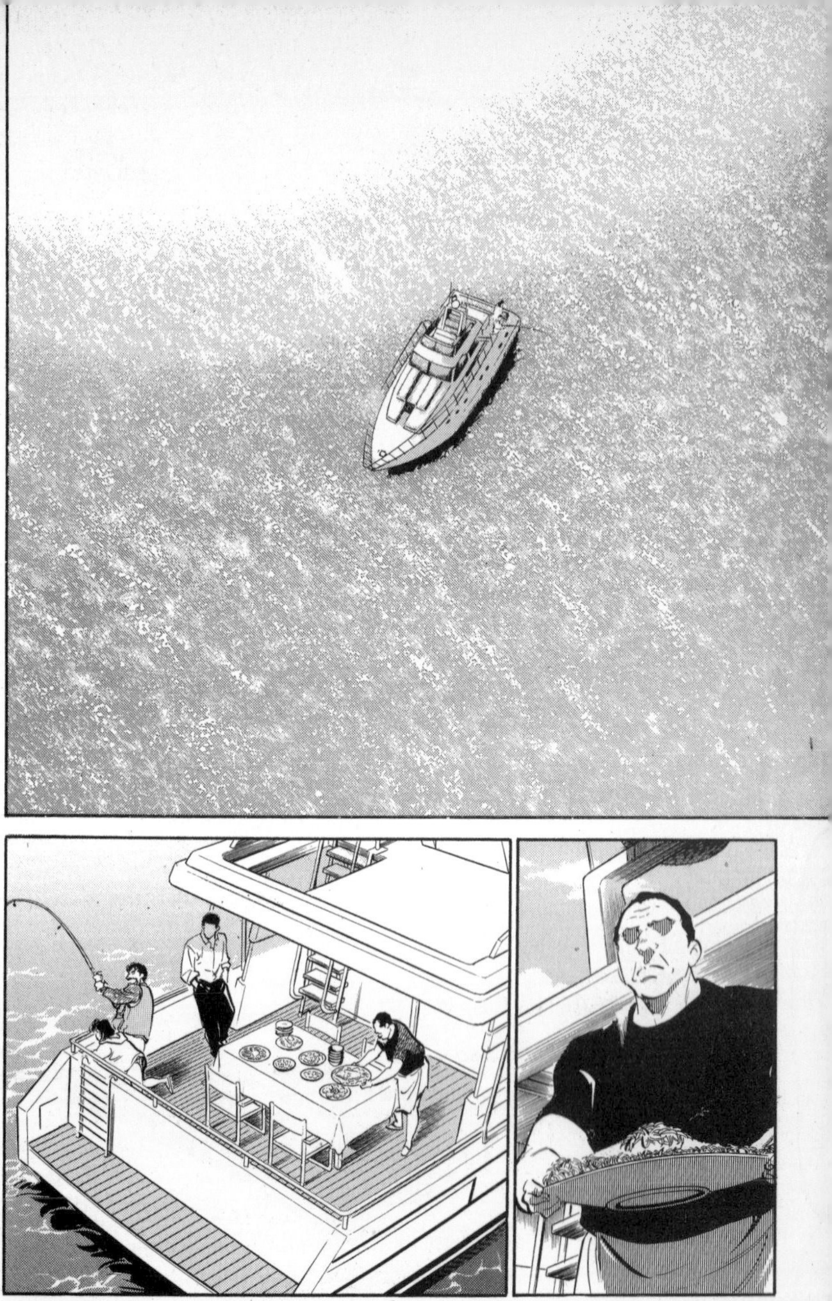

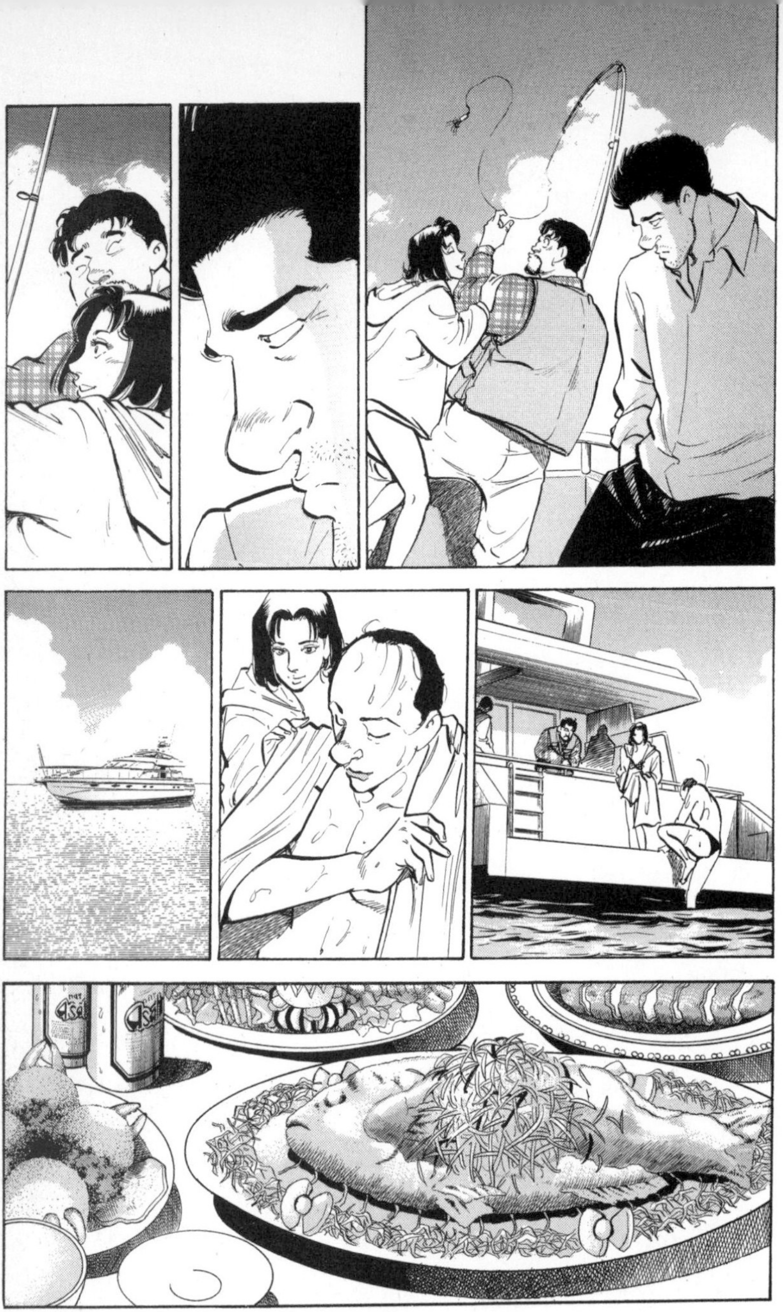

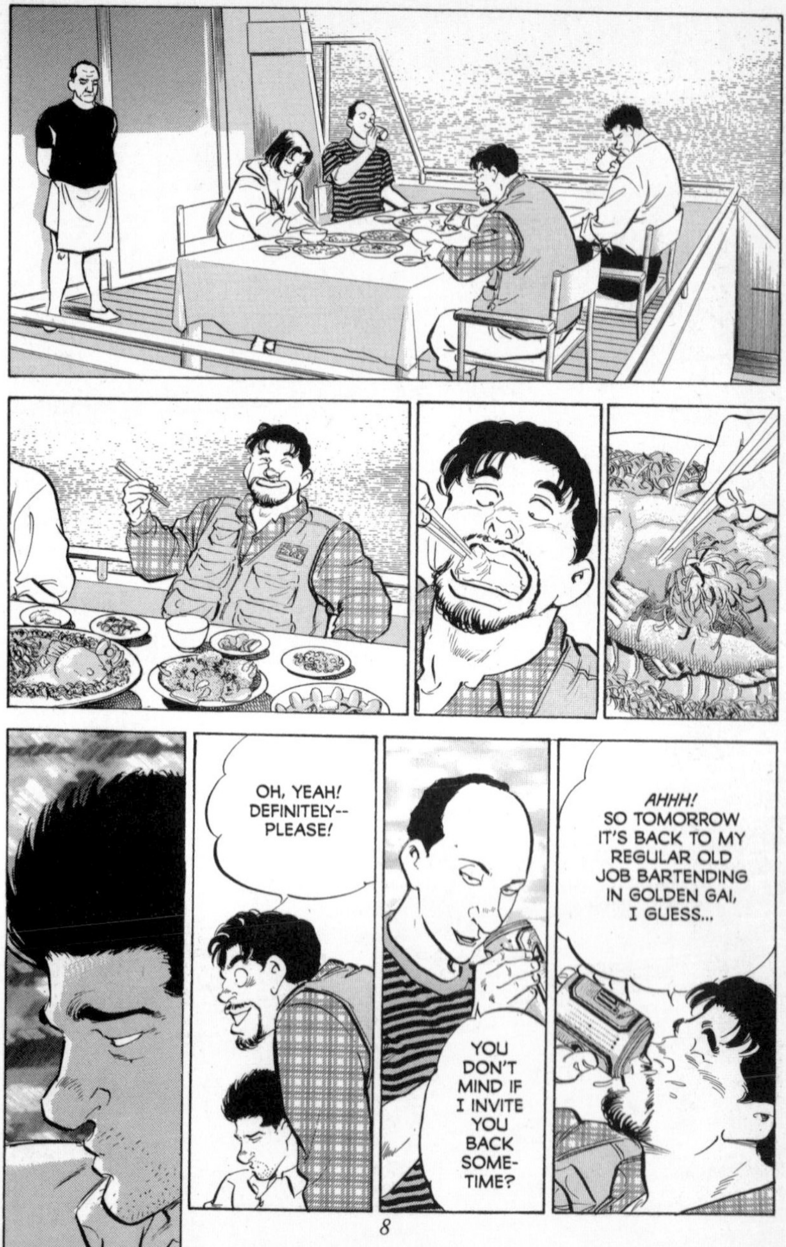

AHHH! SO TOMORROW IT'S BACK TO MY REGULAR OLD JOB BARTENDING IN GOLDEN GAI, I GUESS...
YOU DON'T MIND IF I INVITE YOU BACK SOME-TIME?
OH, YEAH! DEFINITELY-- PLEASE!

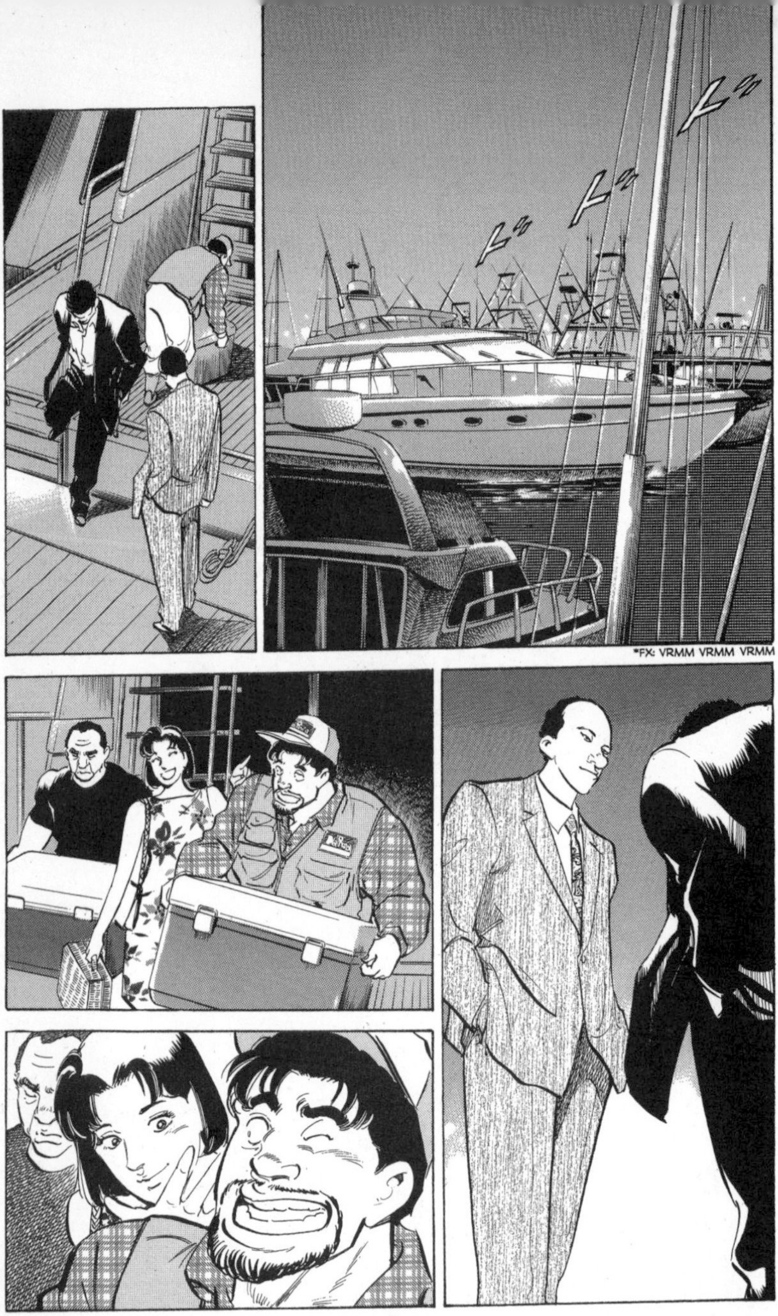
ドッ
ドッ
ドッ
ドッ
*FX: VRMM VRMM VRMM

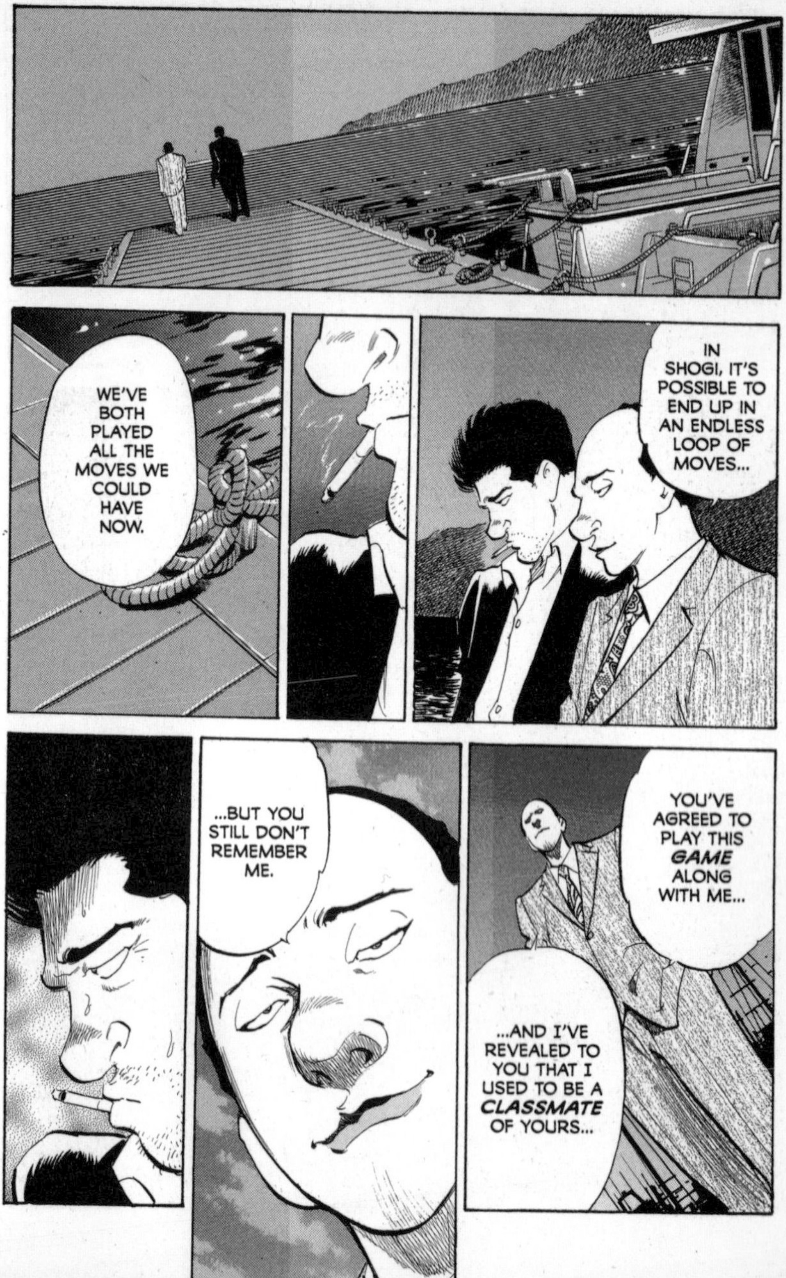
IN SHOGI, IT'S POSSIBLE TO END UP IN AN ENDLESS LOOP OF MOVES...
WE'VE BOTH PLAYED ALL THE MOVES WE COULD HAVE NOW.
YOU'VE AGREED TO PLAY THIS *GAME* ALONG WITH ME...
...AND I'VE REVEALED TO YOU THAT I USED TO BE A *CLASSMATE* OF YOURS...
...BUT YOU STILL DON'T REMEMBER ME.

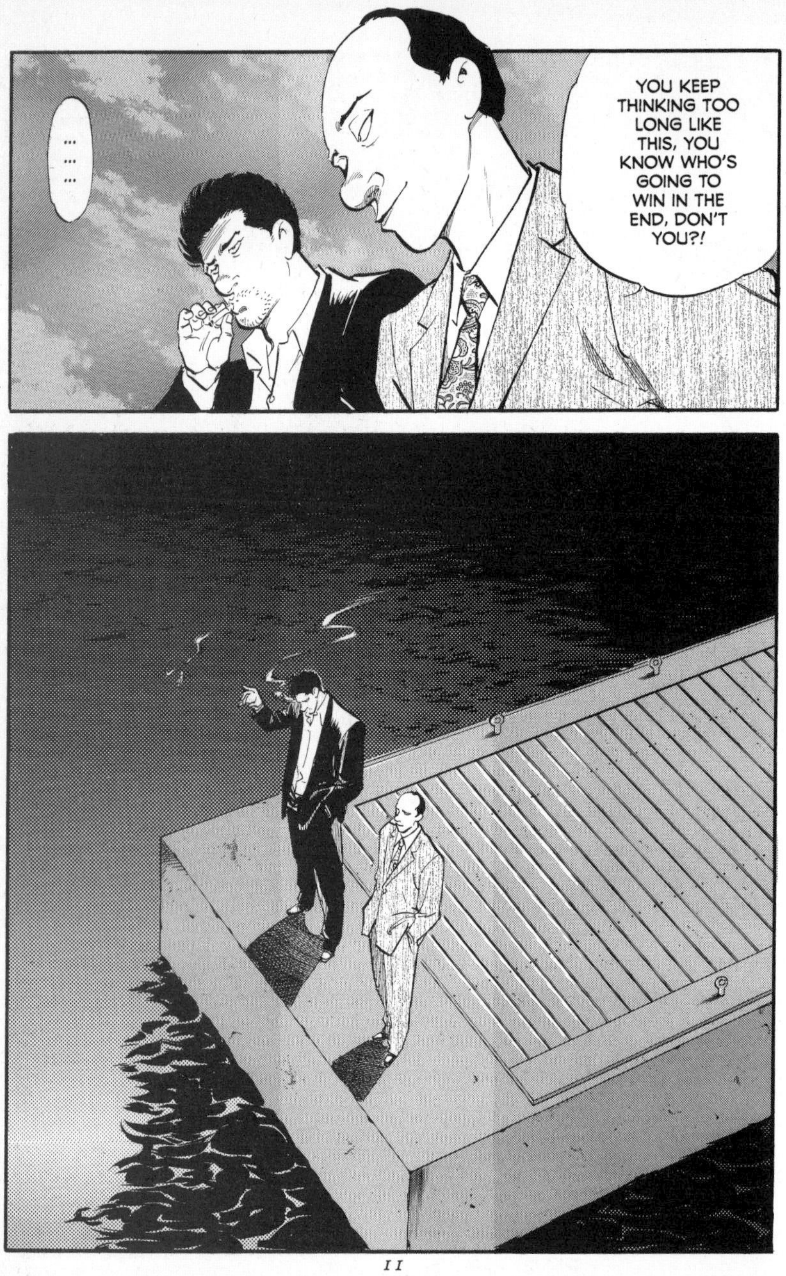
YOU KEEP THINKING TOO LONG LIKE THIS, YOU KNOW WHO'S GOING TO WIN IN THE END, DON'T YOU?!
... ...

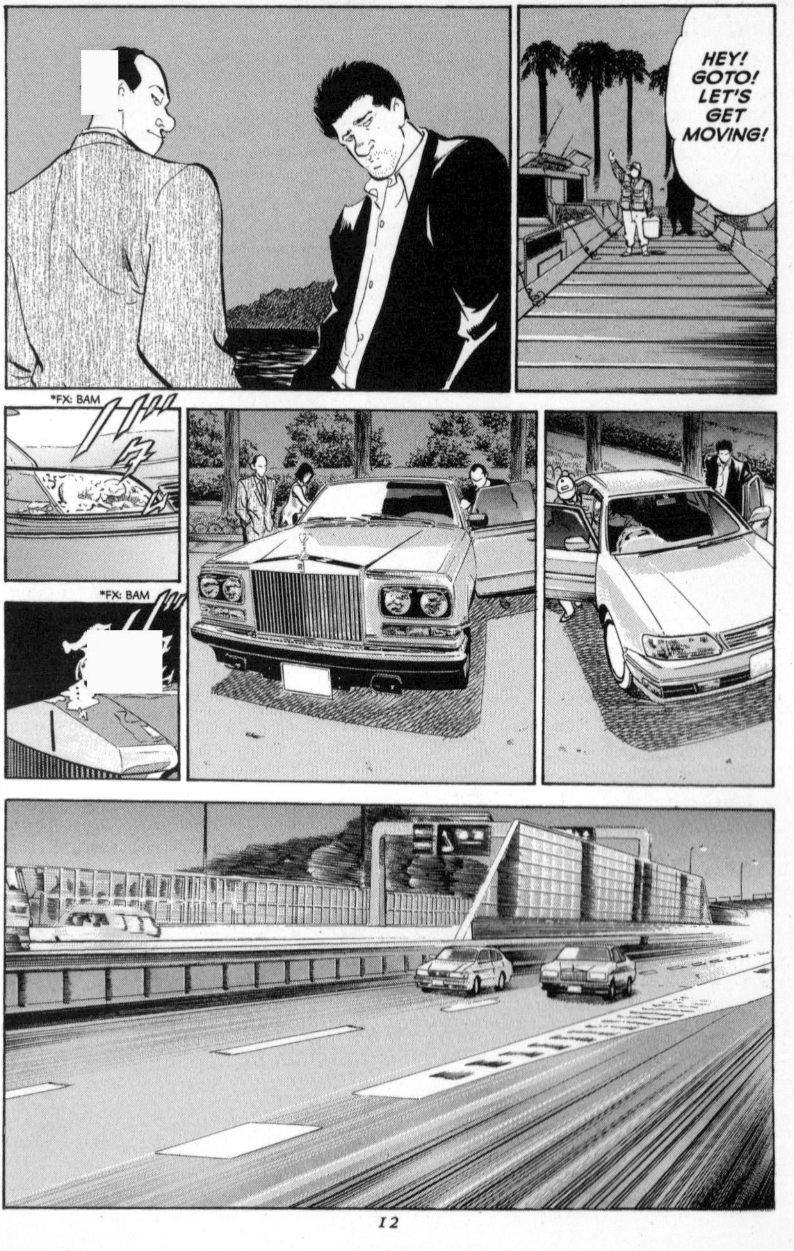
HEY! GOTO! LET'S GET MOVING!
*FX: BAM
*FX: BAM

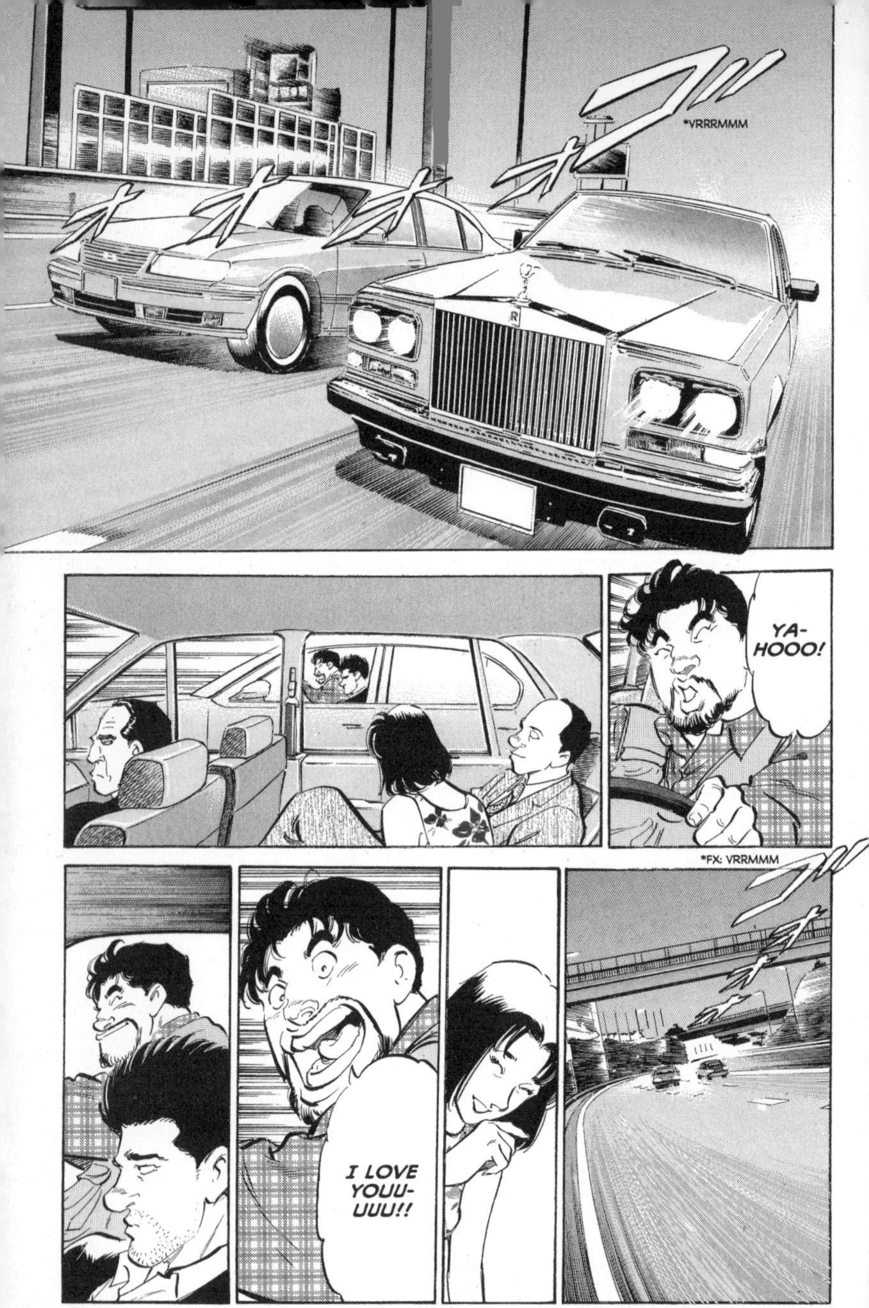
*VRRRMMM
YA-HOOO!
*FX: VRRMMM
I LOVE YOUU-UUU!!

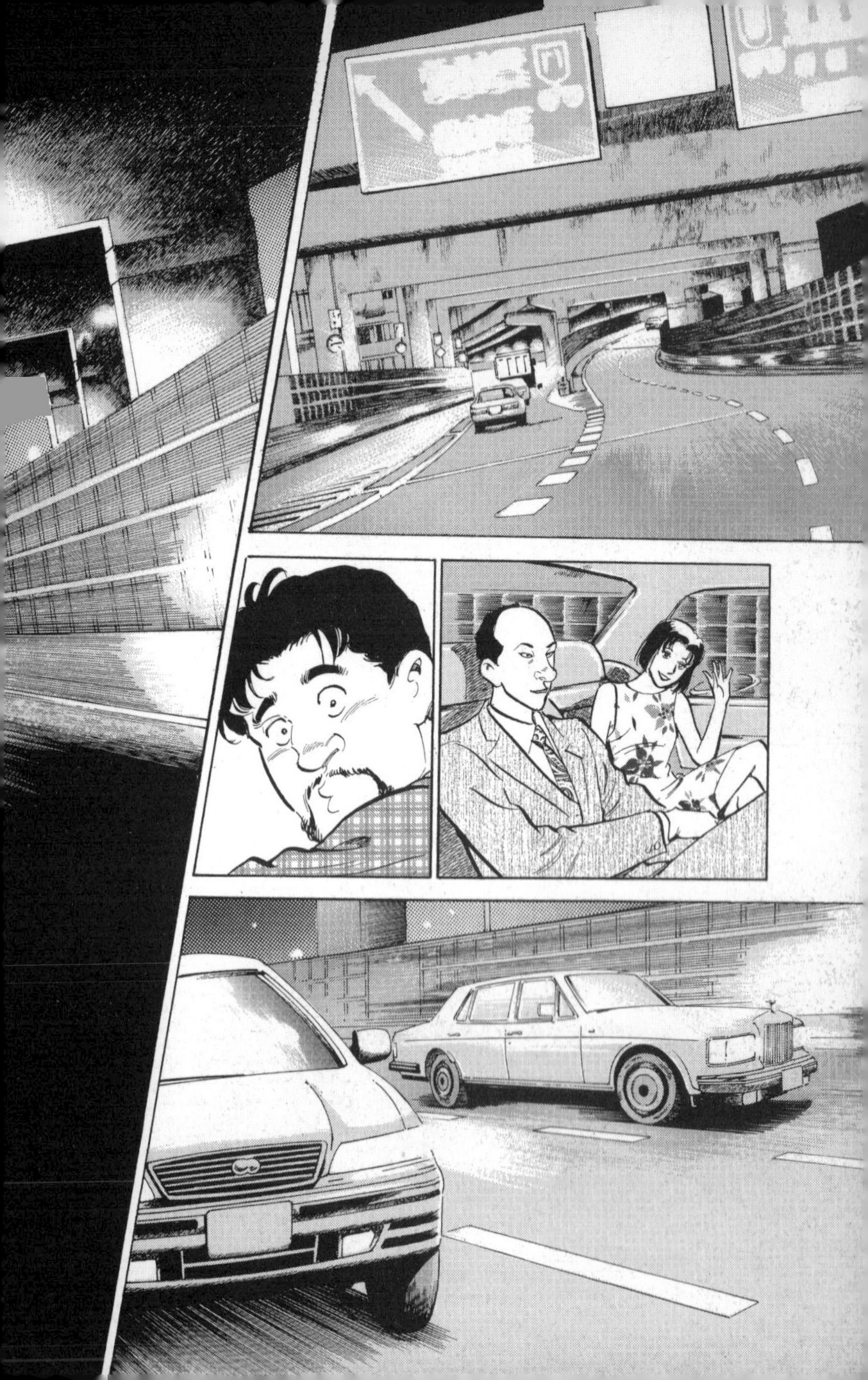

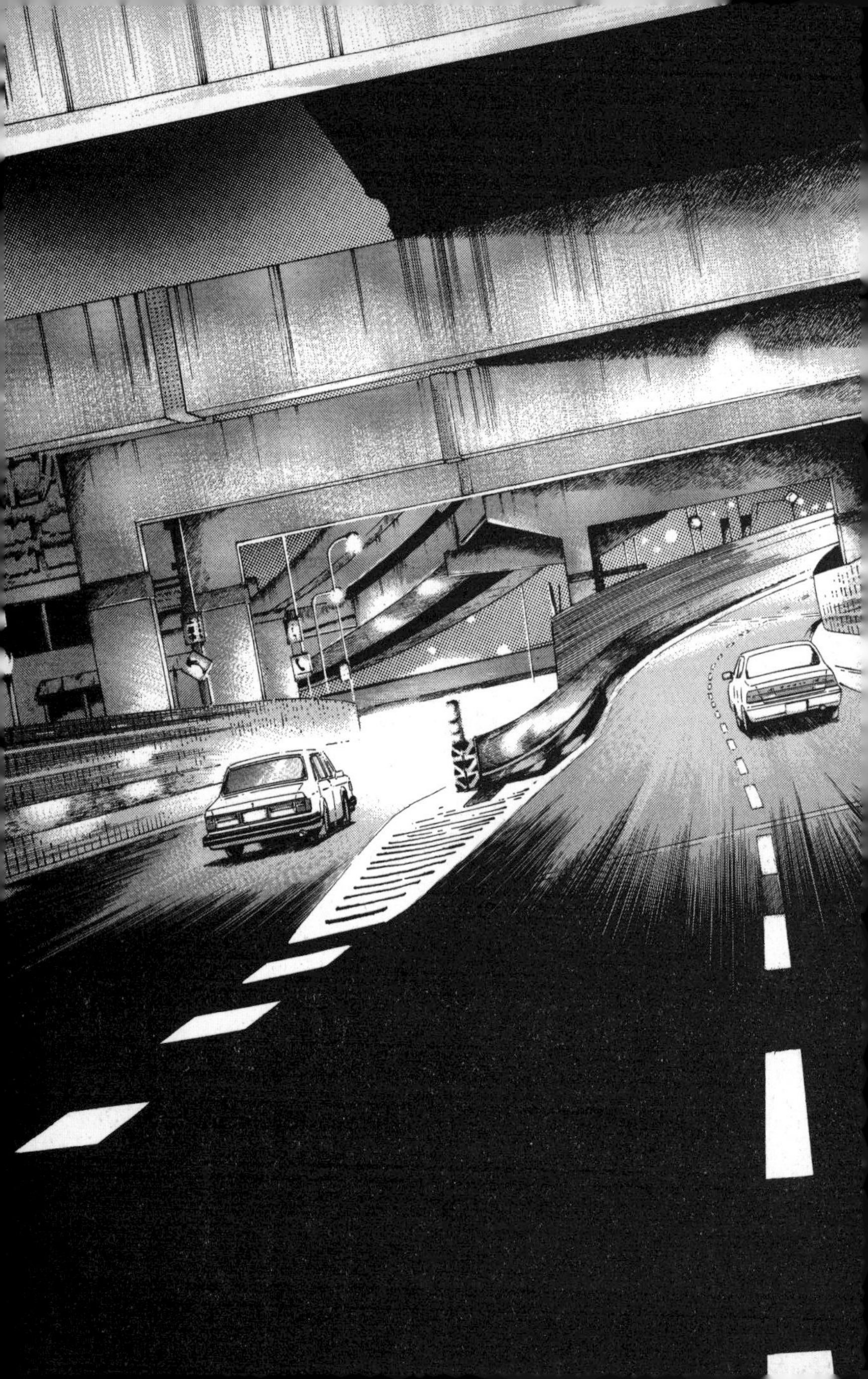

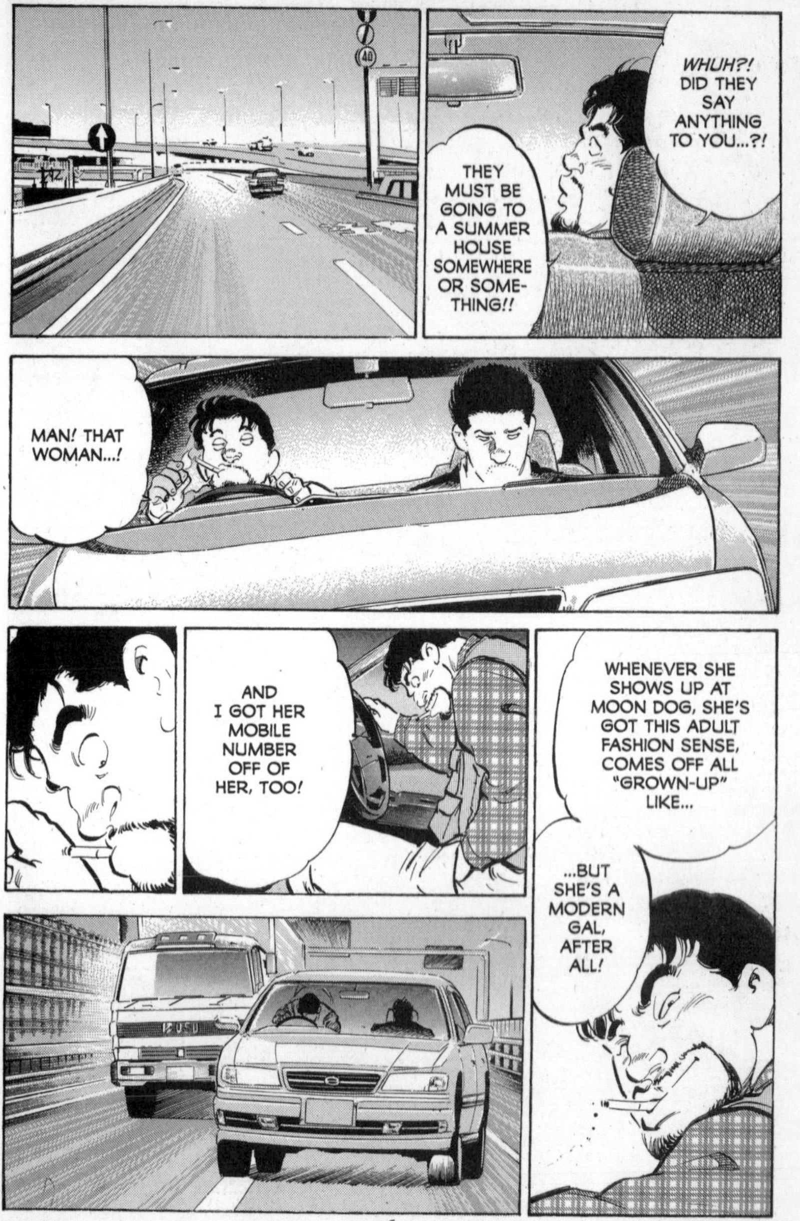
WHUH?! DID THEY SAY ANYTHING TO YOU...?!
THEY MUST BE GOING TO A SUMMER HOUSE SOMEWHERE OR SOME-THING!!
40
MAN! THAT WOMAN...!
WHENEVER SHE SHOWS UP AT MOON DOG, SHE'S GOT THIS ADULT FASHION SENSE, COMES OFF ALL "GROWN-UP" LIKE...
...BUT SHE'S A MODERN GAL, AFTER ALL!
AND I GOT HER MOBILE NUMBER OFF OF HER, TOO!

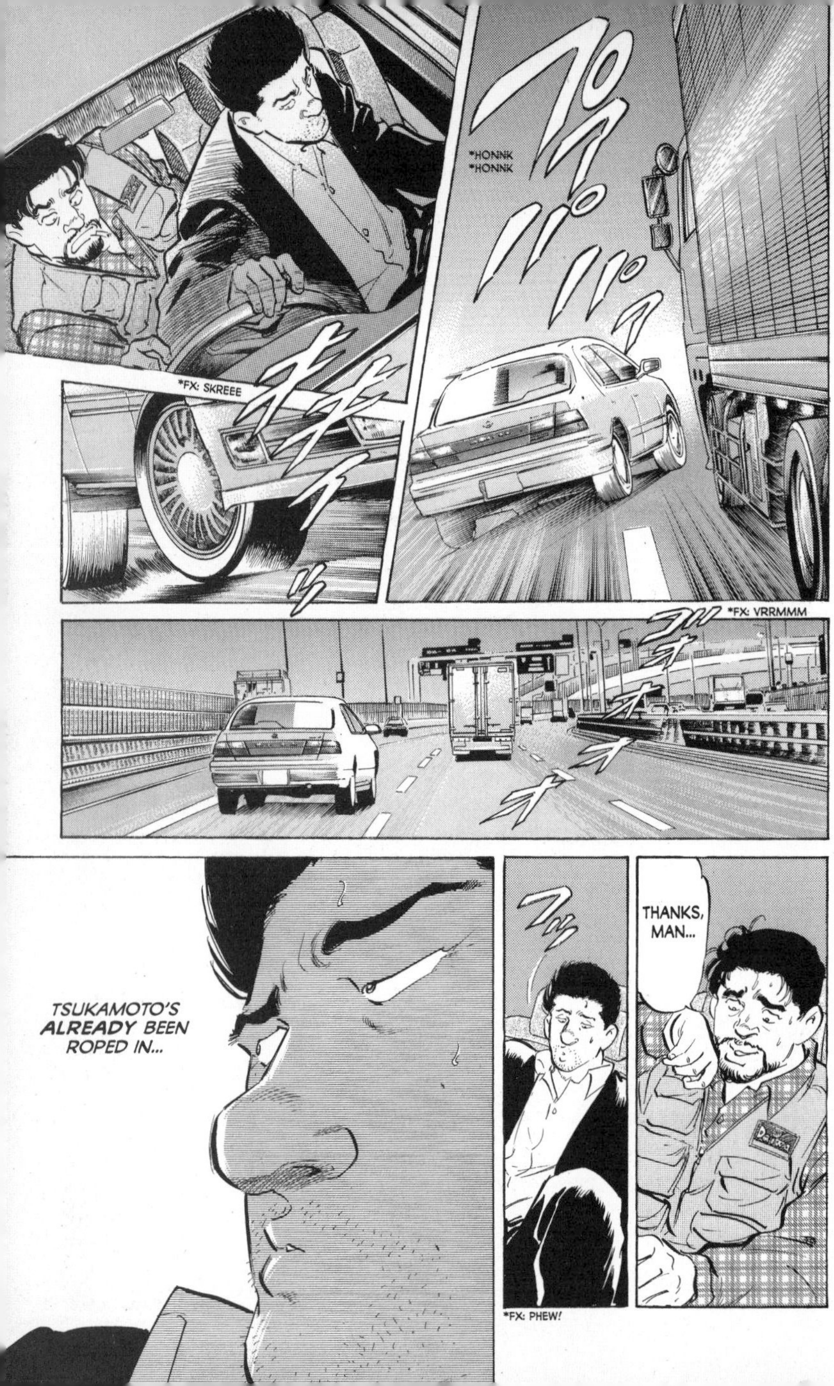
*HONNK
*HONNK
*FX: SKREEE
*FX: VRRMMM
THANKS, MAN...
*FX: PHEW!
TSUKAMOTO'S ALREADY BEEN ROPED IN...

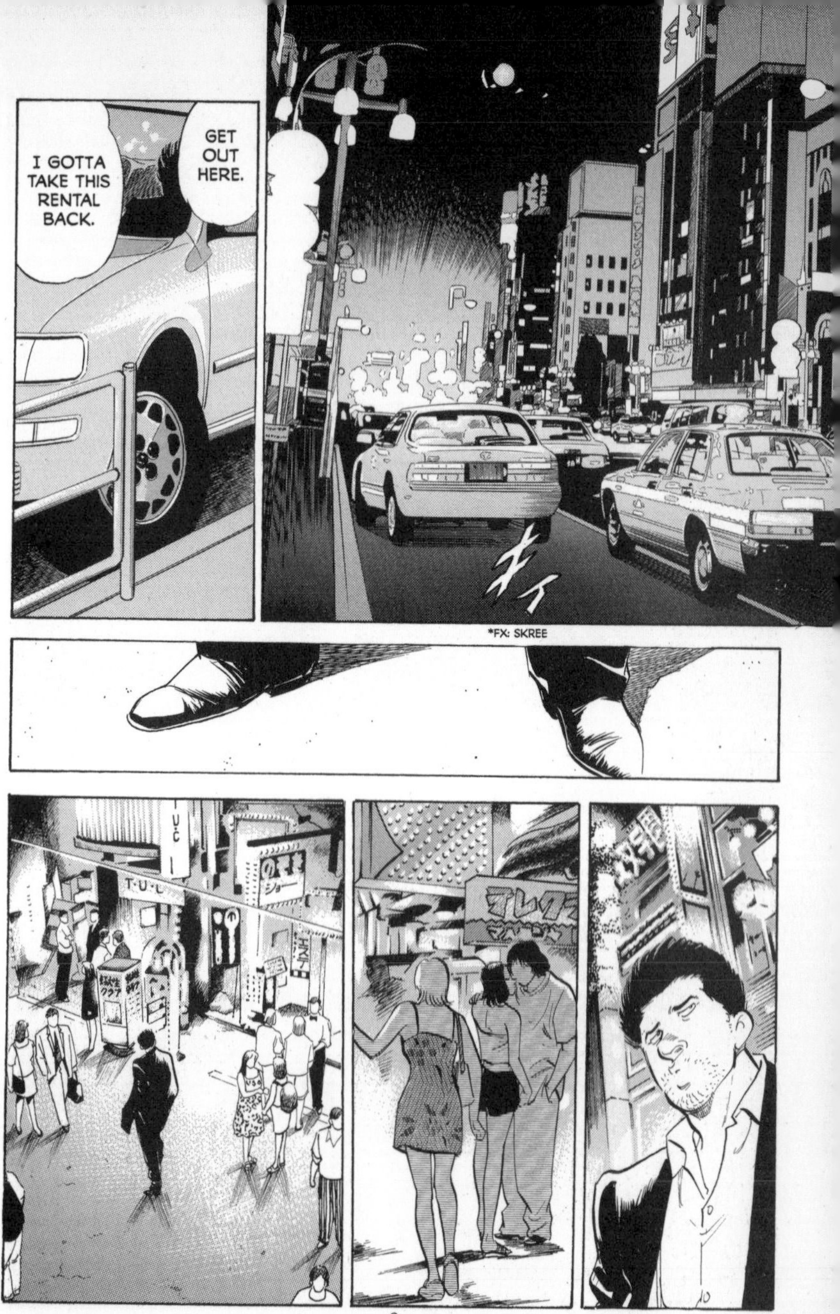
*FX: SKREE
GET OUT HERE.
I GOTTA TAKE THIS RENTAL BACK.

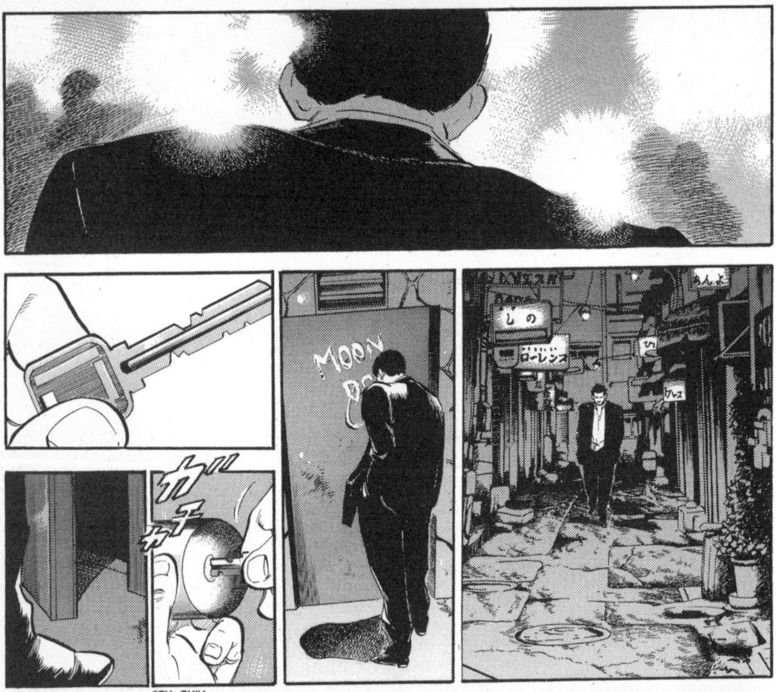
しの
ローレンス
MOON
DO
カチ
*FX: CHIK

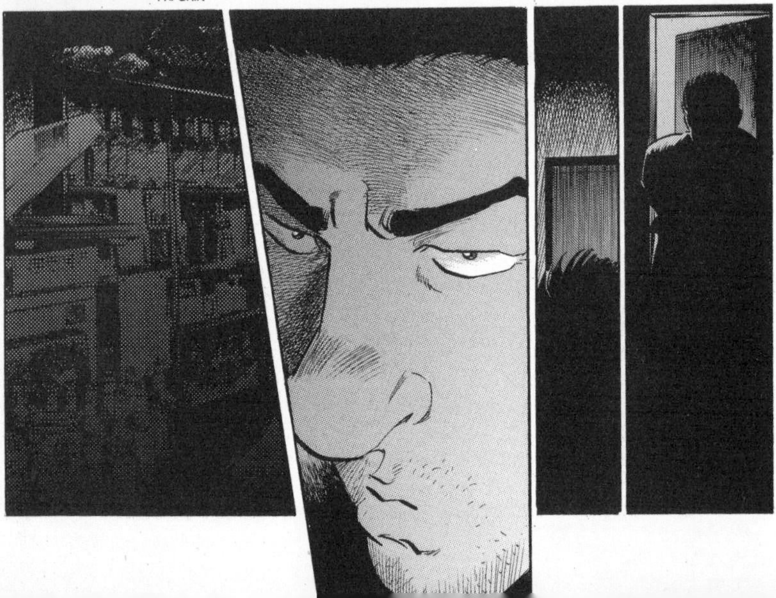

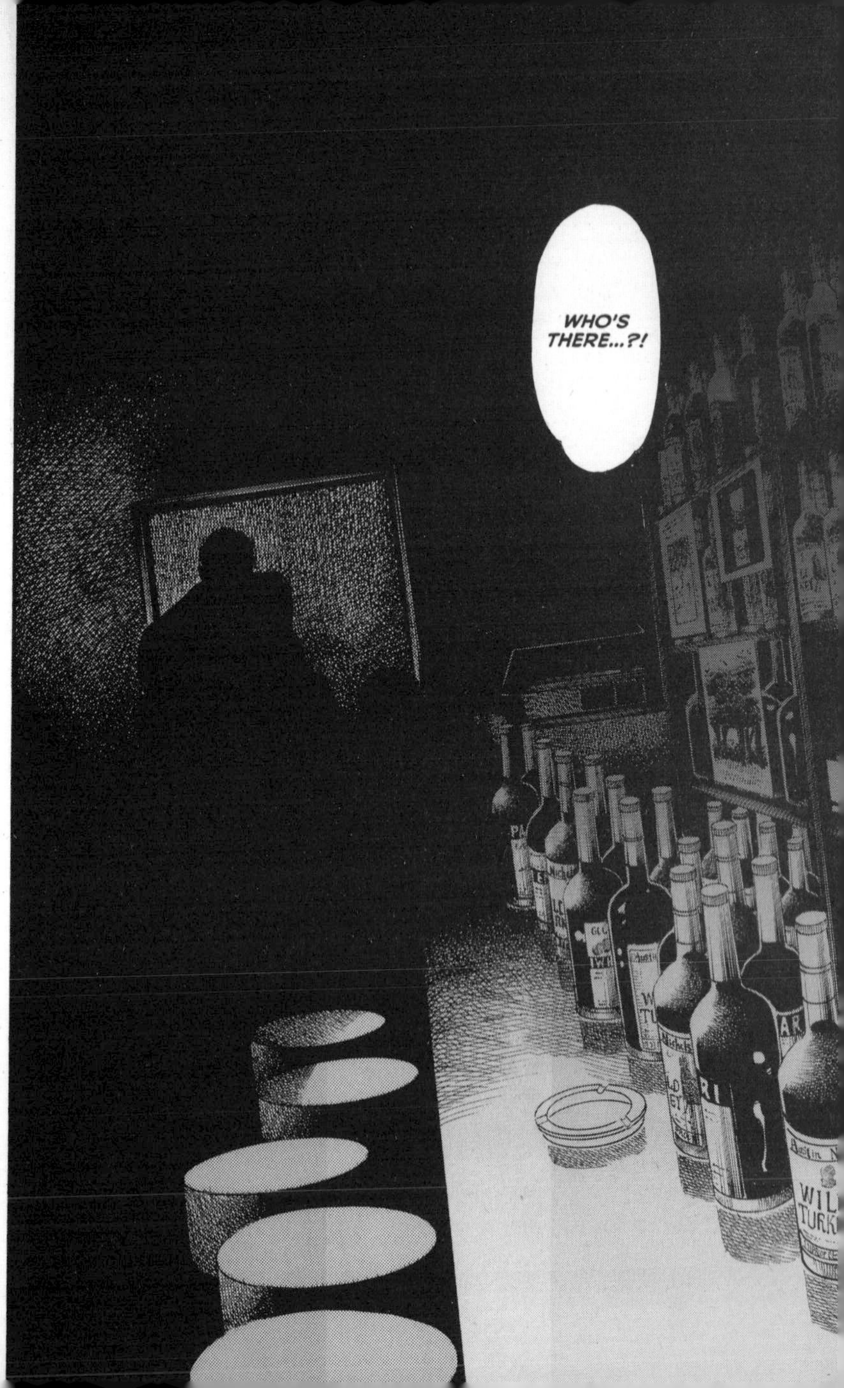
WHO'S THERE...?!

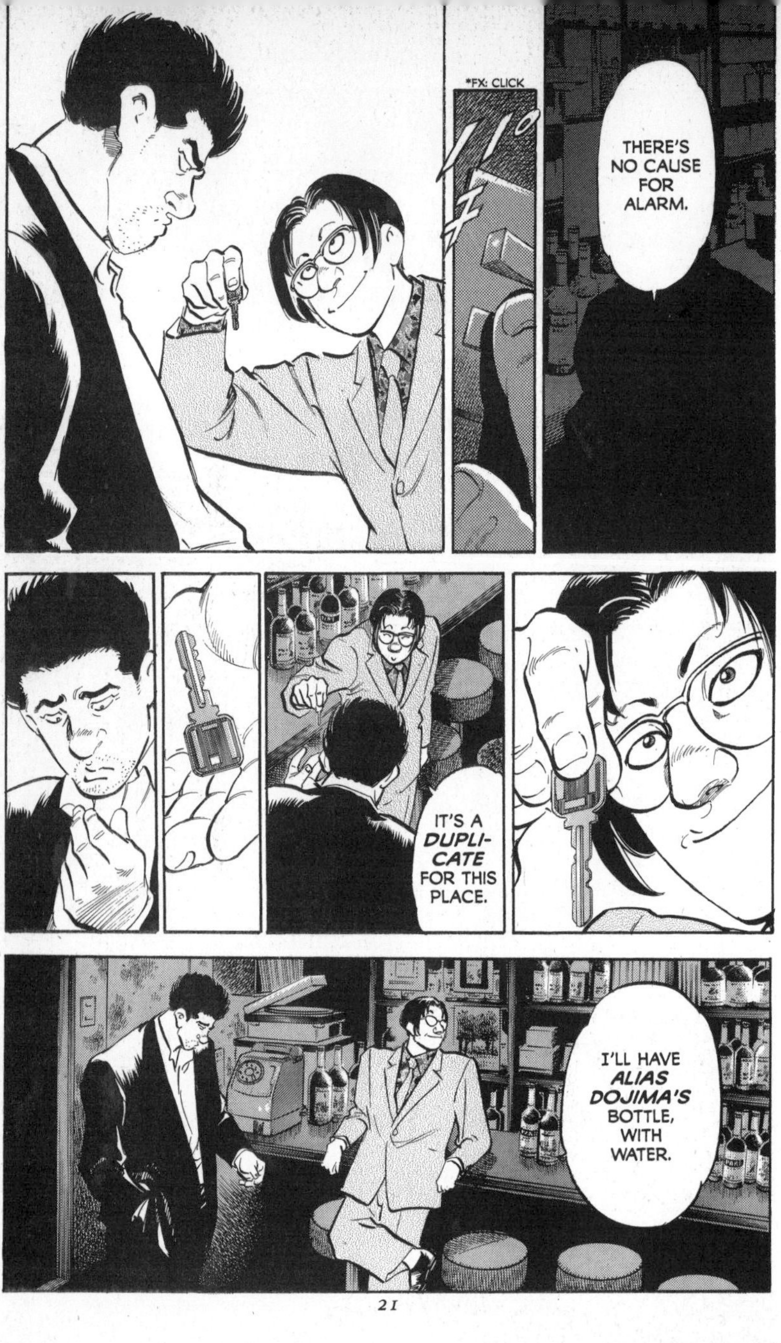
THERE'S NO CAUSE FOR ALARM.
*FX: CLICK
IT'S A *DUPLI-CATE* FOR THIS PLACE.
I'LL HAVE *ALIAS DOJIMA'S* BOTTLE, WITH WATER.

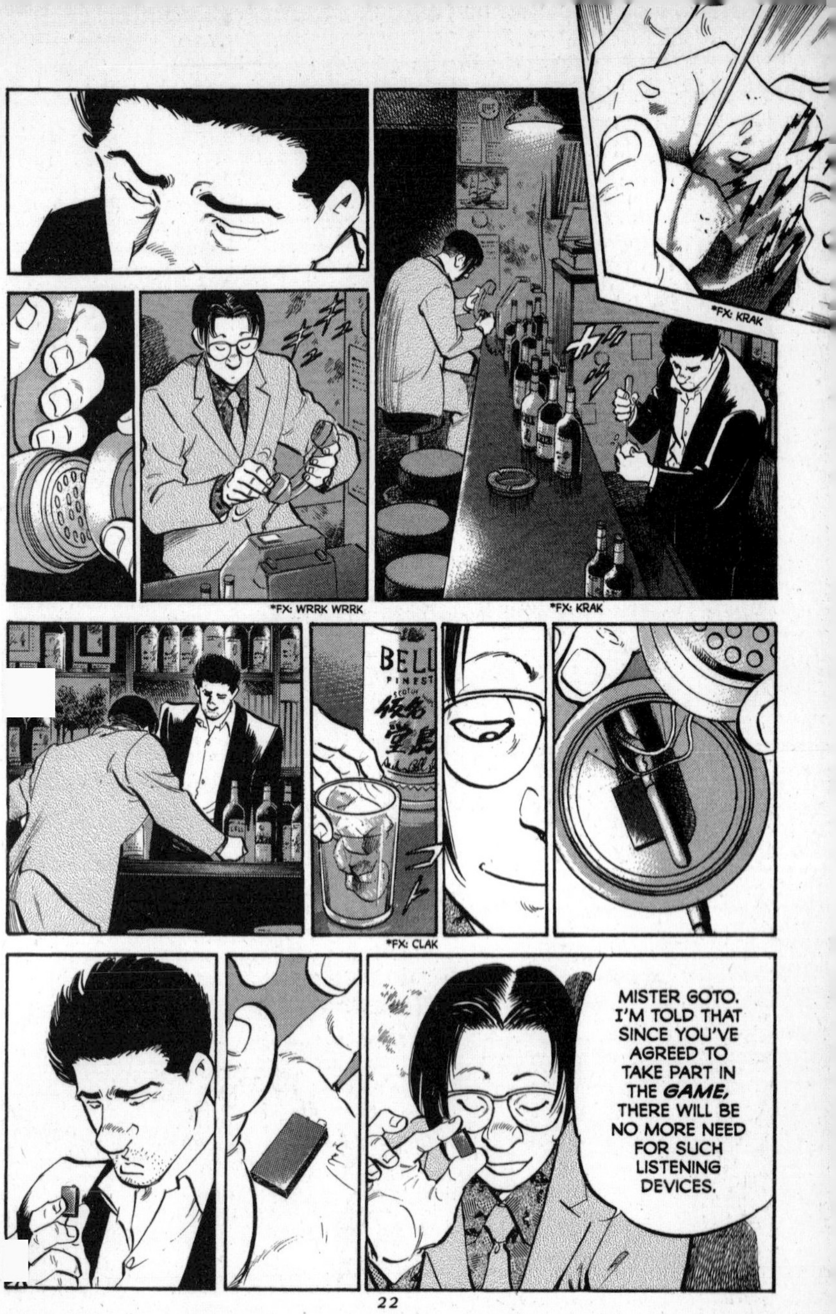
*FX: KRAK
*FX: KRAK
*FX: WRRK WRRK
*FX: CLAK
MISTER GOTO. I'M TOLD THAT SINCE YOU'VE AGREED TO TAKE PART IN THE *GAME,* THERE WILL BE NO MORE NEED FOR SUCH LISTENING DEVICES.

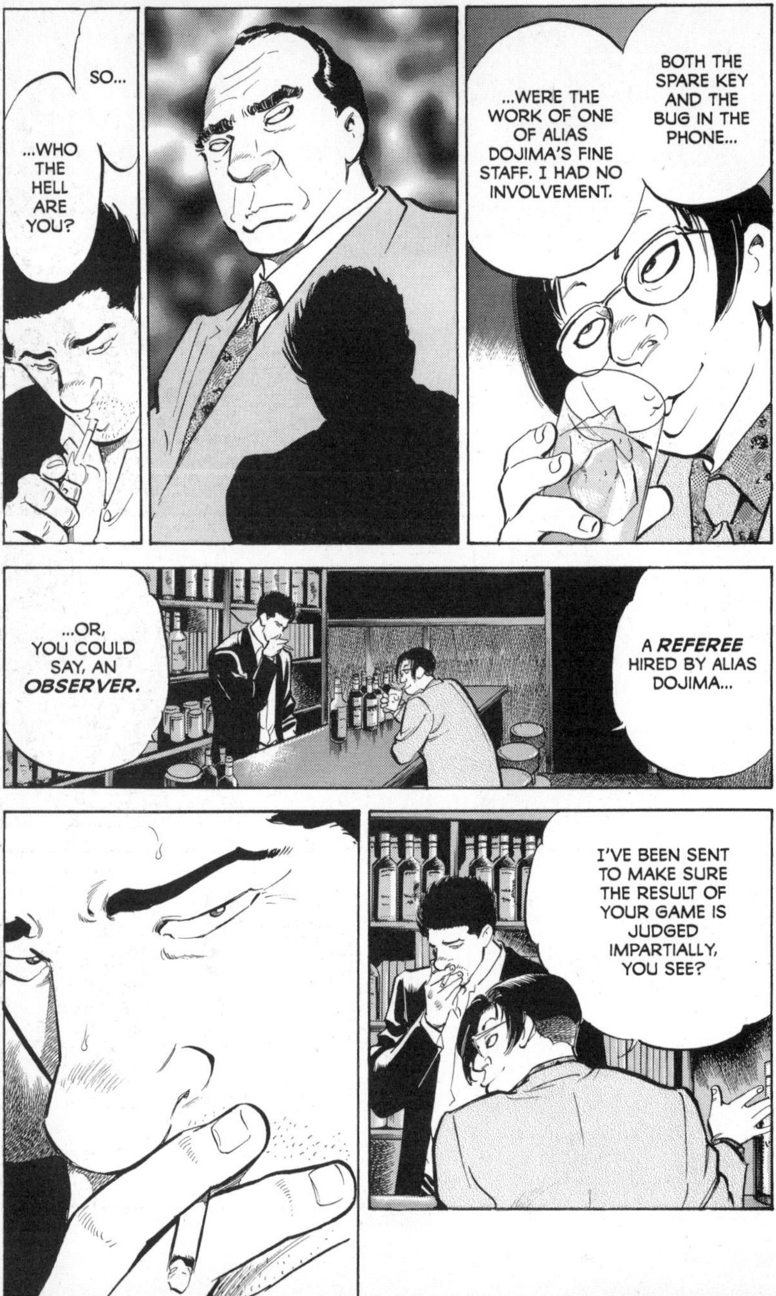
BOTH THE SPARE KEY AND THE BUG IN THE PHONE...
...WERE THE WORK OF ONE OF ALIAS DOJIMA'S FINE STAFF. I HAD NO INVOLVEMENT.
SO...
...WHO THE HELL ARE YOU?
A *REFEREE* HIRED BY ALIAS DOJIMA...
...OR, YOU COULD SAY, AN *OBSERVER.*
I'VE BEEN SENT TO MAKE SURE THE RESULT OF YOUR GAME IS JUDGED IMPARTIALLY, YOU SEE?

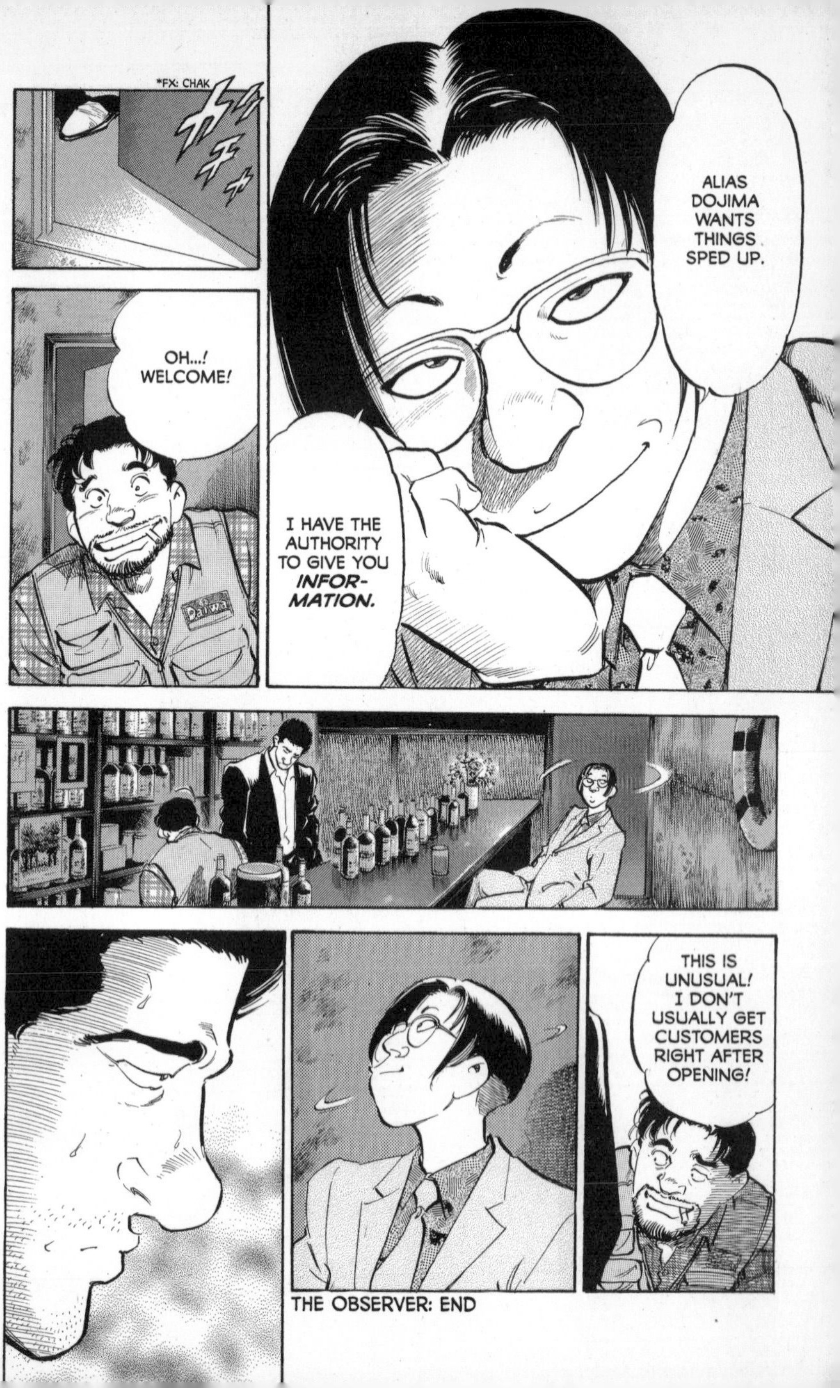
ALIAS DOJIMA WANTS THINGS SPED UP.
I HAVE THE AUTHORITY TO GIVE YOU *INFORMATION.*
*FX: CHAK
OH...! WELCOME!
Daiwa
THIS IS UNUSUAL! I DON'T USUALLY GET CUSTOMERS RIGHT AFTER OPENING!

THE OBSERVER: END

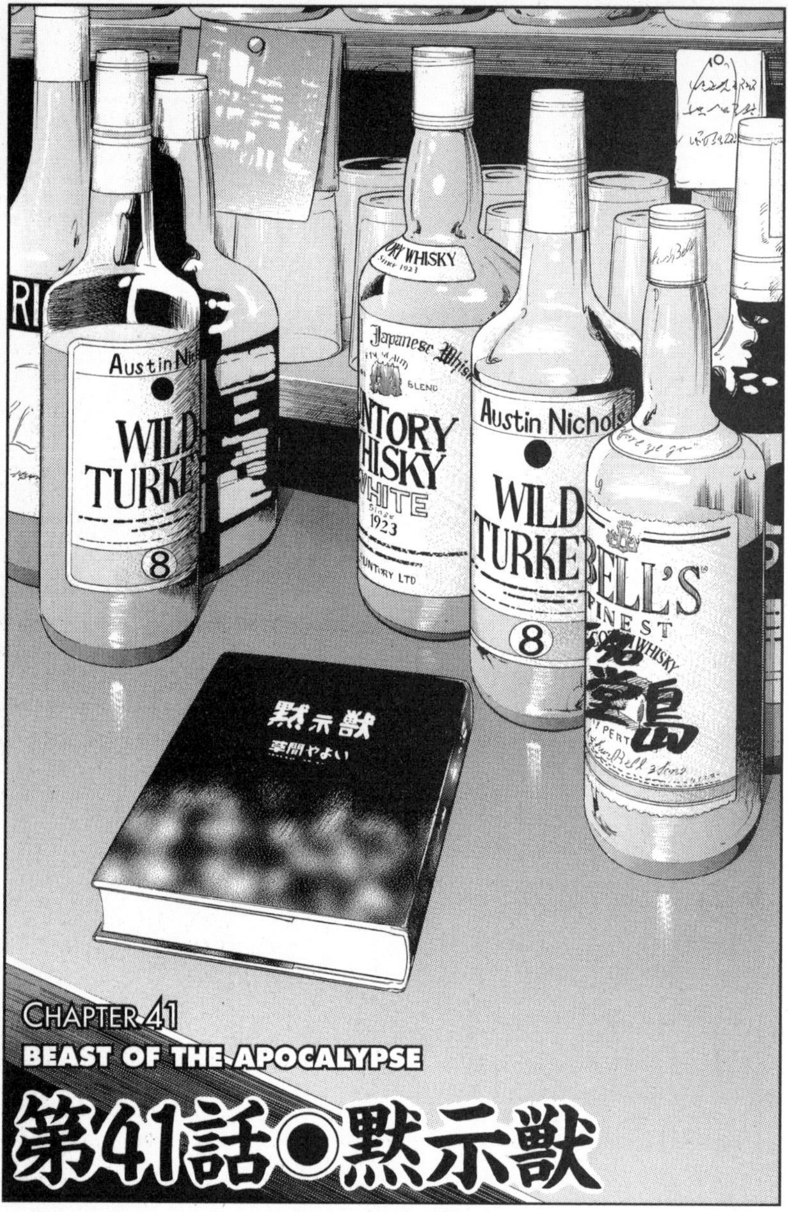
Austin Nichols
WILD TURKEY
8
SUNTORY WHISKY
WHITE
Since 1923
BELL'S
FINEST
黙示獣

CHAPTER 41
BEAST OF THE APOCALYPSE
第41話○黙示獣

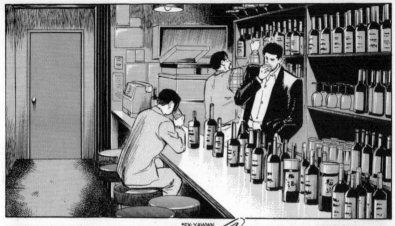

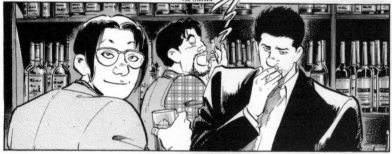

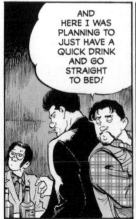

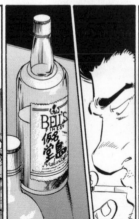

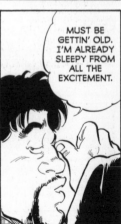

MUST BE GETTIN' OLD. I'M ALREADY SLEEPY FROM ALL THE EXCITEMENT.
BELL'S FINEST
AND HERE I WAS PLANNING TO JUST HAVE A QUICK DRINK AND GO STRAIGHT TO BED!
*FX: YAWWN
*ON LABEL: ALIAS DOJIMA

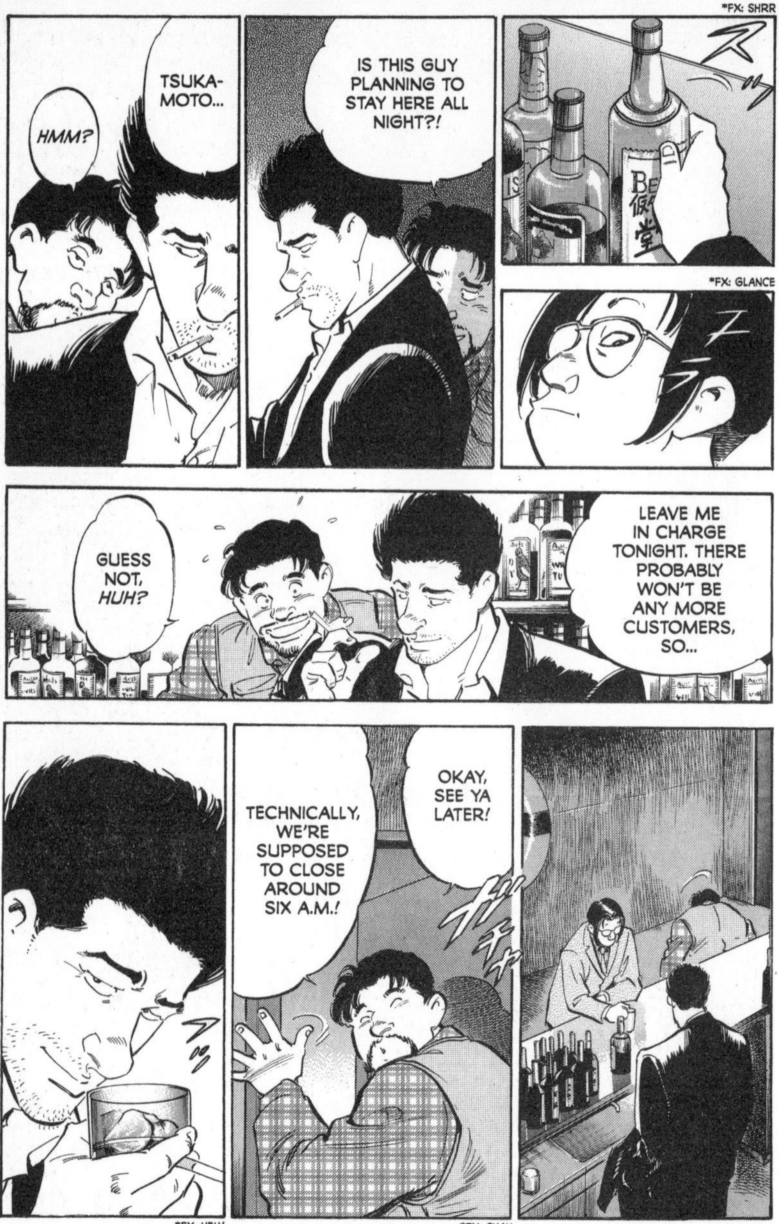
*FX: SHRR
*FX: GLANCE
IS THIS GUY PLANNING TO STAY HERE ALL NIGHT?!
TSUKA-MOTO...
HMM?
LEAVE ME IN CHARGE TONIGHT. THERE PROBABLY WON'T BE ANY MORE CUSTOMERS, SO...
GUESS NOT, HUH?
OKAY, SEE YA LATER!
TECHNICALLY, WE'RE SUPPOSED TO CLOSE AROUND SIX A.M.!
*FX: CHAK
*FX: HEH!

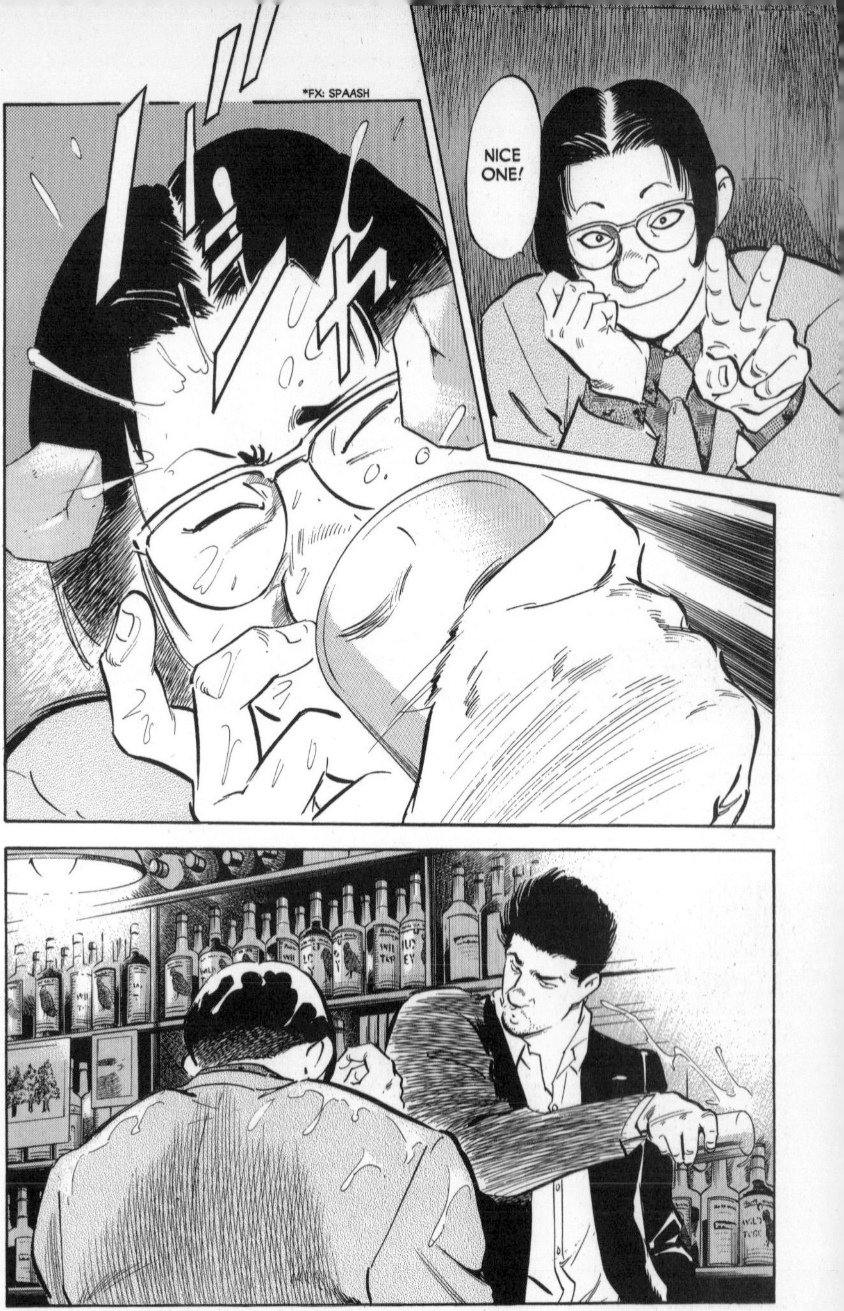
NICE ONE!
*FX: SPAASH

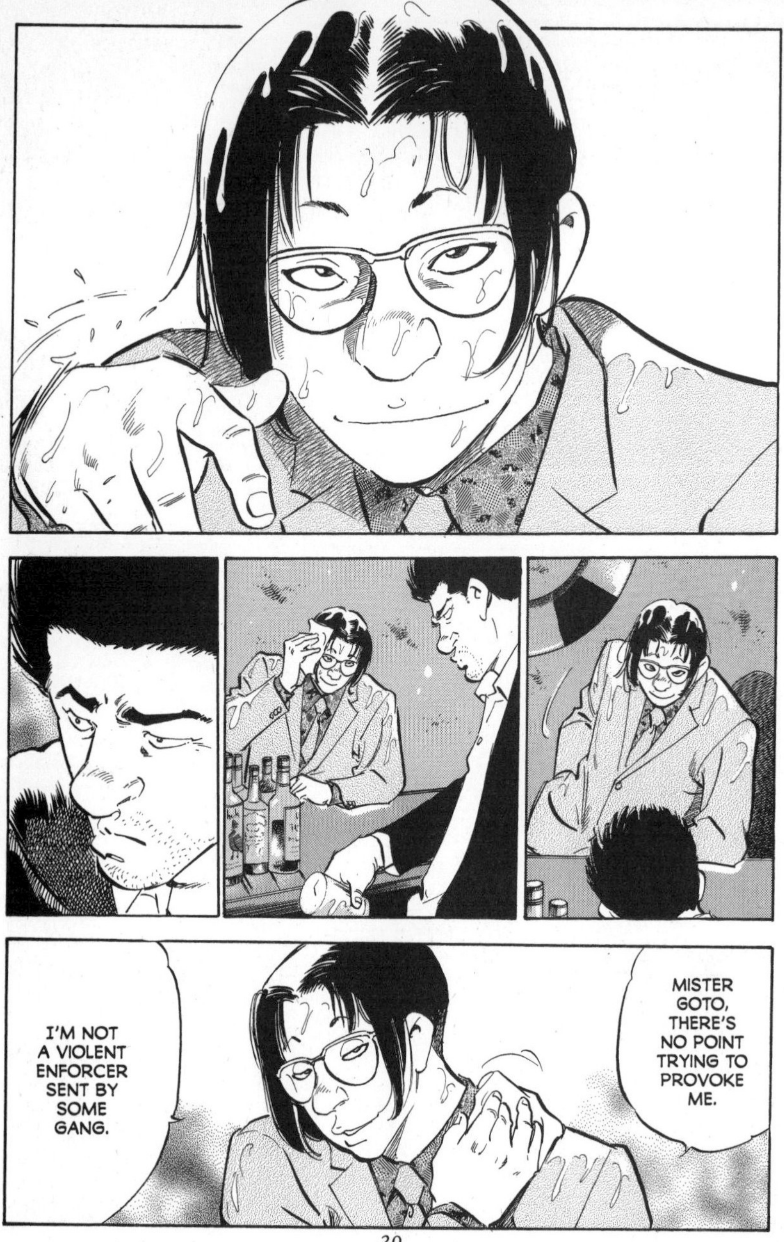
MISTER GOTO, THERE'S NO POINT TRYING TO PROVOKE ME.
I'M NOT A VIOLENT ENFORCER SENT BY SOME GANG.

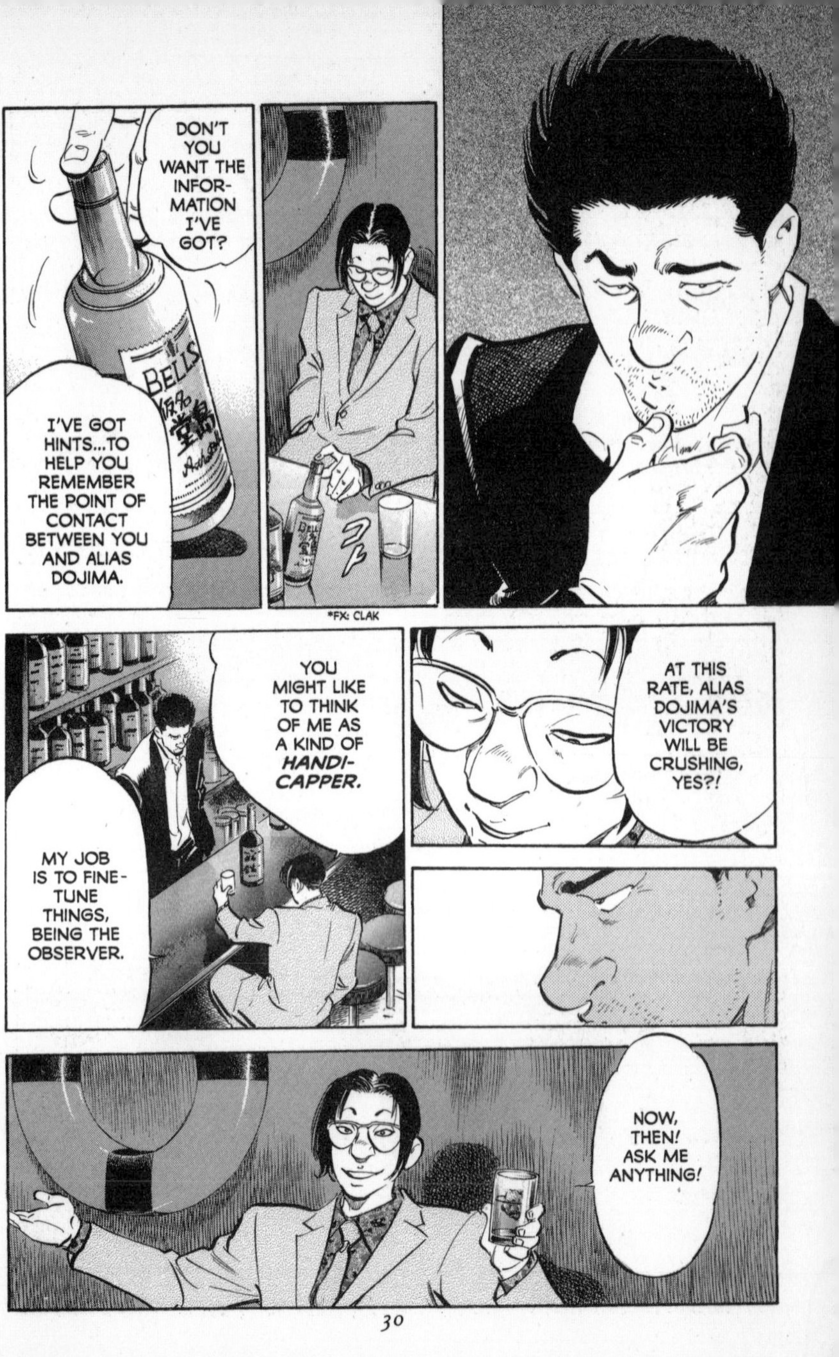
*FX: CLAK
DON'T YOU WANT THE INFORMATION I'VE GOT?
BELLS
I'VE GOT HINTS...TO HELP YOU REMEMBER THE POINT OF CONTACT BETWEEN YOU AND ALIAS DOJIMA.
AT THIS RATE, ALIAS DOJIMA'S VICTORY WILL BE CRUSHING, YES?!
YOU MIGHT LIKE TO THINK OF ME AS A KIND OF ***HANDI-CAPPER.***
MY JOB IS TO FINE-TUNE THINGS, BEING THE OBSERVER.
NOW, THEN! ASK ME ANYTHING!

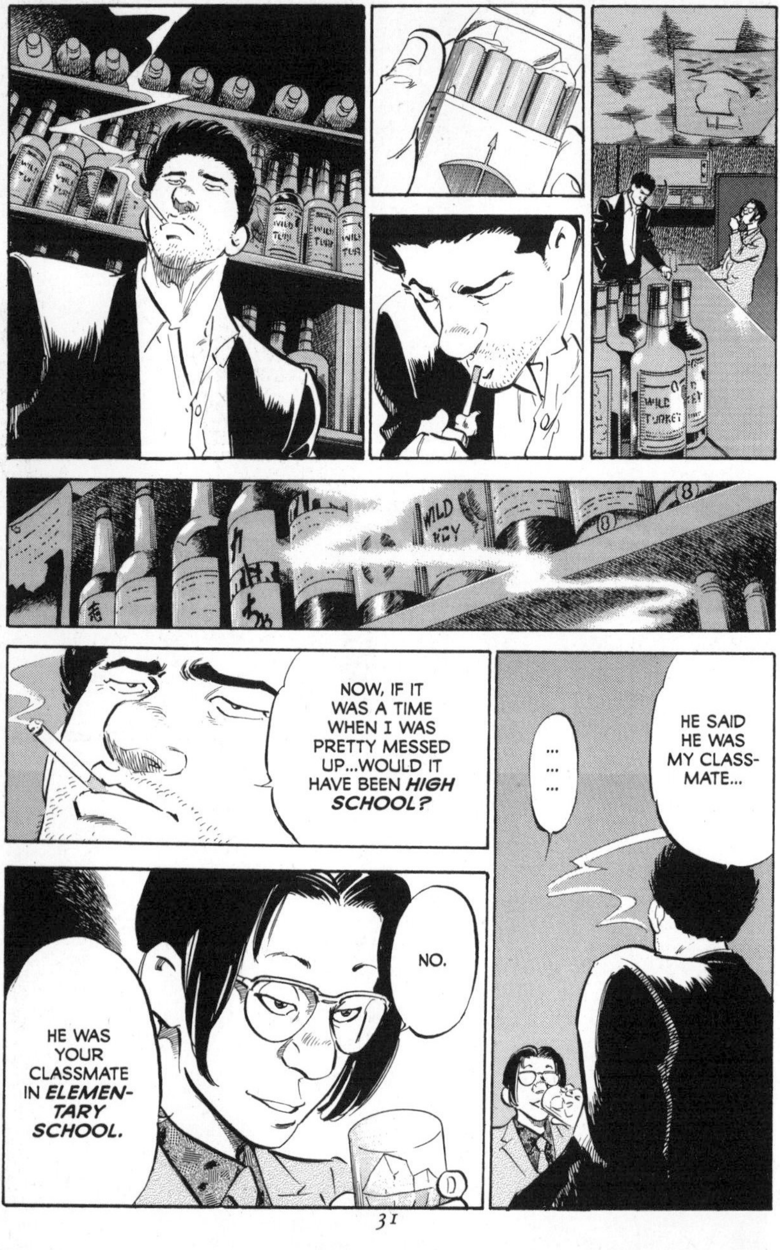
HE SAID HE WAS MY CLASS-MATE...
... ...
NOW, IF IT WAS A TIME WHEN I WAS PRETTY MESSED UP...WOULD IT HAVE BEEN *HIGH SCHOOL?*
NO.
HE WAS YOUR CLASSMATE IN *ELEMEN-TARY SCHOOL.*

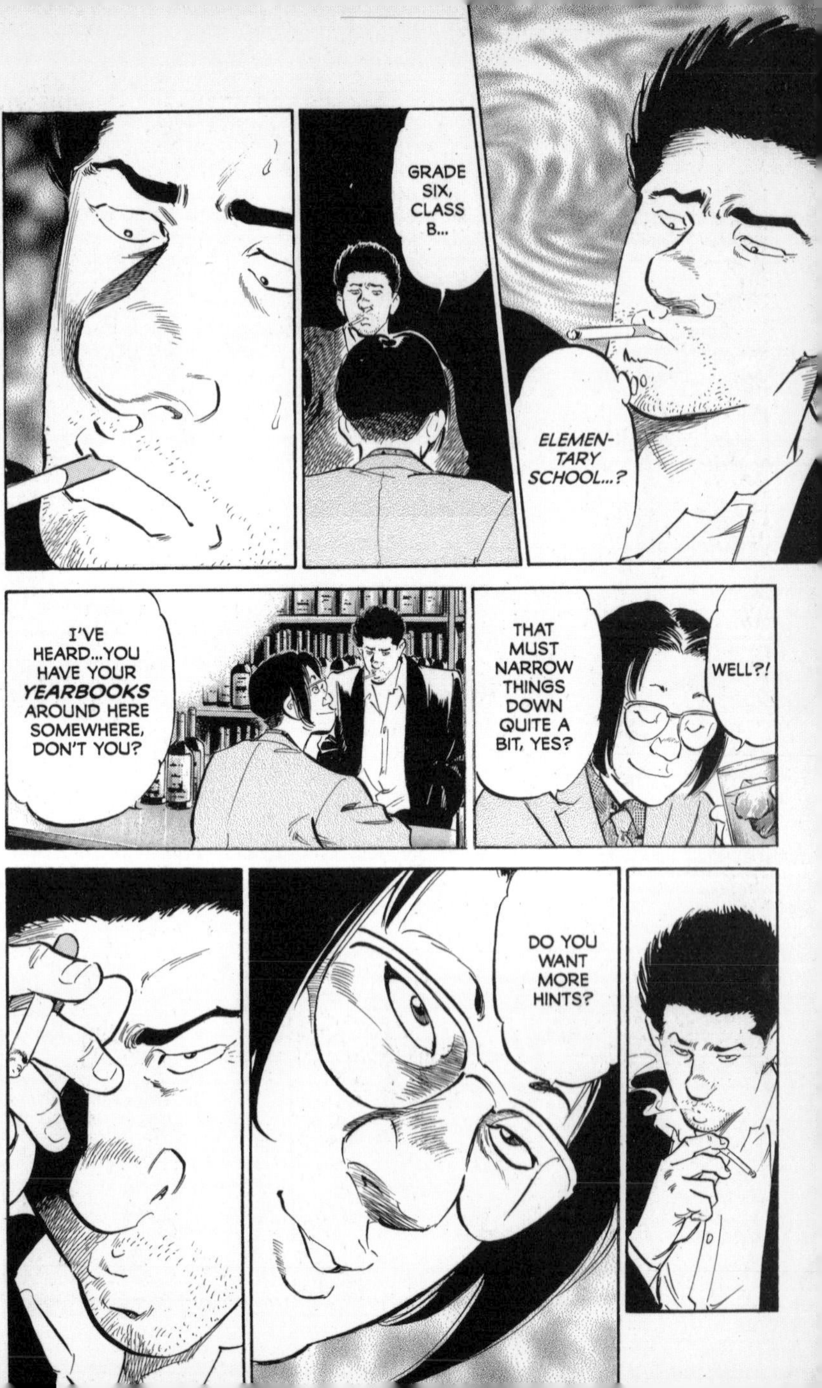
ELEMEN-TARY SCHOOL...?
GRADE SIX, CLASS B...
WELL?!
THAT MUST NARROW THINGS DOWN QUITE A BIT, YES?
I'VE HEARD...YOU HAVE YOUR *YEARBOOKS* AROUND HERE SOMEWHERE, DON'T YOU?
DO YOU WANT MORE HINTS?

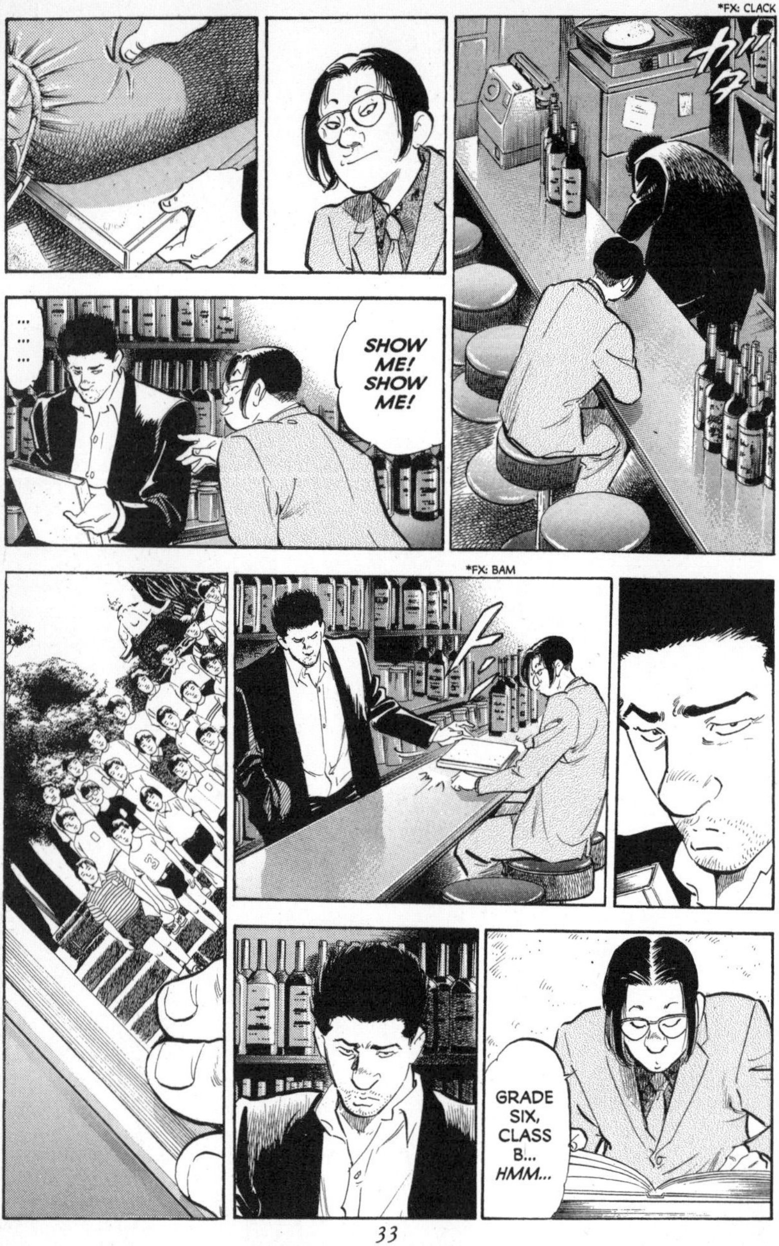
*FX: CLACK
SHOW ME! SHOW ME!
...
...
...
*FX: BAM
GRADE SIX, CLASS B... HMM...

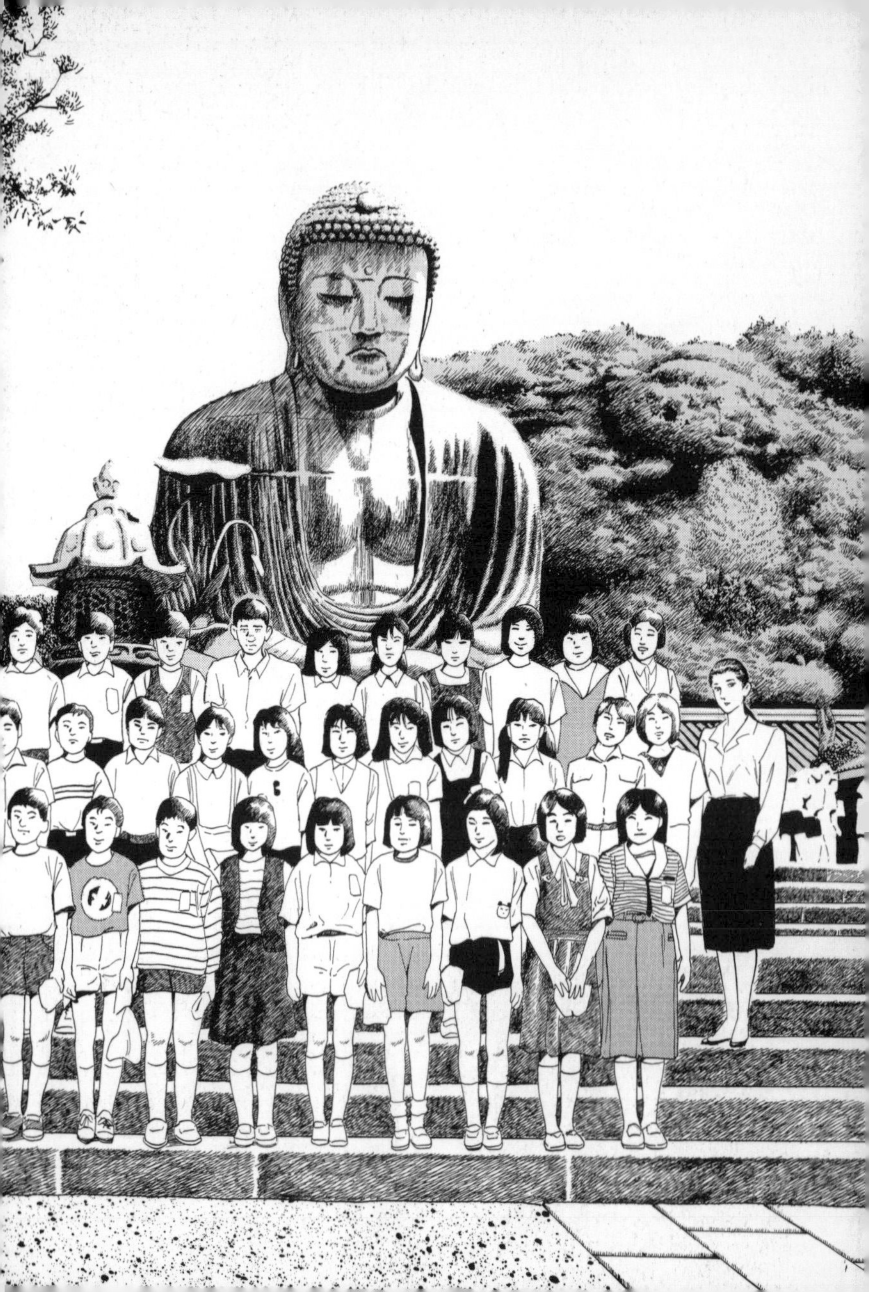

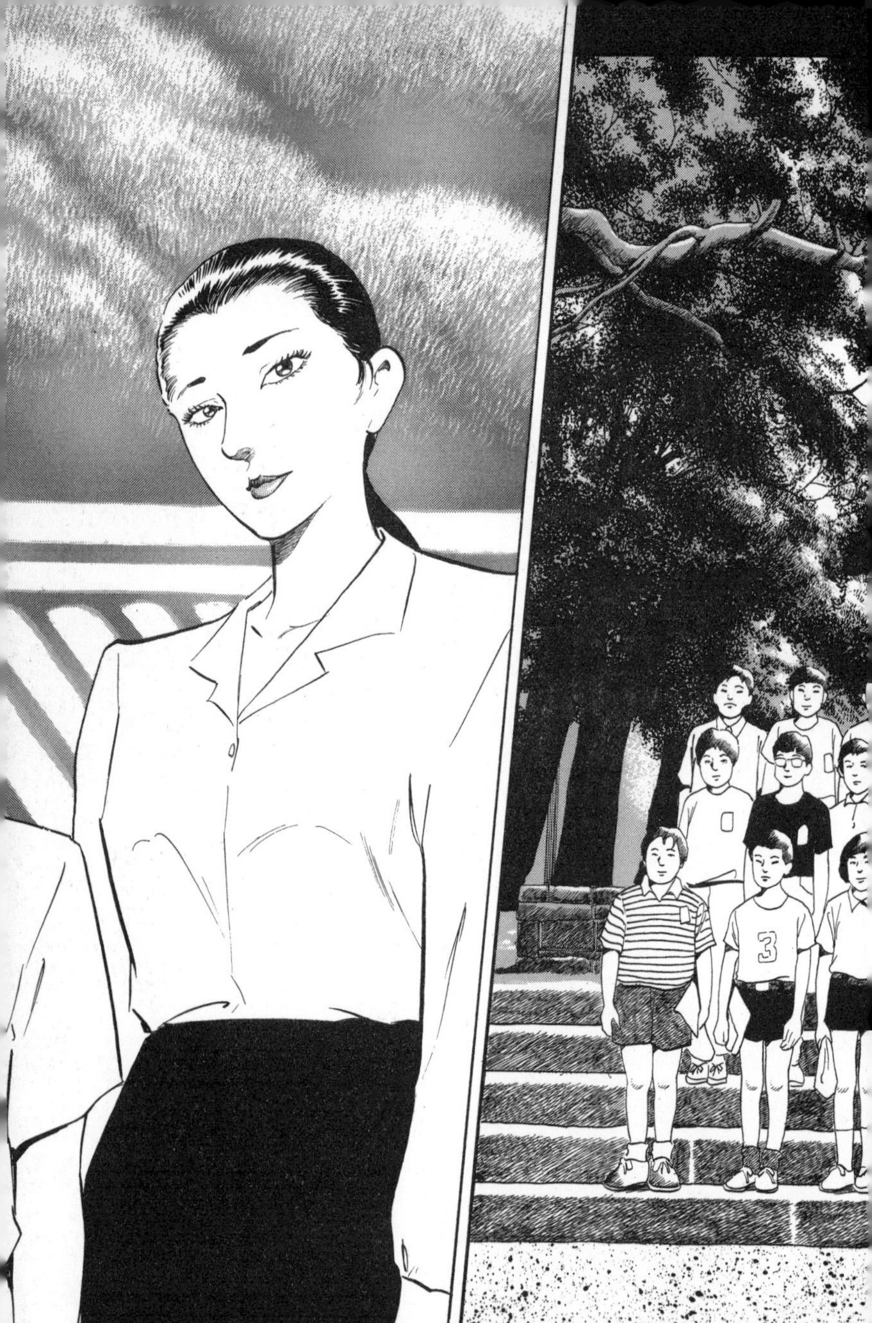

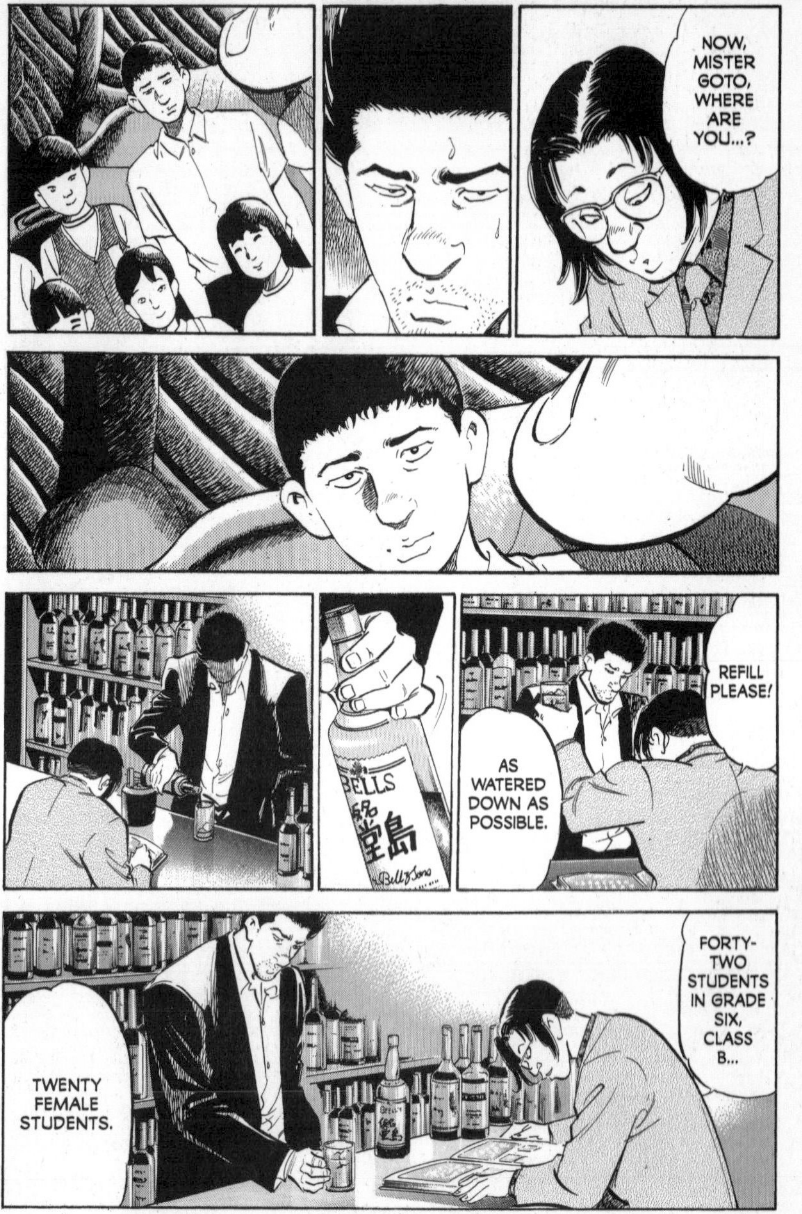
NOW, MISTER GOTO, WHERE ARE YOU...?
REFILL PLEASE!
AS WATERED DOWN AS POSSIBLE.
BELLS
FORTY-TWO STUDENTS IN GRADE SIX, CLASS B...
TWENTY FEMALE STUDENTS.

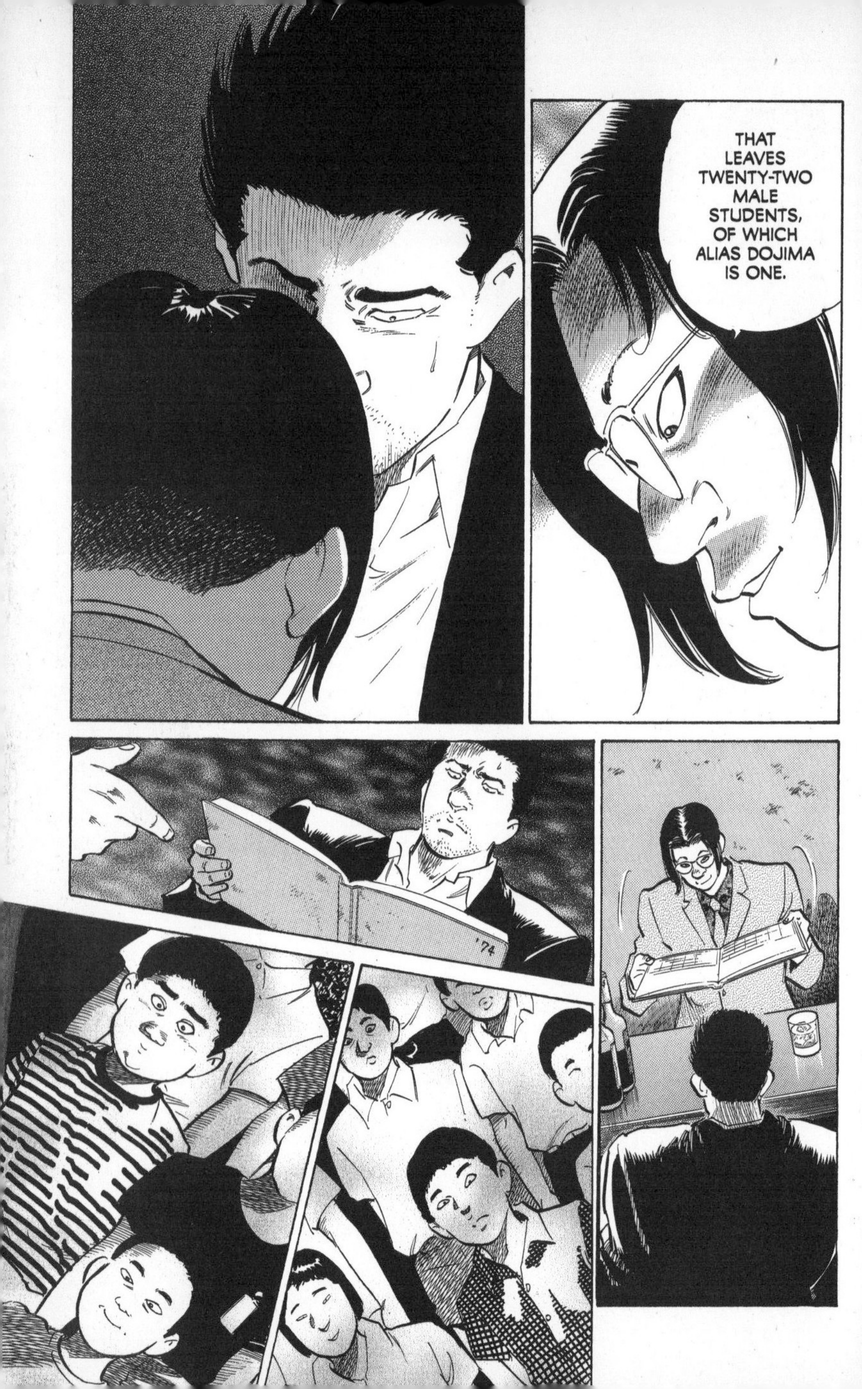
THAT LEAVES TWENTY-TWO MALE STUDENTS, OF WHICH ALIAS DOJIMA IS ONE.
'74

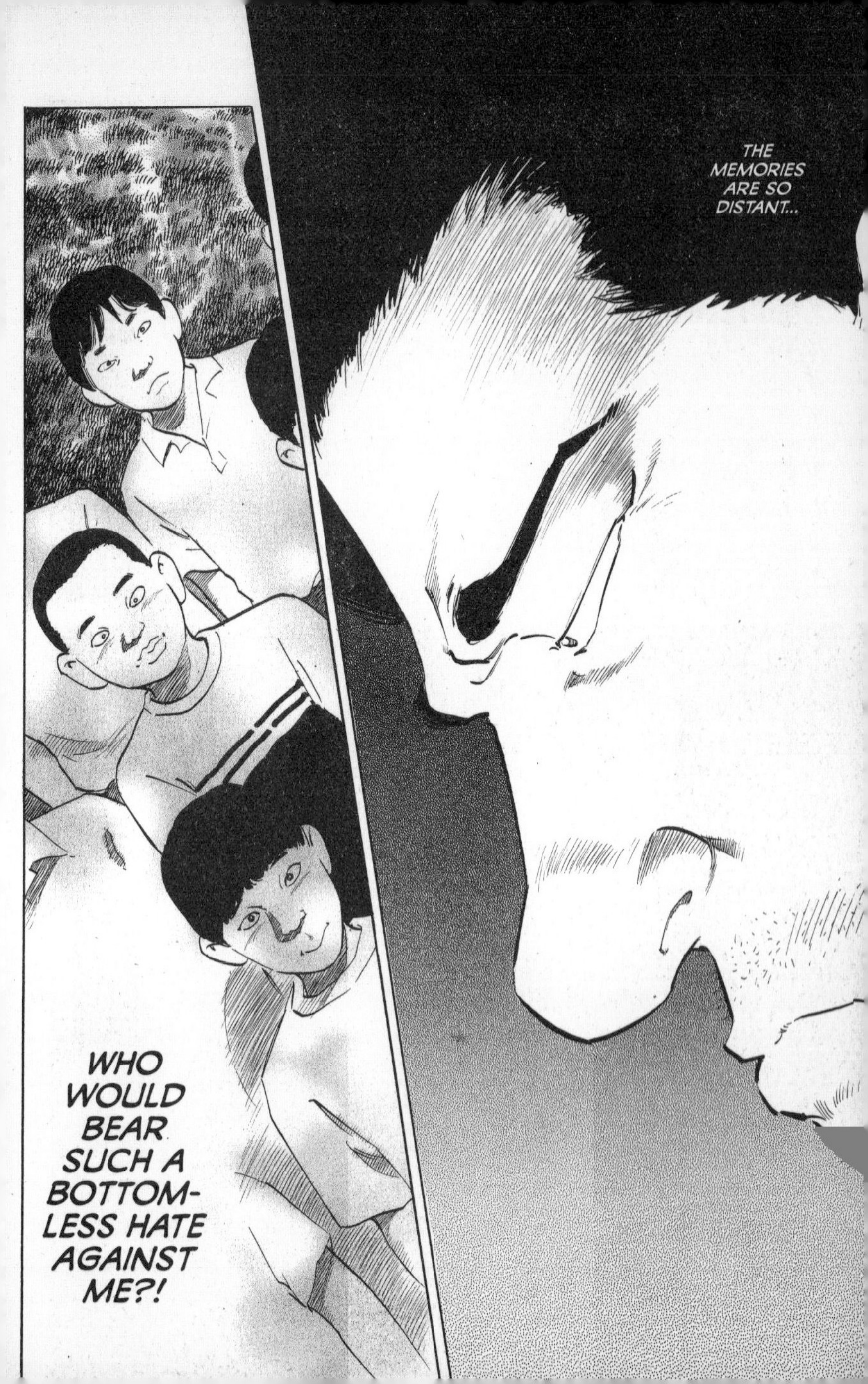
THE MEMORIES ARE SO DISTANT...
WHO WOULD BEAR SUCH A BOTTOM-LESS HATE AGAINST ME?!

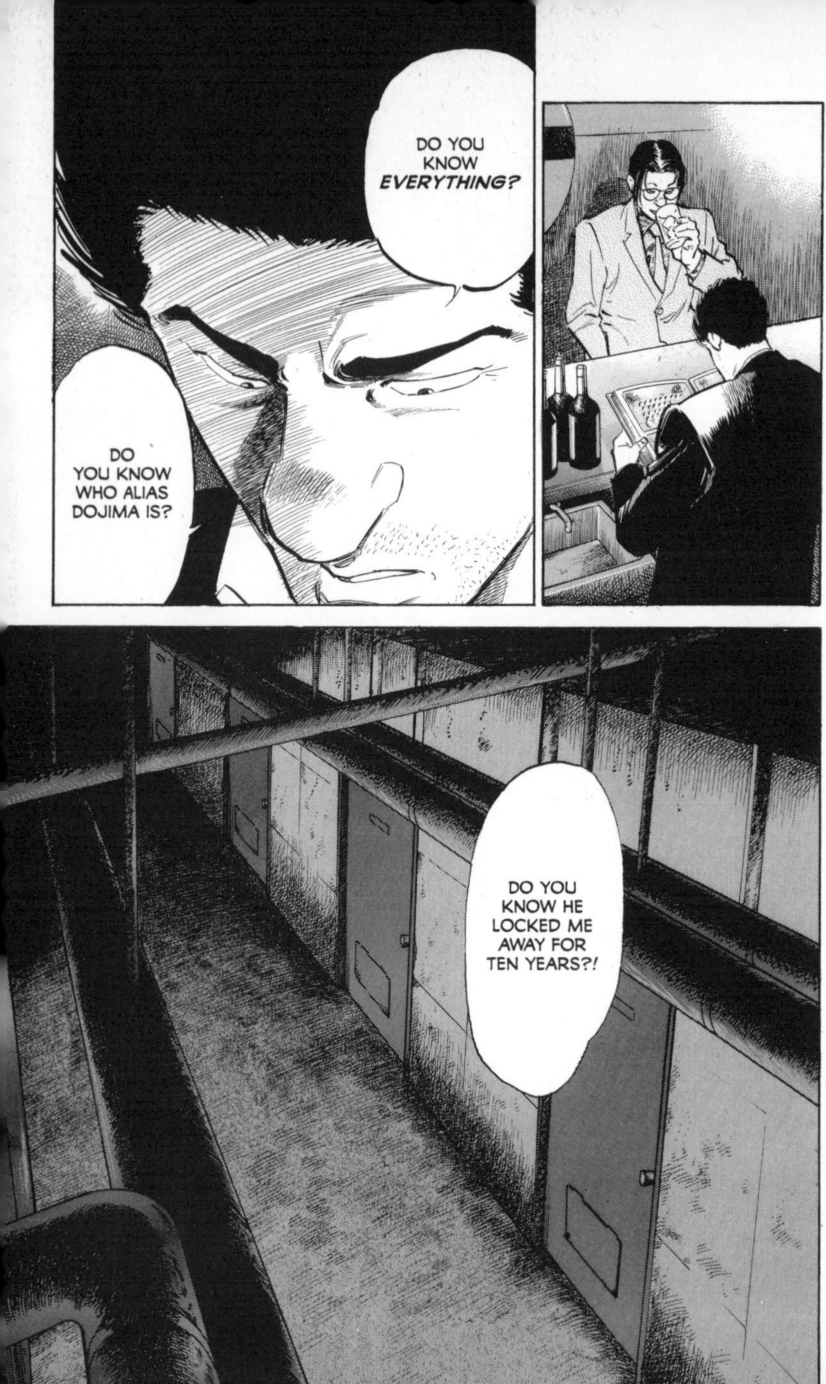
DO YOU KNOW *EVERYTHING?*
DO YOU KNOW WHO ALIAS DOJIMA IS?
DO YOU KNOW HE LOCKED ME AWAY FOR TEN YEARS?!

*FX: KLAK

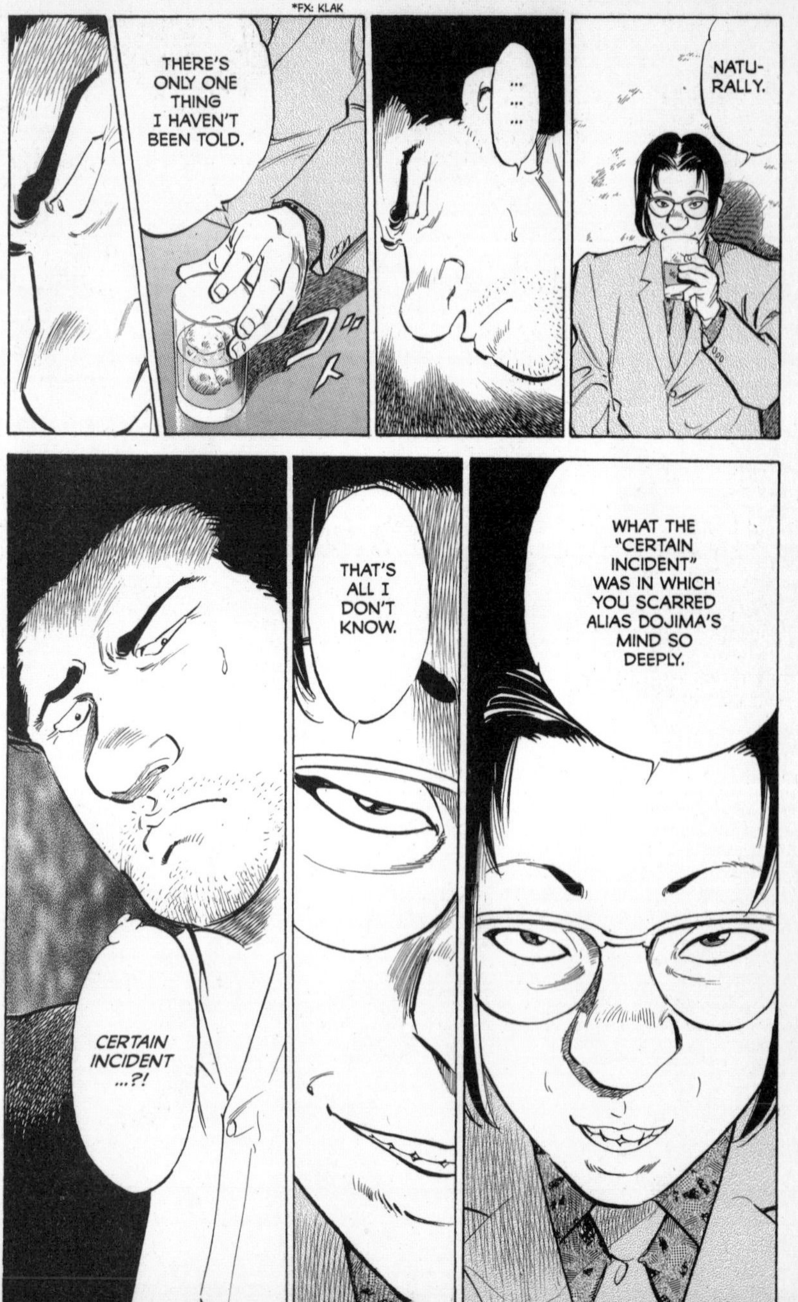
NATU-RALLY.
...
...
...
THERE'S ONLY ONE THING I HAVEN'T BEEN TOLD.
WHAT THE "CERTAIN INCIDENT" WAS IN WHICH YOU SCARRED ALIAS DOJIMA'S MIND SO DEEPLY.
THAT'S ALL I DON'T KNOW.
CERTAIN INCIDENT ...?!

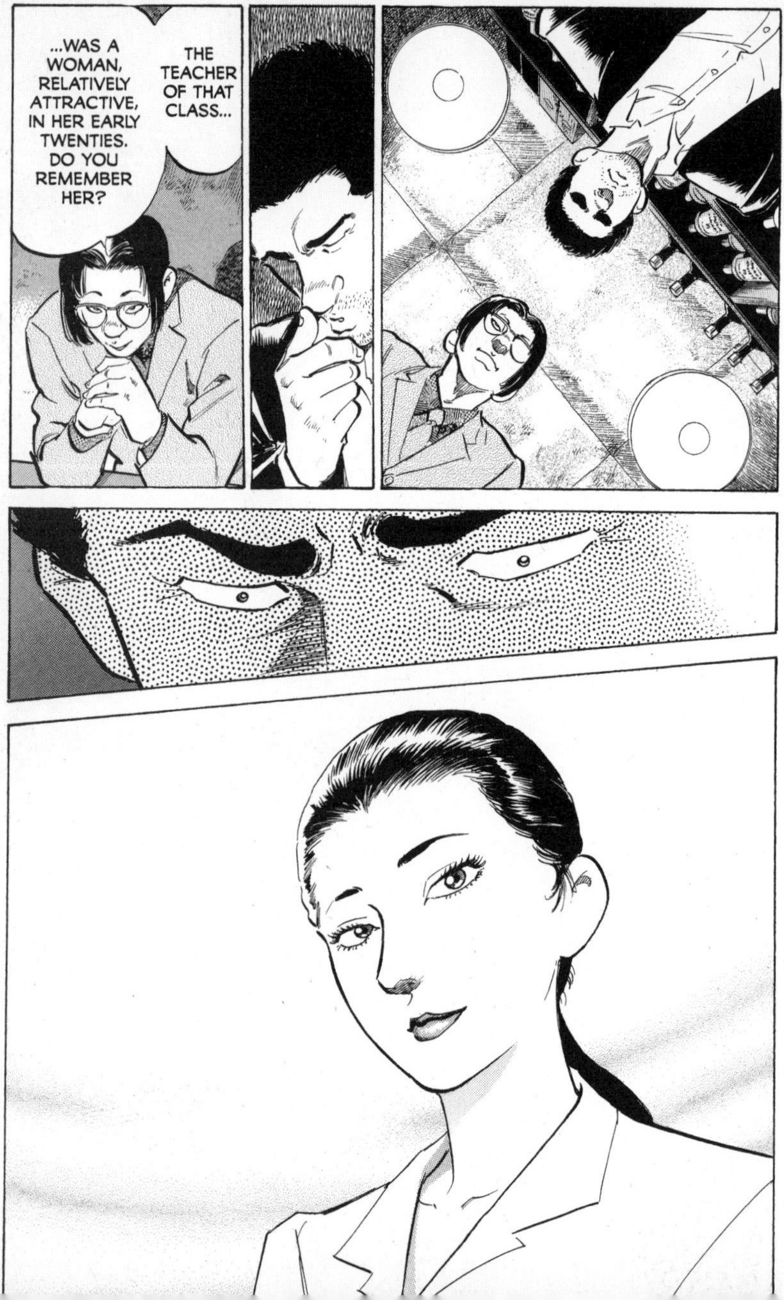
THE TEACHER OF THAT CLASS...
...WAS A WOMAN, RELATIVELY ATTRACTIVE, IN HER EARLY TWENTIES. DO YOU REMEMBER HER?

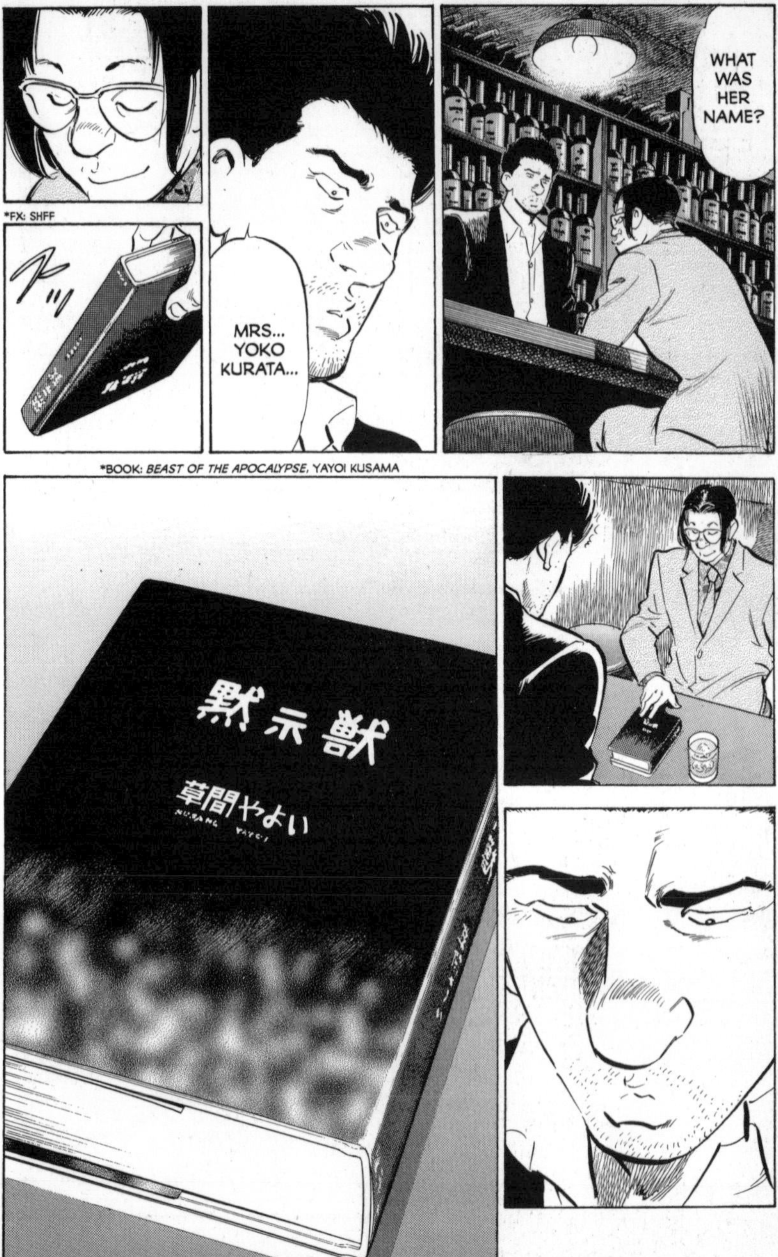
WHAT WAS HER NAME?
MRS... YOKO KURATA...
*FX: SHFF
スッ
*BOOK: *BEAST OF THE APOCALYPSE*, YAYOI KUSAMA
黙示獣
草間やよい

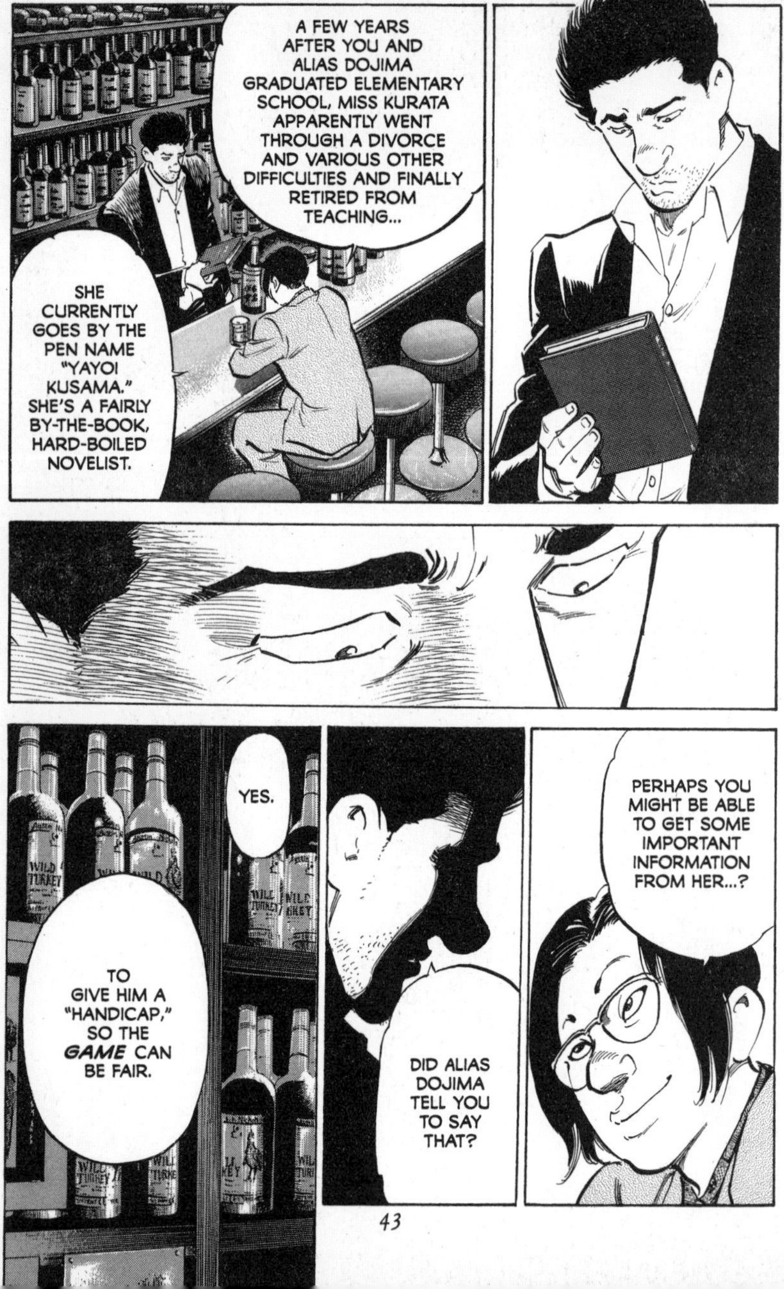
A FEW YEARS AFTER YOU AND ALIAS DOJIMA GRADUATED ELEMENTARY SCHOOL, MISS KURATA APPARENTLY WENT THROUGH A DIVORCE AND VARIOUS OTHER DIFFICULTIES AND FINALLY RETIRED FROM TEACHING...
SHE CURRENTLY GOES BY THE PEN NAME "YAYOI KUSAMA." SHE'S A FAIRLY BY-THE-BOOK, HARD-BOILED NOVELIST.
PERHAPS YOU MIGHT BE ABLE TO GET SOME IMPORTANT INFORMATION FROM HER...?
DID ALIAS DOJIMA TELL YOU TO SAY THAT?
YES.
TO GIVE HIM A "HANDICAP," SO THE *GAME* CAN BE FAIR.

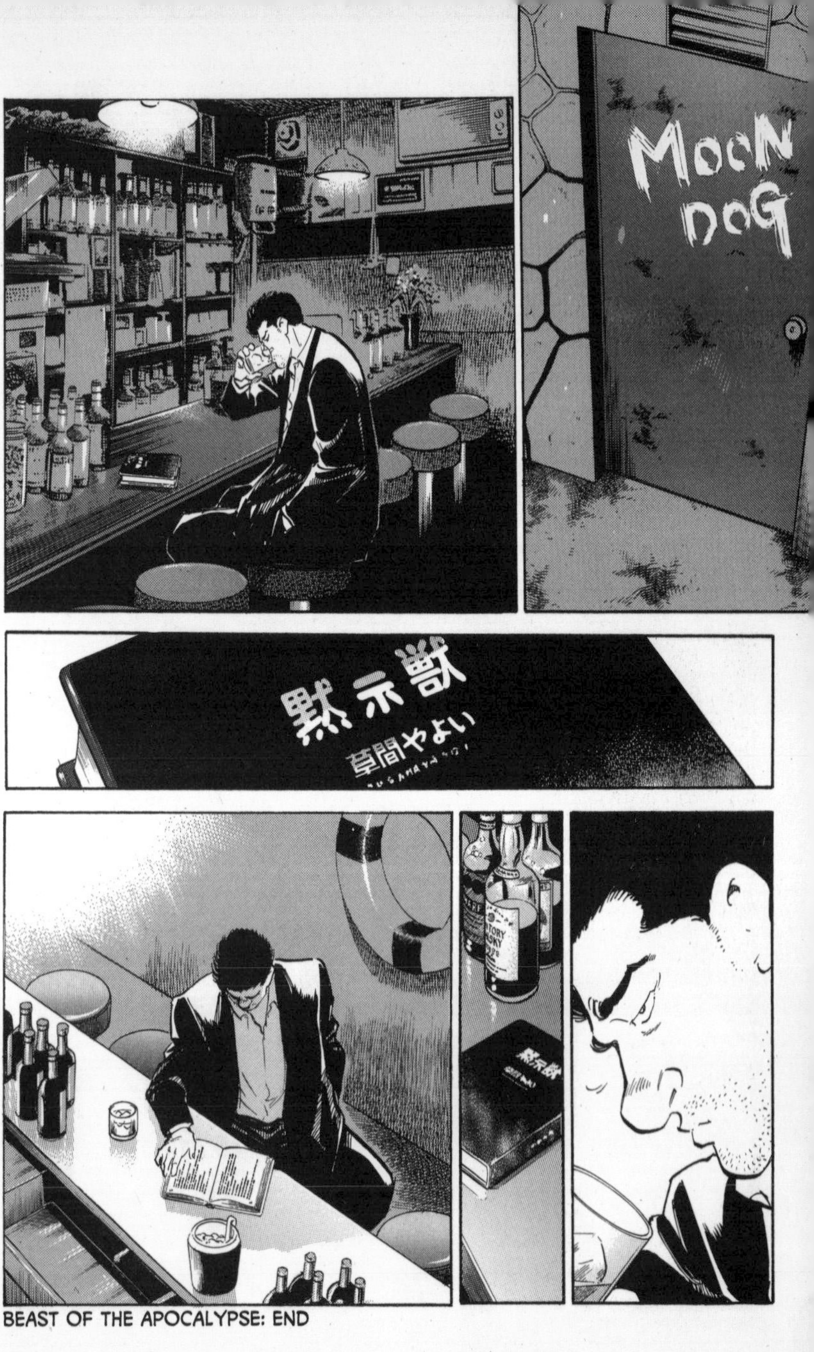
MOON DOG
黙示獣
草間やよい

BEAST OF THE APOCALYPSE: END

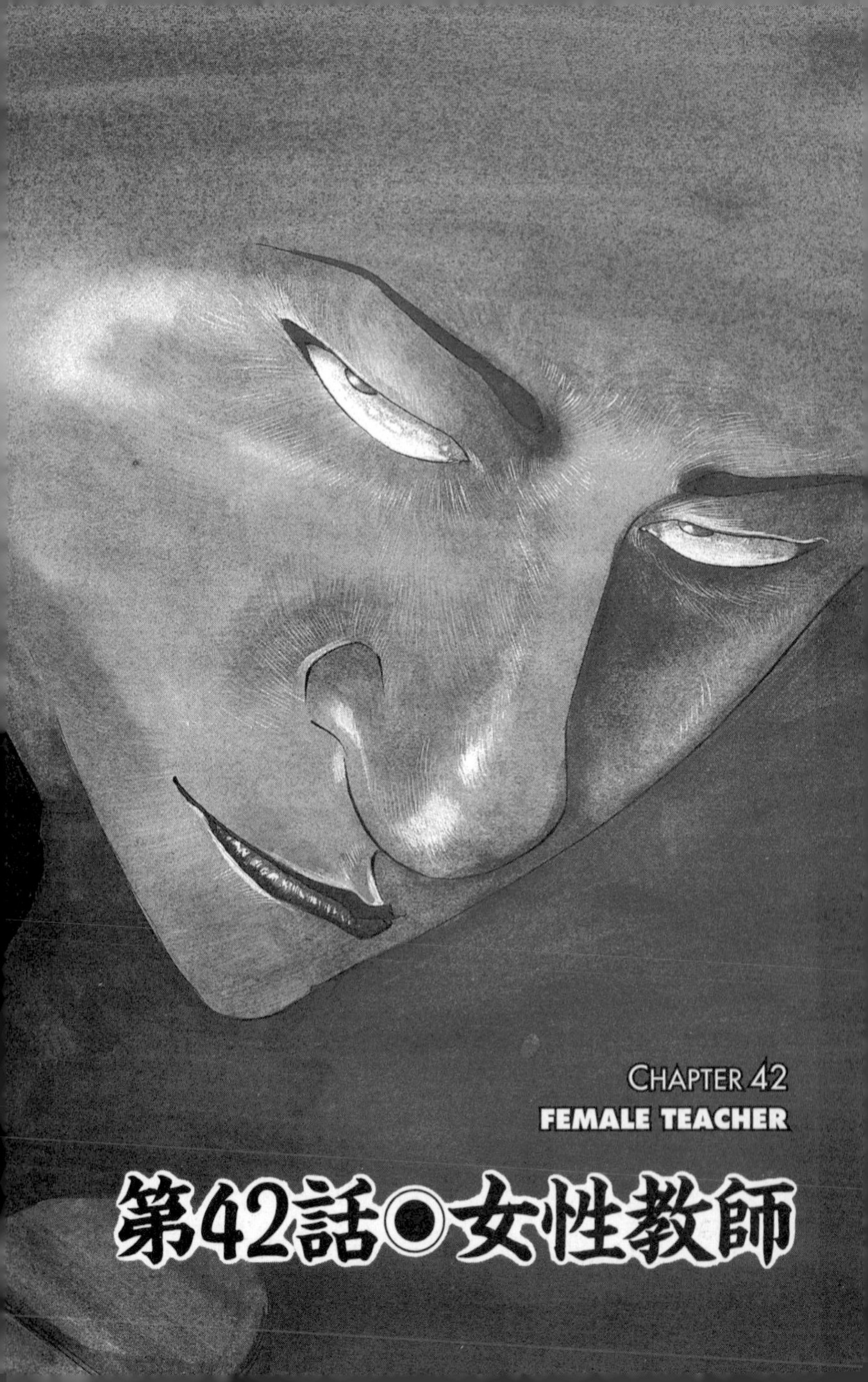
CHAPTER 42
FEMALE TEACHER
第42話◎女性教師

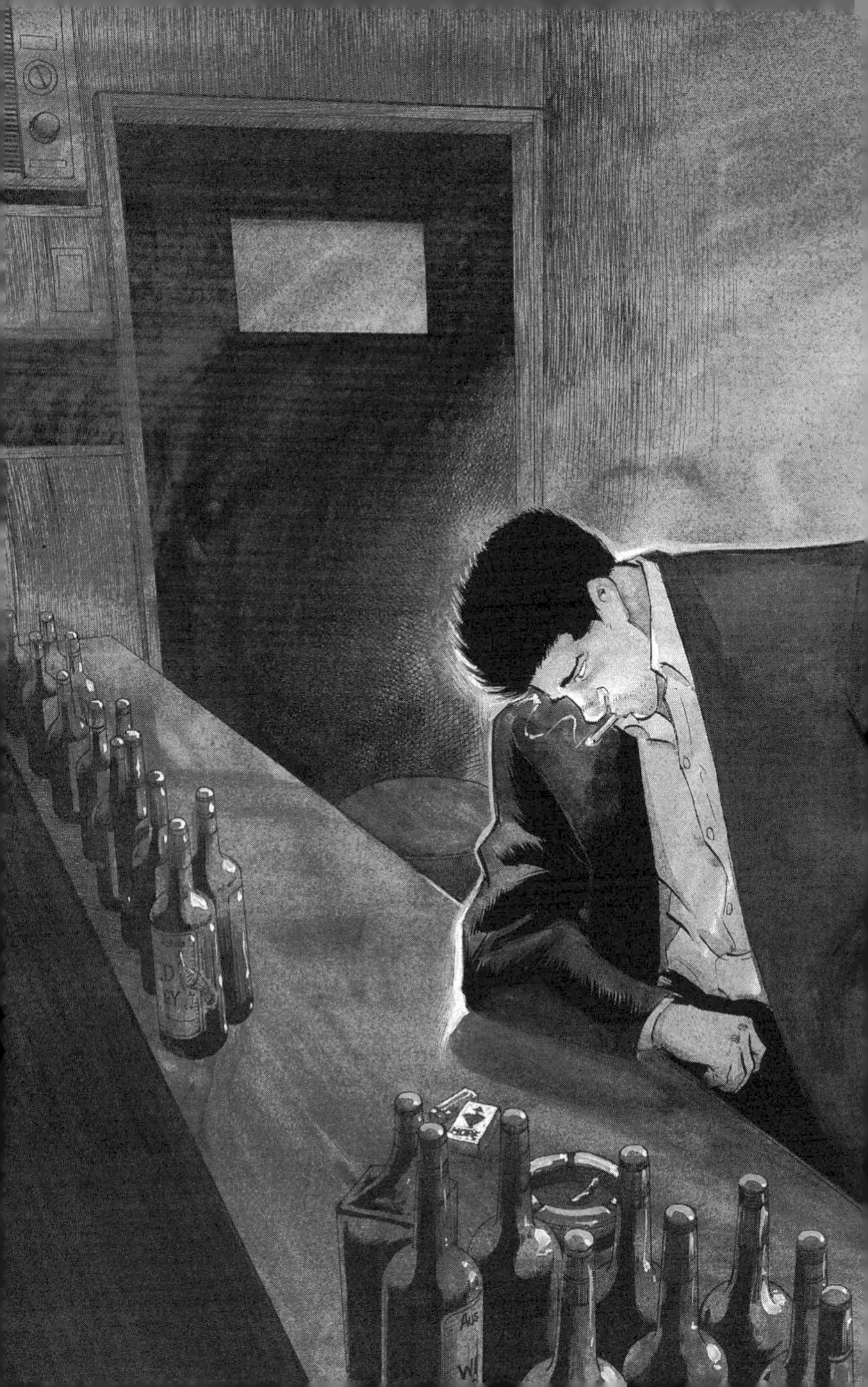

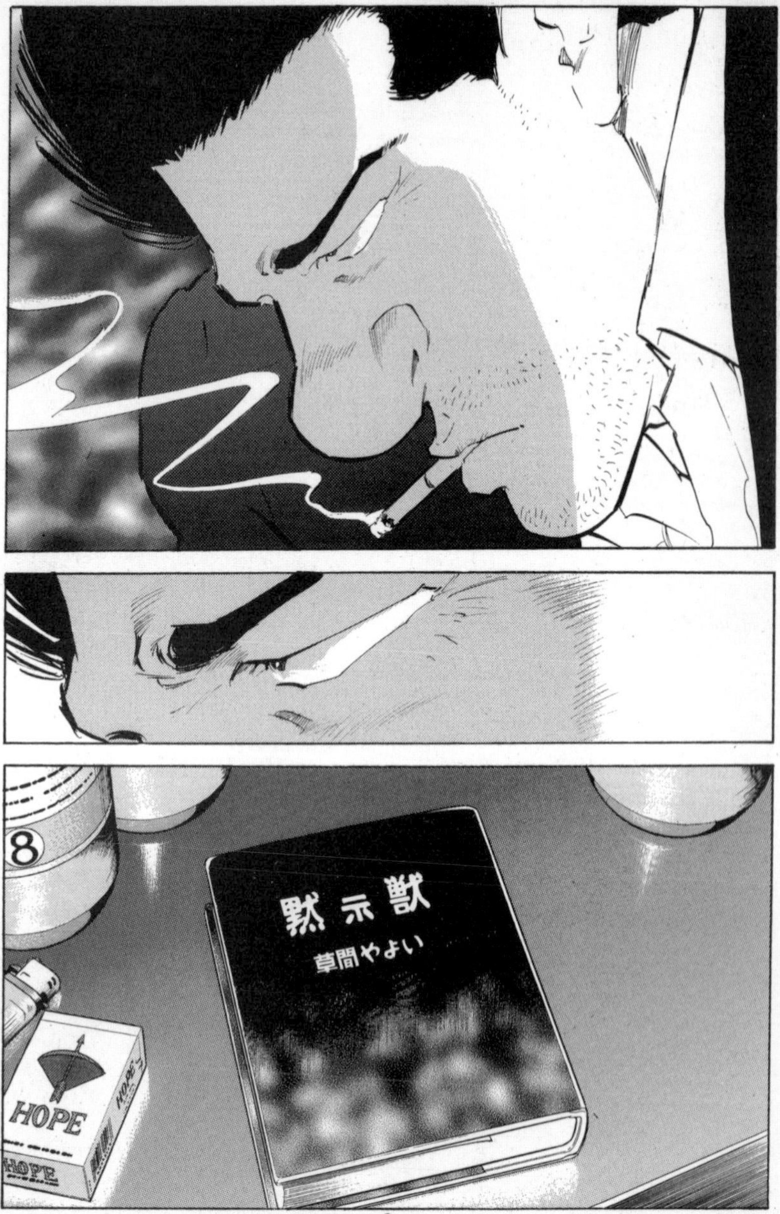
黙示獣
草間やよい
HOPE
HOPE

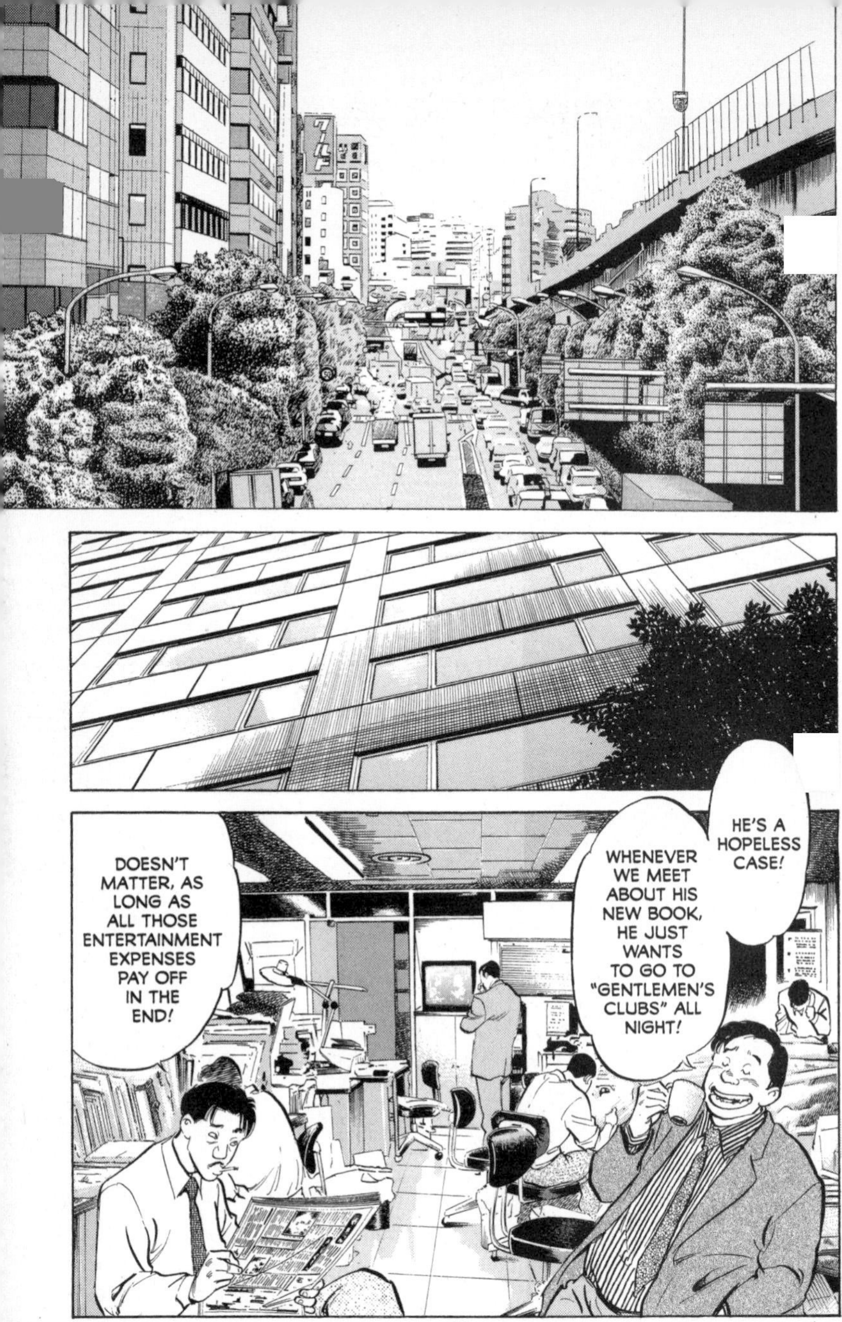
HE'S A HOPELESS CASE!
WHENEVER WE MEET ABOUT HIS NEW BOOK, HE JUST WANTS TO GO TO "GENTLEMEN'S CLUBS" ALL NIGHT!
DOESN'T MATTER, AS LONG AS ALL THOSE ENTERTAINMENT EXPENSES PAY OFF IN THE END!

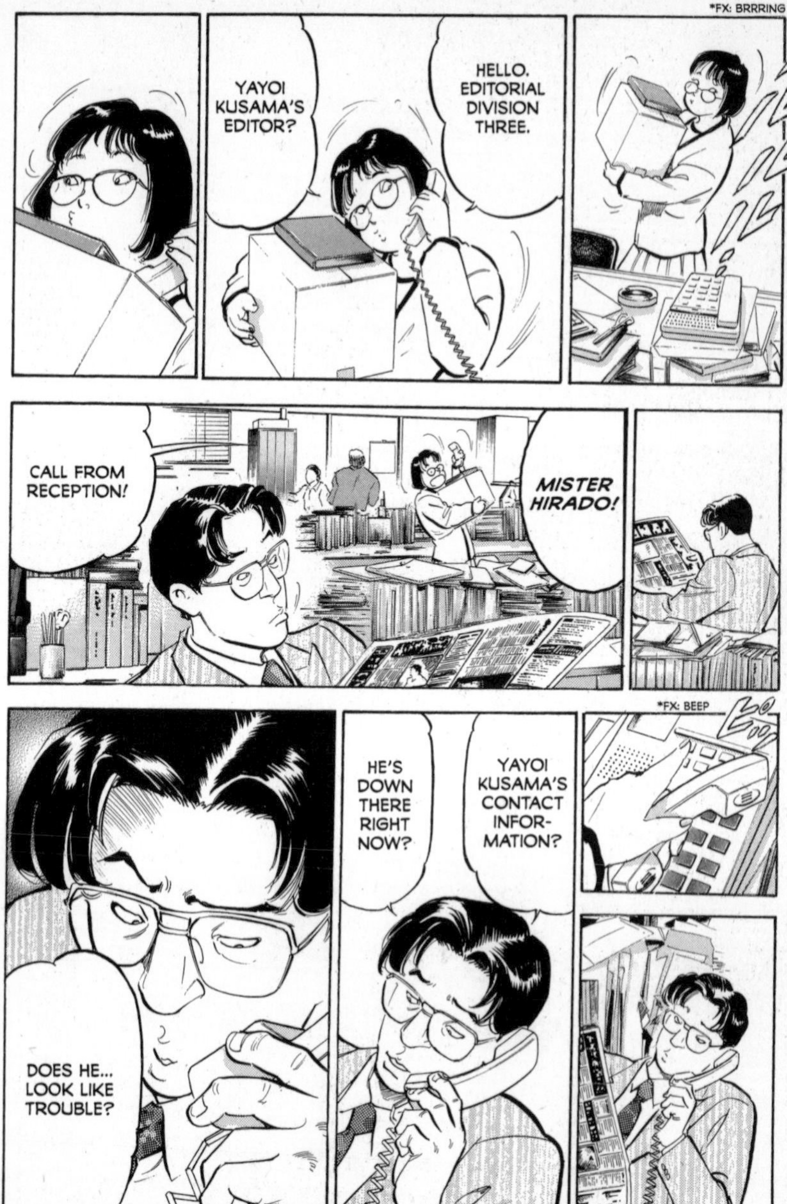
*FX: BRRRING
HELLO. EDITORIAL DIVISION THREE.
YAYOI KUSAMA'S EDITOR?
MISTER HIRADO!
CALL FROM RECEPTION!
*FX: BEEP
YAYOI KUSAMA'S CONTACT INFOR-MATION?
HE'S DOWN THERE RIGHT NOW?
DOES HE... LOOK LIKE TROUBLE?

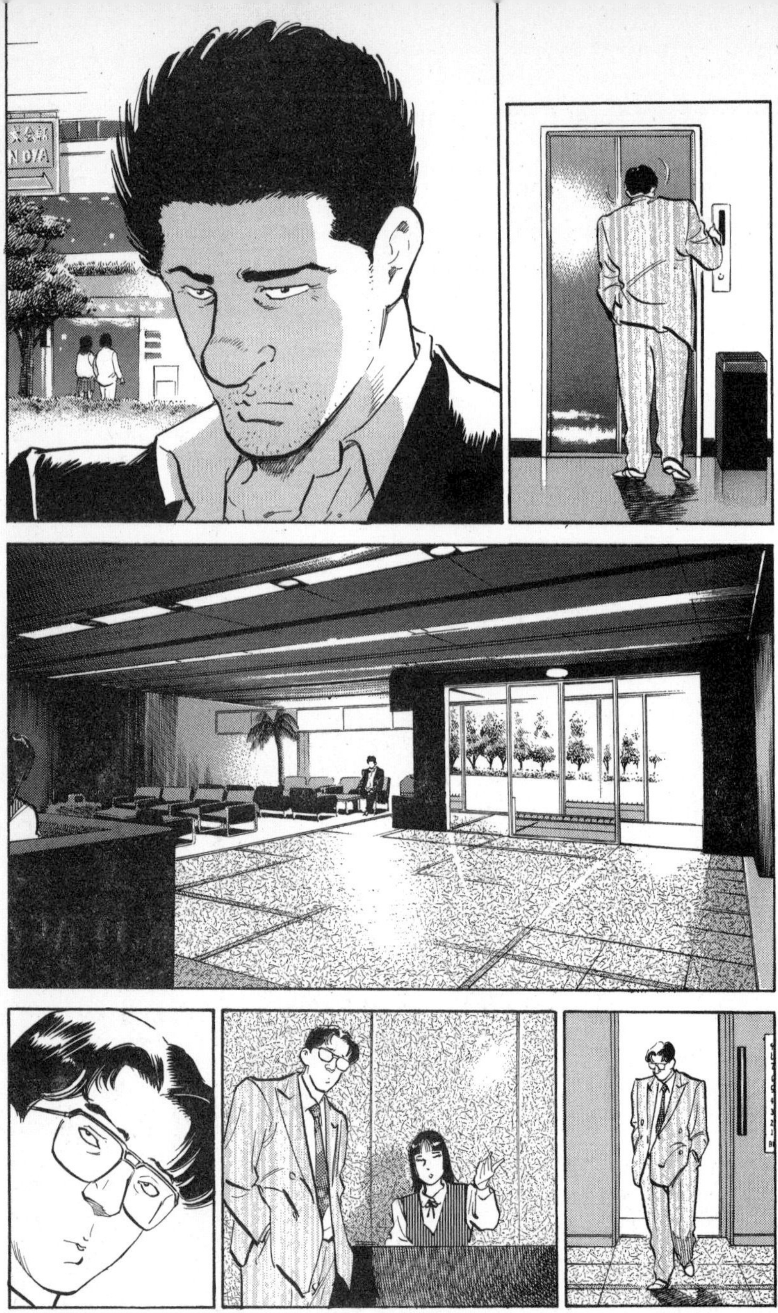

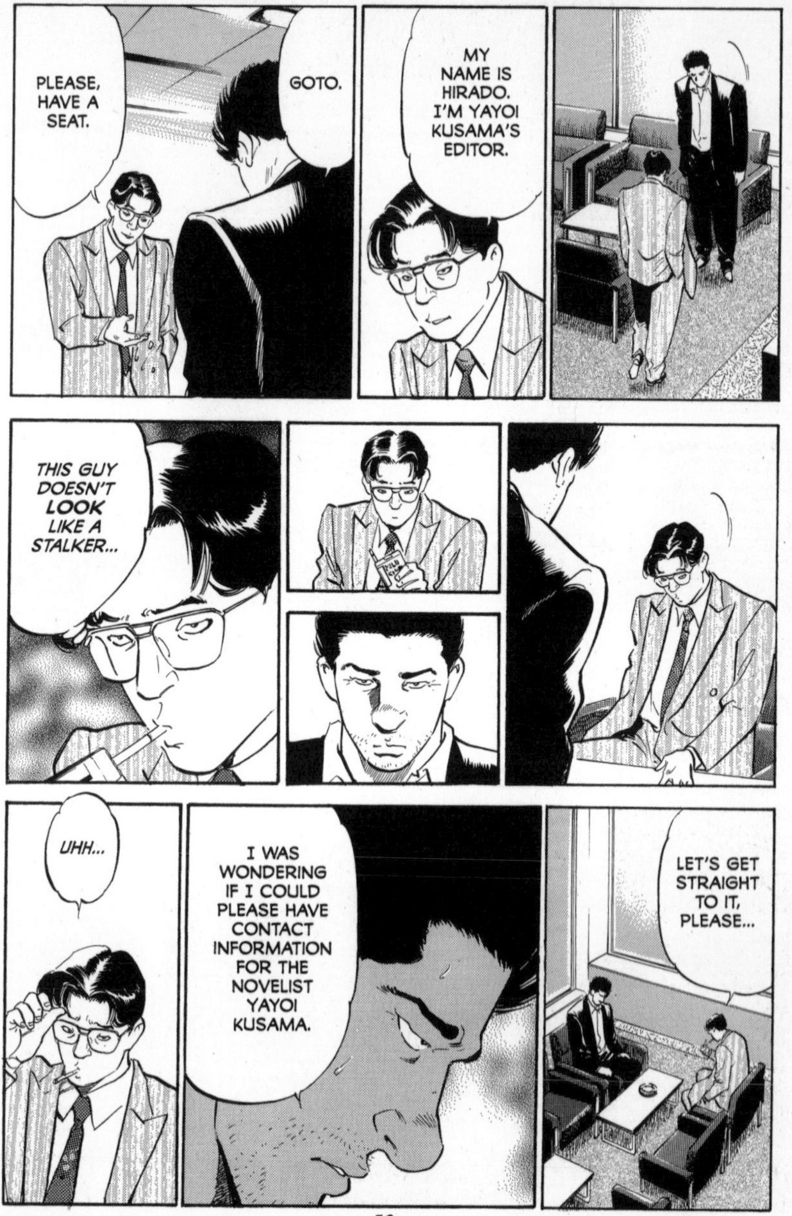
MY NAME IS HIRADO. I'M YAYOI KUSAMA'S EDITOR.
GOTO.
PLEASE, HAVE A SEAT.
THIS GUY DOESN'T **LOOK** LIKE A STALKER...
LET'S GET STRAIGHT TO IT, PLEASE...
I WAS WONDERING IF I COULD PLEASE HAVE CONTACT INFORMATION FOR THE NOVELIST YAYOI KUSAMA.
UHH...

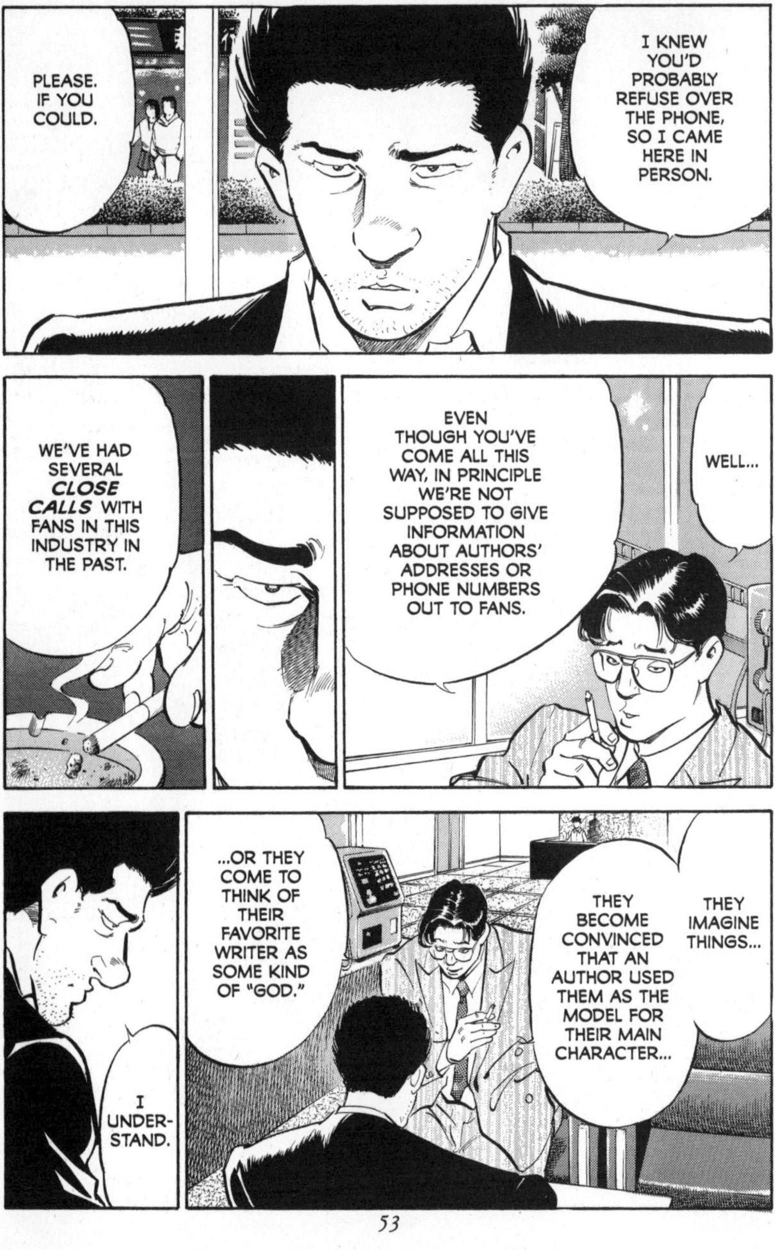
I KNEW YOU'D PROBABLY REFUSE OVER THE PHONE, SO I CAME HERE IN PERSON.
PLEASE. IF YOU COULD.
WELL...
EVEN THOUGH YOU'VE COME ALL THIS WAY, IN PRINCIPLE WE'RE NOT SUPPOSED TO GIVE INFORMATION ABOUT AUTHORS' ADDRESSES OR PHONE NUMBERS OUT TO FANS.
WE'VE HAD SEVERAL *CLOSE CALLS* WITH FANS IN THIS INDUSTRY IN THE PAST.
THEY IMAGINE THINGS...
THEY BECOME CONVINCED THAT AN AUTHOR USED THEM AS THE MODEL FOR THEIR MAIN CHARACTER...
...OR THEY COME TO THINK OF THEIR FAVORITE WRITER AS SOME KIND OF "GOD."
I UNDER-STAND.

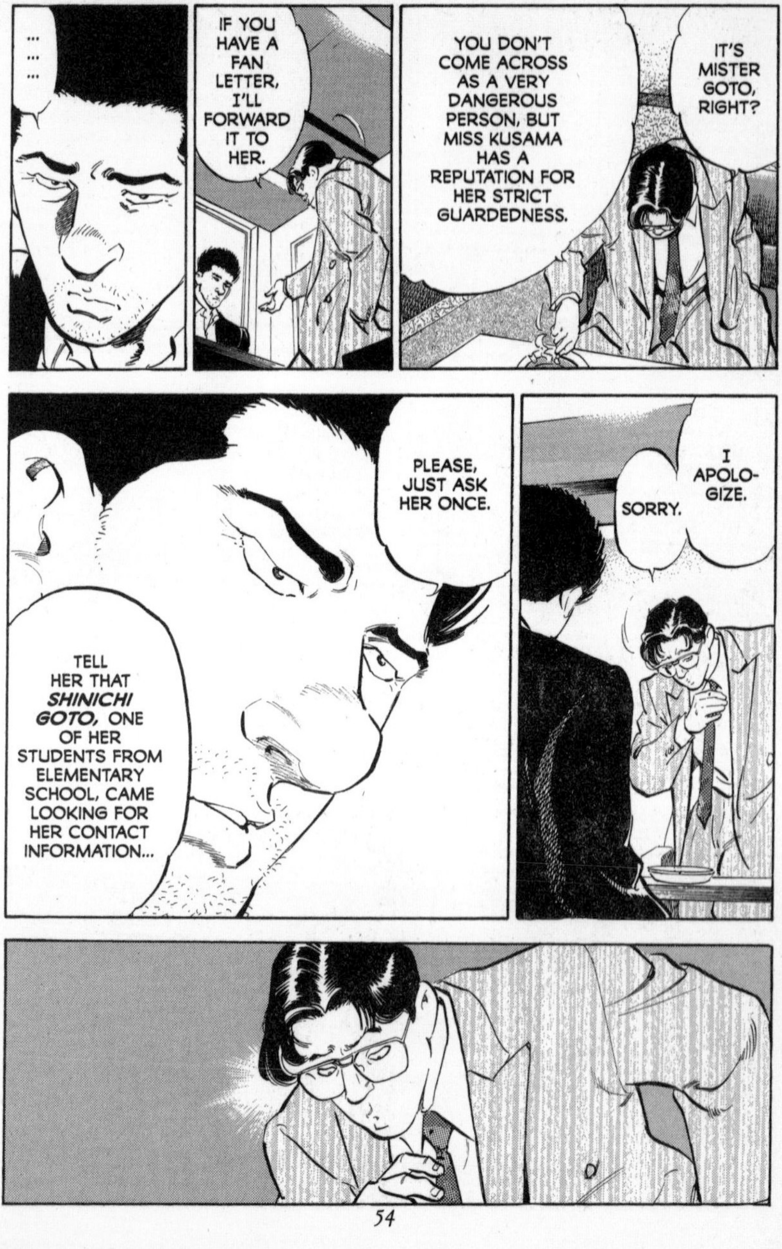
IT'S MISTER GOTO, RIGHT?
YOU DON'T COME ACROSS AS A VERY DANGEROUS PERSON, BUT MISS KUSAMA HAS A REPUTATION FOR HER STRICT GUARDEDNESS.
IF YOU HAVE A FAN LETTER, I'LL FORWARD IT TO HER.
... ...
I APOLOGIZE.
SORRY.
PLEASE, JUST ASK HER ONCE.
TELL HER THAT ***SHINICHI GOTO,*** ONE OF HER STUDENTS FROM ELEMENTARY SCHOOL, CAME LOOKING FOR HER CONTACT INFORMATION...

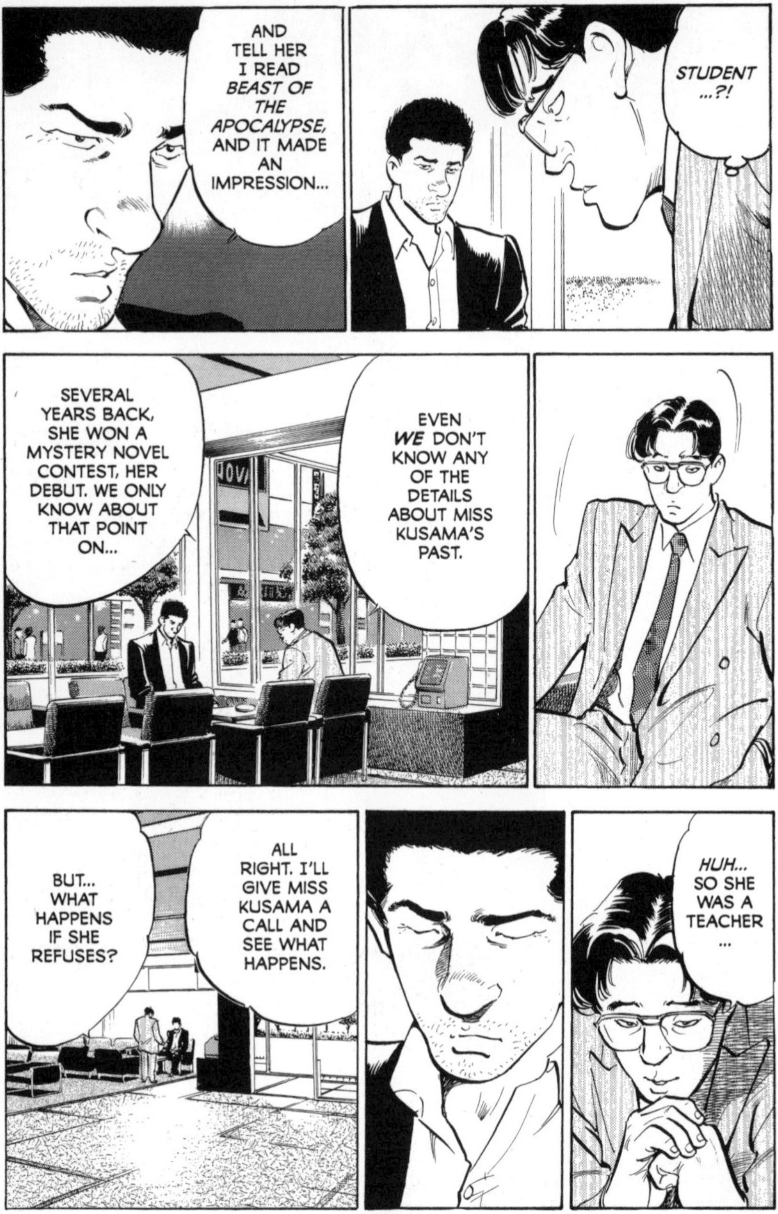
STUDENT ...?!
AND TELL HER I READ *BEAST OF THE APOCALYPSE,* AND IT MADE AN IMPRESSION...
EVEN ***WE*** DON'T KNOW ANY OF THE DETAILS ABOUT MISS KUSAMA'S PAST.
SEVERAL YEARS BACK, SHE WON A MYSTERY NOVEL CONTEST, HER DEBUT. WE ONLY KNOW ABOUT THAT POINT ON...
HUH... SO SHE WAS A TEACHER ...
ALL RIGHT. I'LL GIVE MISS KUSAMA A CALL AND SEE WHAT HAPPENS.
BUT... WHAT HAPPENS IF SHE REFUSES?

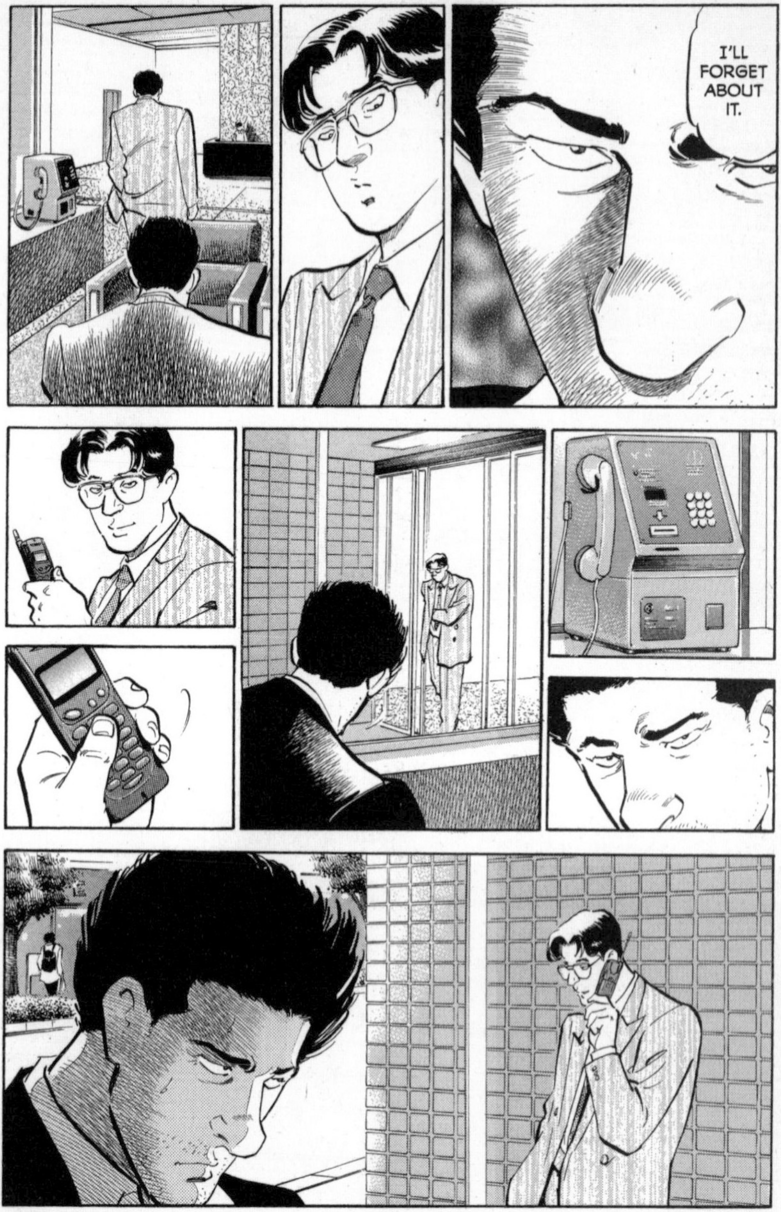
I'LL FORGET ABOUT IT.

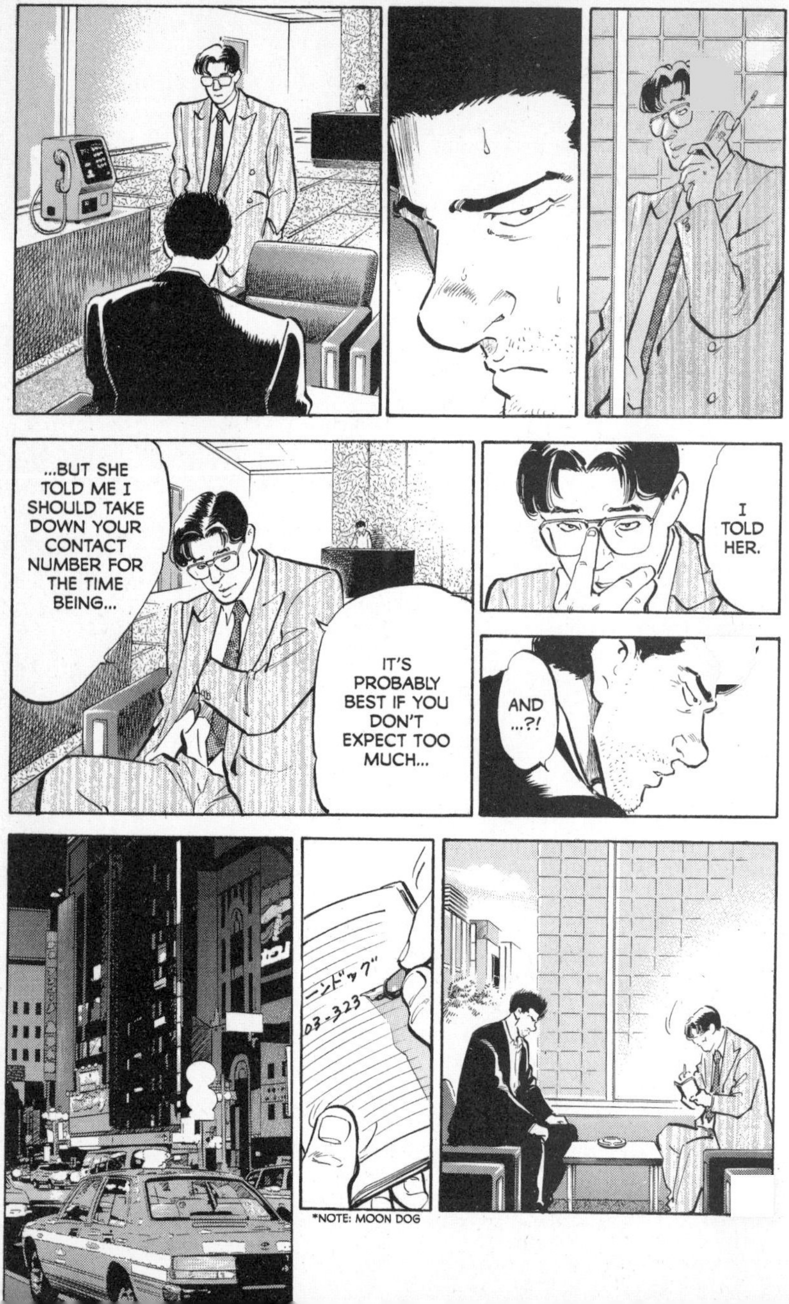
I TOLD HER.
AND ...?!
...BUT SHE TOLD ME I SHOULD TAKE DOWN YOUR CONTACT NUMBER FOR THE TIME BEING...
IT'S PROBABLY BEST IF YOU DON'T EXPECT TOO MUCH...
ーンドッグ
03-323

*NOTE: MOON DOG

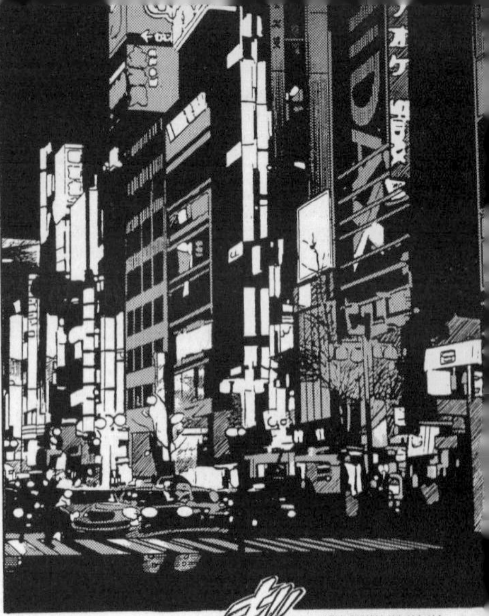

*SIGN: SHINJUKU GOLDEN GAI

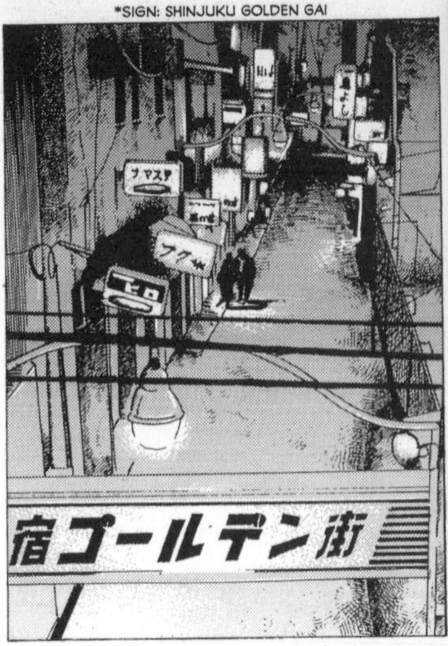
宿ゴールデン街

*FX: BWAH HA HA HA

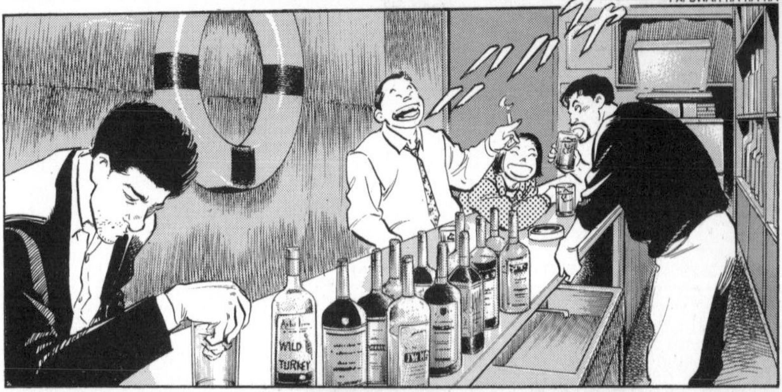

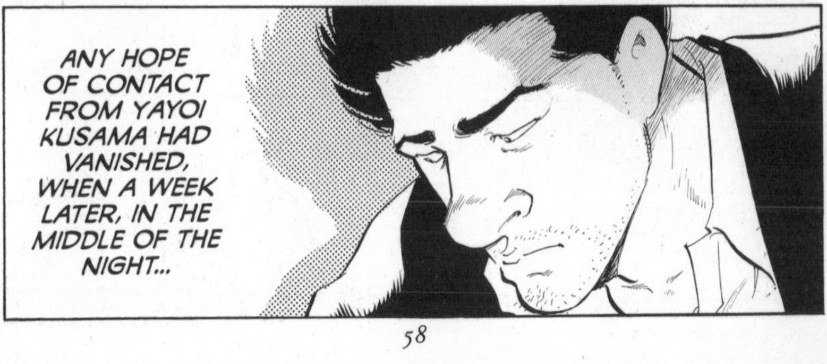
ANY HOPE OF CONTACT FROM YAYOI KUSAMA HAD VANISHED, WHEN A WEEK LATER, IN THE MIDDLE OF THE NIGHT...

GUY NAMED *HIRADO* FROM SOME PUBLISHING COMPANY!

HEY, GOTO!

*FX: BRRRIINNG

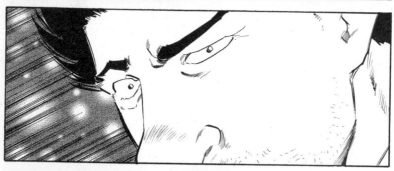

HELLO ...?

PHONE CALL FOR YA, *EH...?*

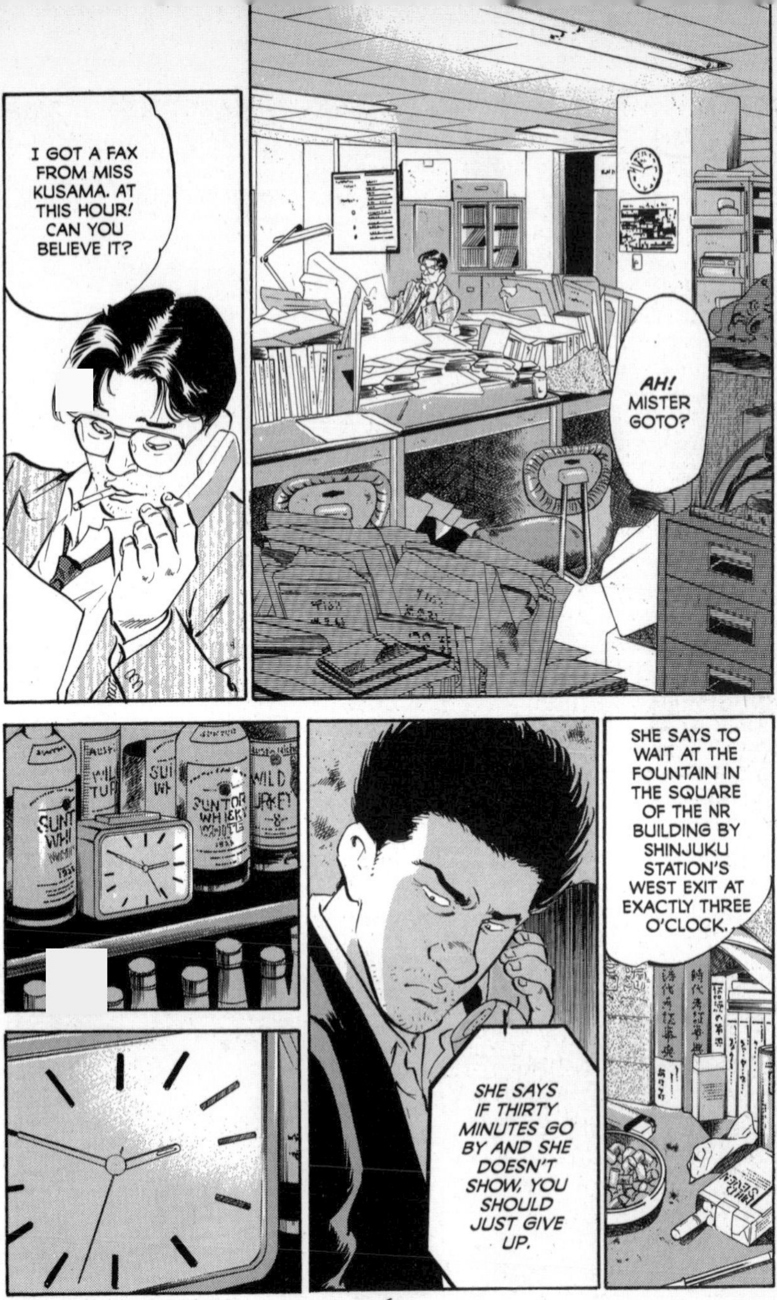
AH! MISTER GOTO?
I GOT A FAX FROM MISS KUSAMA. AT THIS HOUR! CAN YOU BELIEVE IT?
SHE SAYS TO WAIT AT THE FOUNTAIN IN THE SQUARE OF THE NR BUILDING BY SHINJUKU STATION'S WEST EXIT AT EXACTLY THREE O'CLOCK...
SHE SAYS IF THIRTY MINUTES GO BY AND SHE DOESN'T SHOW, YOU SHOULD JUST GIVE UP.

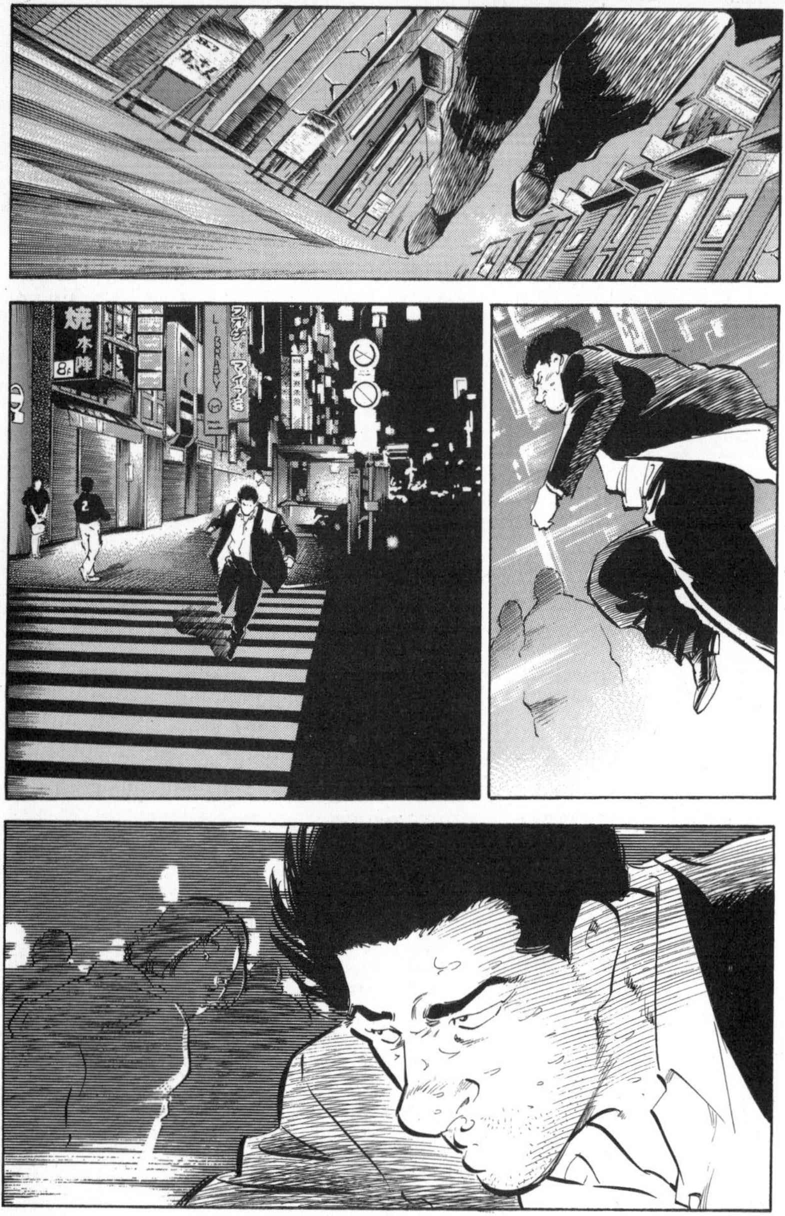
焼
本陣
8F
LIBRARY

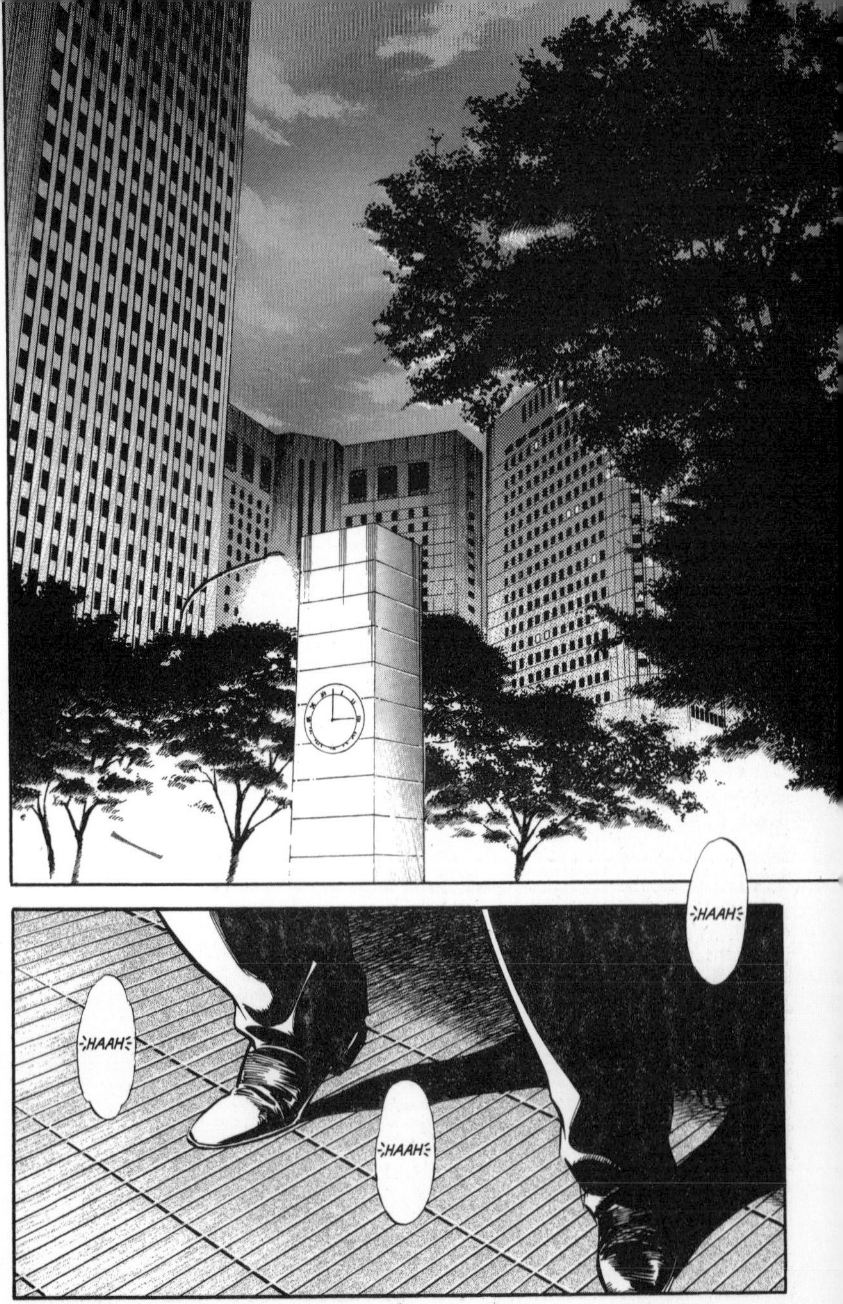
HAAH
HAAH
HAAH

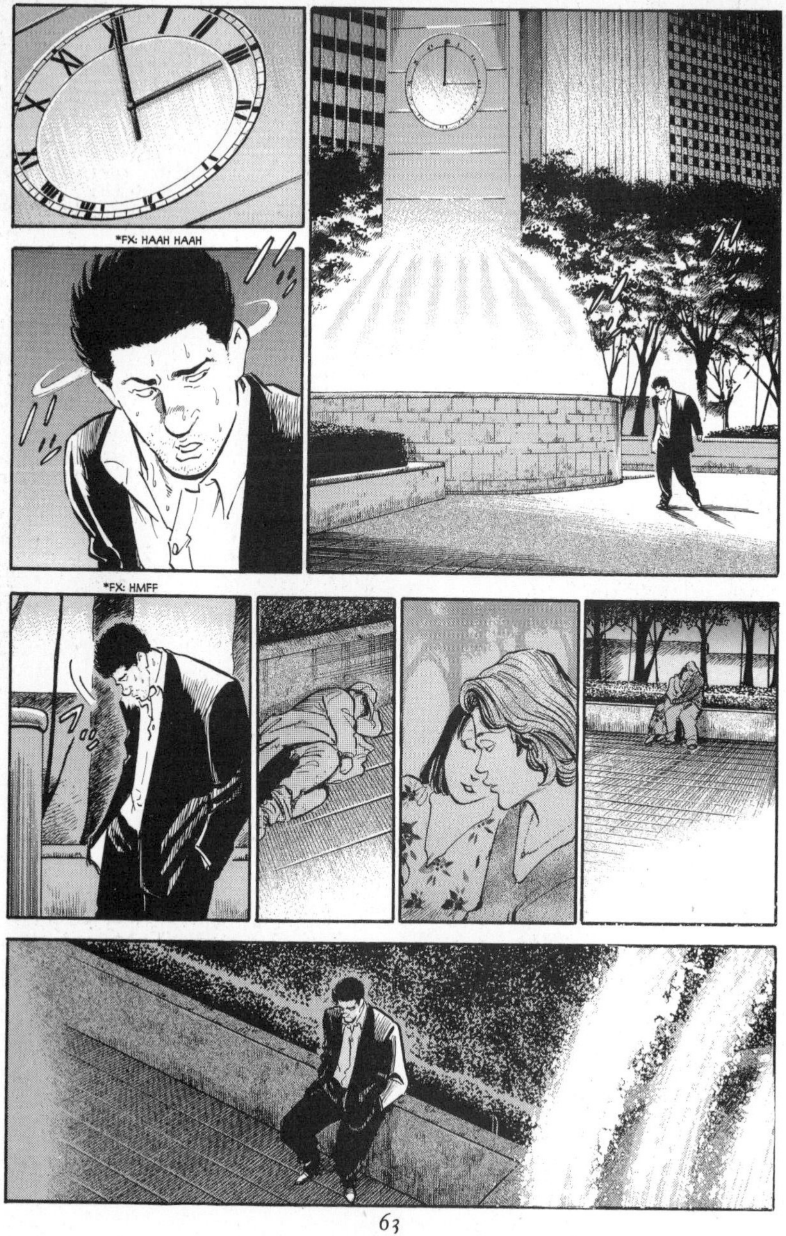
*FX: HAAH HAAH
*FX: HMFF

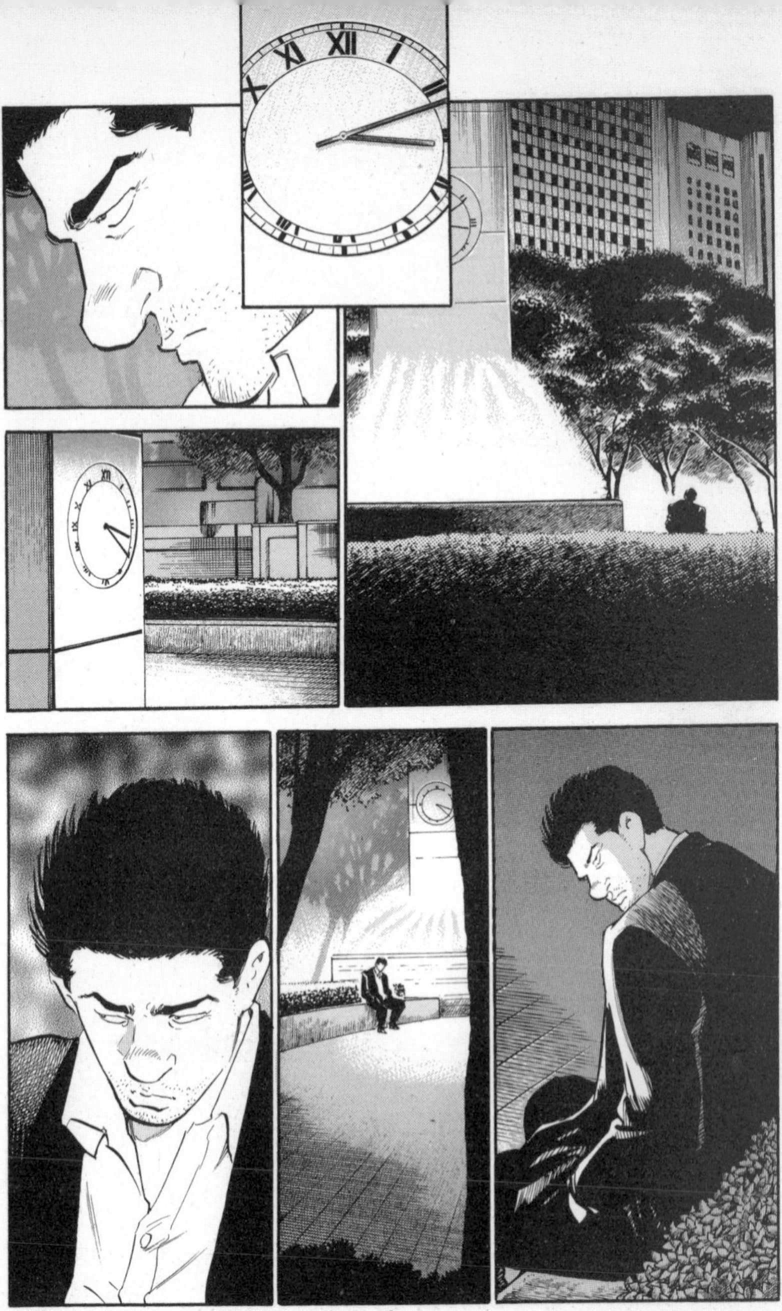

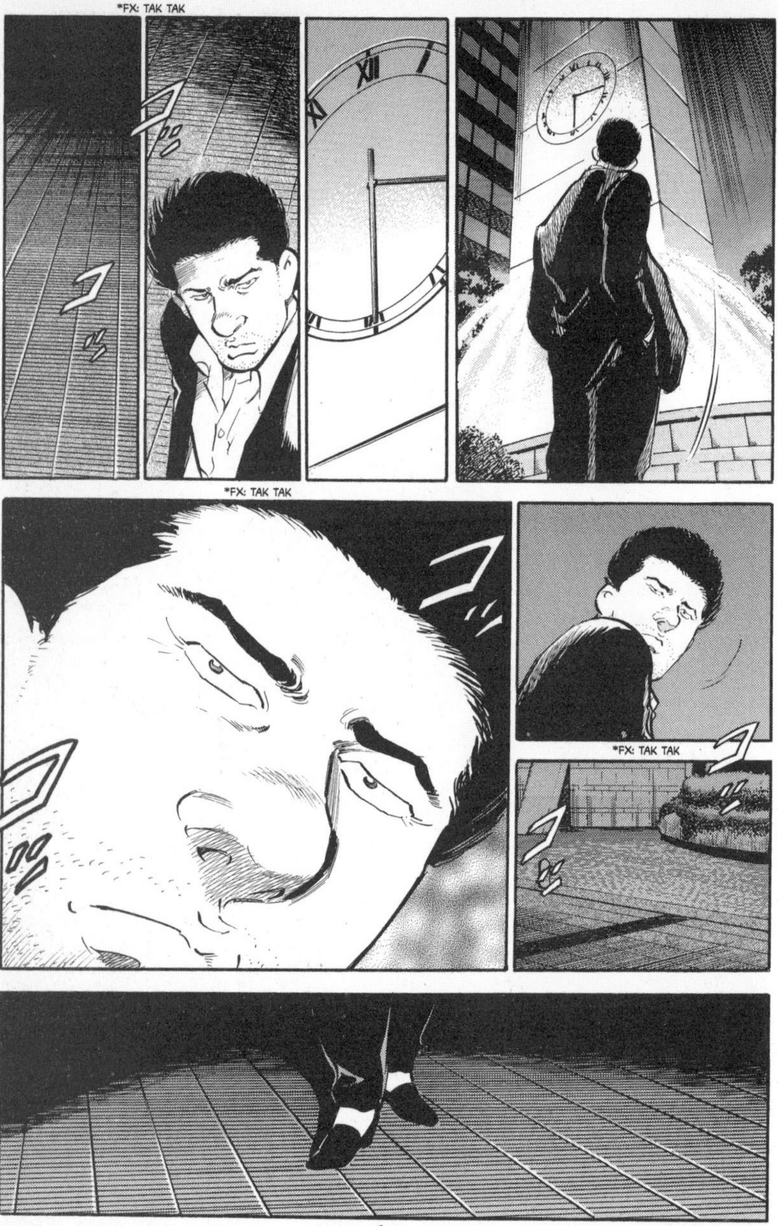
*FX: TAK TAK
*FX: TAK TAK
*FX: TAK TAK

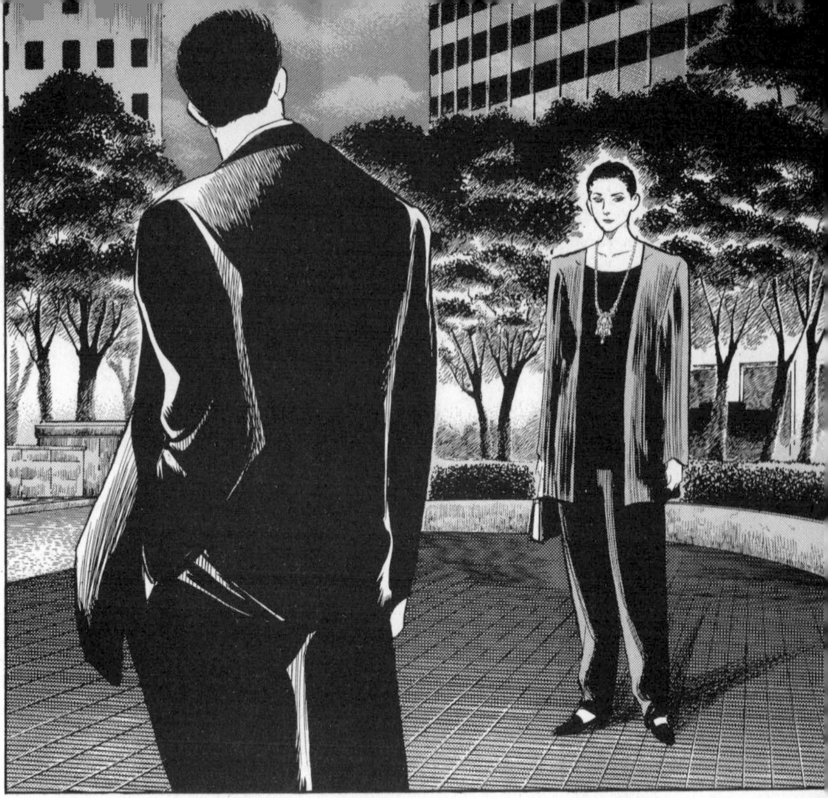
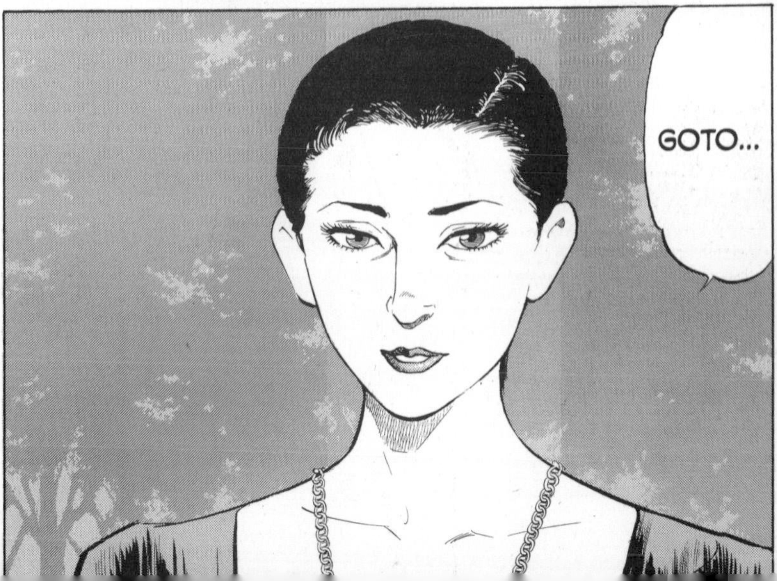
GOTO...

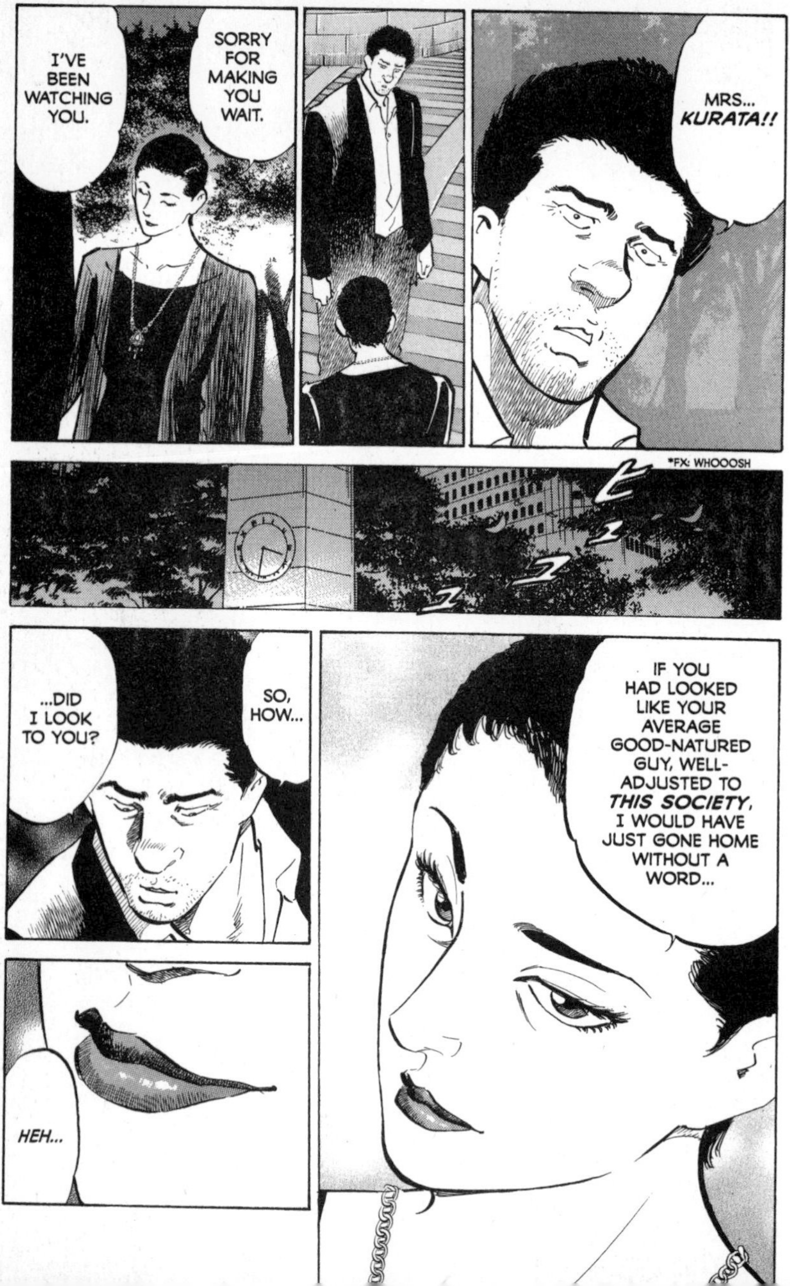
MRS... KURATA!!
SORRY FOR MAKING YOU WAIT.
I'VE BEEN WATCHING YOU.
*FX: WHOOOSH
IF YOU HAD LOOKED LIKE YOUR AVERAGE GOOD-NATURED GUY, WELL-ADJUSTED TO THIS SOCIETY, I WOULD HAVE JUST GONE HOME WITHOUT A WORD...
SO, HOW...
...DID I LOOK TO YOU?
HEH...

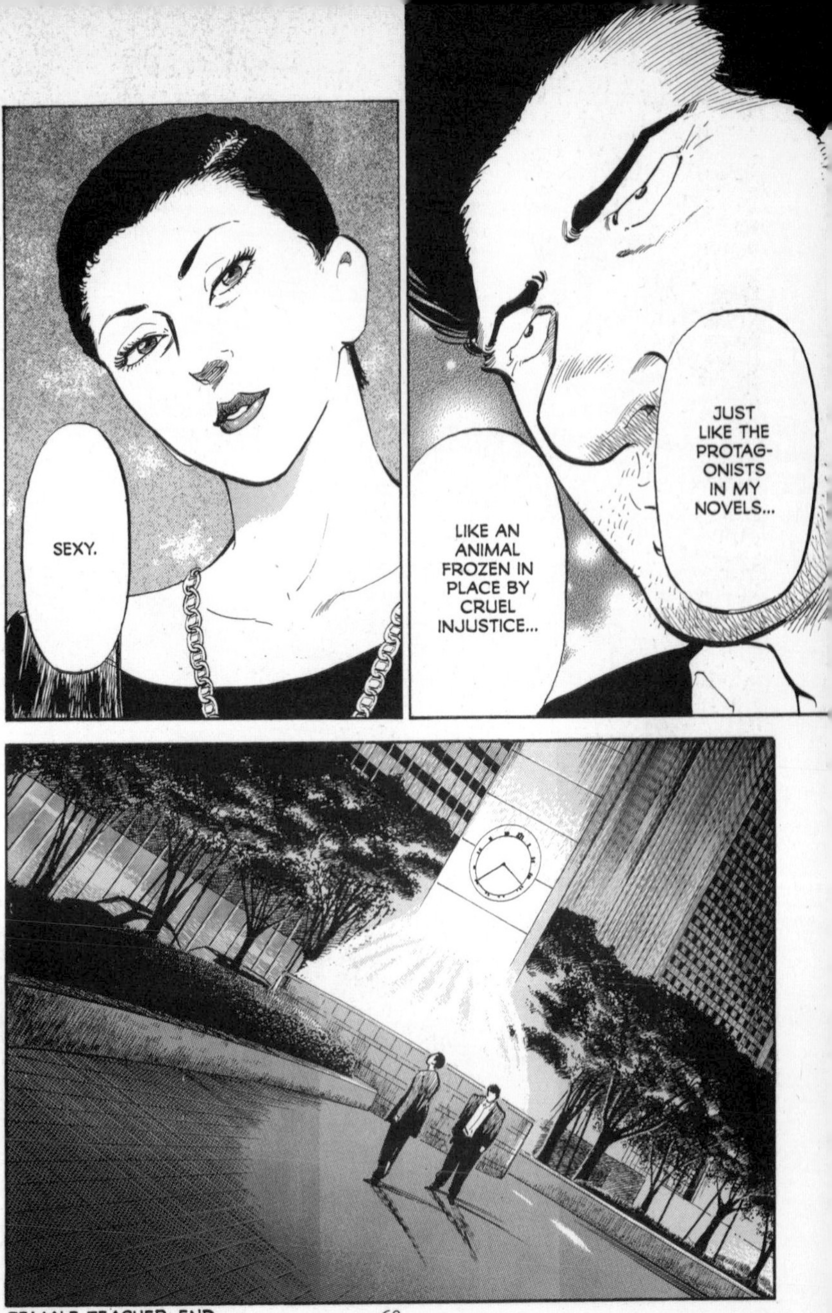
JUST LIKE THE PROTAG- ONISTS IN MY NOVELS...
LIKE AN ANIMAL FROZEN IN PLACE BY CRUEL INJUSTICE...
SEXY.

FEMALE TEACHER: END

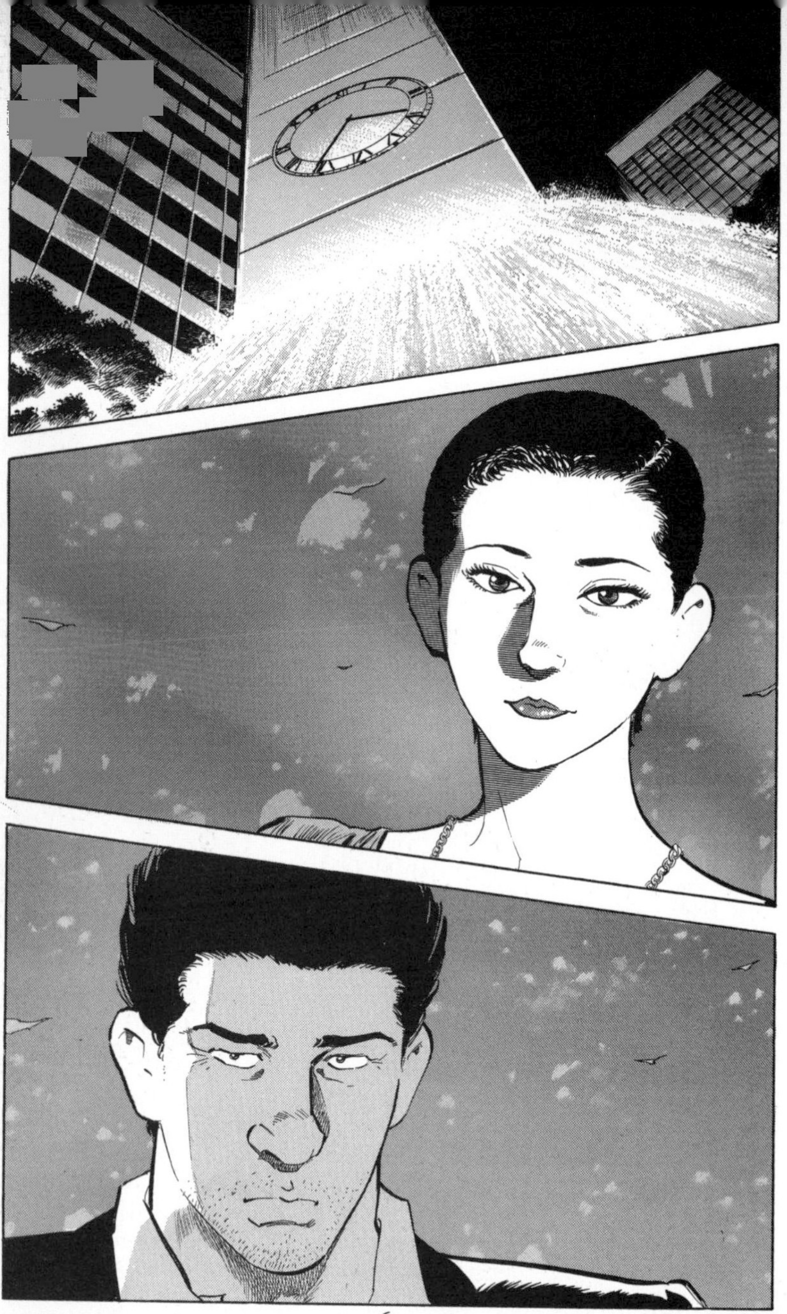

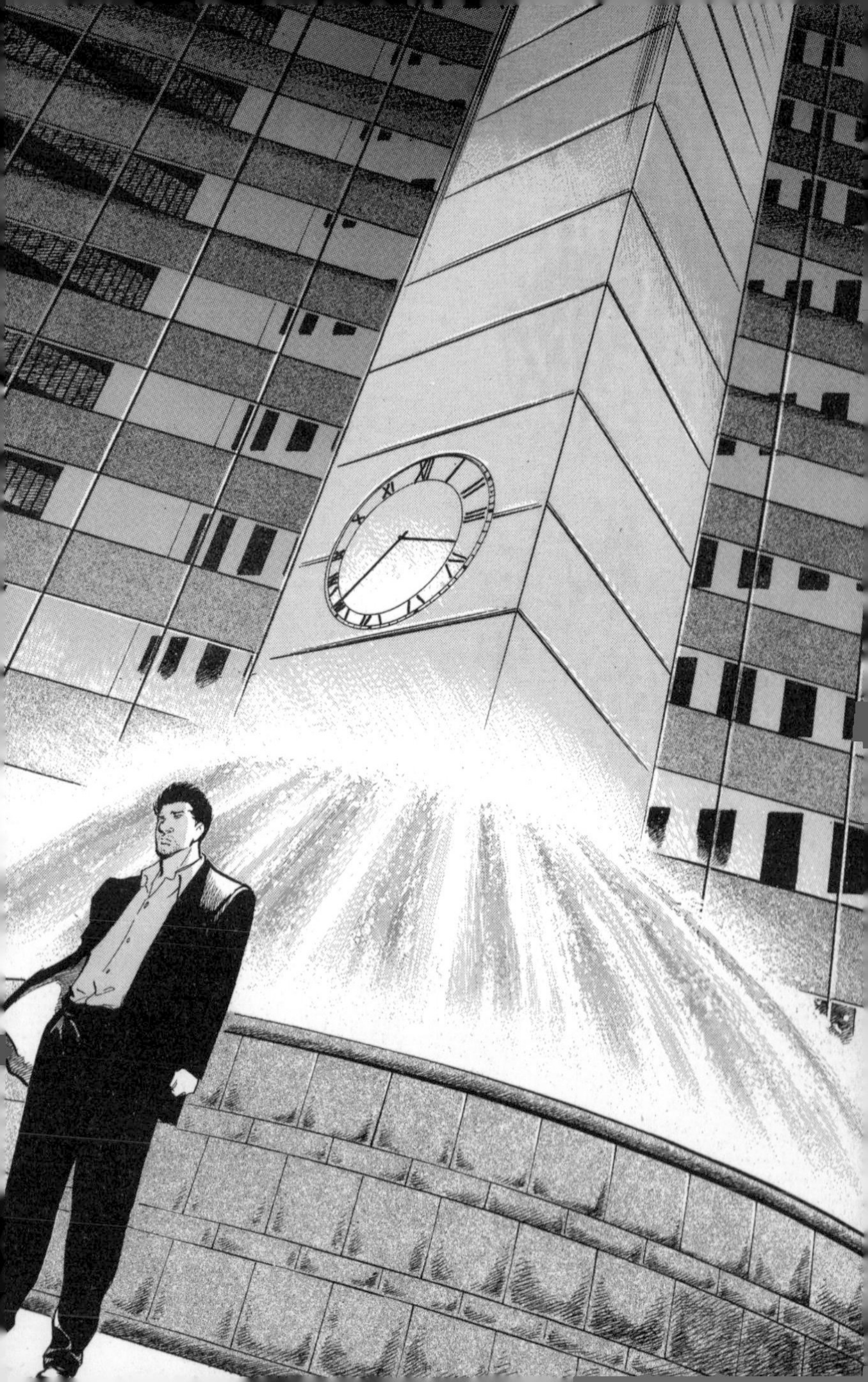

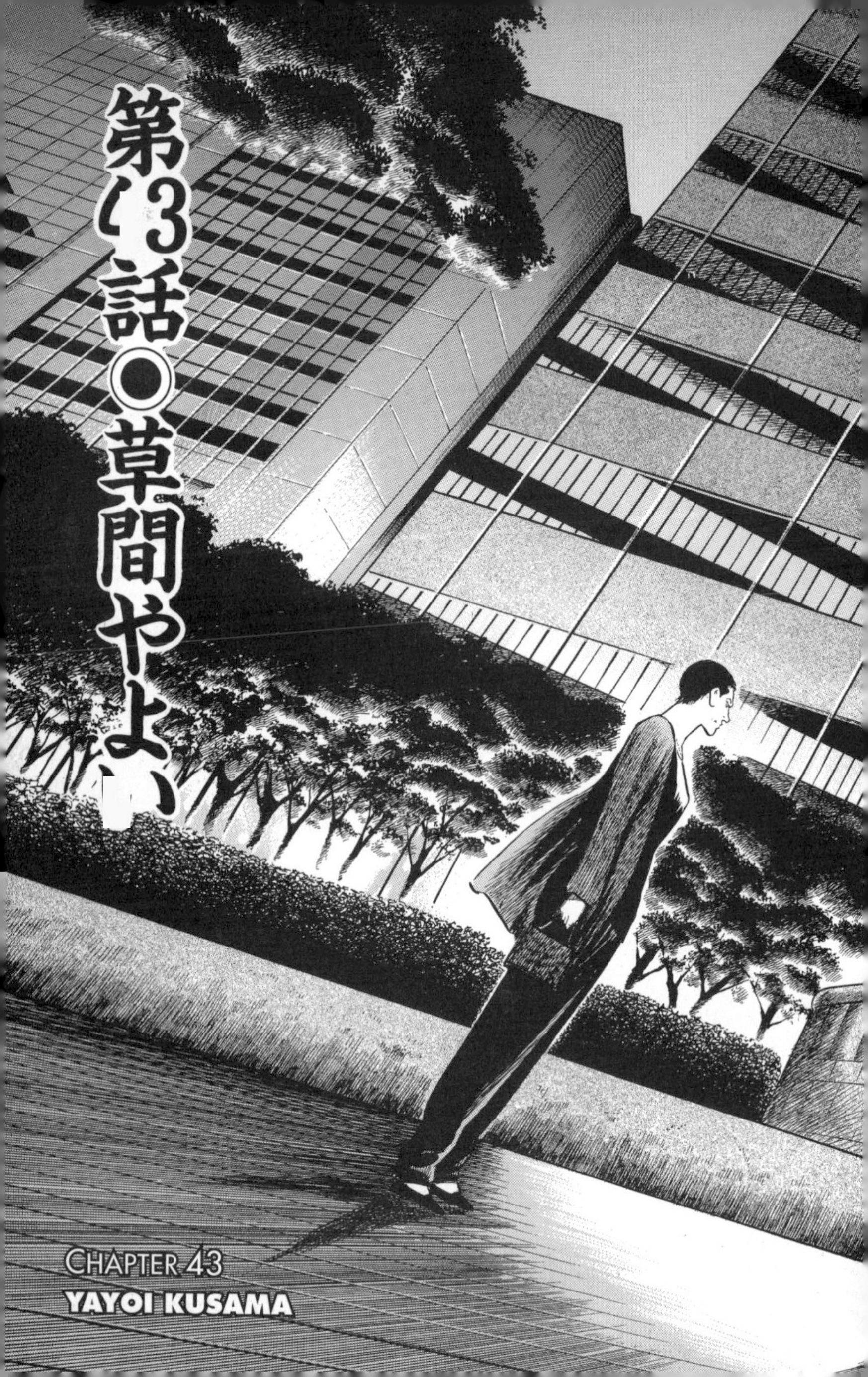
第3話◎草間やよい
CHAPTER 43
YAYOI KUSAMA

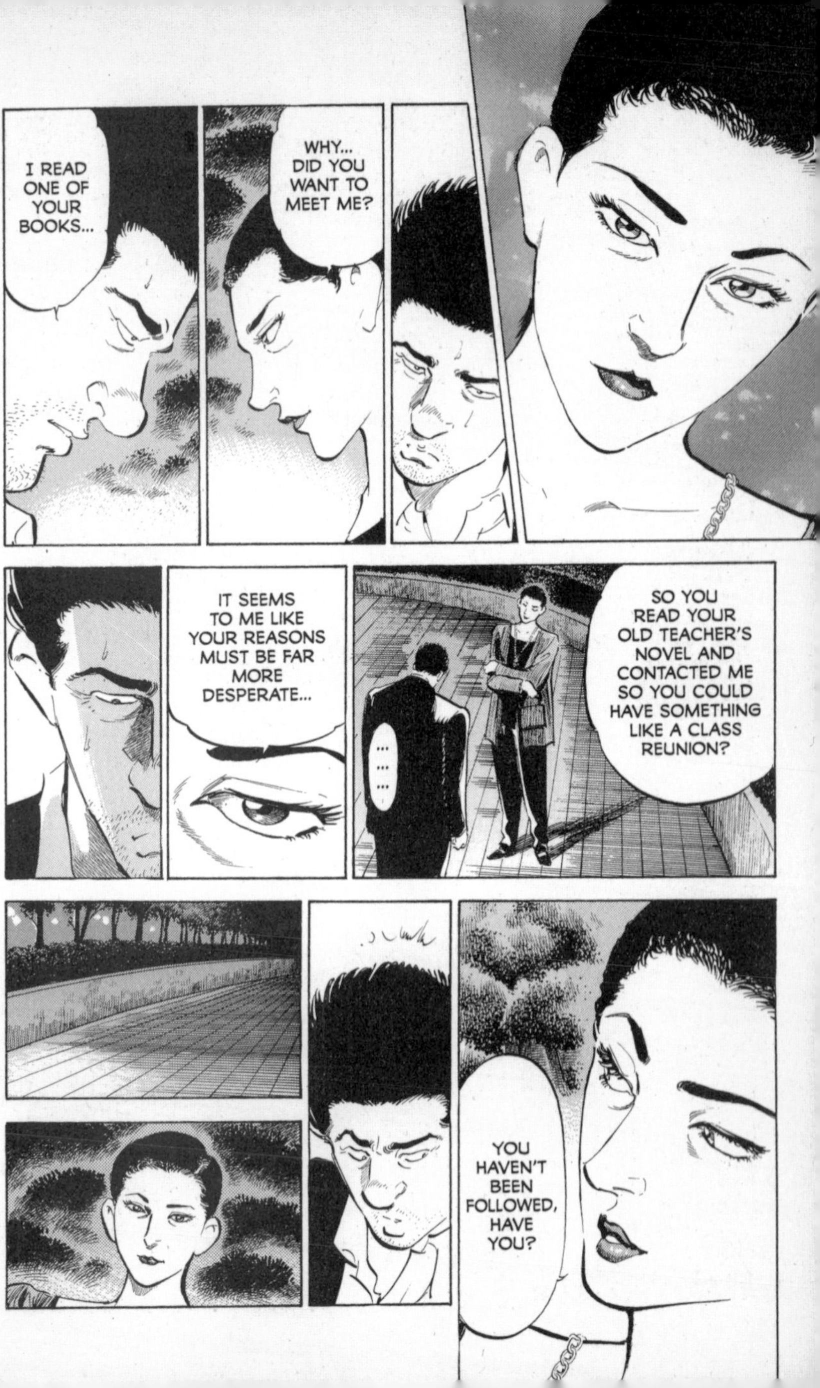
WHY... DID YOU WANT TO MEET ME?
I READ ONE OF YOUR BOOKS...
SO YOU READ YOUR OLD TEACHER'S NOVEL AND CONTACTED ME SO YOU COULD HAVE SOMETHING LIKE A CLASS REUNION?
... ...
IT SEEMS TO ME LIKE YOUR REASONS MUST BE FAR MORE DESPERATE...
YOU HAVEN'T BEEN FOLLOWED, HAVE YOU?

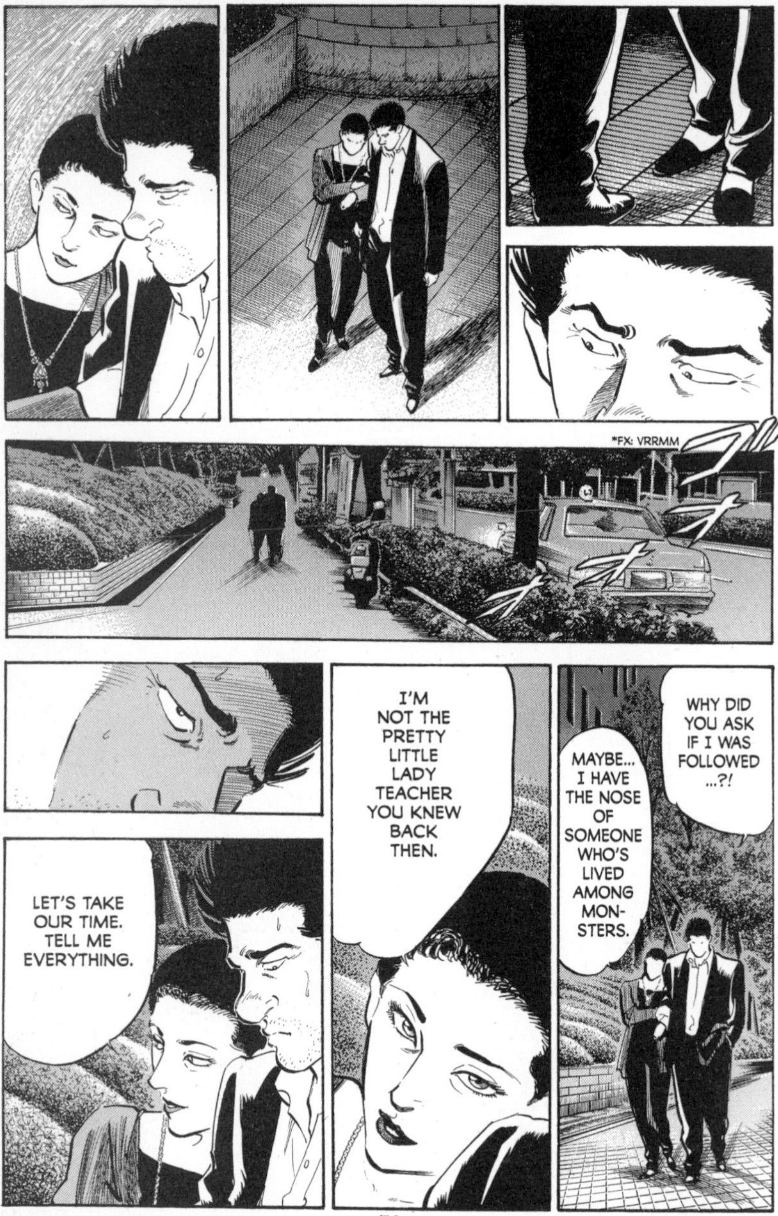
*FX: VRRMM
WHY DID YOU ASK IF I WAS FOLLOWED ...?!
MAYBE... I HAVE THE NOSE OF SOMEONE WHO'S LIVED AMONG MON-STERS.
I'M NOT THE PRETTY LITTLE LADY TEACHER YOU KNEW BACK THEN.
LET'S TAKE OUR TIME. TELL ME EVERYTHING.

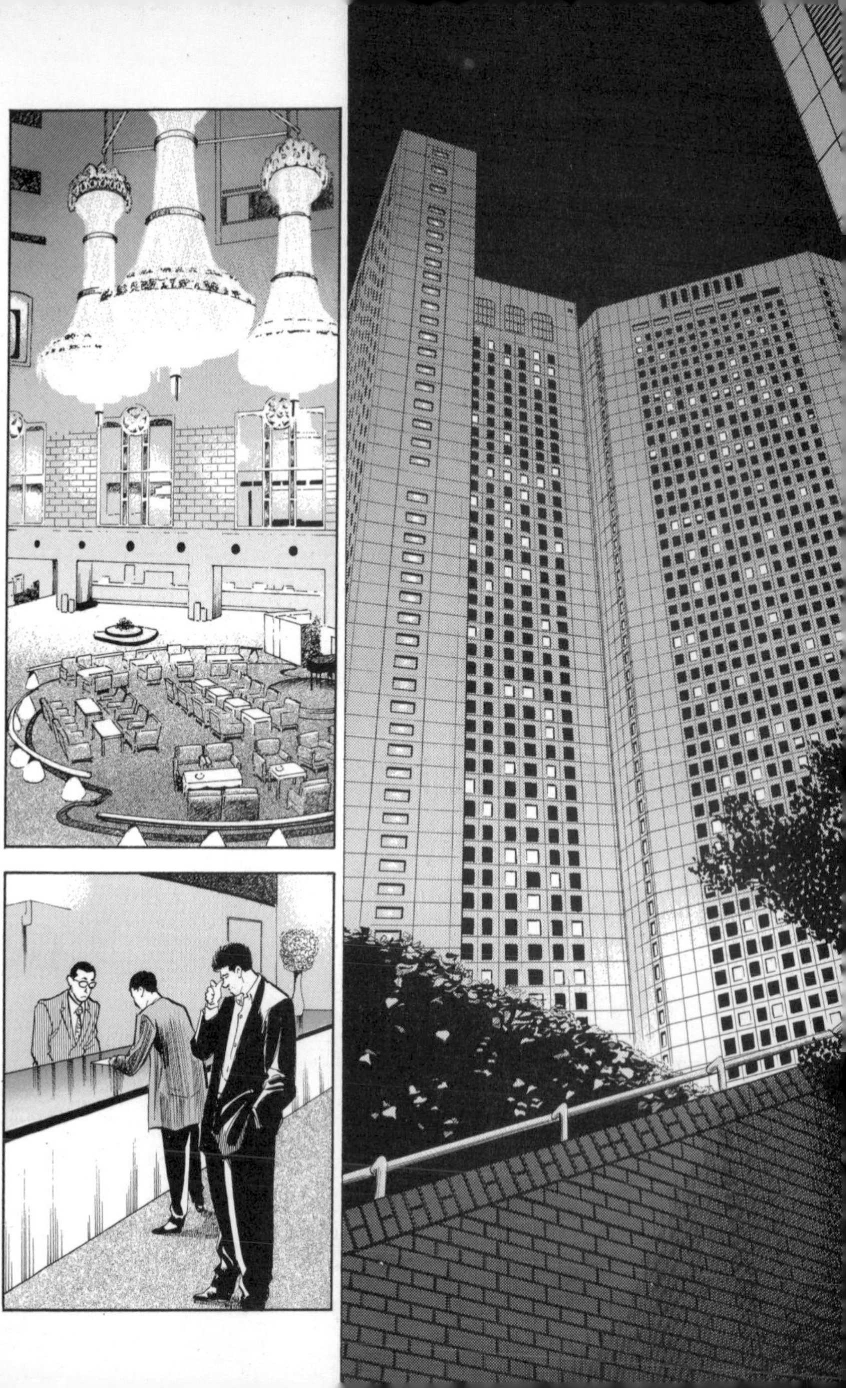

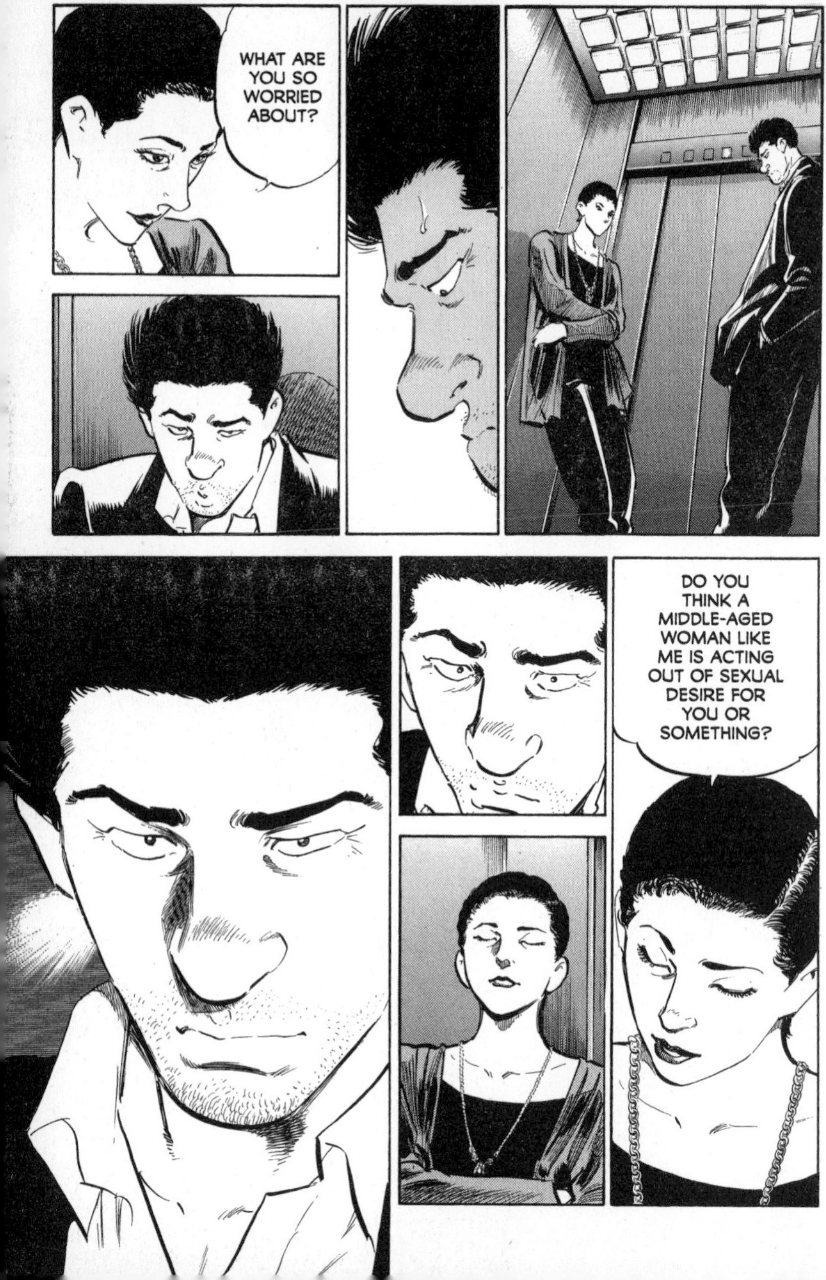
WHAT ARE YOU SO WORRIED ABOUT?
DO YOU THINK A MIDDLE-AGED WOMAN LIKE ME IS ACTING OUT OF SEXUAL DESIRE FOR YOU OR SOMETHING?

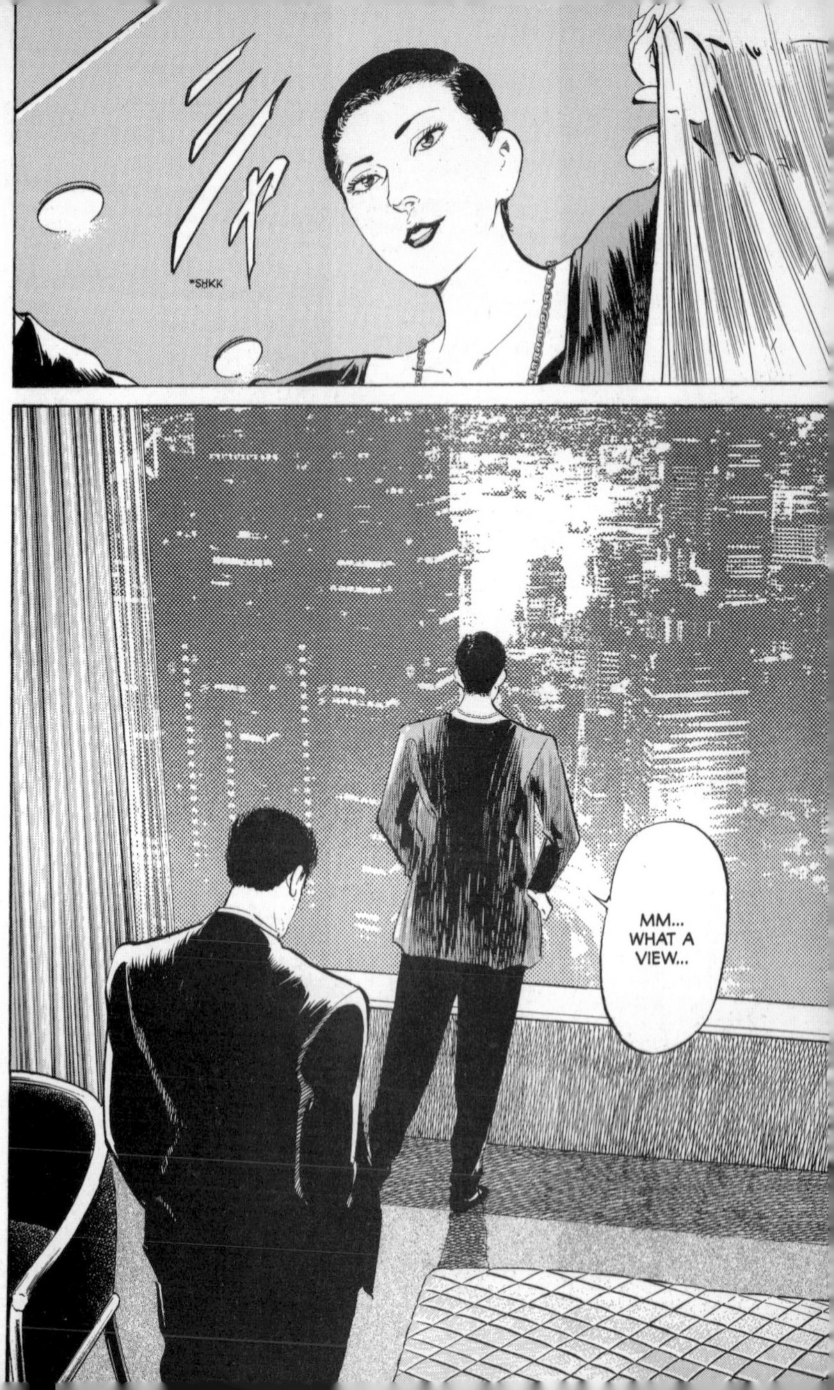

*SHKK
MM... WHAT A VIEW...

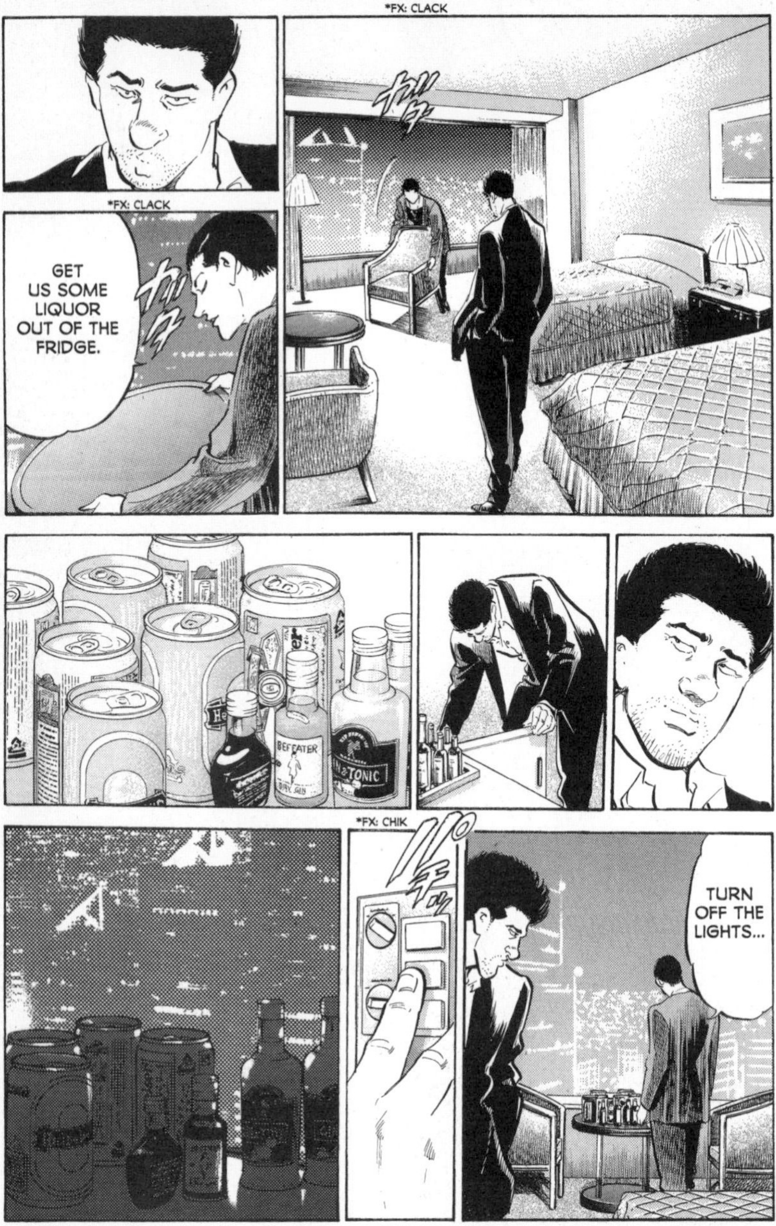
*FX: CLACK
*FX: CLACK
GET US SOME LIQUOR OUT OF THE FRIDGE.
*FX: CHIK
TURN OFF THE LIGHTS...

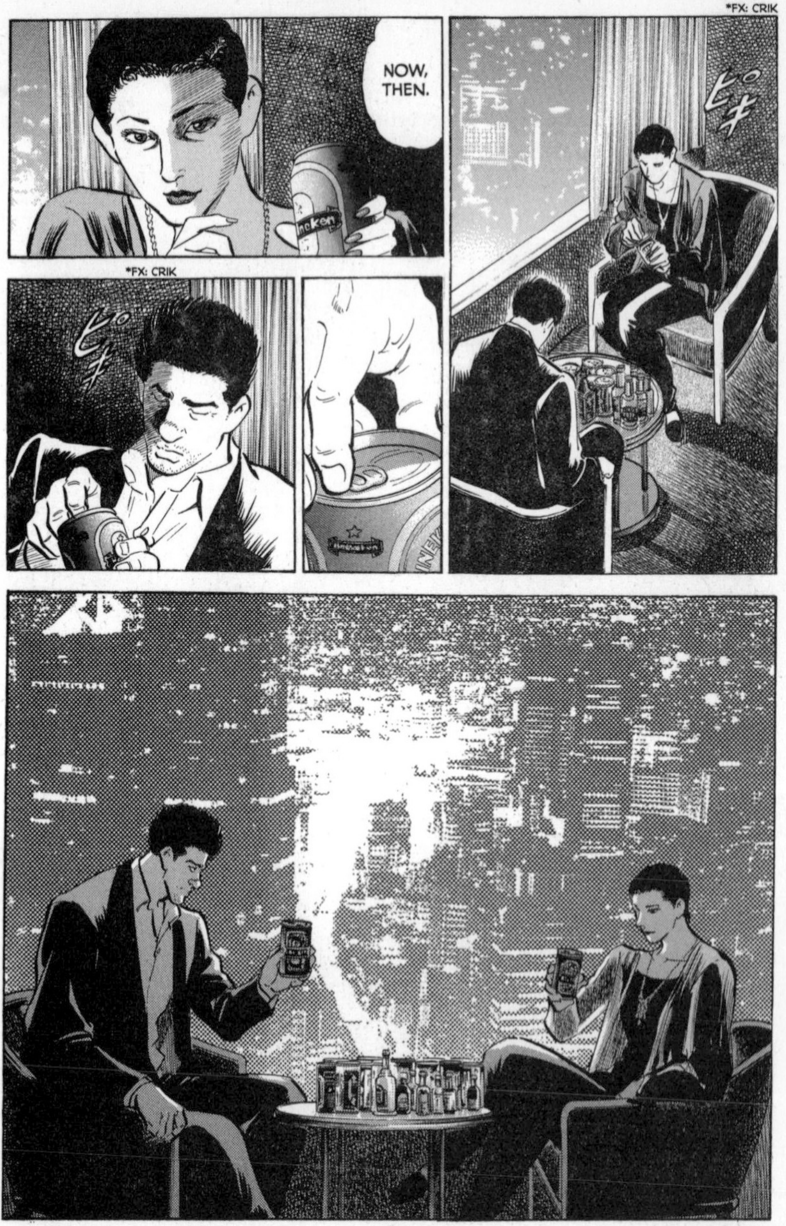
*FX: CRIK
ピキ
NOW, THEN.
*FX: CRIK
ピキ

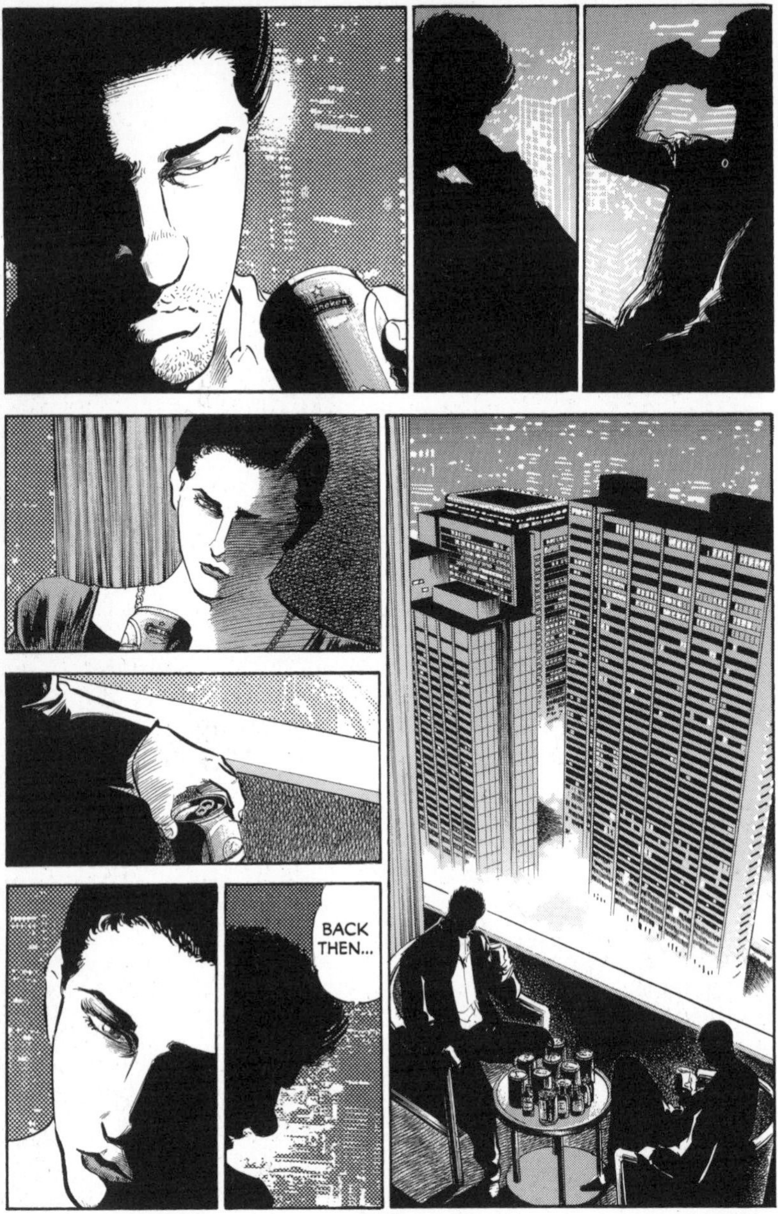
BACK THEN...

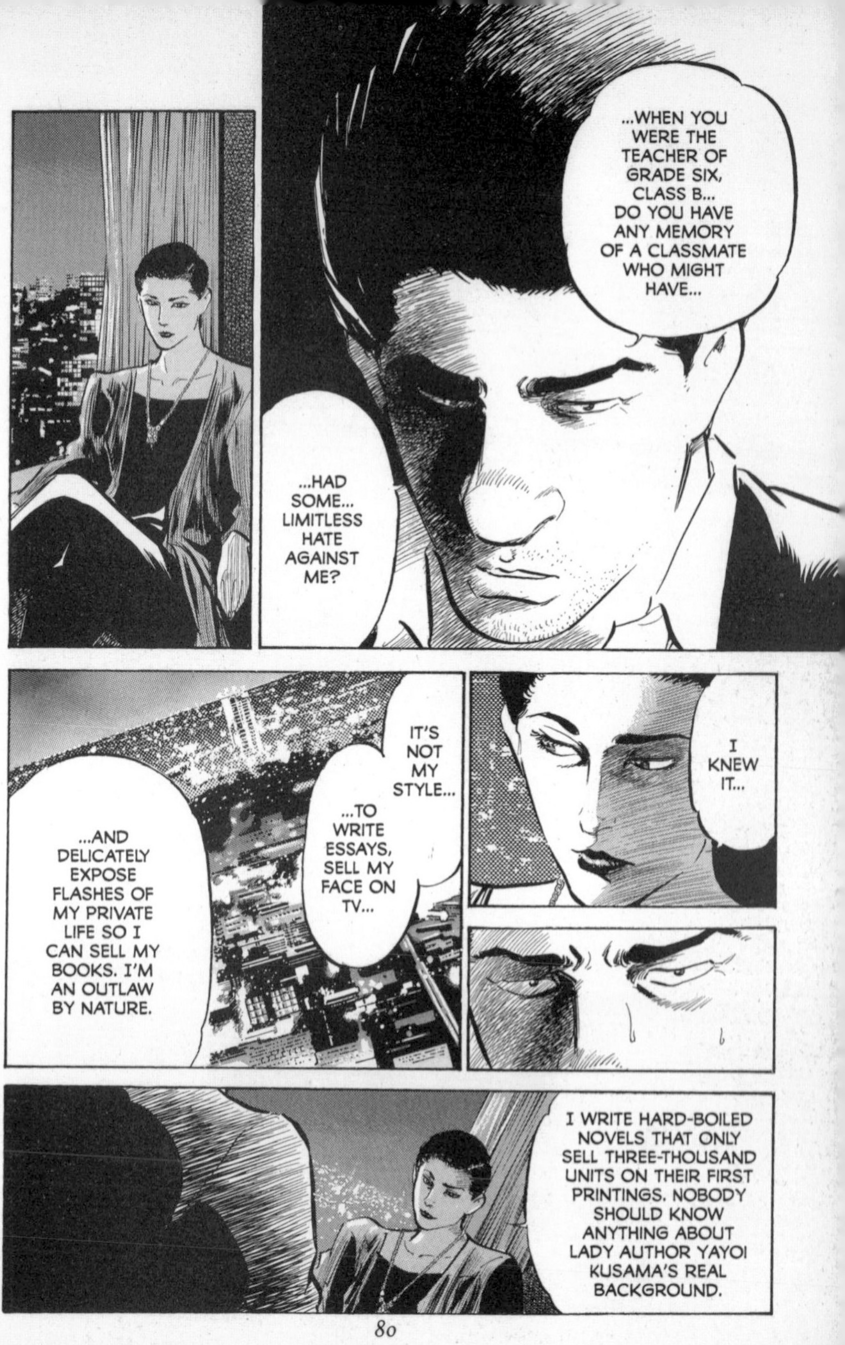
...WHEN YOU WERE THE TEACHER OF GRADE SIX, CLASS B... DO YOU HAVE ANY MEMORY OF A CLASSMATE WHO MIGHT HAVE...
...HAD SOME... LIMITLESS HATE AGAINST ME?
I KNEW IT...
IT'S NOT MY STYLE...
...TO WRITE ESSAYS, SELL MY FACE ON TV...
...AND DELICATELY EXPOSE FLASHES OF MY PRIVATE LIFE SO I CAN SELL MY BOOKS. I'M AN OUTLAW BY NATURE.
I WRITE HARD-BOILED NOVELS THAT ONLY SELL THREE-THOUSAND UNITS ON THEIR FIRST PRINTINGS. NOBODY SHOULD KNOW ANYTHING ABOUT LADY AUTHOR YAYOI KUSAMA'S REAL BACKGROUND.

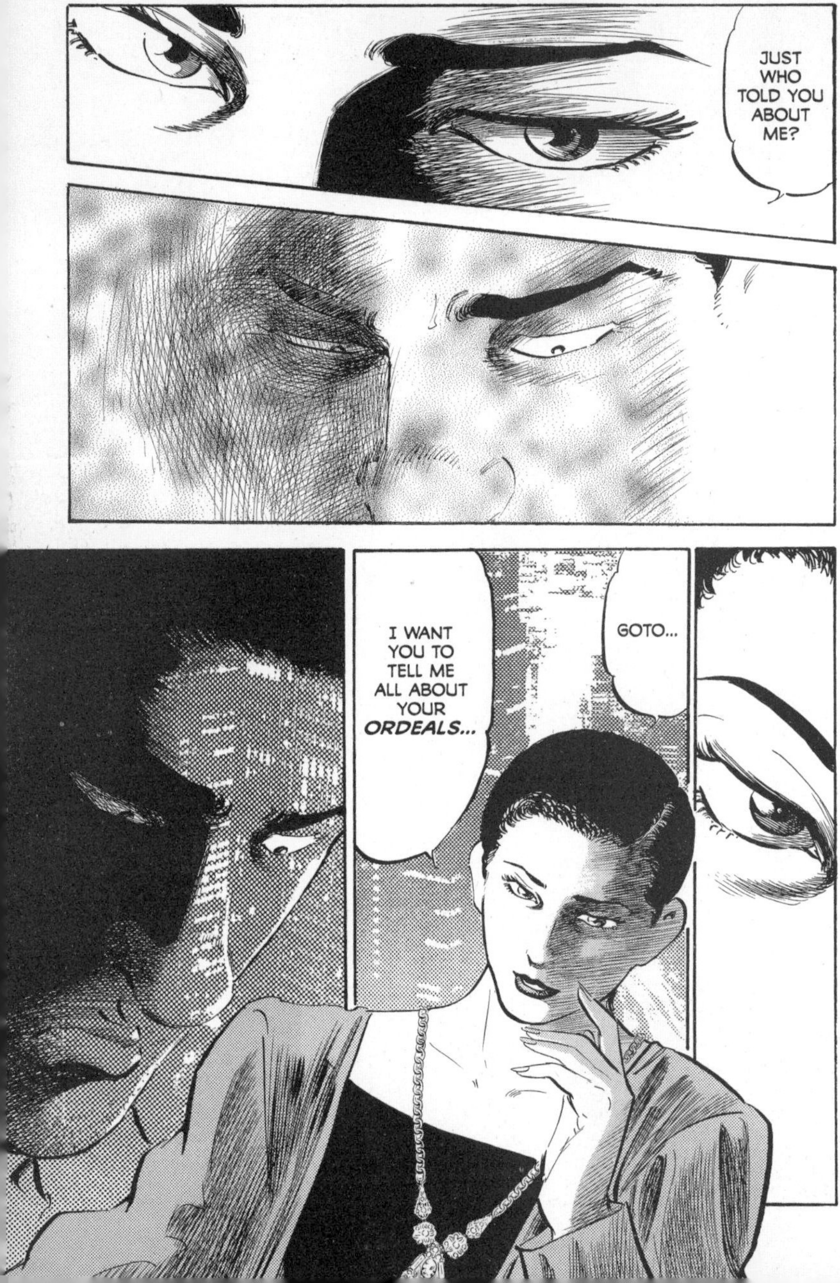
JUST WHO TOLD YOU ABOUT ME?
GOTO...
I WANT YOU TO TELL ME ALL ABOUT YOUR *ORDEALS...*

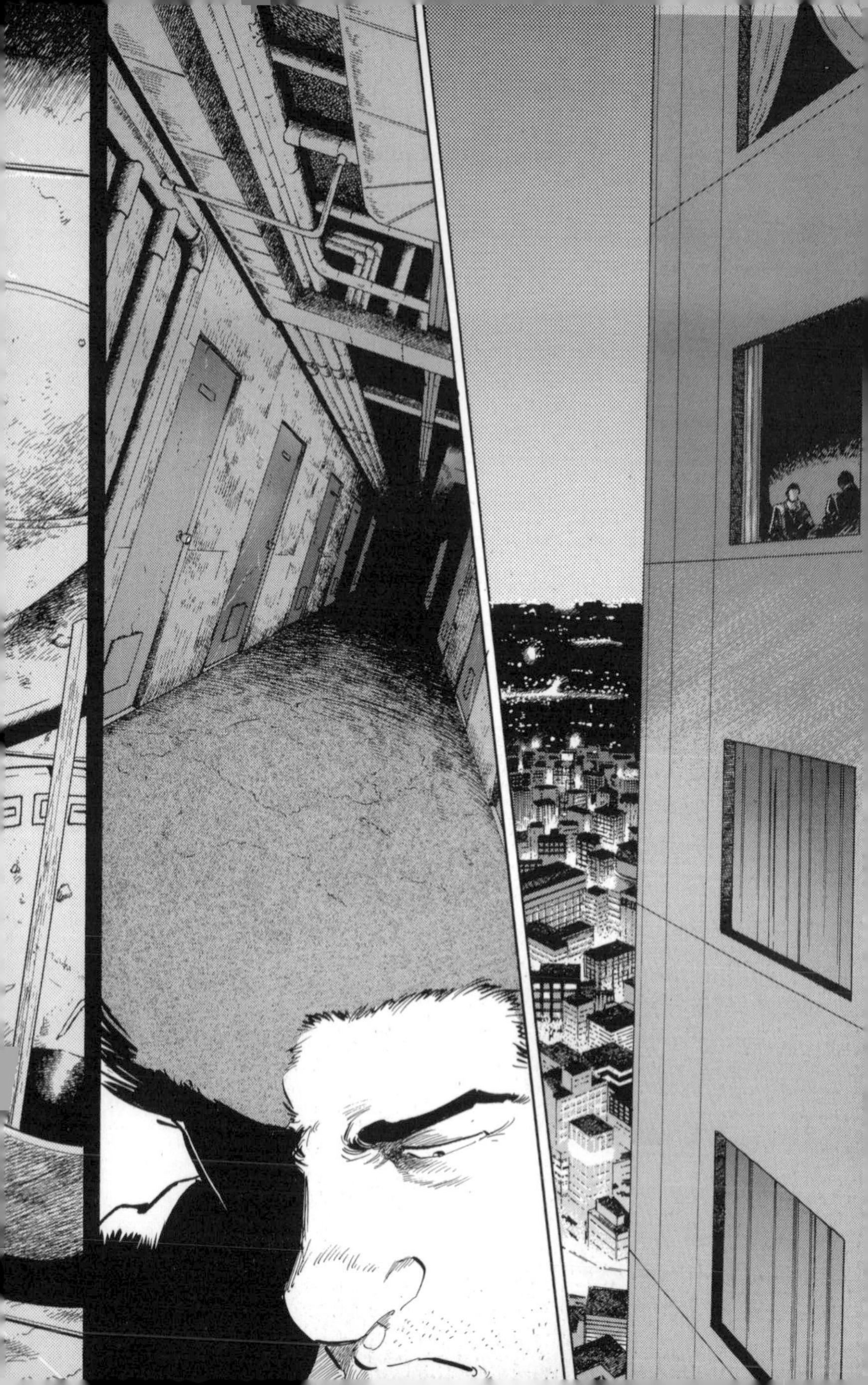

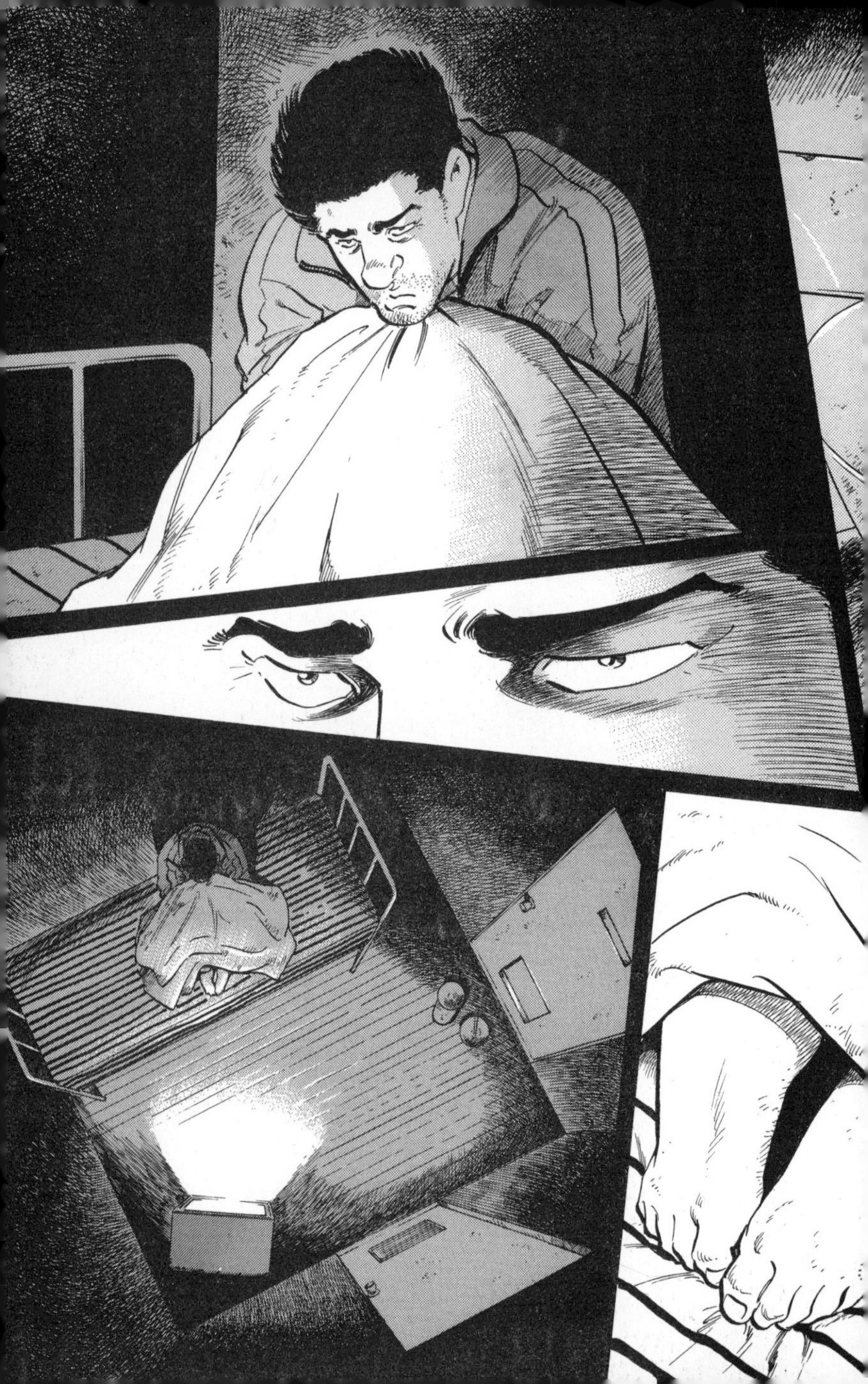

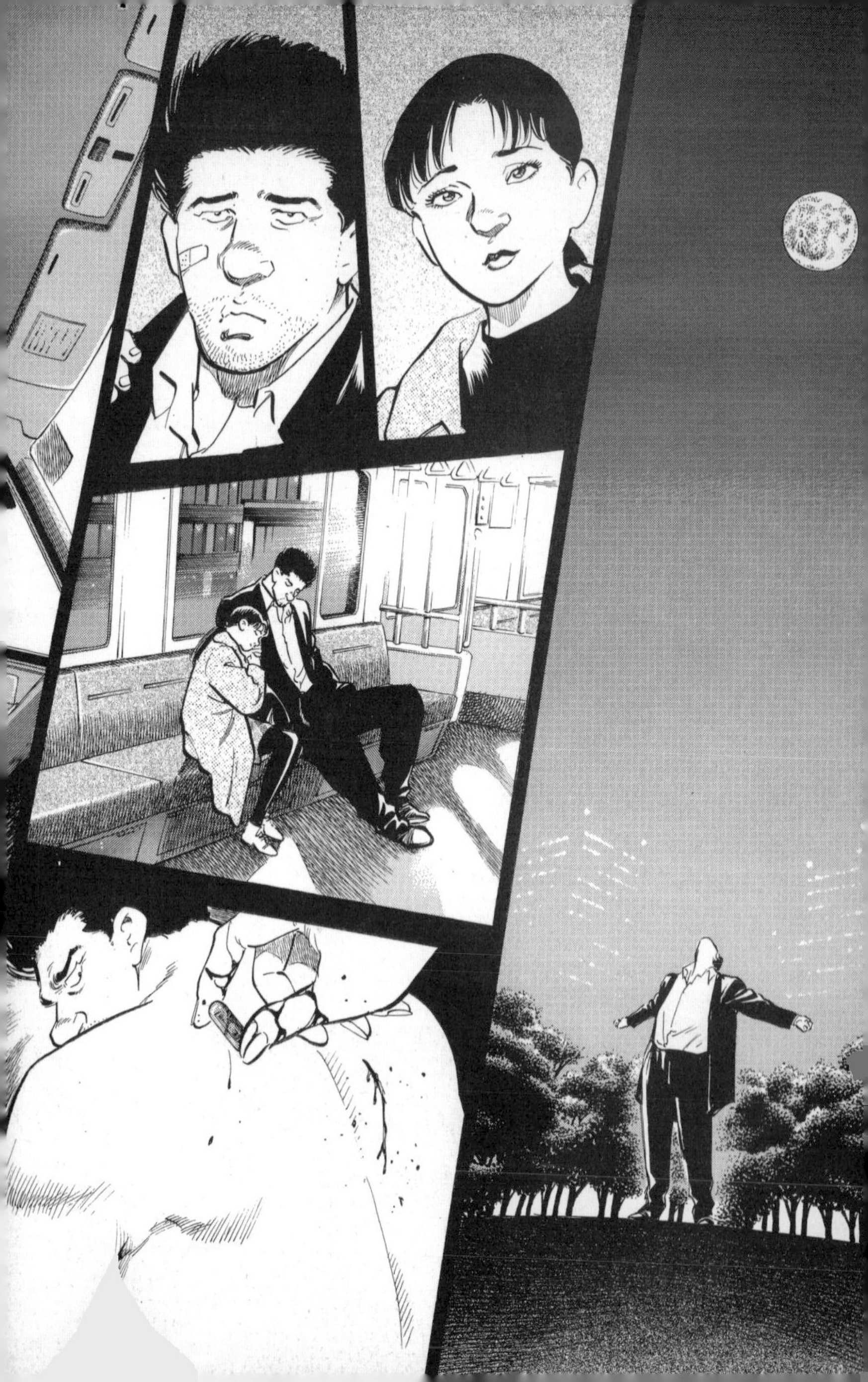

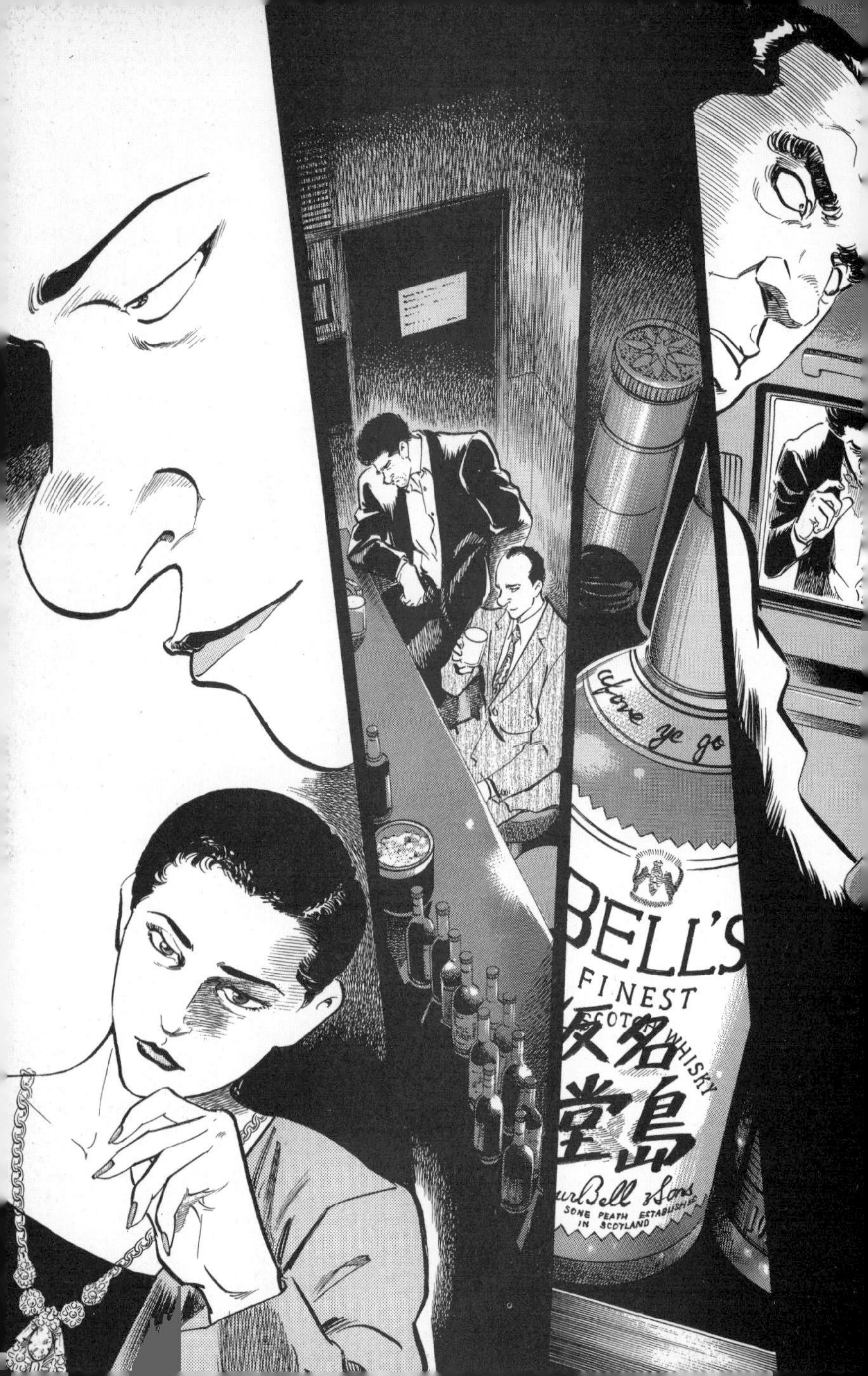
ye go
BELL'S
FINEST
WHISKY
IN SCOTLAND

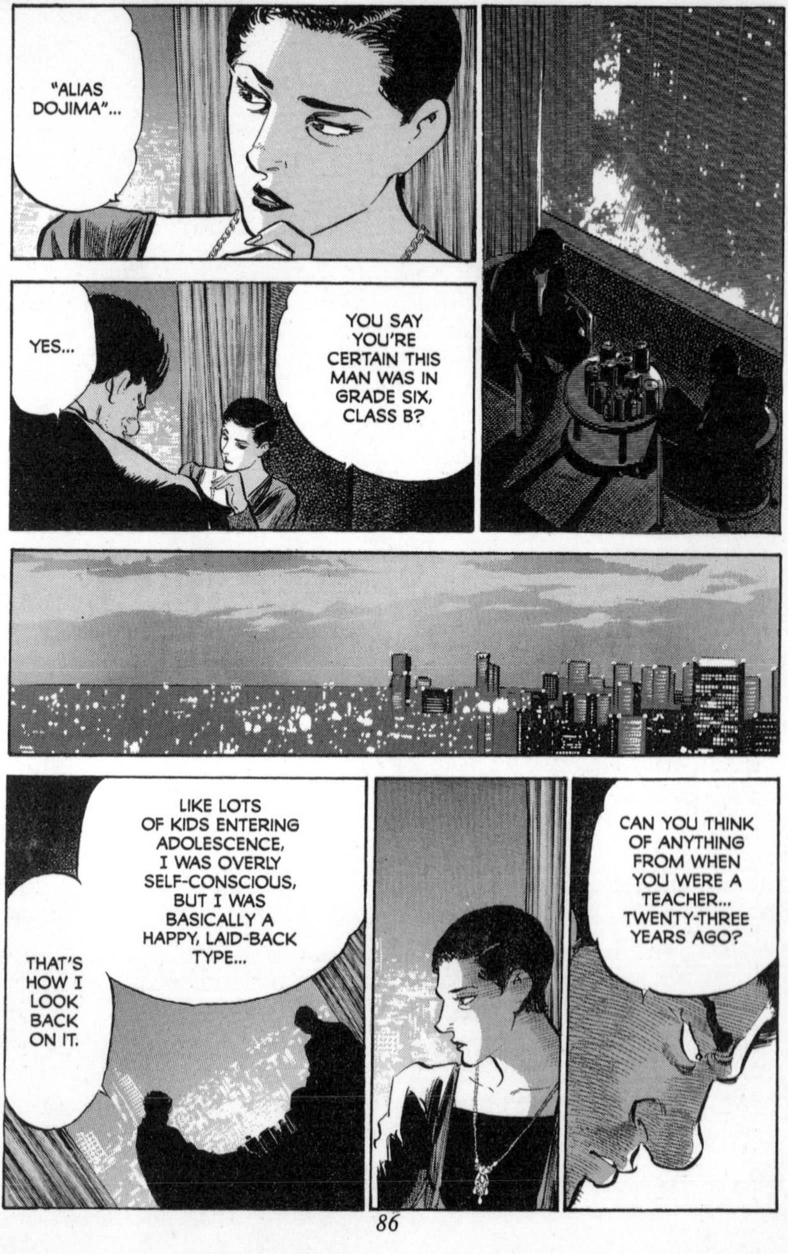
"ALIAS DOJIMA"...
YOU SAY YOU'RE CERTAIN THIS MAN WAS IN GRADE SIX, CLASS B?
YES...
CAN YOU THINK OF ANYTHING FROM WHEN YOU WERE A TEACHER... TWENTY-THREE YEARS AGO?
LIKE LOTS OF KIDS ENTERING ADOLESCENCE, I WAS OVERLY SELF-CONSCIOUS, BUT I WAS BASICALLY A HAPPY, LAID-BACK TYPE...
THAT'S HOW I LOOK BACK ON IT.

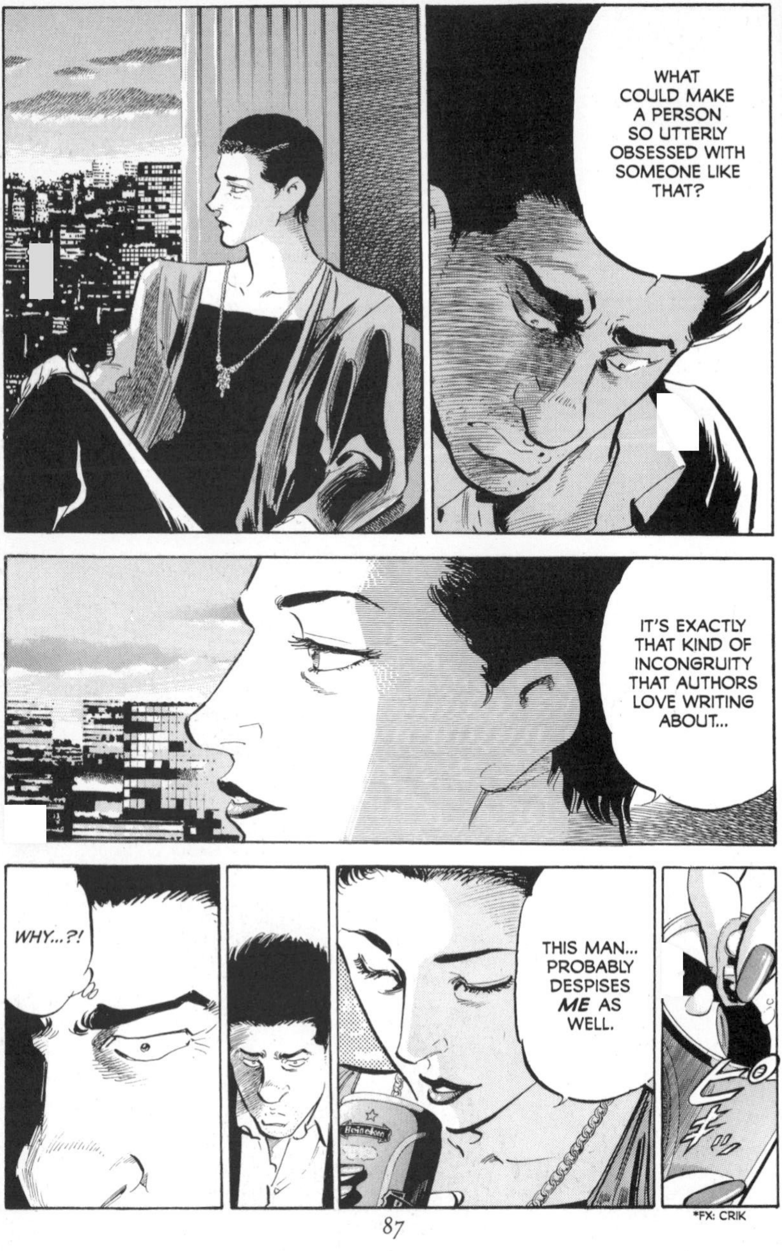
WHAT COULD MAKE A PERSON SO UTTERLY OBSESSED WITH SOMEONE LIKE THAT?
IT'S EXACTLY THAT KIND OF INCONGRUITY THAT AUTHORS LOVE WRITING ABOUT...
THIS MAN... PROBABLY DESPISES *ME* AS WELL.
WHY...?!
Heineken

*FX: CRIK

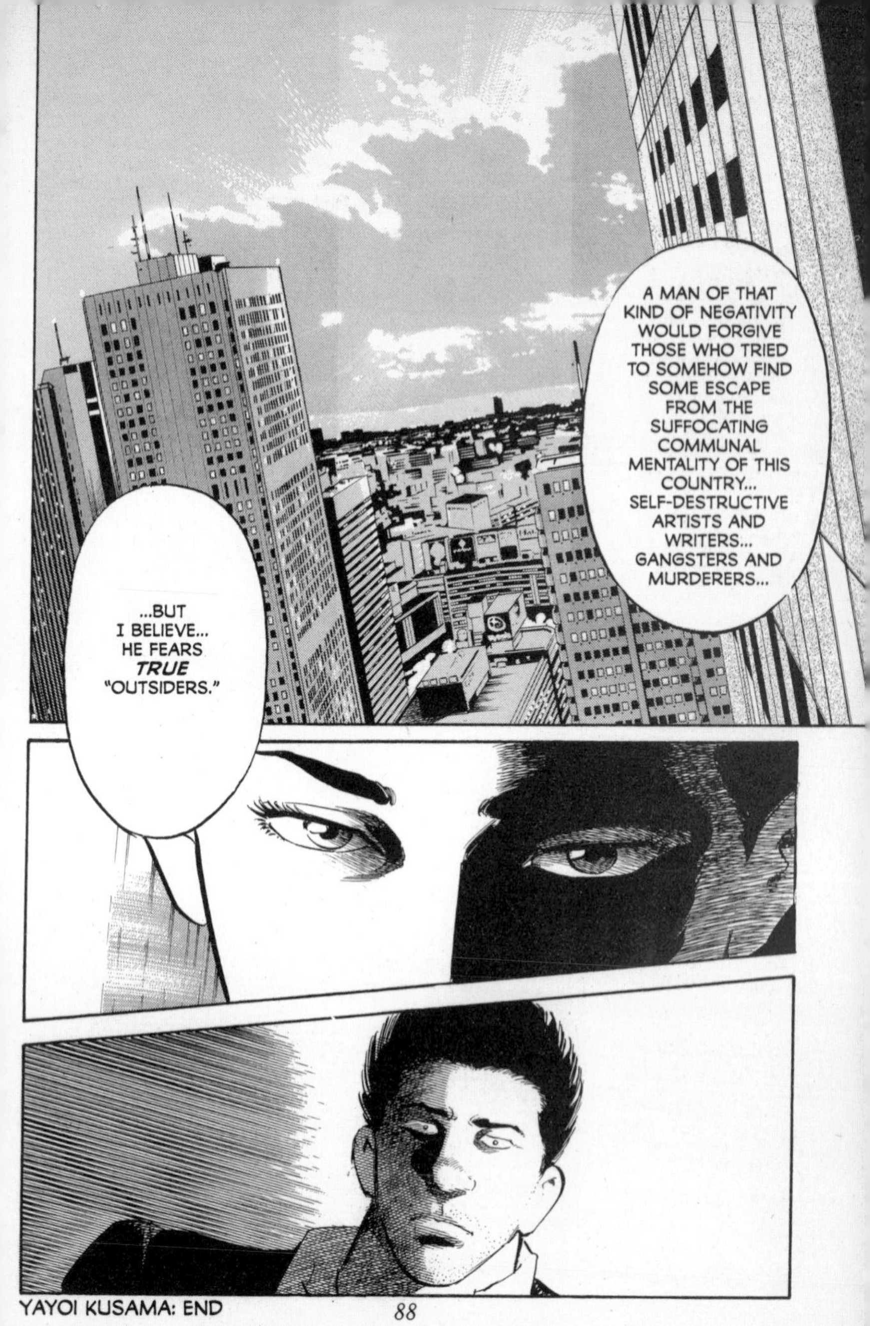
A MAN OF THAT KIND OF NEGATIVITY WOULD FORGIVE THOSE WHO TRIED TO SOMEHOW FIND SOME ESCAPE FROM THE SUFFOCATING COMMUNAL MENTALITY OF THIS COUNTRY... SELF-DESTRUCTIVE ARTISTS AND WRITERS... GANGSTERS AND MURDERERS...
...BUT I BELIEVE... HE FEARS ***TRUE*** "OUTSIDERS."

YAYOI KUSAMA: END

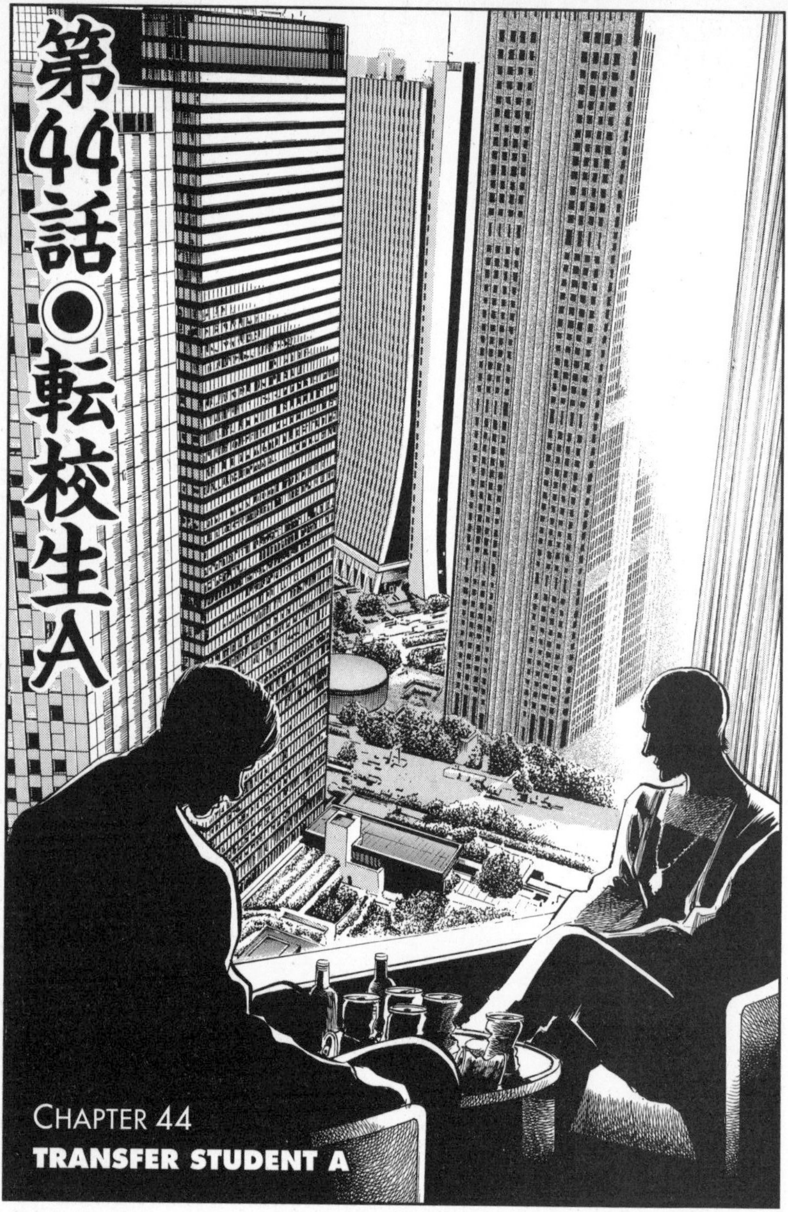
第44話●転校生A
CHAPTER 44
TRANSFER STUDENT A

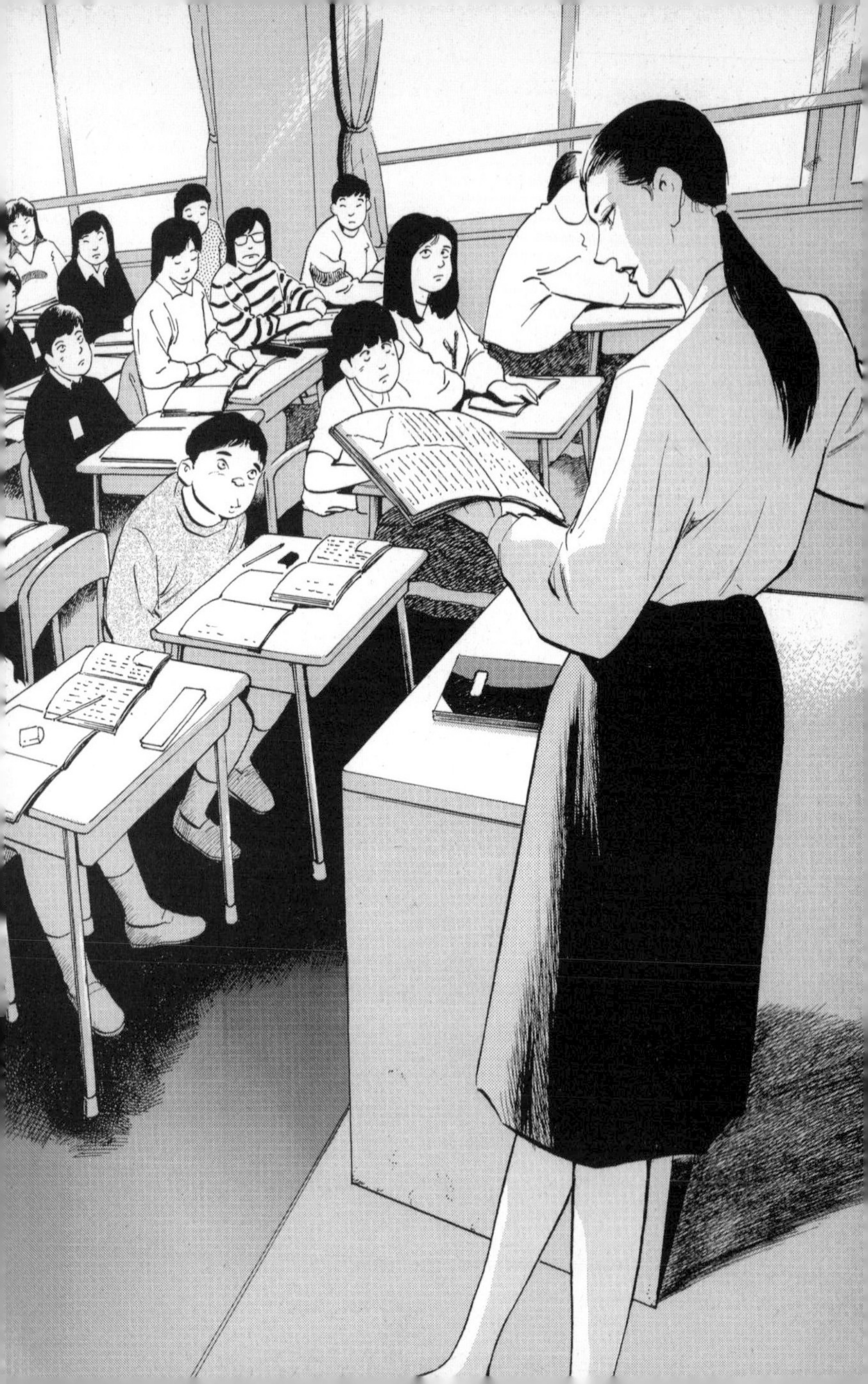

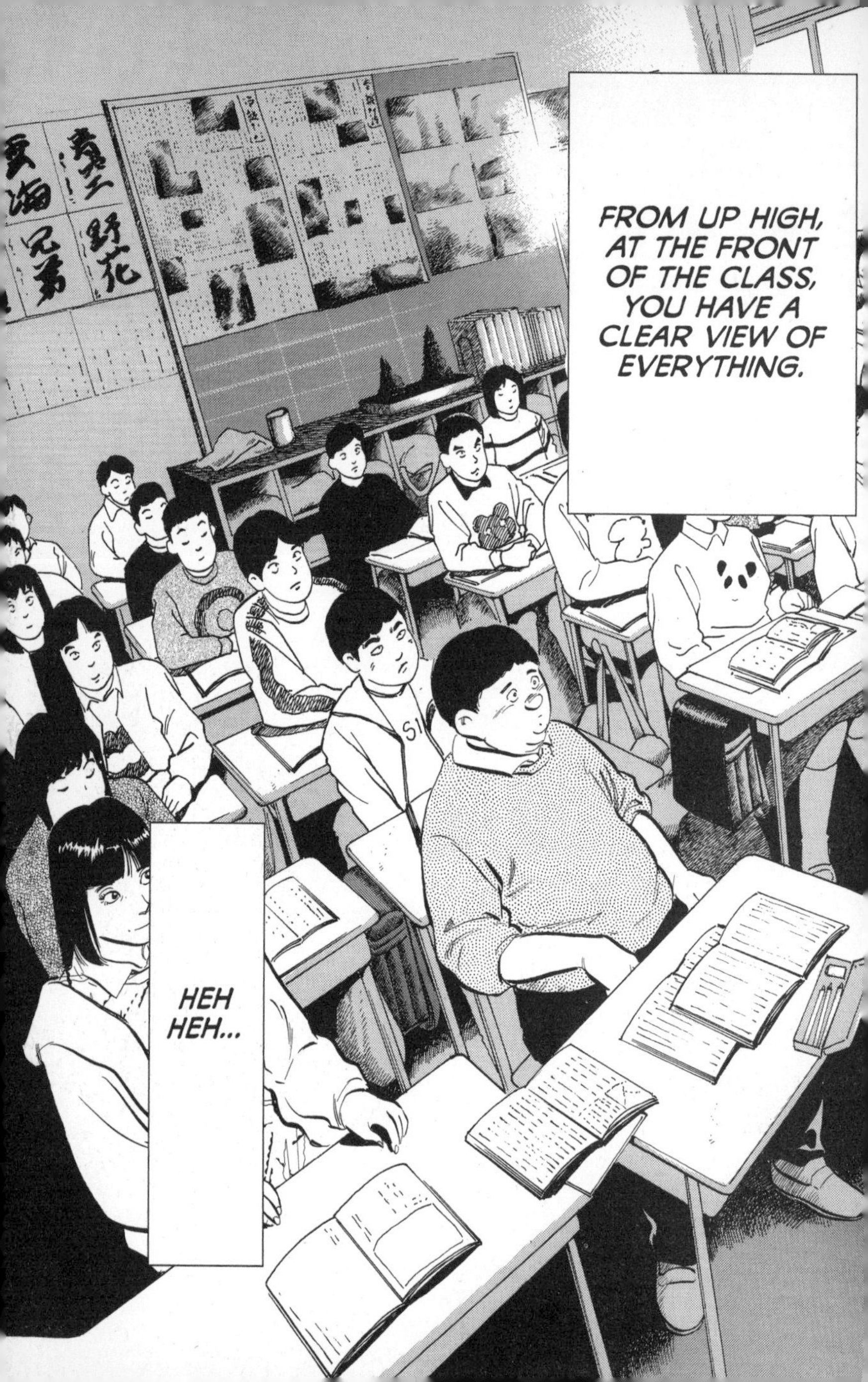
FROM UP HIGH, AT THE FRONT OF THE CLASS, YOU HAVE A CLEAR VIEW OF EVERYTHING.
HEH HEH...

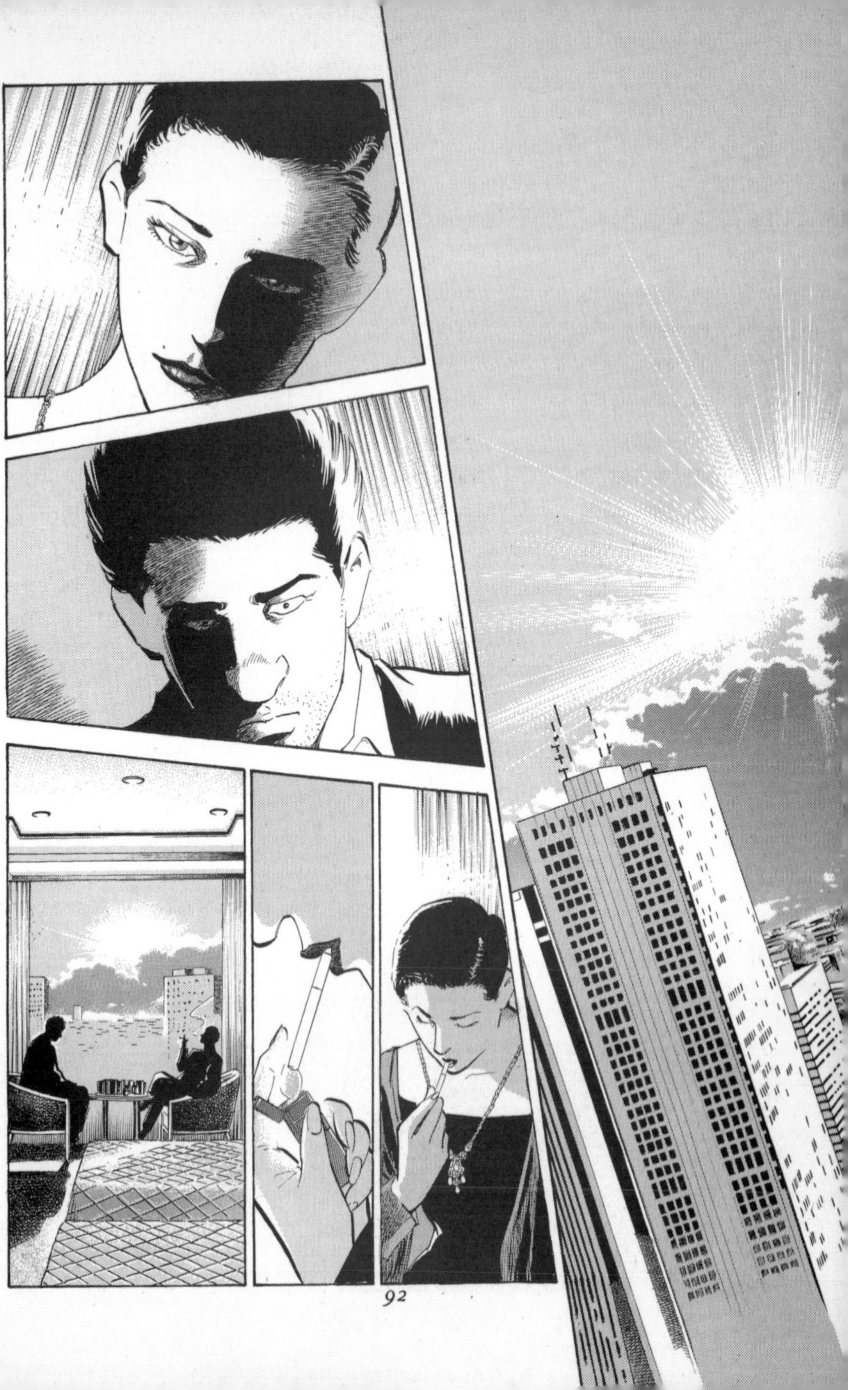

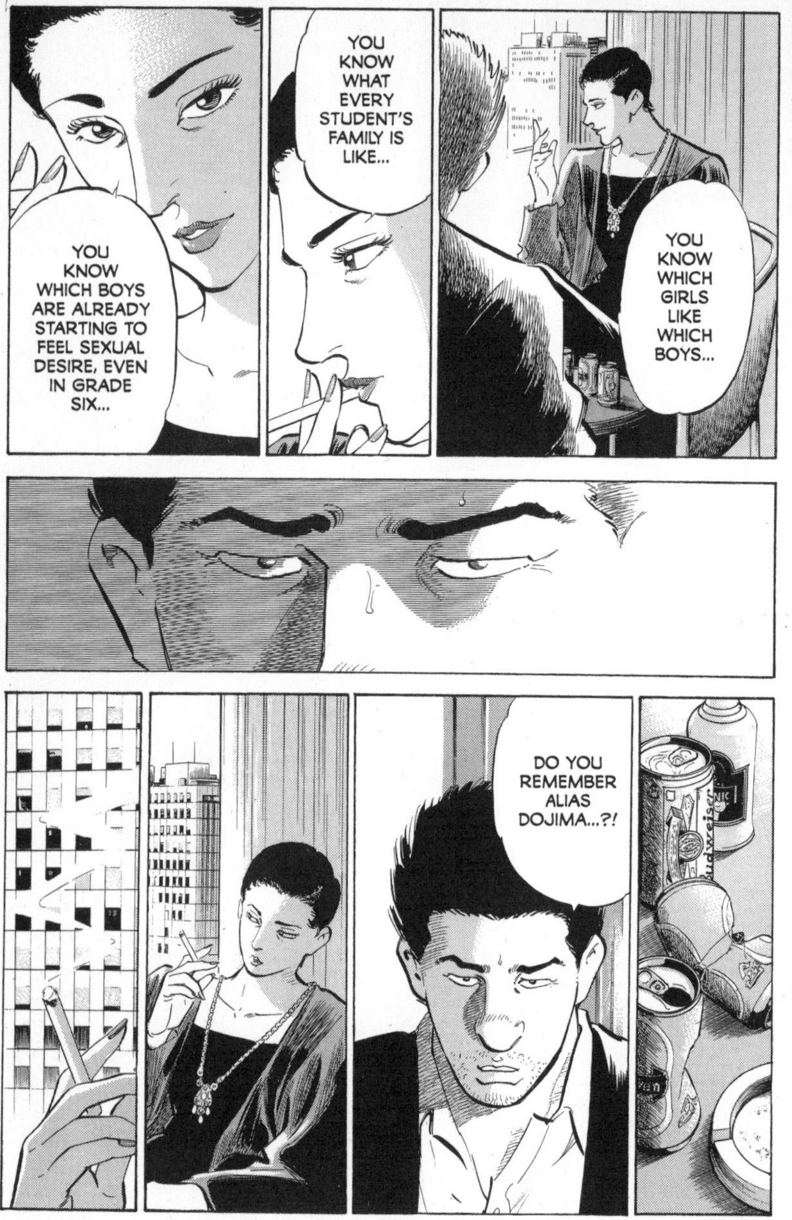
YOU KNOW WHICH GIRLS LIKE WHICH BOYS...
YOU KNOW WHAT EVERY STUDENT'S FAMILY IS LIKE...
YOU KNOW WHICH BOYS ARE ALREADY STARTING TO FEEL SEXUAL DESIRE, EVEN IN GRADE SIX...
DO YOU REMEMBER ALIAS DOJIMA...?!

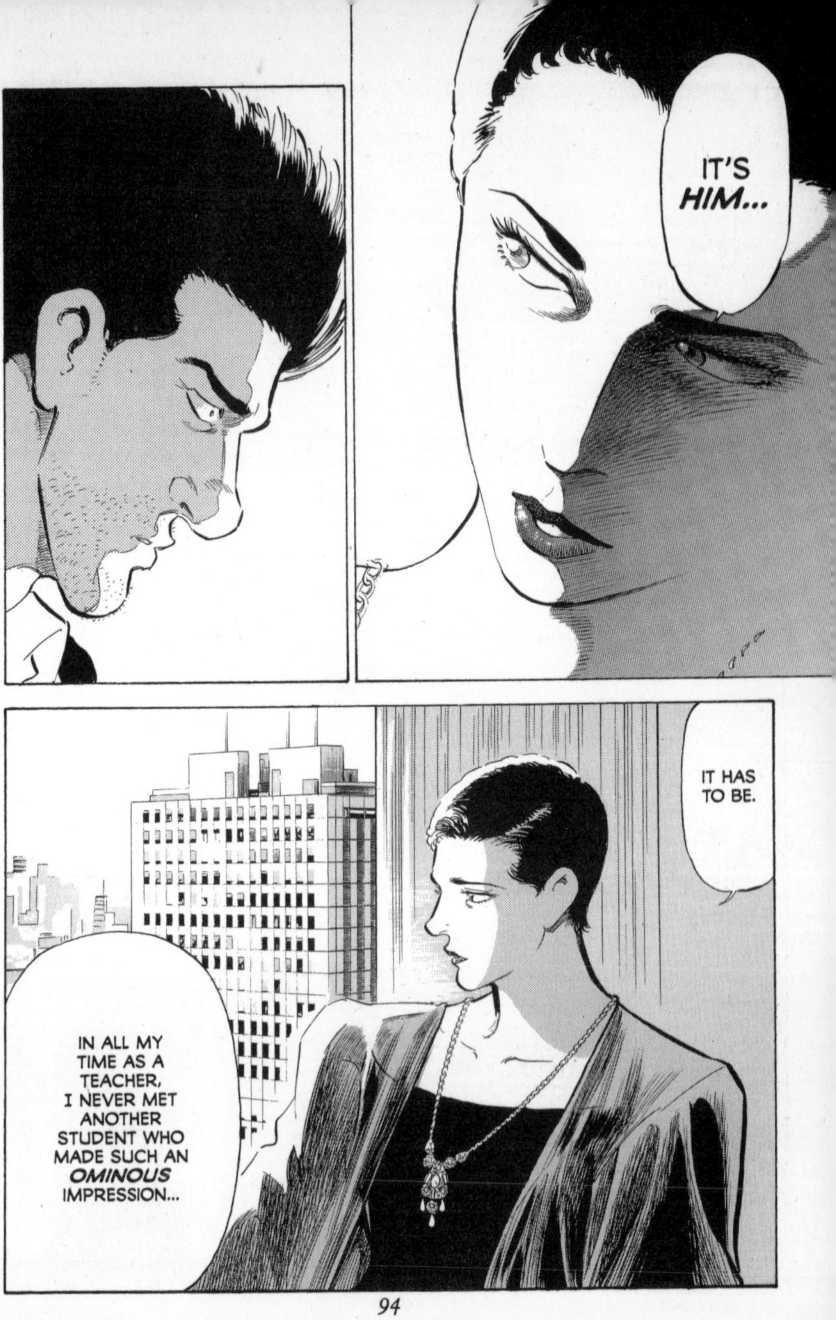
IT'S *HIM...*
IT HAS TO BE.
IN ALL MY TIME AS A TEACHER, I NEVER MET ANOTHER STUDENT WHO MADE SUCH AN *OMINOUS* IMPRESSION...

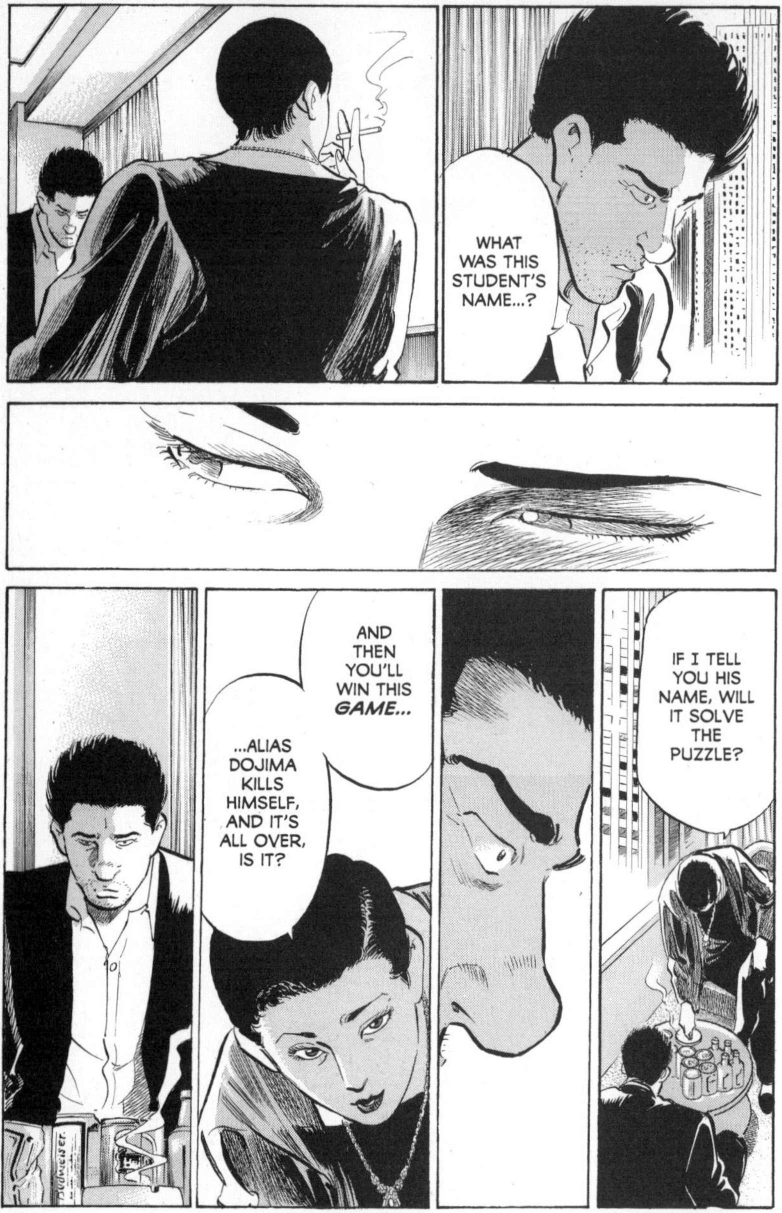
WHAT WAS THIS STUDENT'S NAME...?
IF I TELL YOU HIS NAME, WILL IT SOLVE THE PUZZLE?
AND THEN YOU'LL WIN THIS *GAME...*
...ALIAS DOJIMA KILLS HIMSELF, AND IT'S ALL OVER, IS IT?

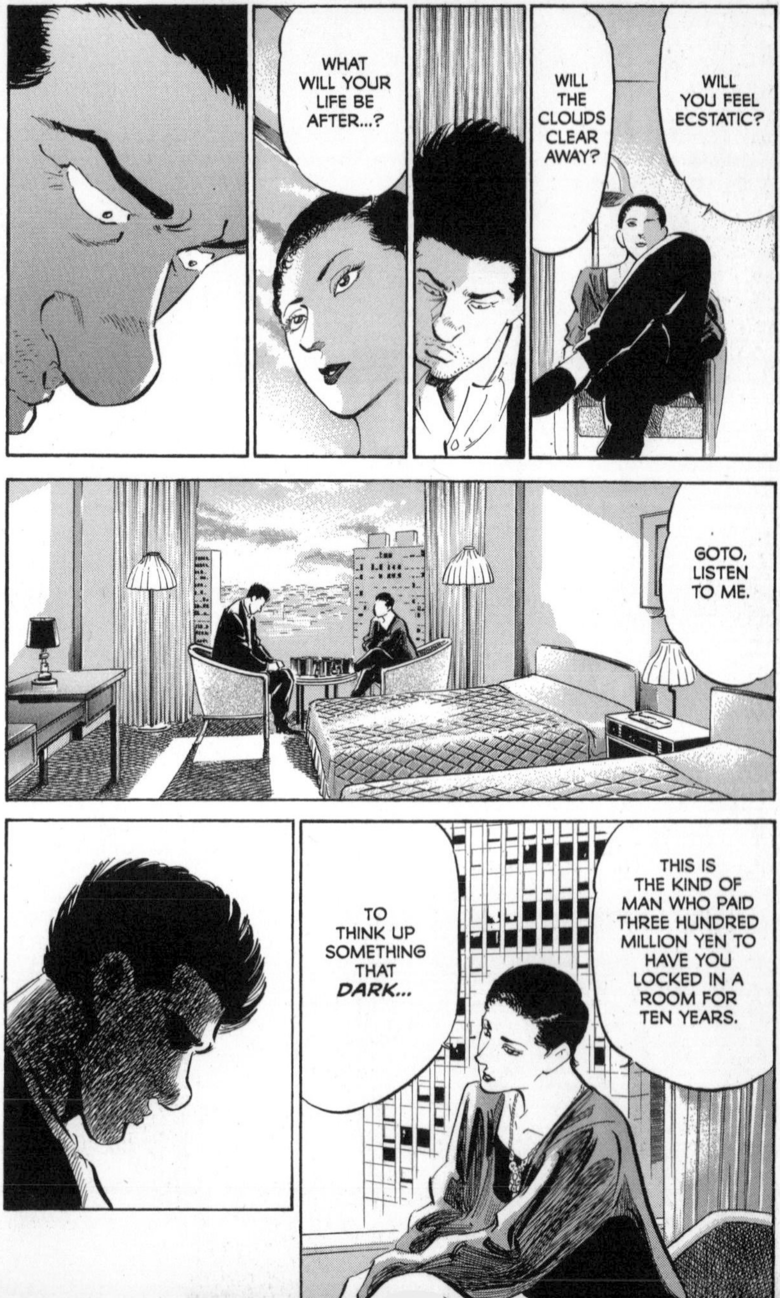
WILL YOU FEEL ECSTATIC?
WILL THE CLOUDS CLEAR AWAY?
WHAT WILL YOUR LIFE BE AFTER...?
GOTO, LISTEN TO ME.
THIS IS THE KIND OF MAN WHO PAID THREE HUNDRED MILLION YEN TO HAVE YOU LOCKED IN A ROOM FOR TEN YEARS.
TO THINK UP SOMETHING THAT *DARK*...

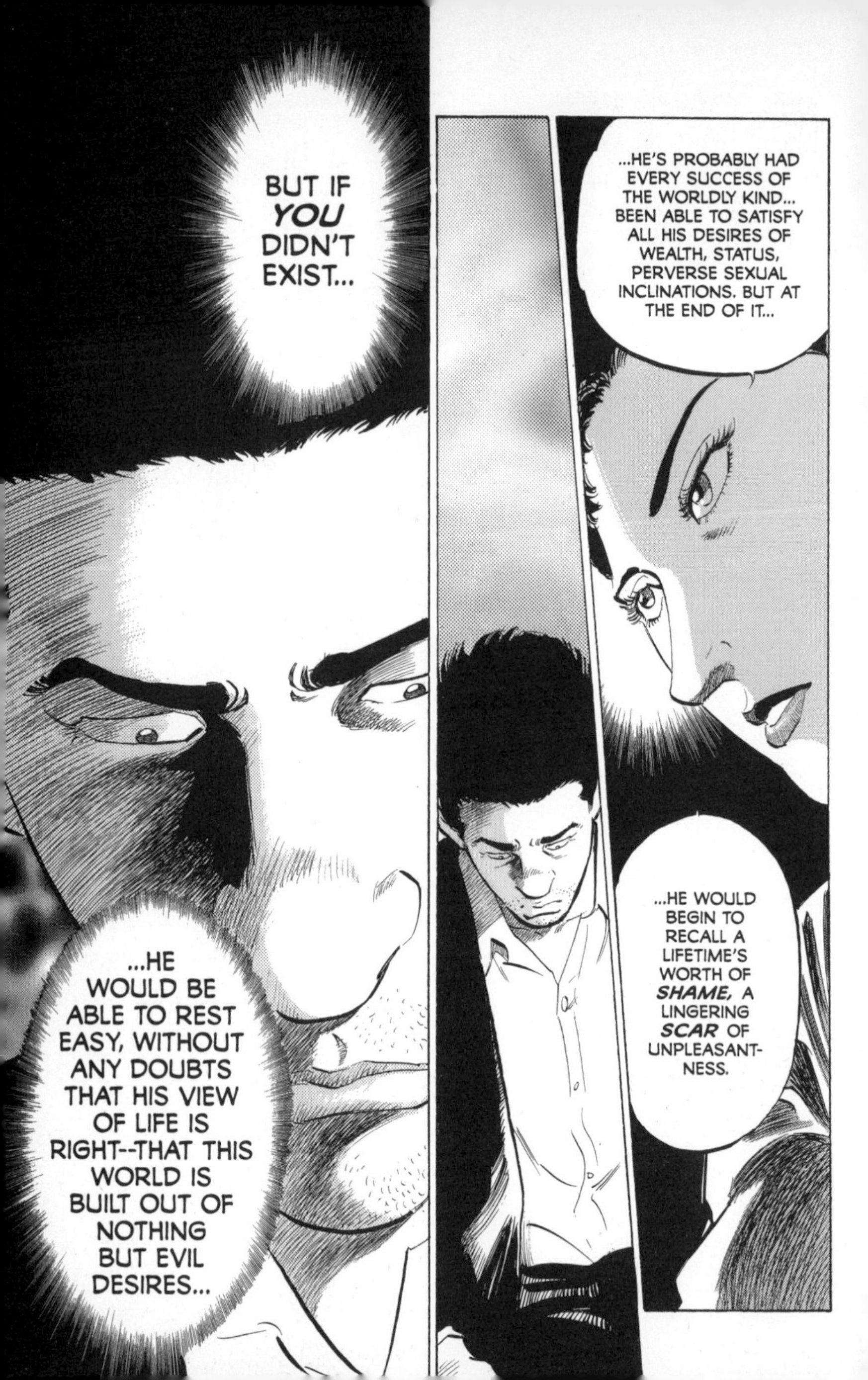
...HE'S PROBABLY HAD EVERY SUCCESS OF THE WORLDLY KIND... BEEN ABLE TO SATISFY ALL HIS DESIRES OF WEALTH, STATUS, PERVERSE SEXUAL INCLINATIONS. BUT AT THE END OF IT...
...HE WOULD BEGIN TO RECALL A LIFETIME'S WORTH OF *SHAME,* A LINGERING *SCAR* OF UNPLEASANT-NESS.
BUT IF *YOU* DIDN'T EXIST...
...HE WOULD BE ABLE TO REST EASY, WITHOUT ANY DOUBTS THAT HIS VIEW OF LIFE IS RIGHT--THAT THIS WORLD IS BUILT OUT OF NOTHING BUT EVIL DESIRES...

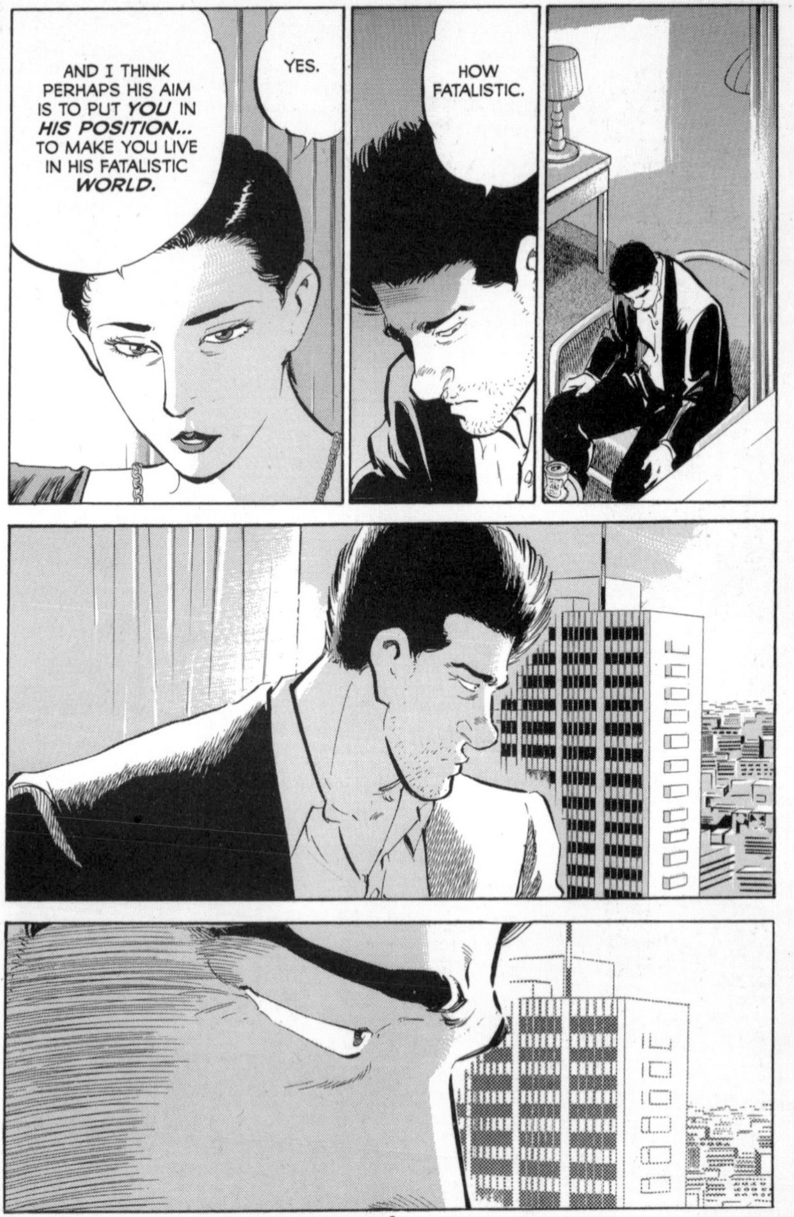
HOW FATALISTIC.
YES.
AND I THINK PERHAPS HIS AIM IS TO PUT ***YOU*** IN ***HIS POSITION...*** TO MAKE YOU LIVE IN HIS FATALISTIC ***WORLD.***

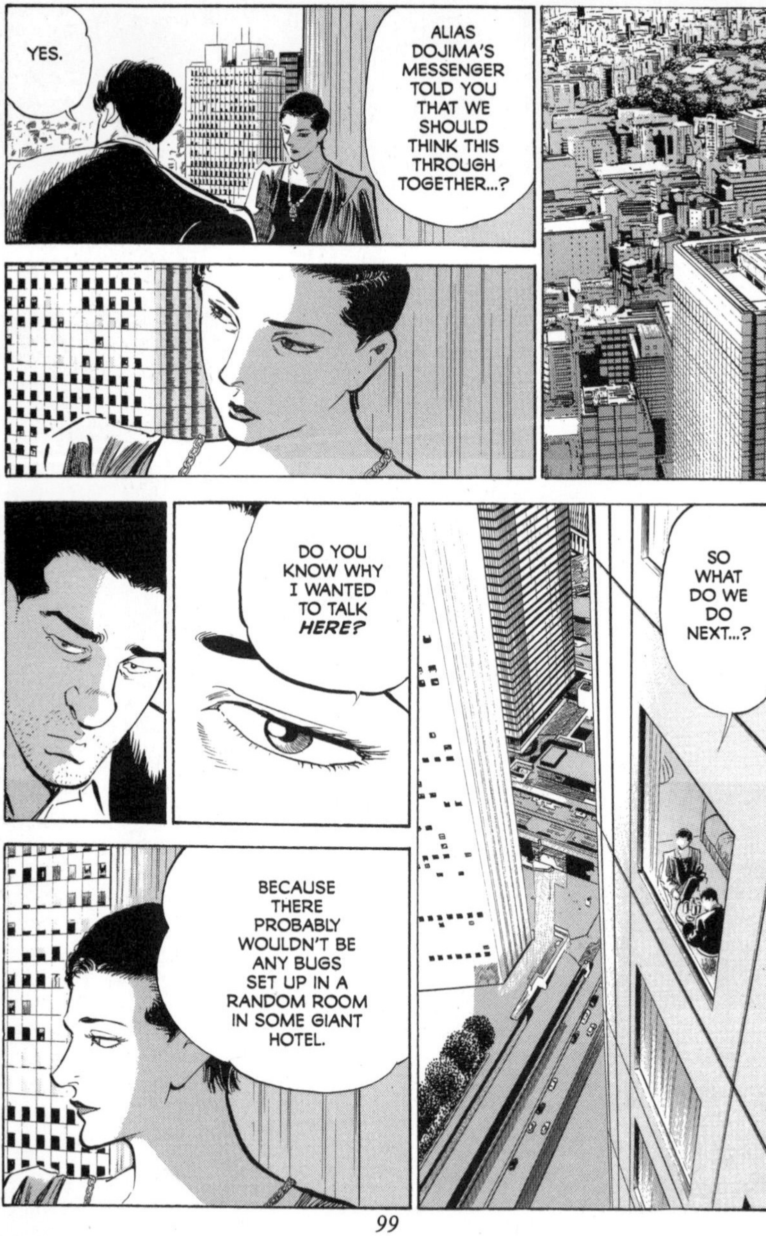
ALIAS DOJIMA'S MESSENGER TOLD YOU THAT WE SHOULD THINK THIS THROUGH TOGETHER...?
YES.
SO WHAT DO WE DO NEXT...?
DO YOU KNOW WHY I WANTED TO TALK *HERE?*
BECAUSE THERE PROBABLY WOULDN'T BE ANY BUGS SET UP IN A RANDOM ROOM IN SOME GIANT HOTEL.

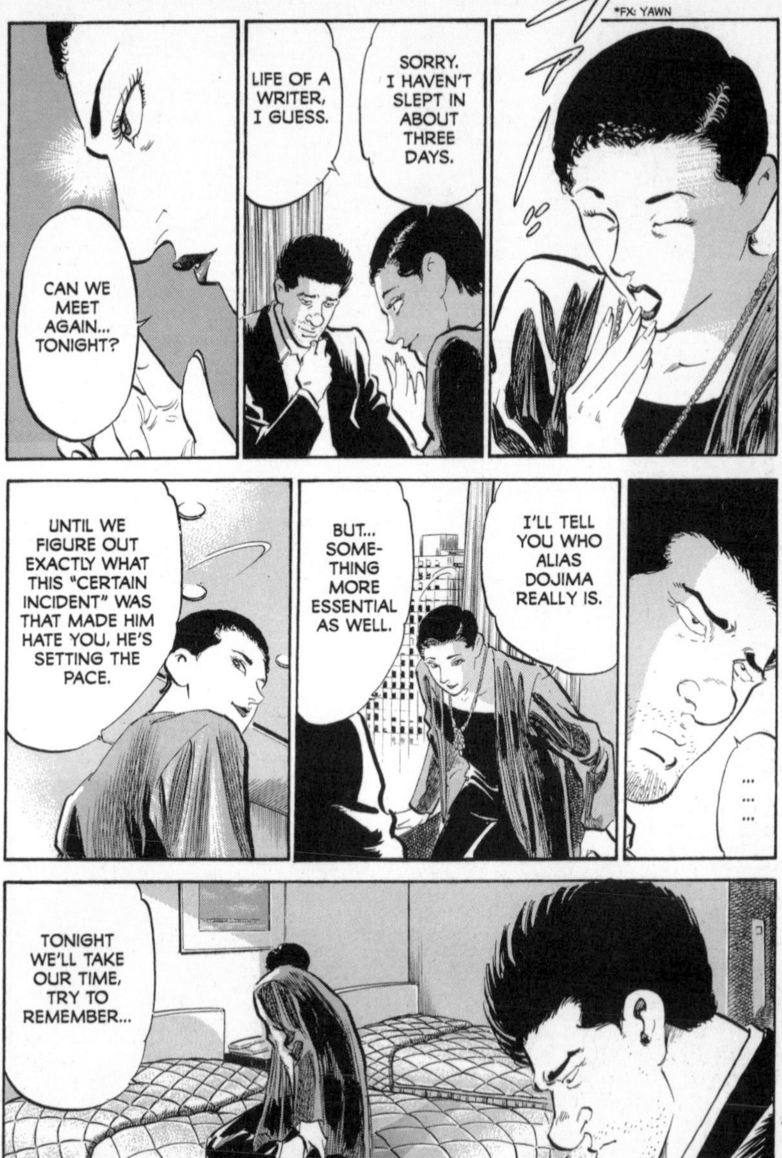
*FX: YAWN
SORRY. I HAVEN'T SLEPT IN ABOUT THREE DAYS.
LIFE OF A WRITER, I GUESS.
CAN WE MEET AGAIN... TONIGHT?
...
...
...
I'LL TELL YOU WHO ALIAS DOJIMA REALLY IS.
BUT... SOME-THING MORE ESSENTIAL AS WELL.
UNTIL WE FIGURE OUT EXACTLY WHAT THIS "CERTAIN INCIDENT" WAS THAT MADE HIM HATE YOU, HE'S SETTING THE PACE.
TONIGHT WE'LL TAKE OUR TIME, TRY TO REMEMBER...

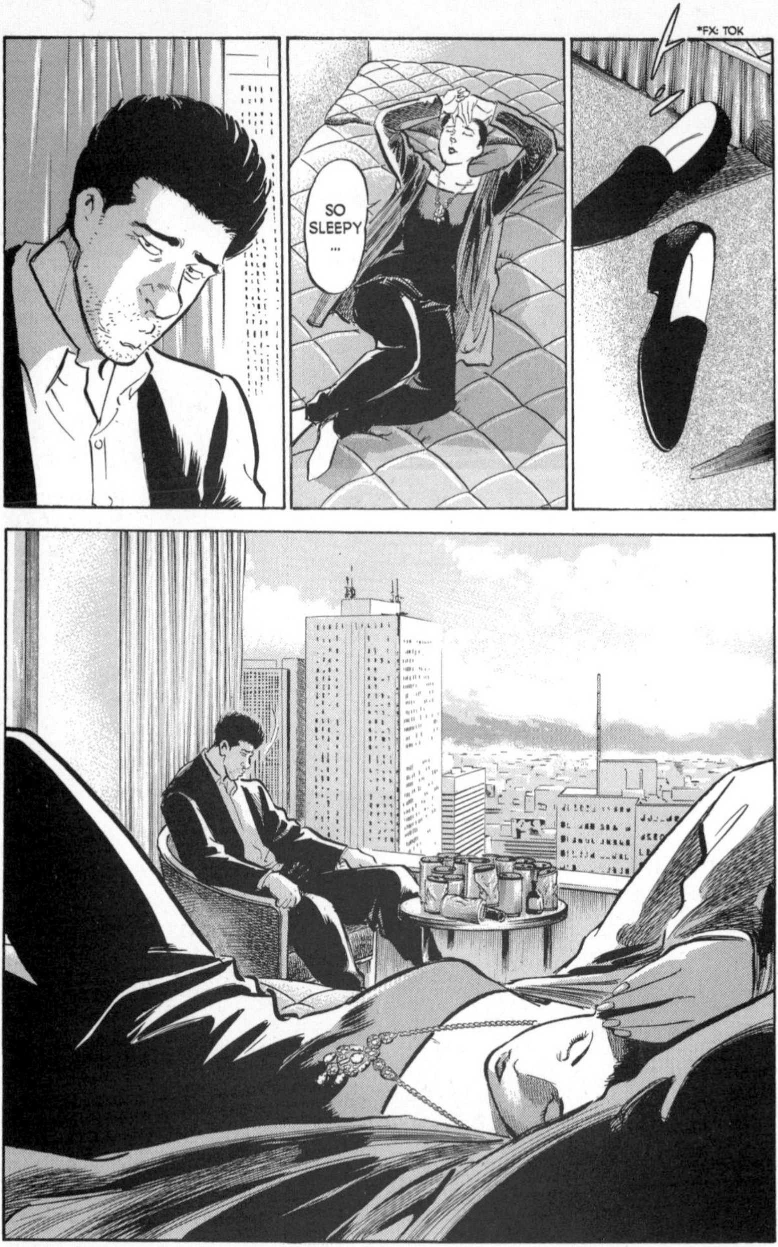
*FX: TOK
SO SLEEPY ...

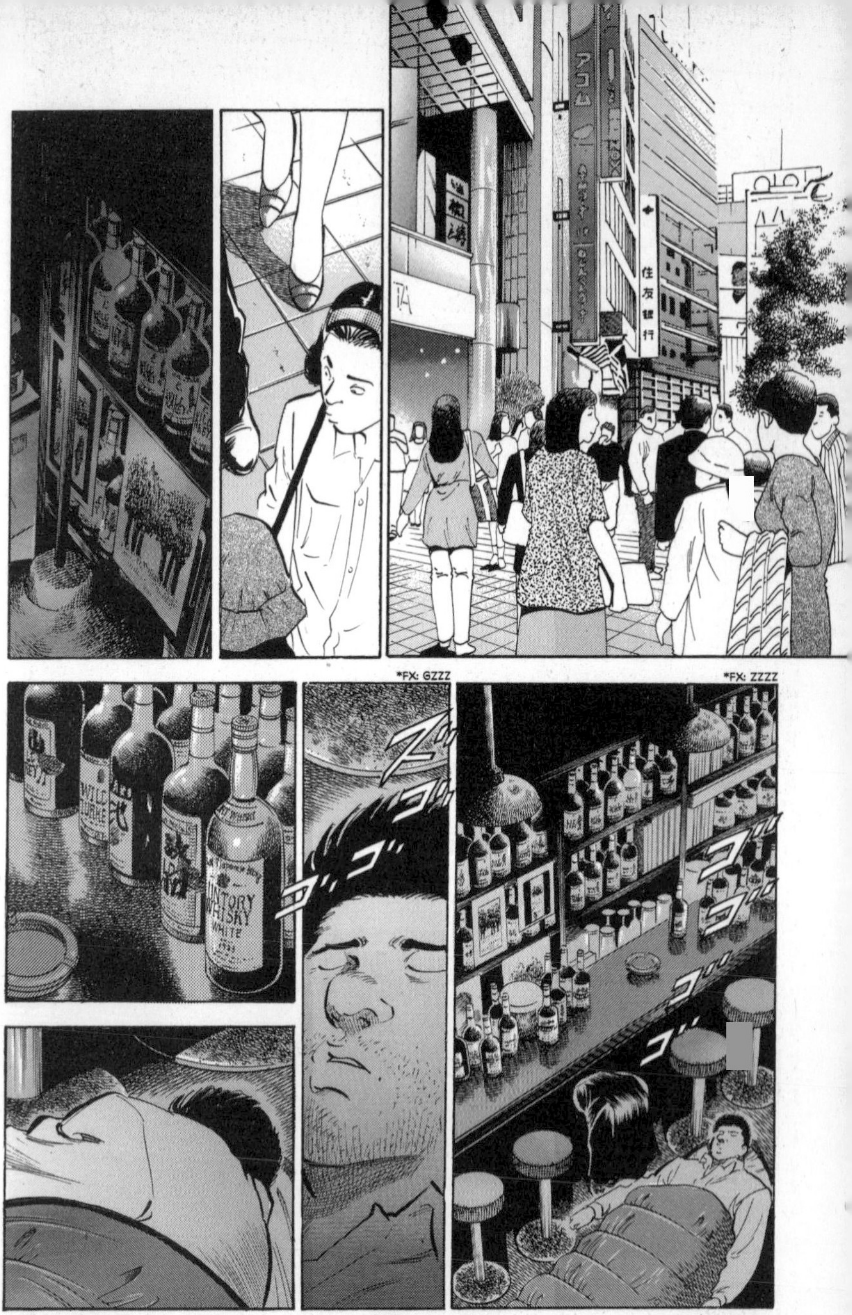
*FX: ZZZZ
*FX: GZZZ

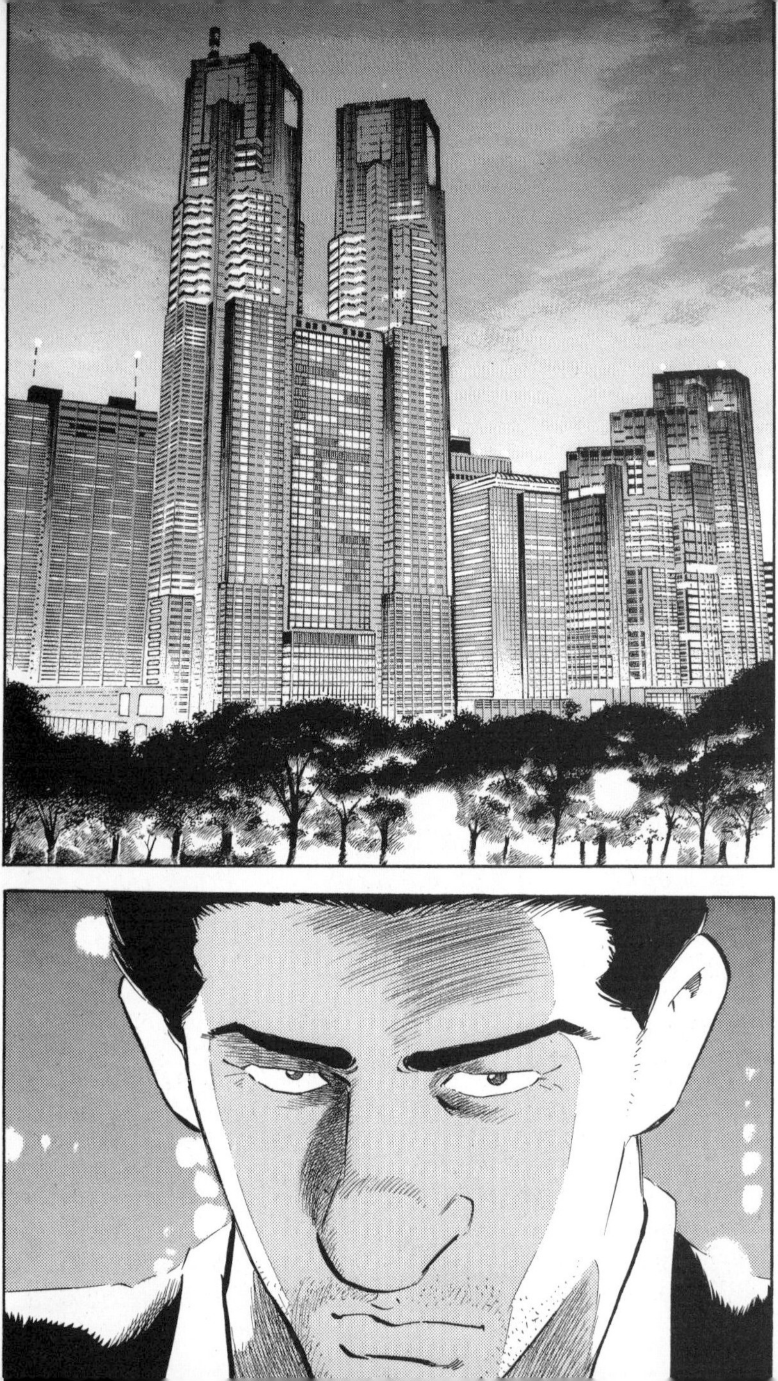

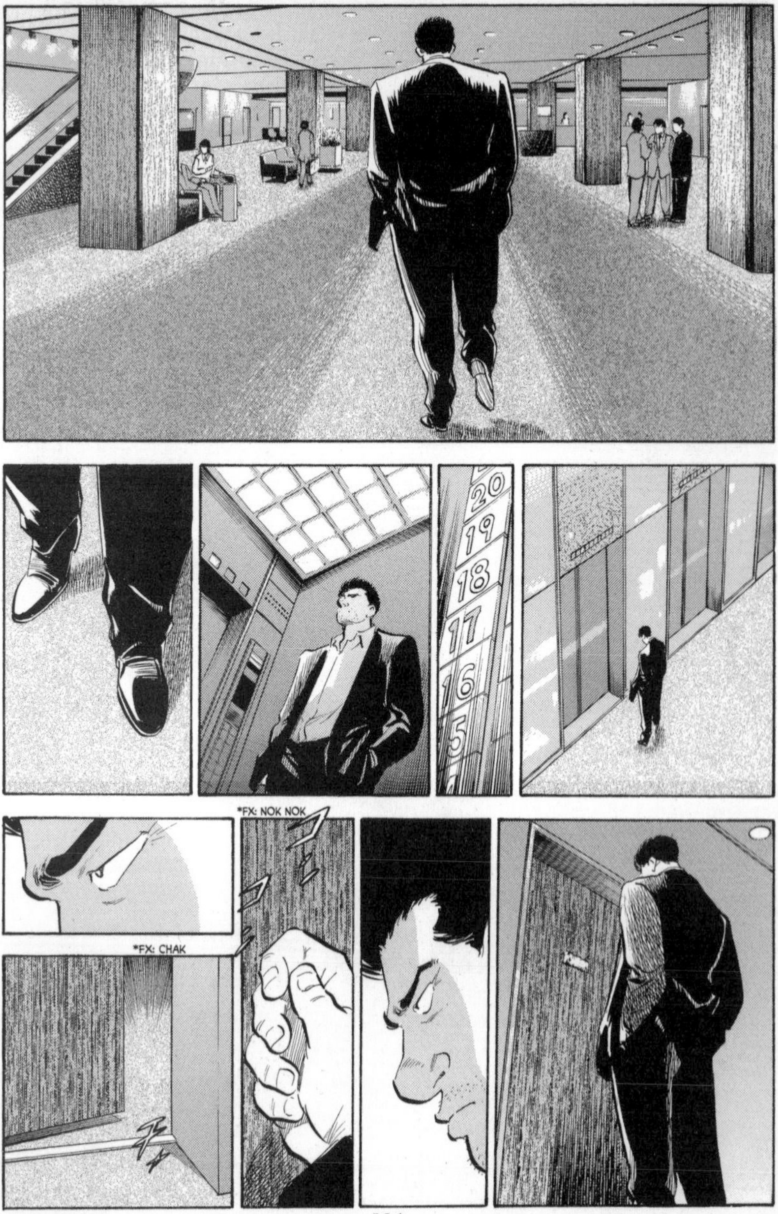
20 19 18 17 16 5
*FX: NOK NOK
*FX: CHAK

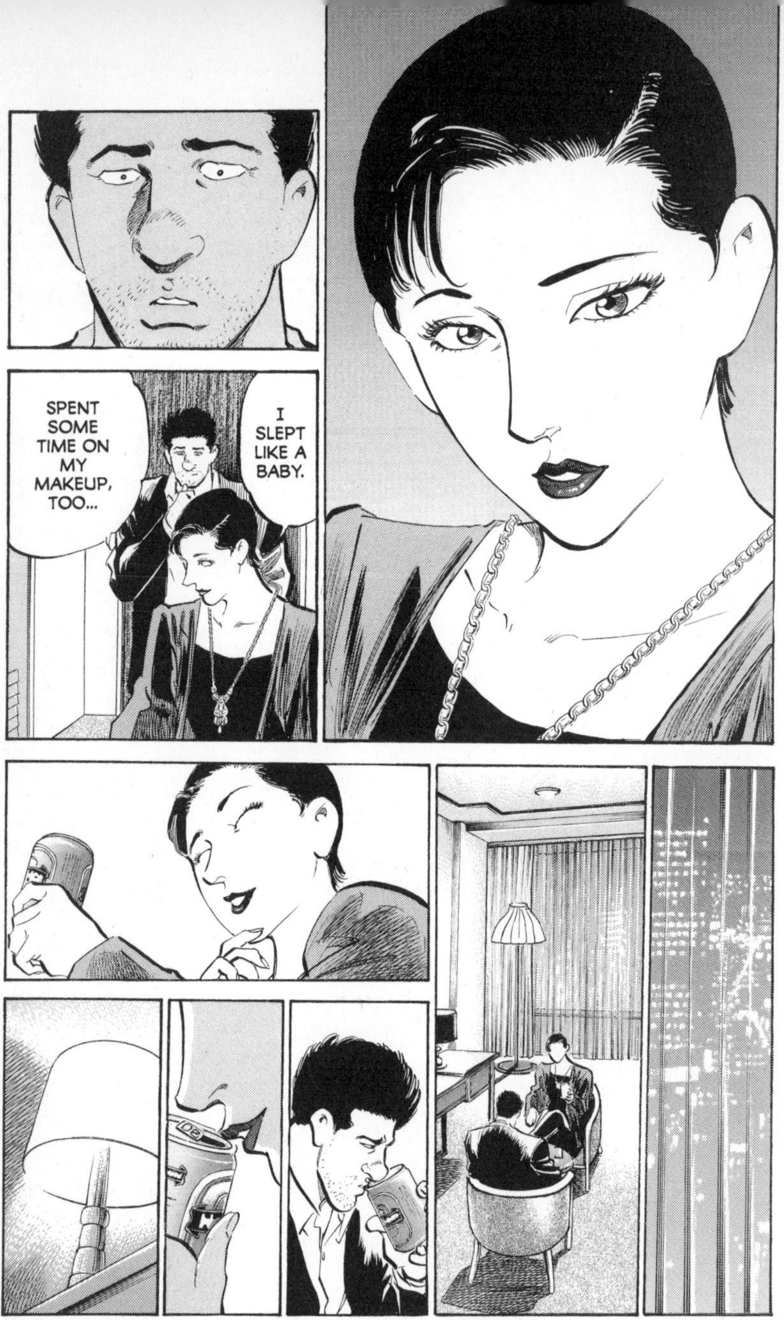
I SLEPT LIKE A BABY.
SPENT SOME TIME ON MY MAKEUP, TOO...

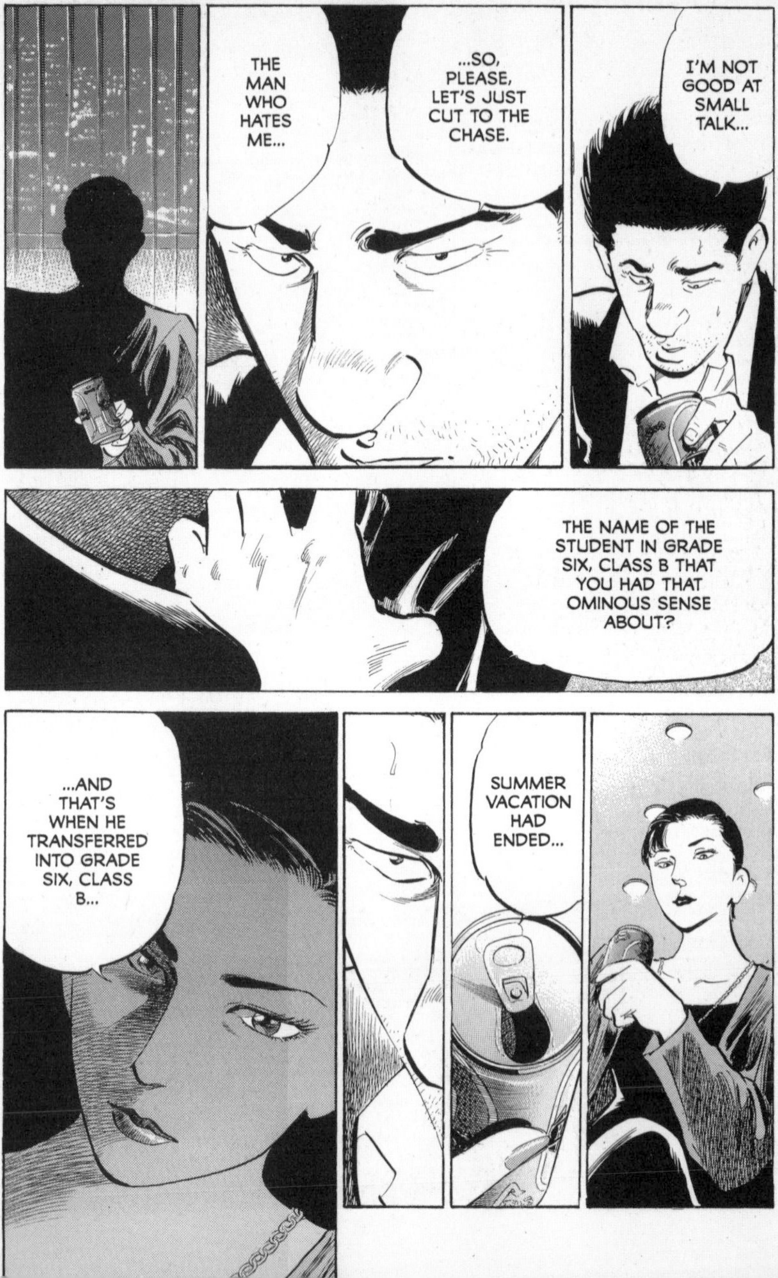
I'M NOT GOOD AT SMALL TALK...
...SO, PLEASE, LET'S JUST CUT TO THE CHASE.
THE MAN WHO HATES ME...
THE NAME OF THE STUDENT IN GRADE SIX, CLASS B THAT YOU HAD THAT OMINOUS SENSE ABOUT?
SUMMER VACATION HAD ENDED...
...AND THAT'S WHEN HE TRANSFERRED INTO GRADE SIX, CLASS B...

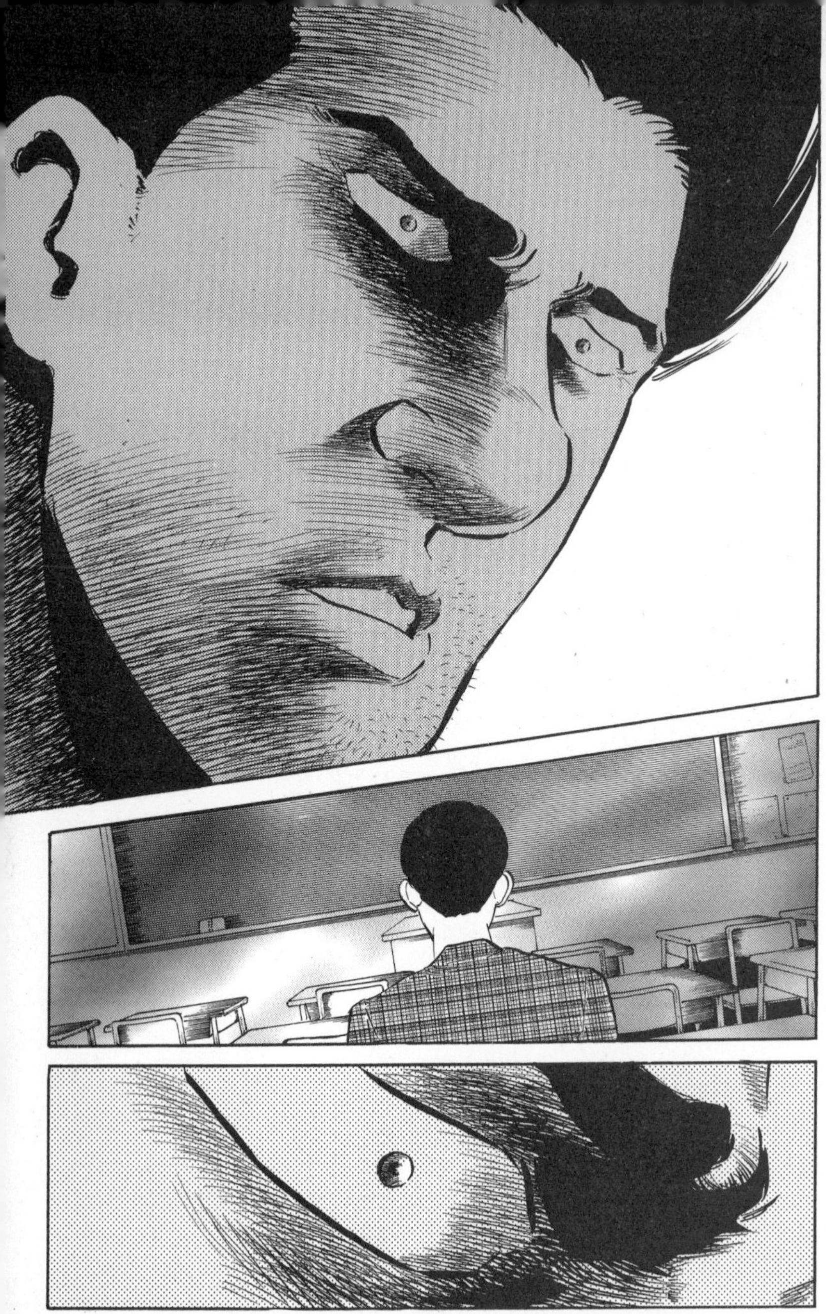

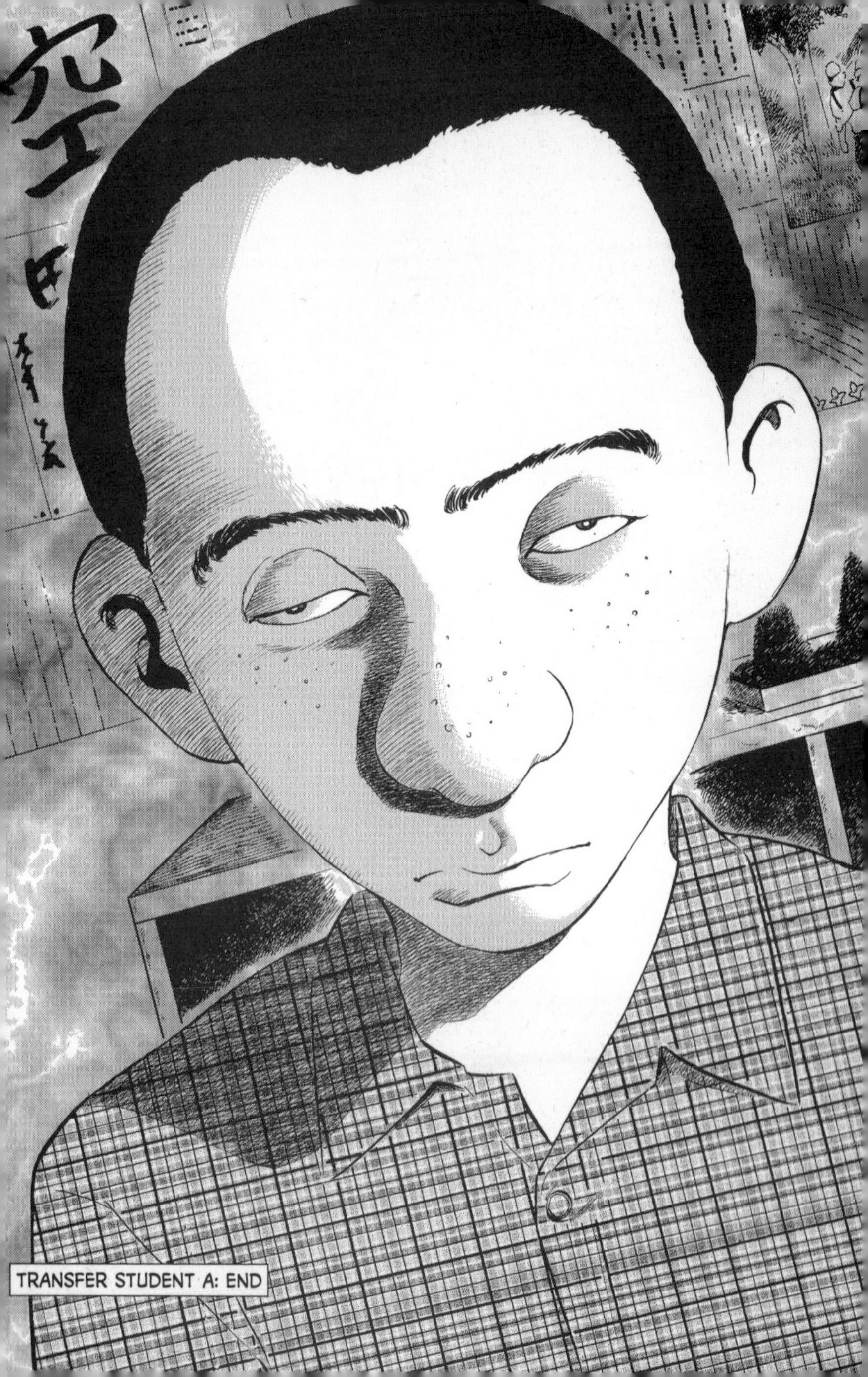
TRANSFER STUDENT A: END

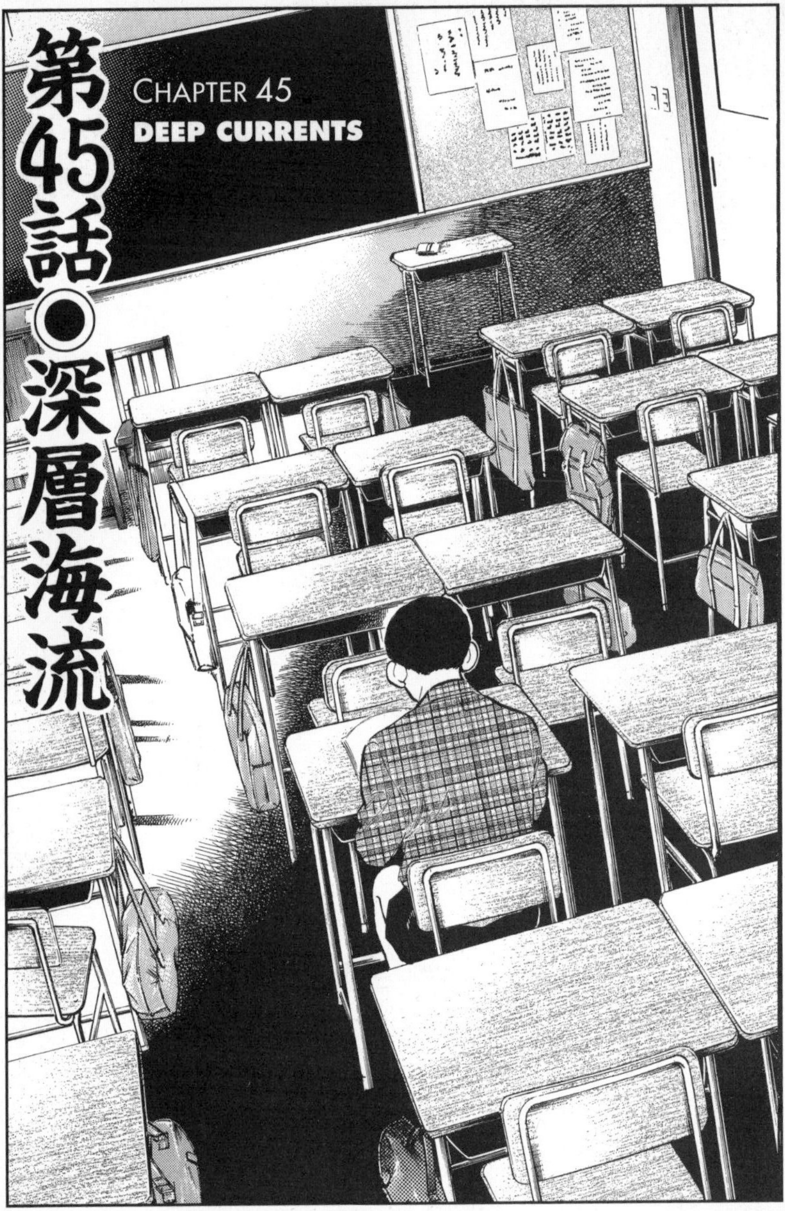
第45話◉深層海流
CHAPTER 45
DEEP CURRENTS

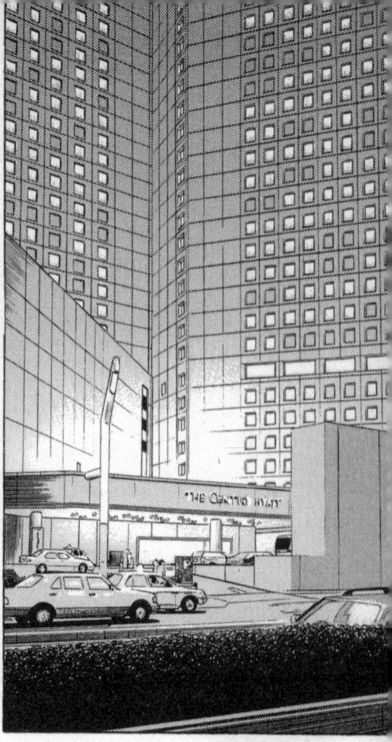

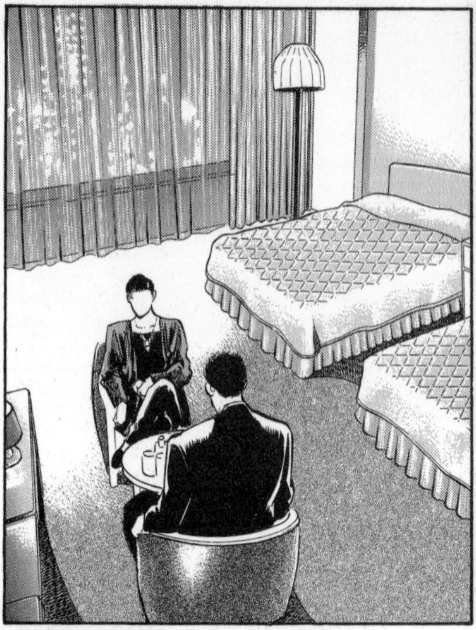

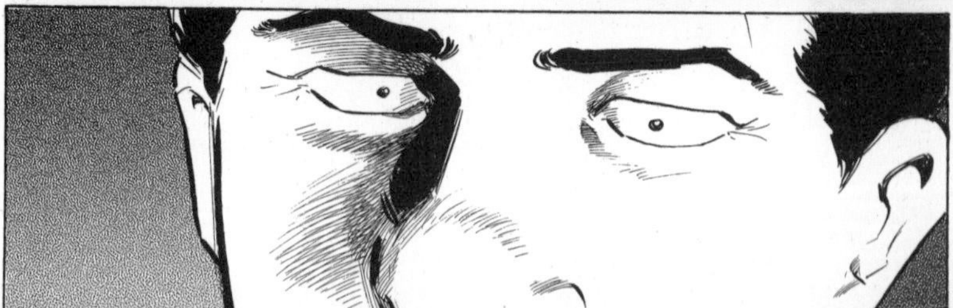

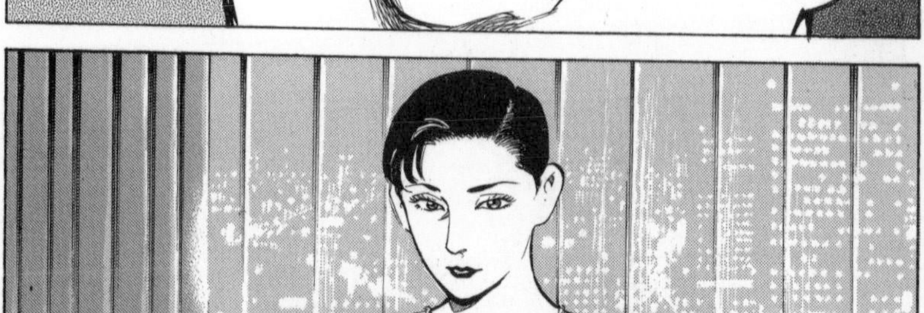

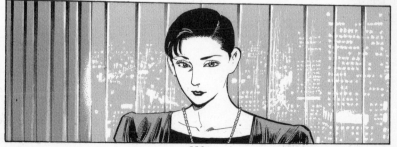

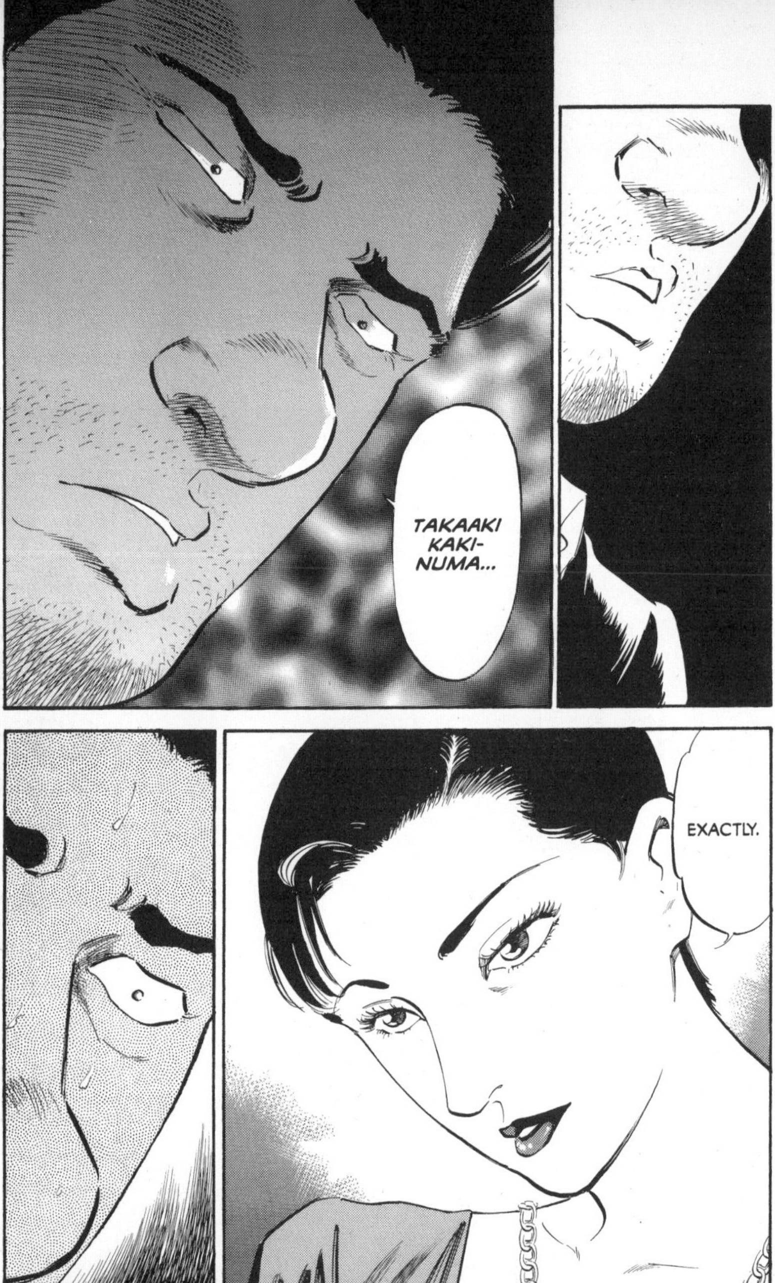
TAKAAKI KAKI-NUMA...
EXACTLY.

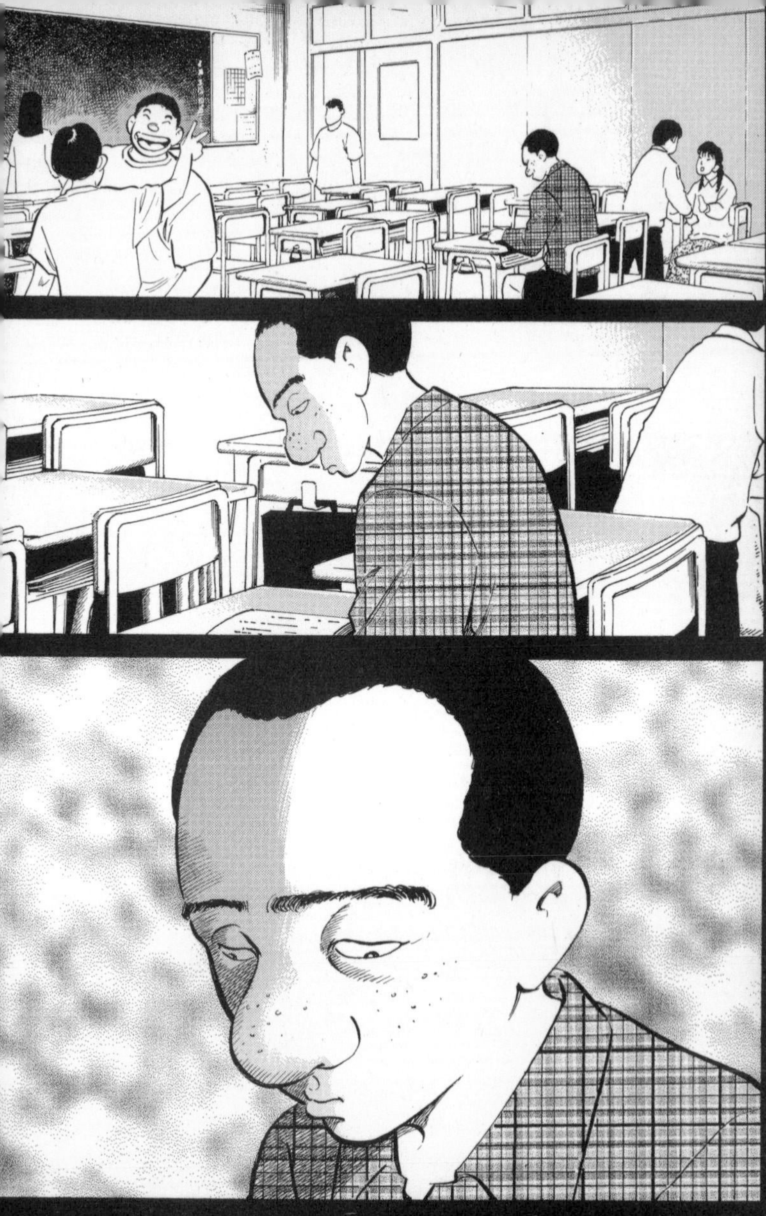

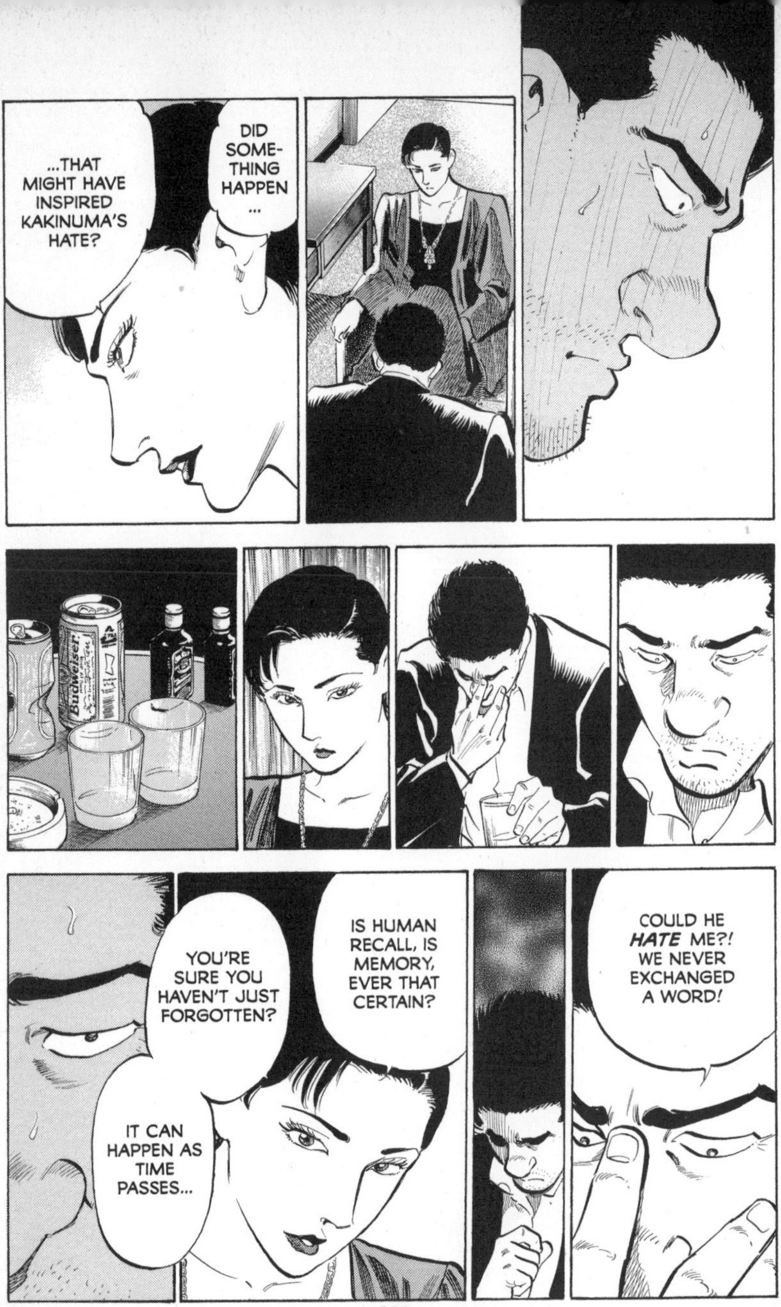
DID SOMETHING HAPPEN ...
...THAT MIGHT HAVE INSPIRED KAKINUMA'S HATE?
Budweiser
COULD HE *HATE* ME?! WE NEVER EXCHANGED A WORD!
IS HUMAN RECALL, IS MEMORY, EVER THAT CERTAIN?
YOU'RE SURE YOU HAVEN'T JUST FORGOTTEN?
IT CAN HAPPEN AS TIME PASSES...

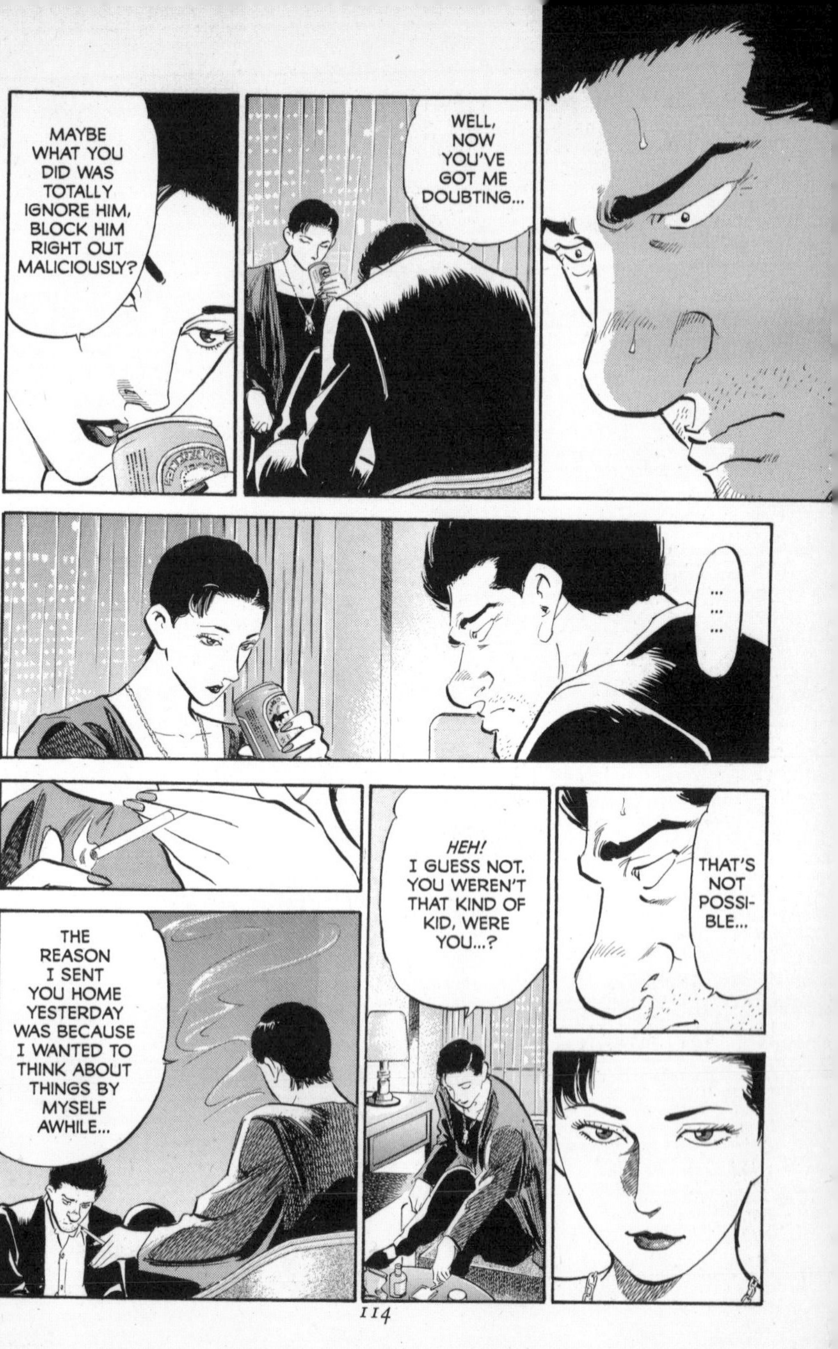

WELL, NOW YOU'VE GOT ME DOUBTING...
MAYBE WHAT YOU DID WAS TOTALLY IGNORE HIM, BLOCK HIM RIGHT OUT MALICIOUSLY?
....
THAT'S NOT POSSI-BLE...
HEH! I GUESS NOT. YOU WEREN'T THAT KIND OF KID, WERE YOU...?
THE REASON I SENT YOU HOME YESTERDAY WAS BECAUSE I WANTED TO THINK ABOUT THINGS BY MYSELF AWHILE...

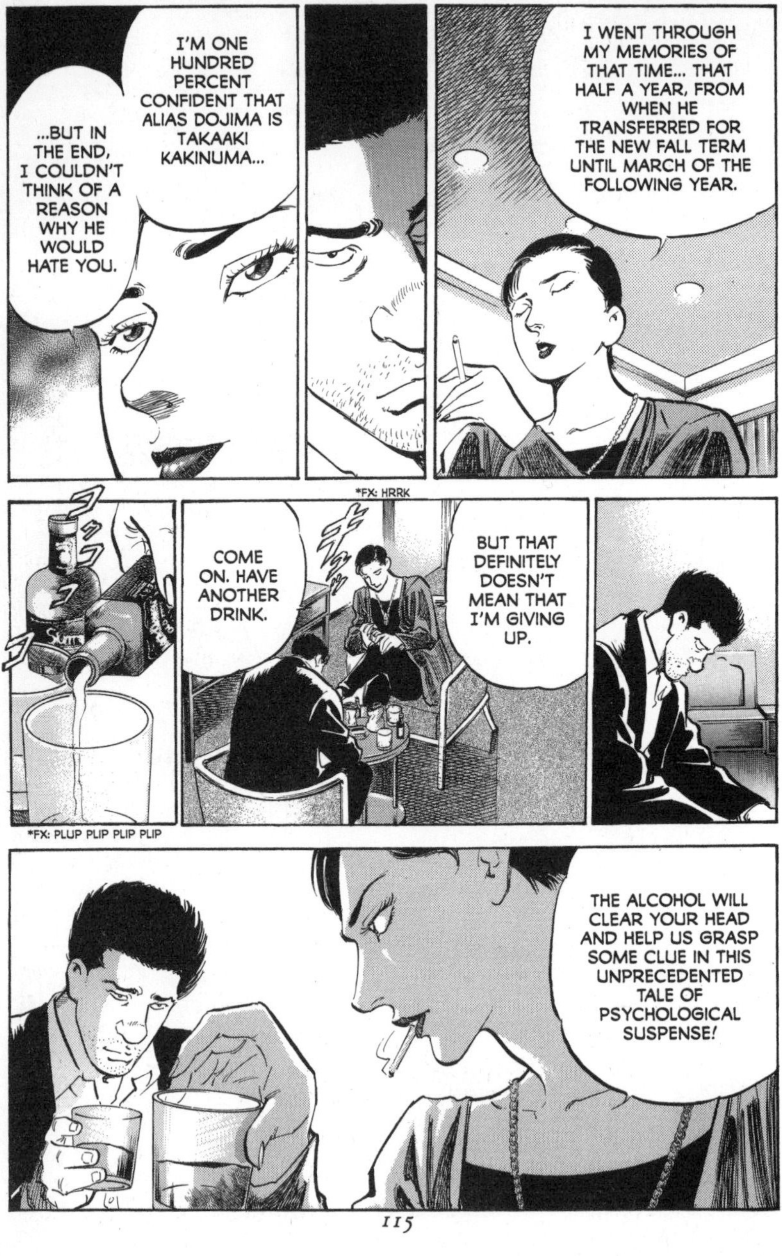
I WENT THROUGH MY MEMORIES OF THAT TIME... THAT HALF A YEAR, FROM WHEN HE TRANSFERRED FOR THE NEW FALL TERM UNTIL MARCH OF THE FOLLOWING YEAR.
*FX: HRRK
I'M ONE HUNDRED PERCENT CONFIDENT THAT ALIAS DOJIMA IS TAKAAKI KAKINUMA...
...BUT IN THE END, I COULDN'T THINK OF A REASON WHY HE WOULD HATE YOU.
BUT THAT DEFINITELY DOESN'T MEAN THAT I'M GIVING UP.
COME ON. HAVE ANOTHER DRINK.
*FX: PLUP PLIP PLIP PLIP
THE ALCOHOL WILL CLEAR YOUR HEAD AND HELP US GRASP SOME CLUE IN THIS UNPRECEDENTED TALE OF PSYCHOLOGICAL SUSPENSE!

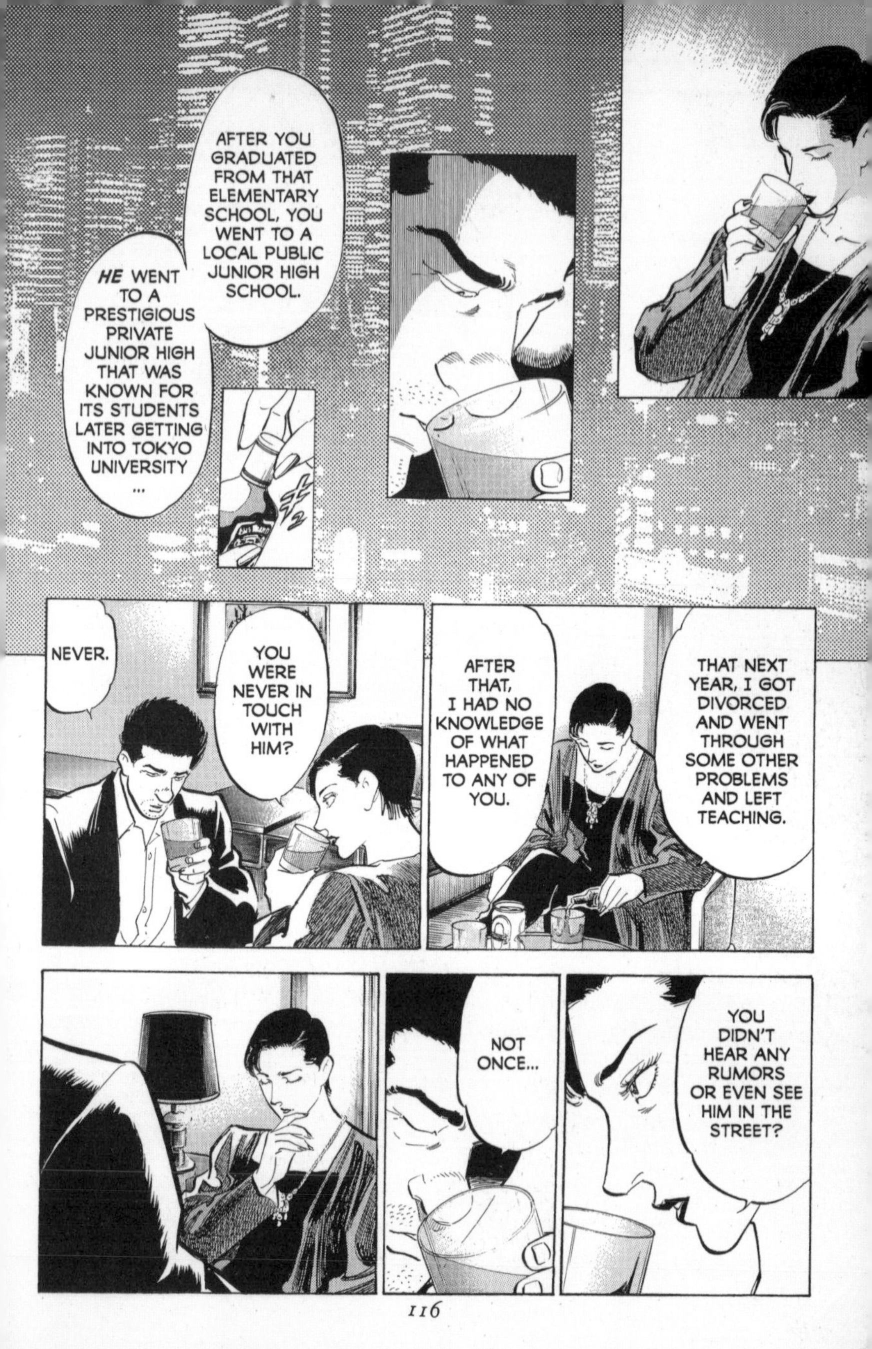
AFTER YOU GRADUATED FROM THAT ELEMENTARY SCHOOL, YOU WENT TO A LOCAL PUBLIC JUNIOR HIGH SCHOOL.
HE WENT TO A PRESTIGIOUS PRIVATE JUNIOR HIGH THAT WAS KNOWN FOR ITS STUDENTS LATER GETTING INTO TOKYO UNIVERSITY ...
THAT NEXT YEAR, I GOT DIVORCED AND WENT THROUGH SOME OTHER PROBLEMS AND LEFT TEACHING.
AFTER THAT, I HAD NO KNOWLEDGE OF WHAT HAPPENED TO ANY OF YOU.
YOU WERE NEVER IN TOUCH WITH HIM?
NEVER.
YOU DIDN'T HEAR ANY RUMORS OR EVEN SEE HIM IN THE STREET?
NOT ONCE...

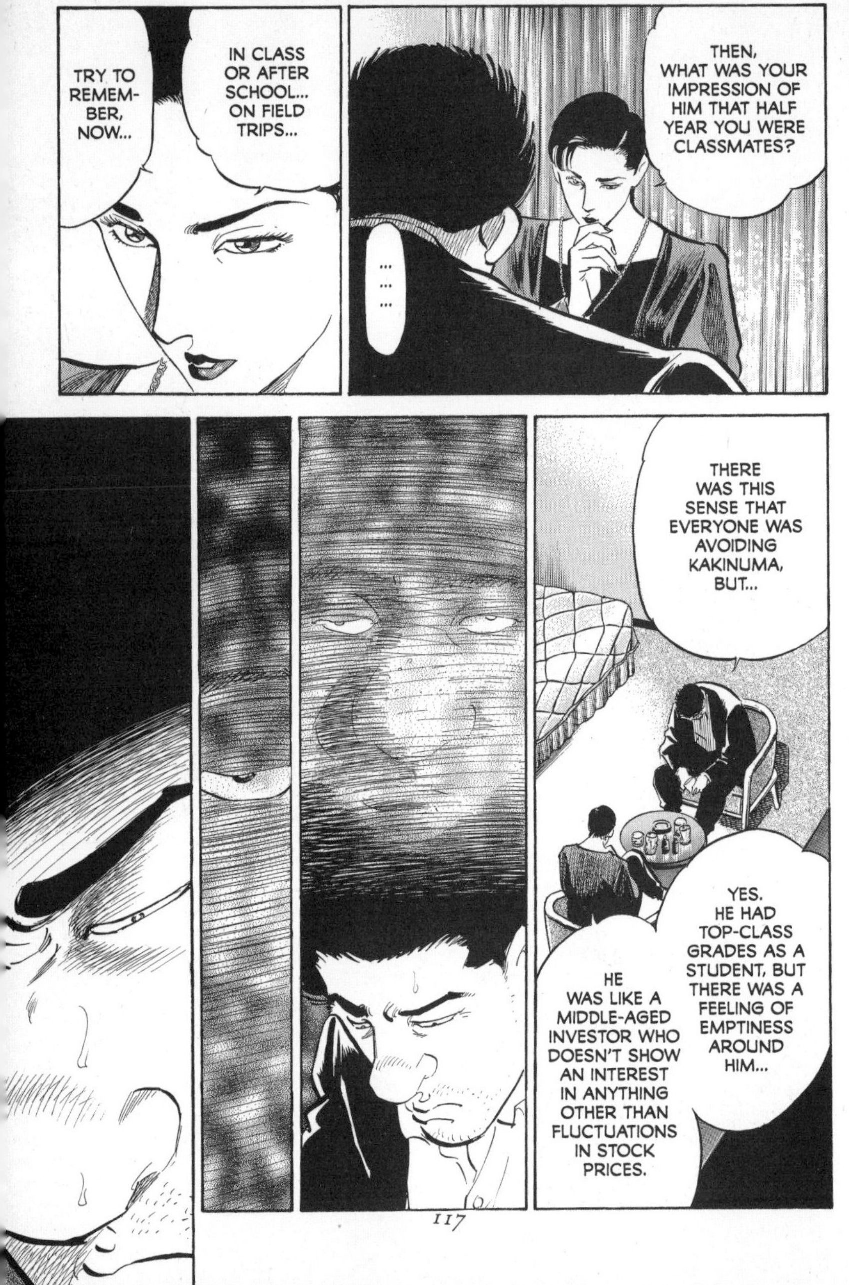
THEN, WHAT WAS YOUR IMPRESSION OF HIM THAT HALF YEAR YOU WERE CLASSMATES?
... ...
IN CLASS OR AFTER SCHOOL... ON FIELD TRIPS...
TRY TO REMEMBER, NOW...
THERE WAS THIS SENSE THAT EVERYONE WAS AVOIDING KAKINUMA, BUT...
YES. HE HAD TOP-CLASS GRADES AS A STUDENT, BUT THERE WAS A FEELING OF EMPTINESS AROUND HIM...
HE WAS LIKE A MIDDLE-AGED INVESTOR WHO DOESN'T SHOW AN INTEREST IN ANYTHING OTHER THAN FLUCTUATIONS IN STOCK PRICES.

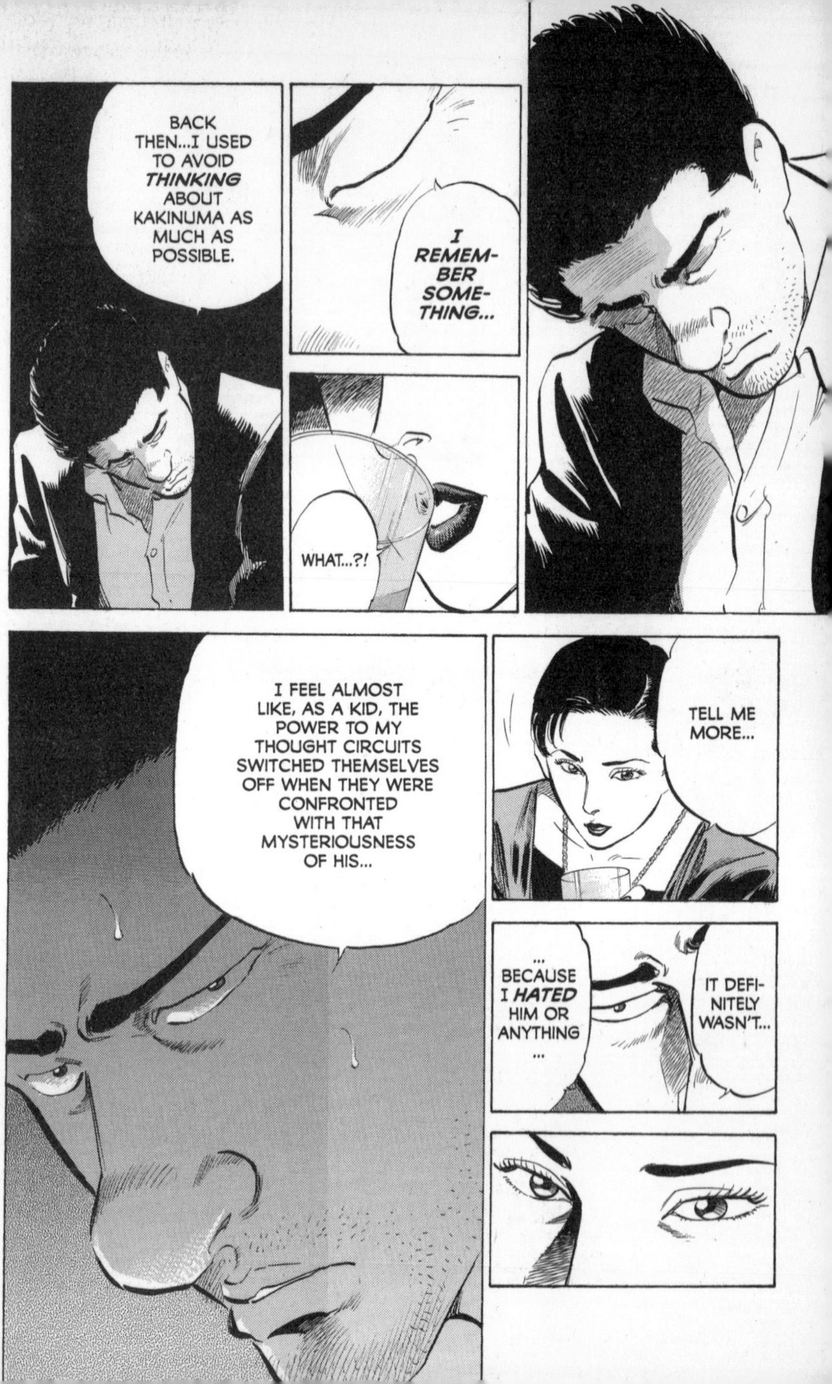
I REMEMBER-BER SOMETHING...
WHAT...?!
BACK THEN...I USED TO AVOID THINKING ABOUT KAKINUMA AS MUCH AS POSSIBLE.
TELL ME MORE...
IT DEFI-NITELY WASN'T...
...BECAUSE I HATED HIM OR ANYTHING...
I FEEL ALMOST LIKE, AS A KID, THE POWER TO MY THOUGHT CIRCUITS SWITCHED THEMSELVES OFF WHEN THEY WERE CONFRONTED WITH THAT MYSTERIOUSNESS OF HIS...

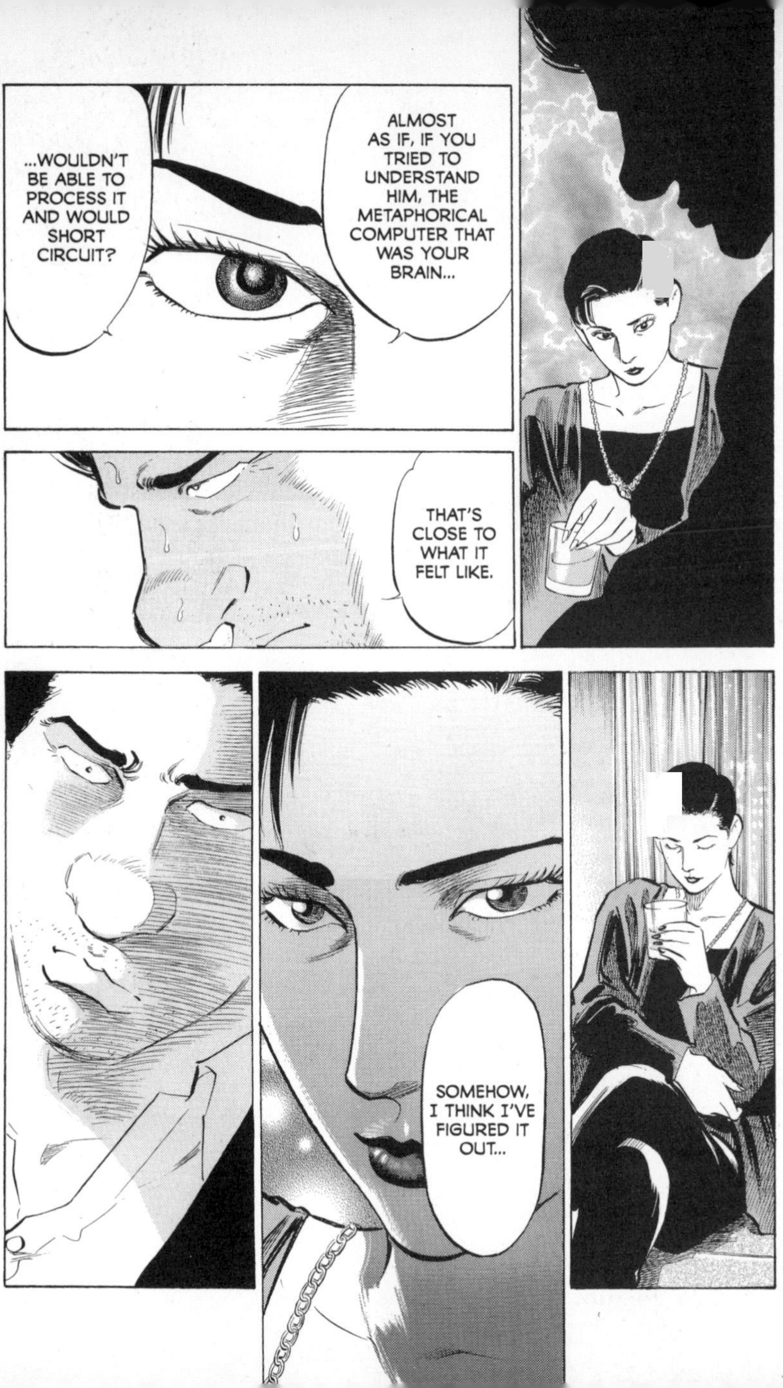
ALMOST AS IF, IF YOU TRIED TO UNDERSTAND HIM, THE METAPHORICAL COMPUTER THAT WAS YOUR BRAIN...
...WOULDN'T BE ABLE TO PROCESS IT AND WOULD SHORT CIRCUIT?
THAT'S CLOSE TO WHAT IT FELT LIKE.
SOMEHOW, I THINK I'VE FIGURED IT OUT...

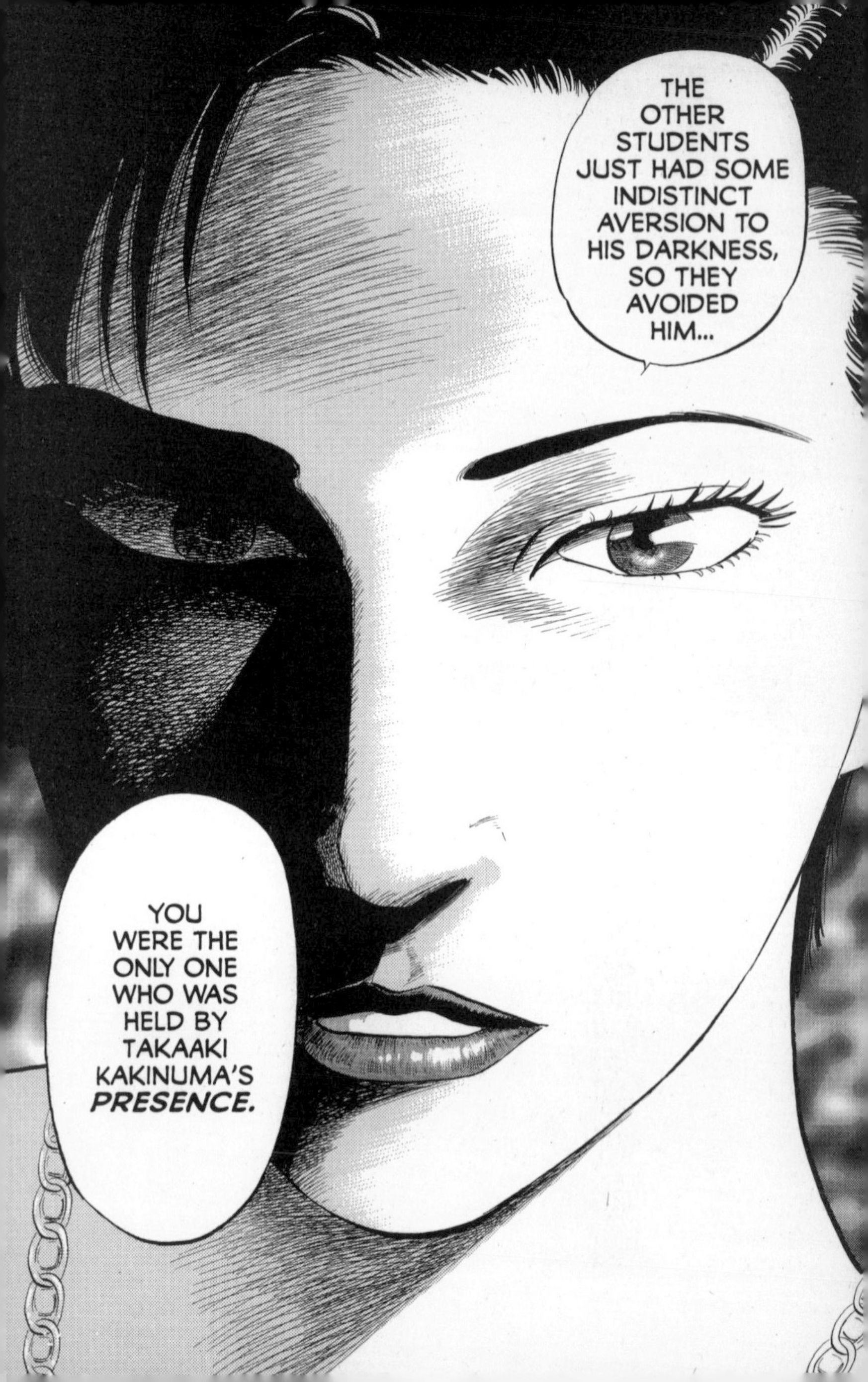
THE OTHER STUDENTS JUST HAD SOME INDISTINCT AVERSION TO HIS DARKNESS, SO THEY AVOIDED HIM...
YOU WERE THE ONLY ONE WHO WAS HELD BY TAKAAKI KAKINUMA'S ***PRESENCE.***

UNTIL THIS MOMENT TONIGHT, YOU'VE HAD HIM LOCKED UP *SO DEEP* IN YOUR SUBCONSCIOUS THAT YOU COULDN'T EVEN REMEMBER HIM.

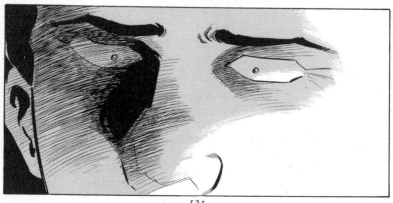

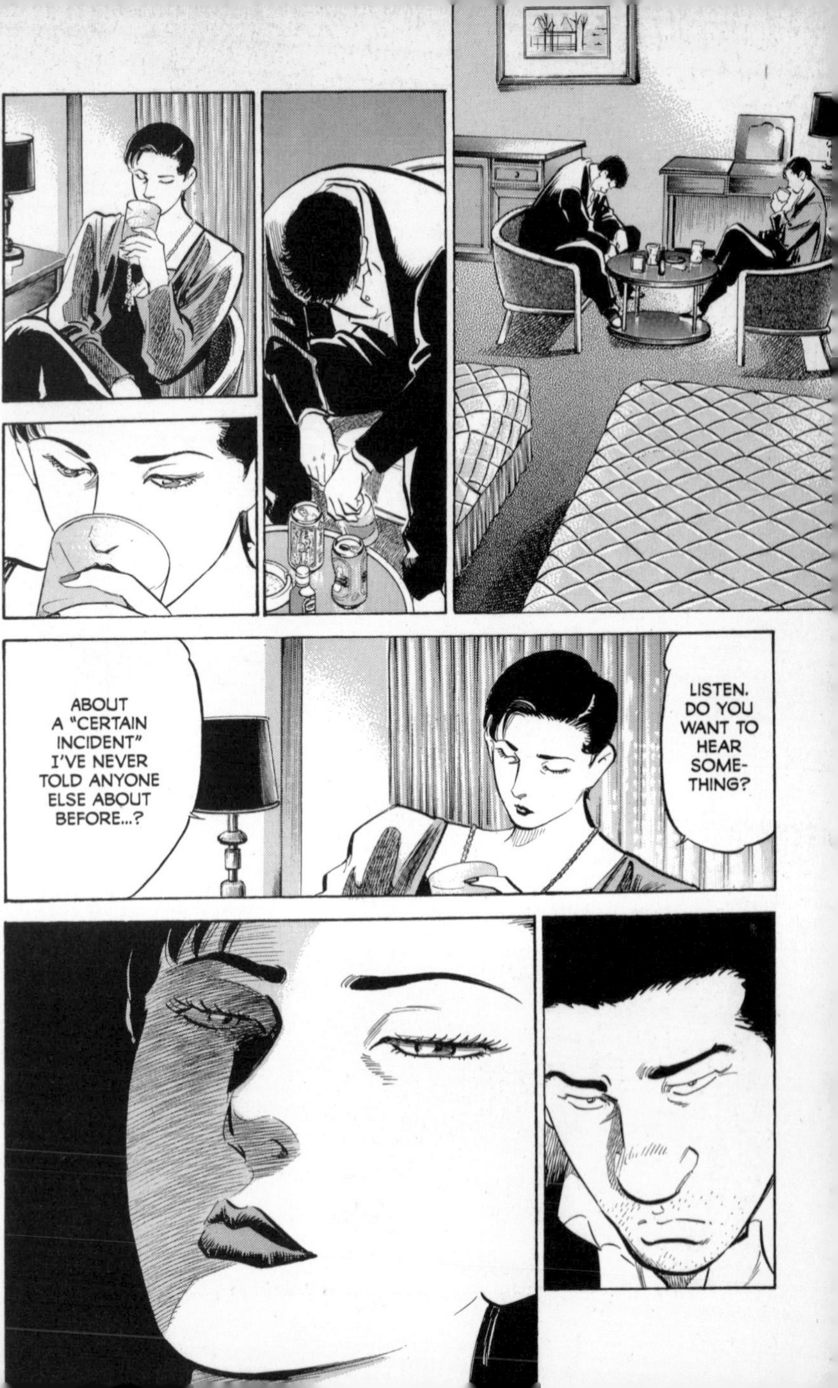
LISTEN. DO YOU WANT TO HEAR SOME-THING?
ABOUT A "CERTAIN INCIDENT" I'VE NEVER TOLD ANYONE ELSE ABOUT BEFORE...?

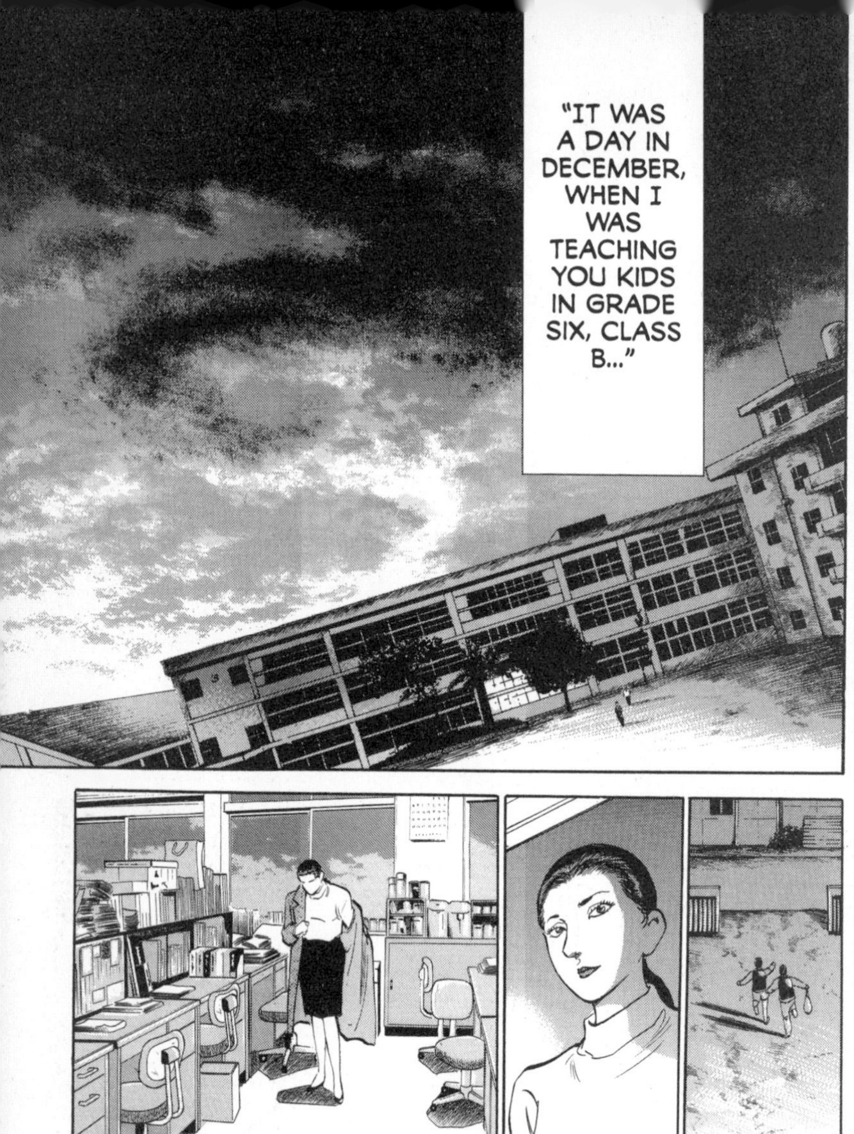
"IT WAS A DAY IN DECEMBER, WHEN I WAS TEACHING YOU KIDS IN GRADE SIX, CLASS B..."

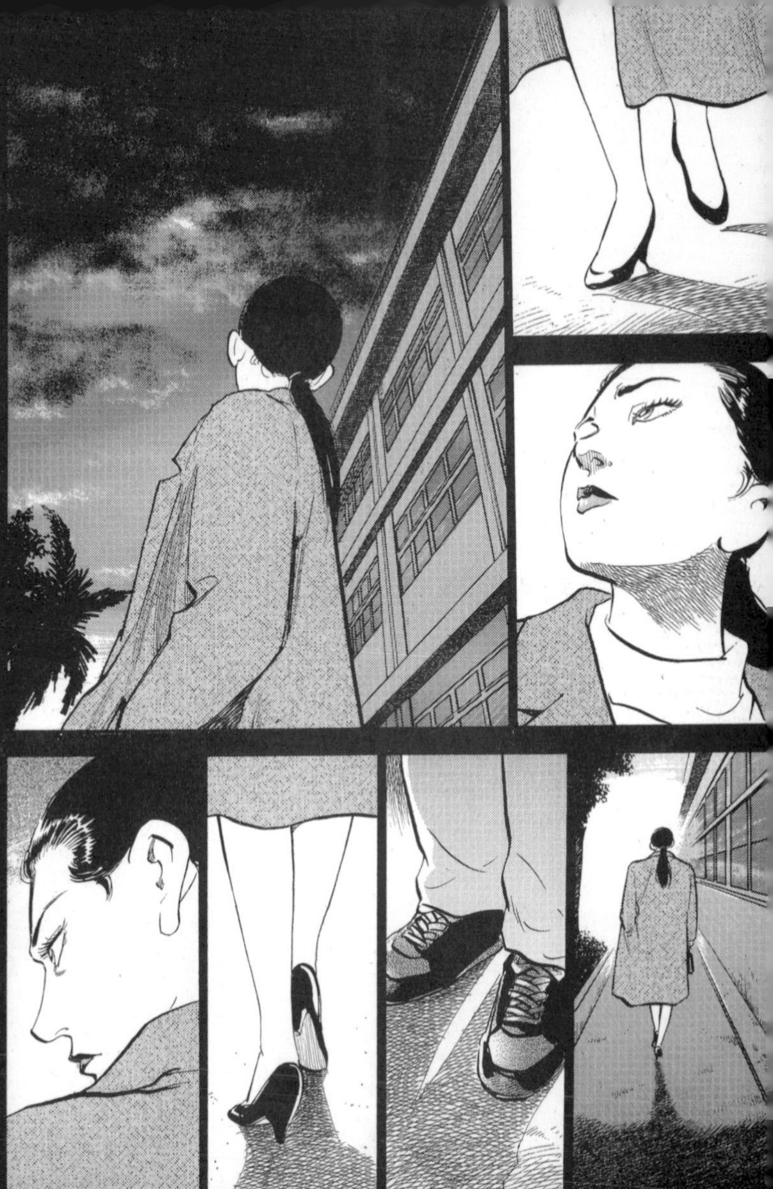

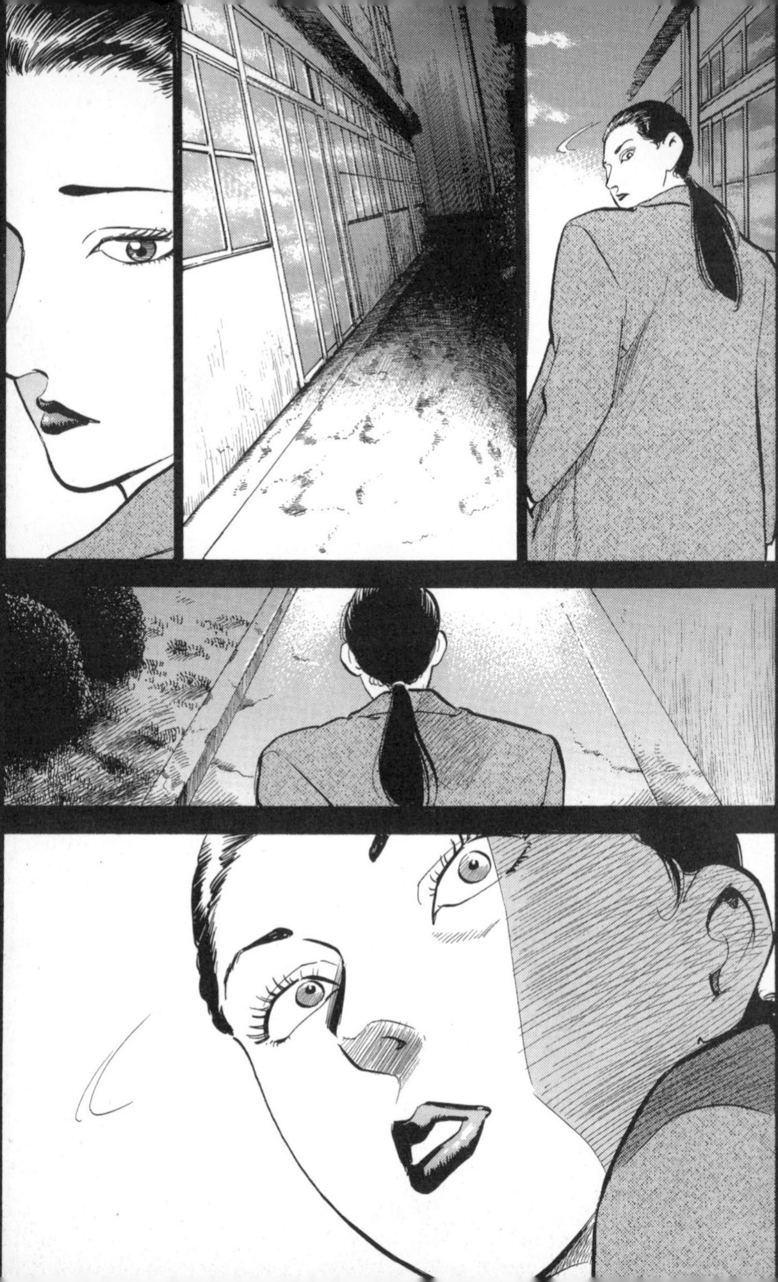

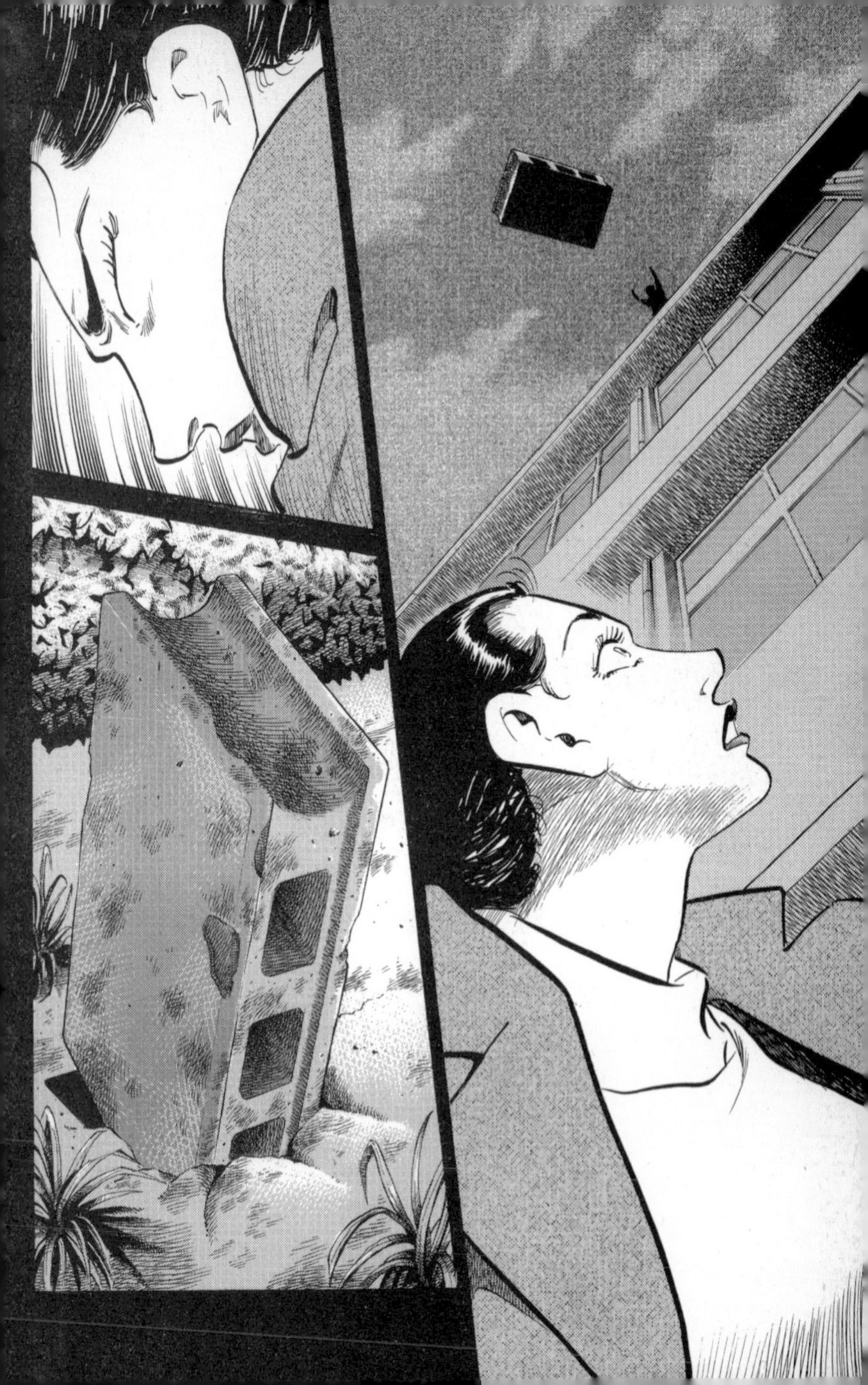

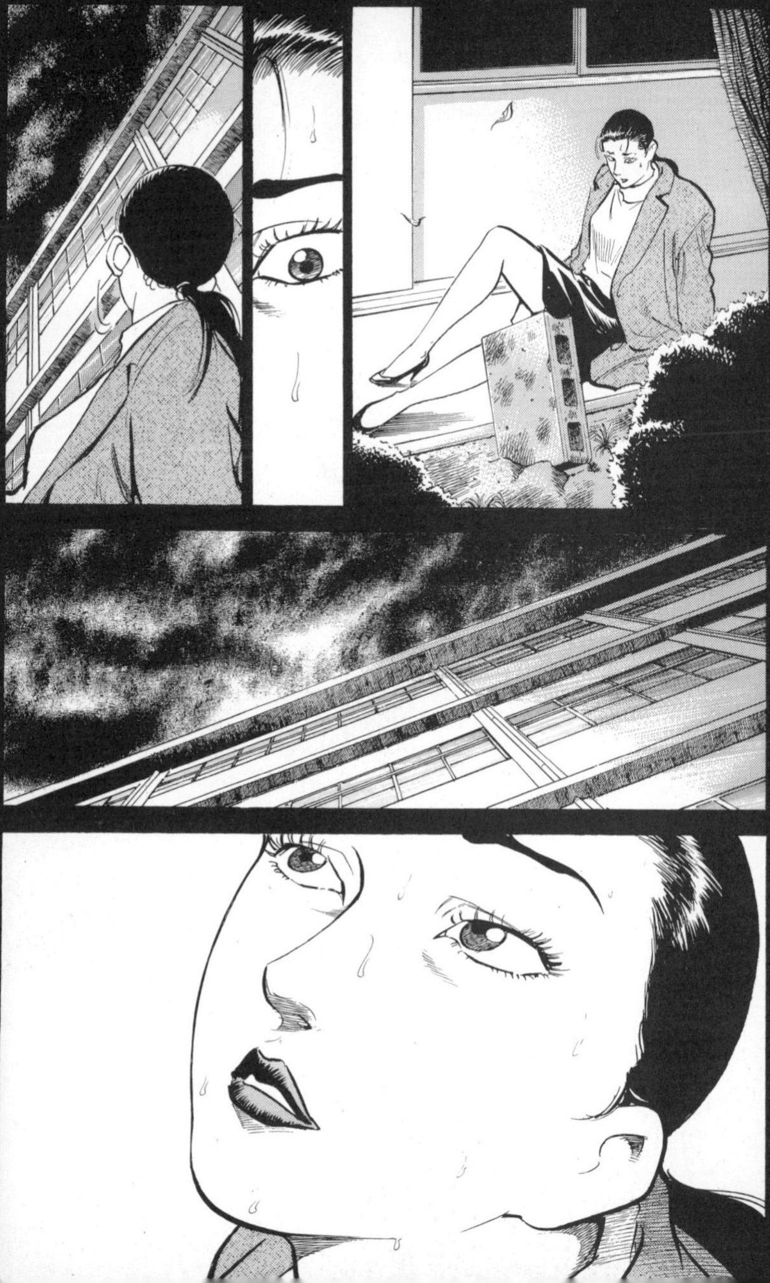

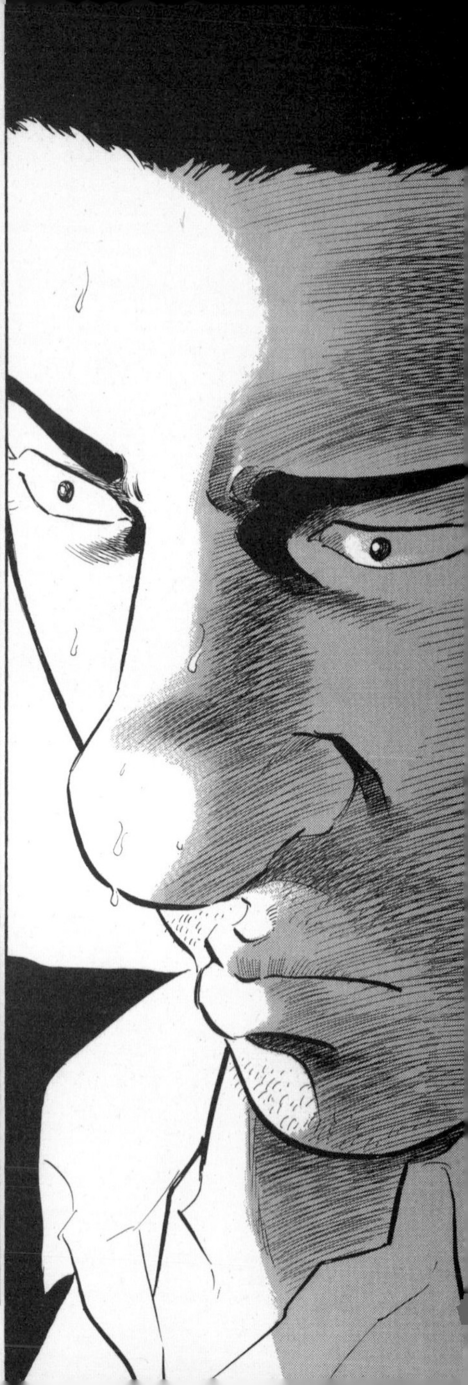

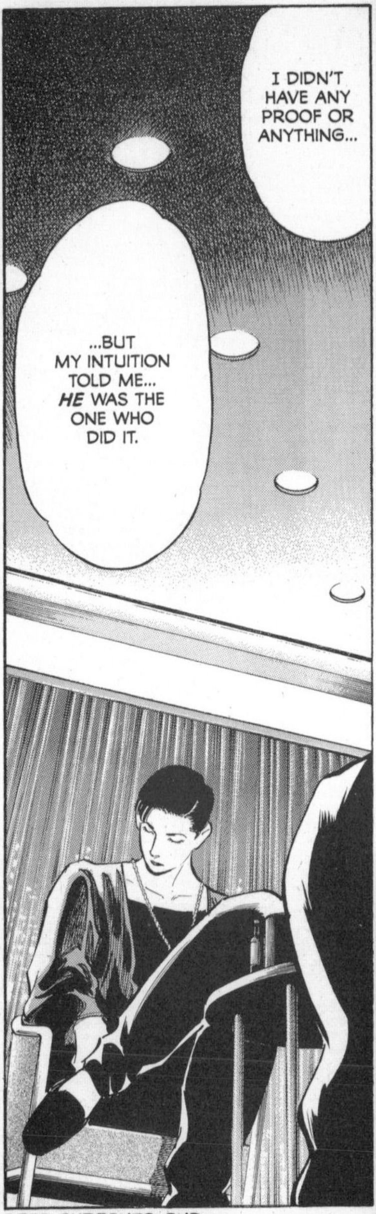
I DIDN'T HAVE ANY PROOF OR ANYTHING...
...BUT MY INTUITION TOLD ME... *HE* WAS THE ONE WHO DID IT.

DEEP CURRENTS: END

第46話◎絶対視線

CHAPTER 46
ABSOLUTE GAZE

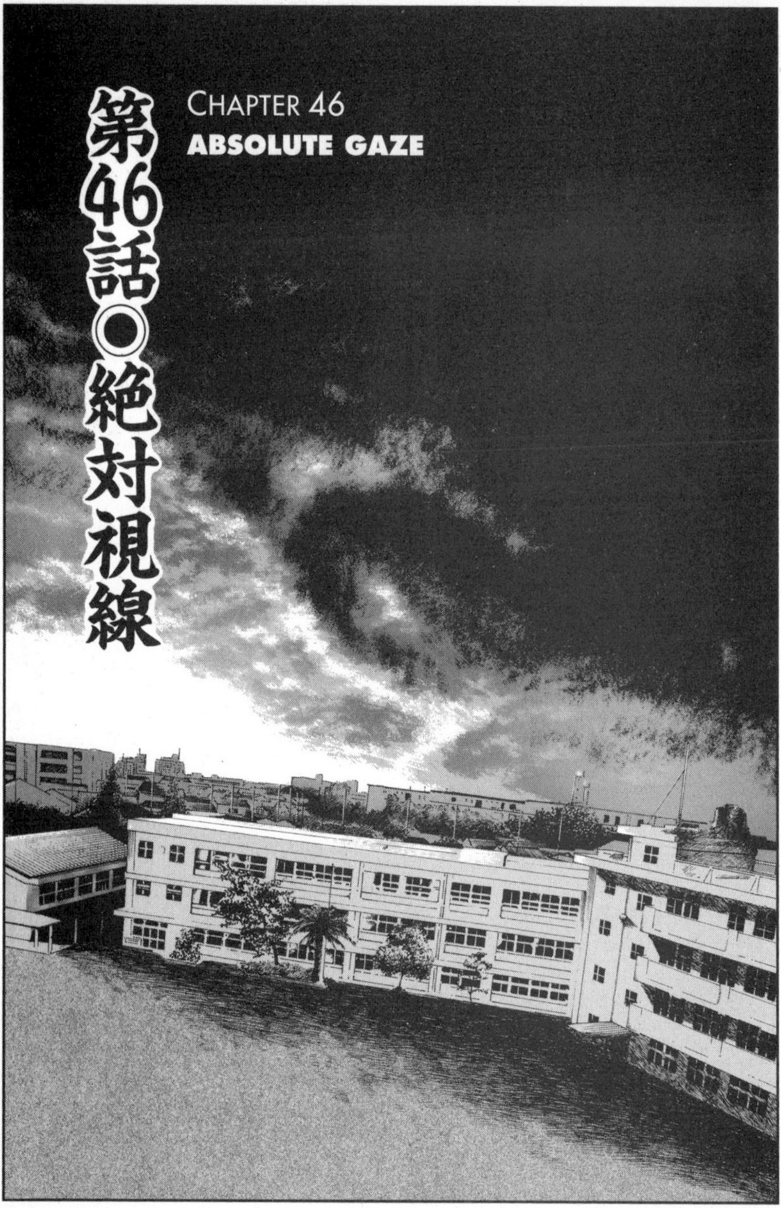

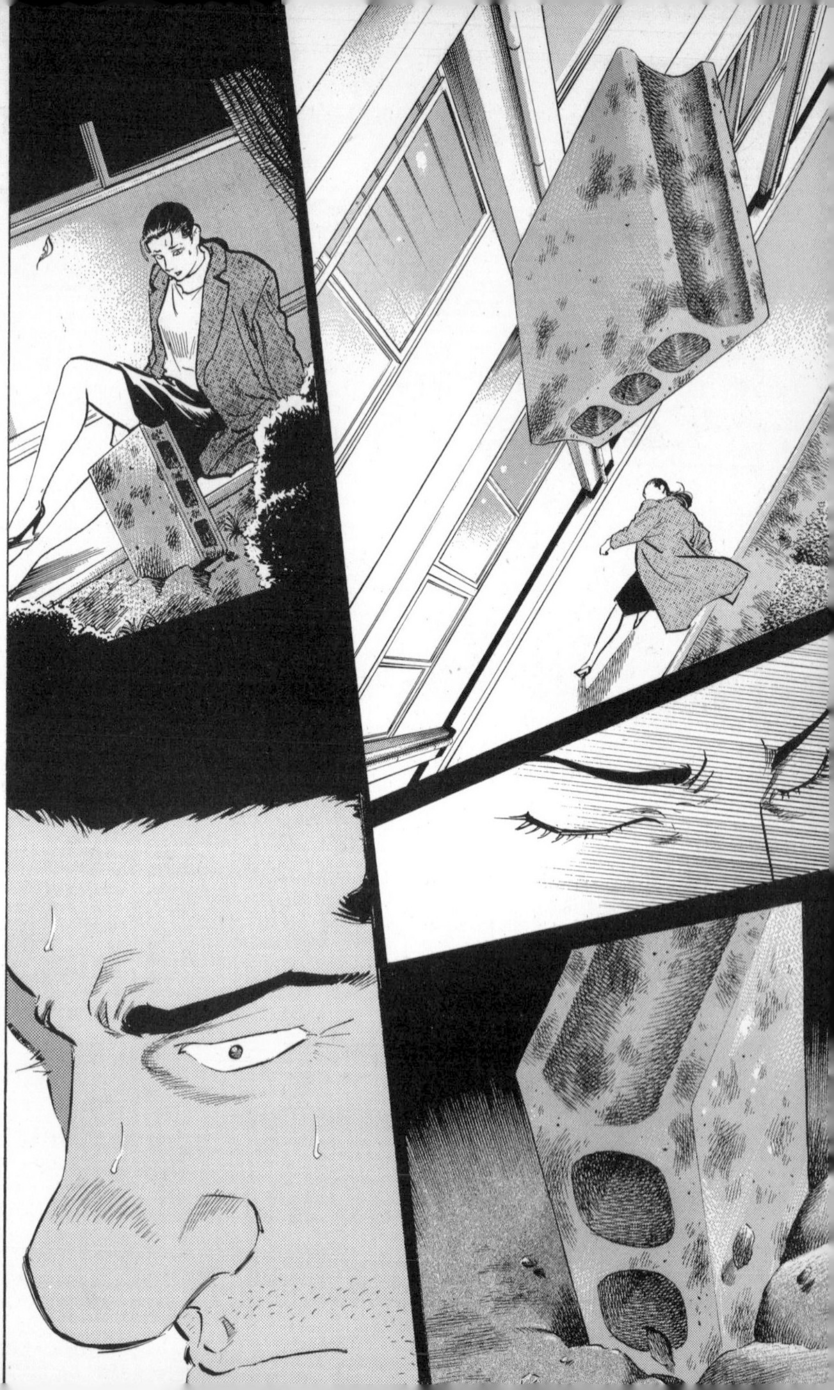

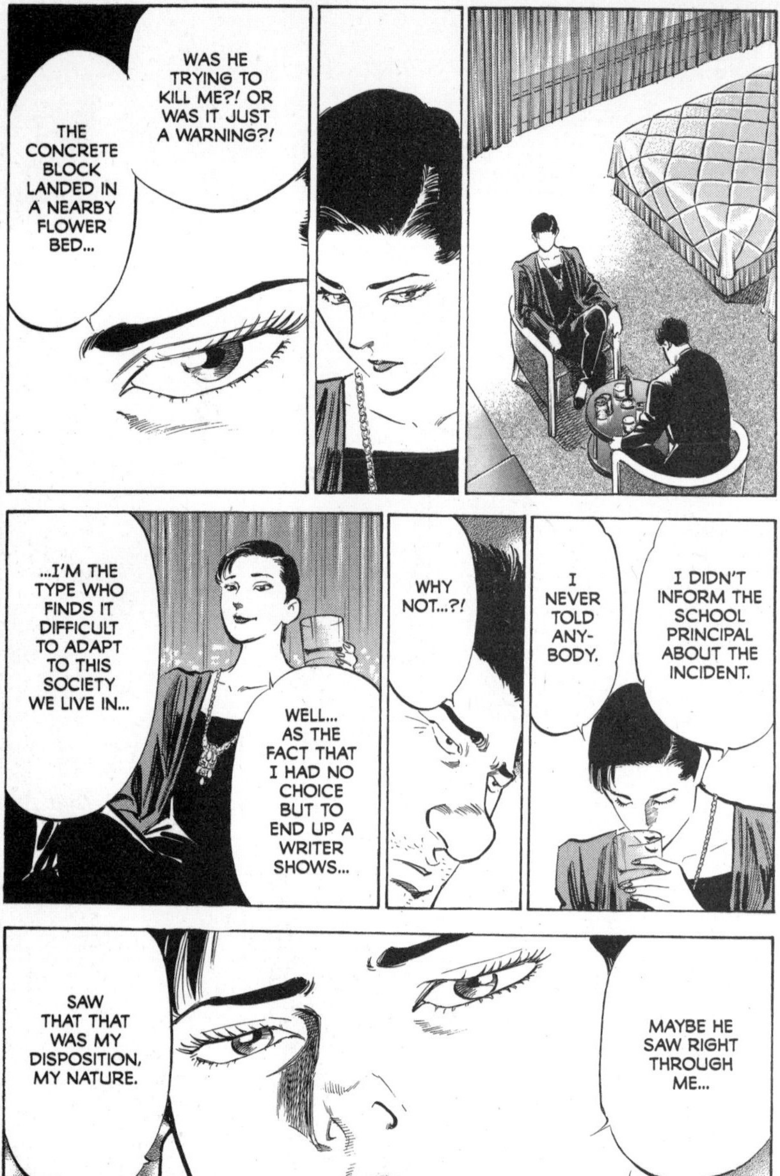
WAS HE TRYING TO KILL ME?! OR WAS IT JUST A WARNING?!
THE CONCRETE BLOCK LANDED IN A NEARBY FLOWER BED...
I DIDN'T INFORM THE SCHOOL PRINCIPAL ABOUT THE INCIDENT.
I NEVER TOLD ANY-BODY.
WHY NOT...?!
WELL... AS THE FACT THAT I HAD NO CHOICE BUT TO END UP A WRITER SHOWS...
...I'M THE TYPE WHO FINDS IT DIFFICULT TO ADAPT TO THIS SOCIETY WE LIVE IN...
MAYBE HE SAW RIGHT THROUGH ME...
SAW THAT THAT WAS MY DISPOSITION, MY NATURE.

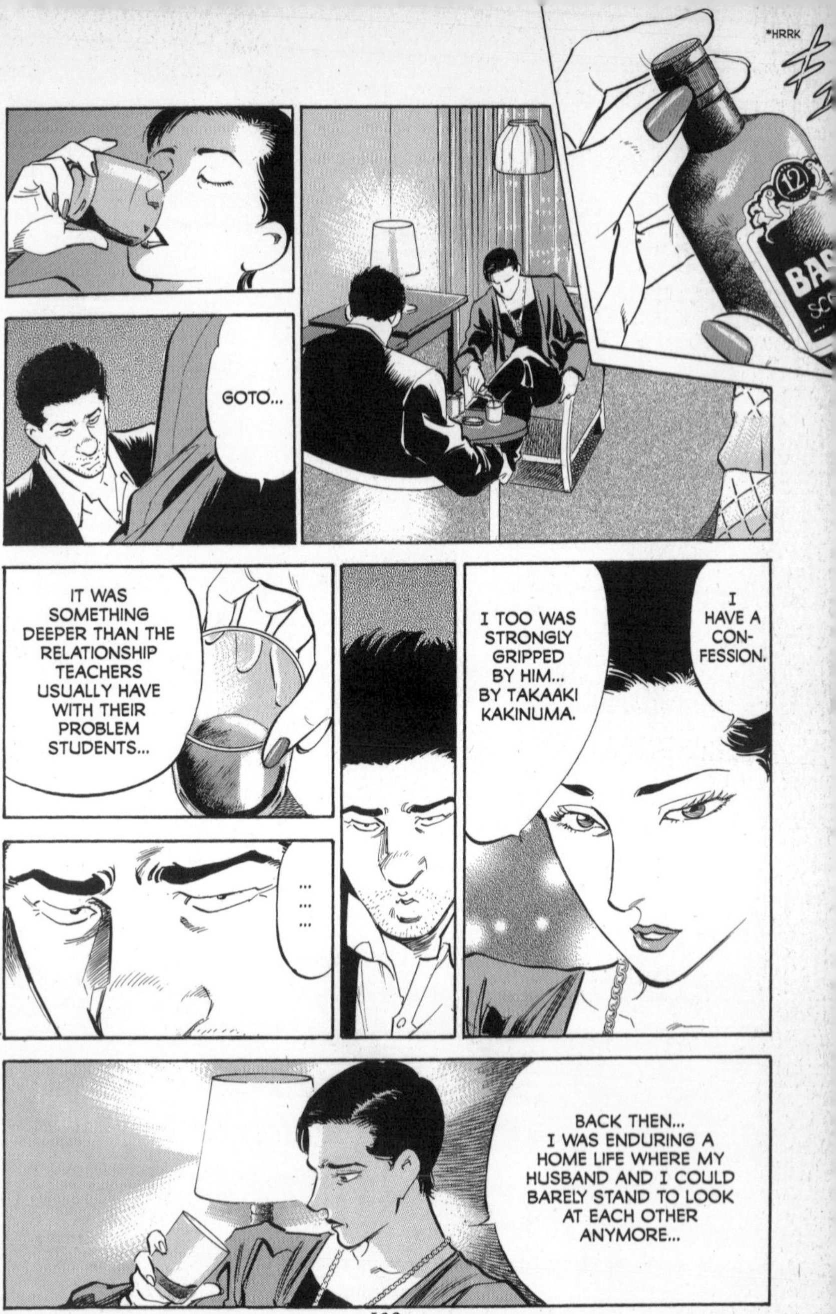
*HRRK
GOTO...
I HAVE A CON-FESSION.
I TOO WAS STRONGLY GRIPPED BY HIM... BY TAKAAKI KAKINUMA.
IT WAS SOMETHING DEEPER THAN THE RELATIONSHIP TEACHERS USUALLY HAVE WITH THEIR PROBLEM STUDENTS...
......
BACK THEN... I WAS ENDURING A HOME LIFE WHERE MY HUSBAND AND I COULD BARELY STAND TO LOOK AT EACH OTHER ANYMORE...

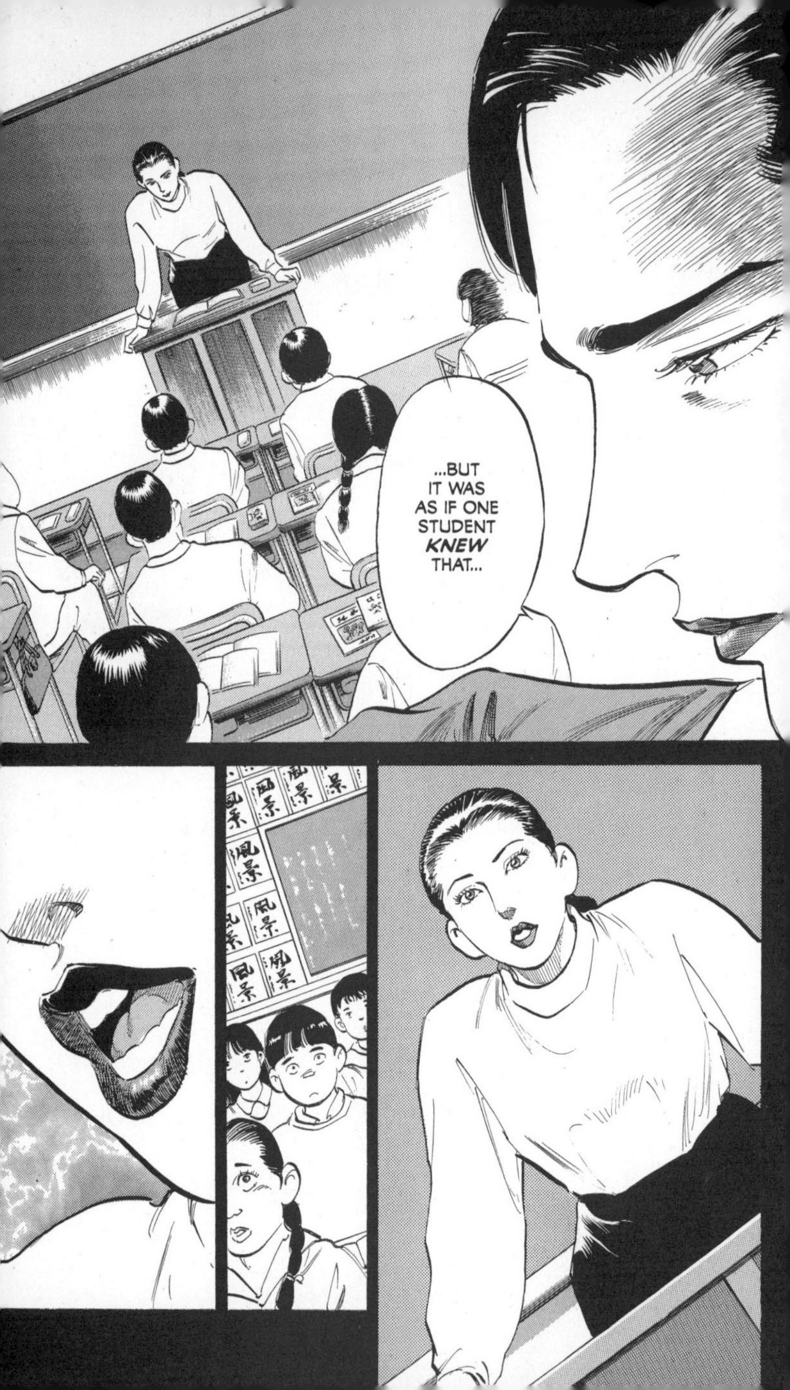
...BUT IT WAS AS IF ONE STUDENT *KNEW* THAT...

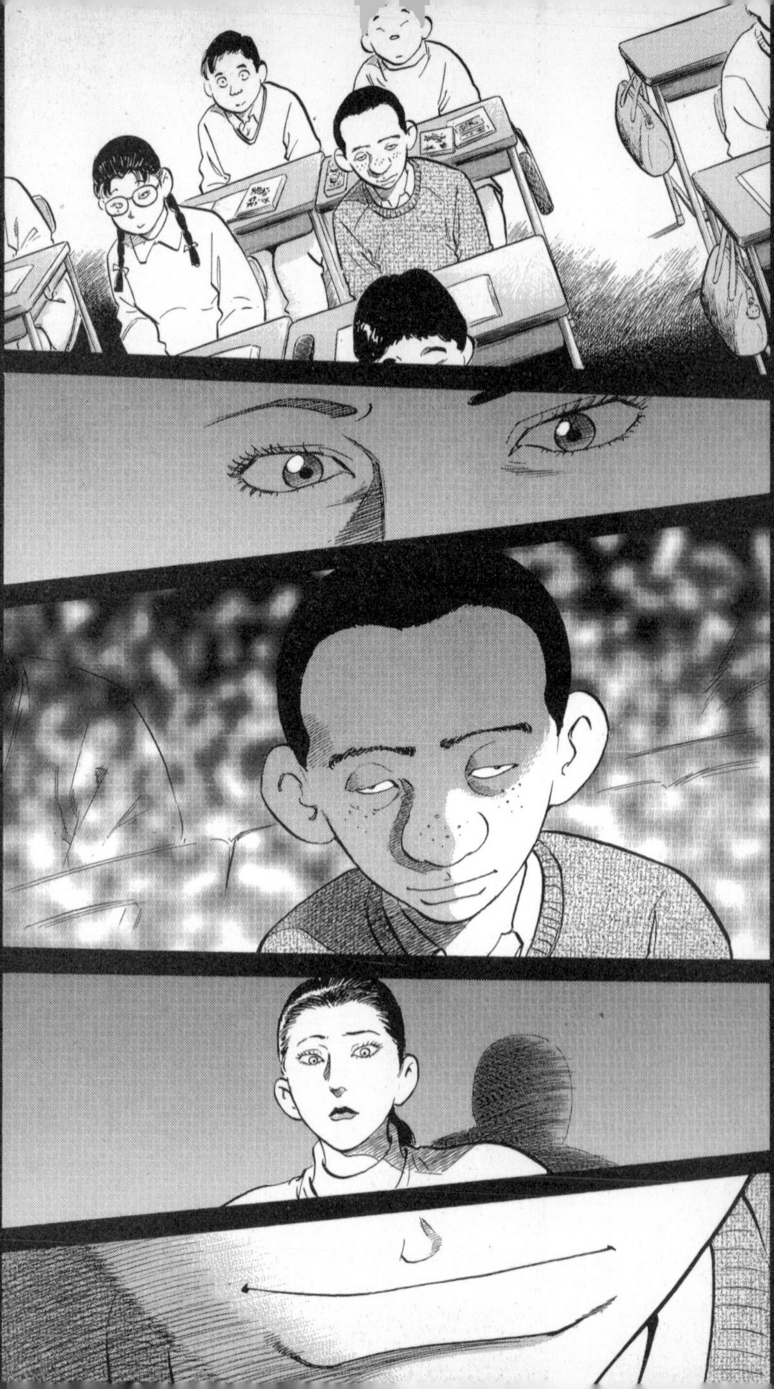

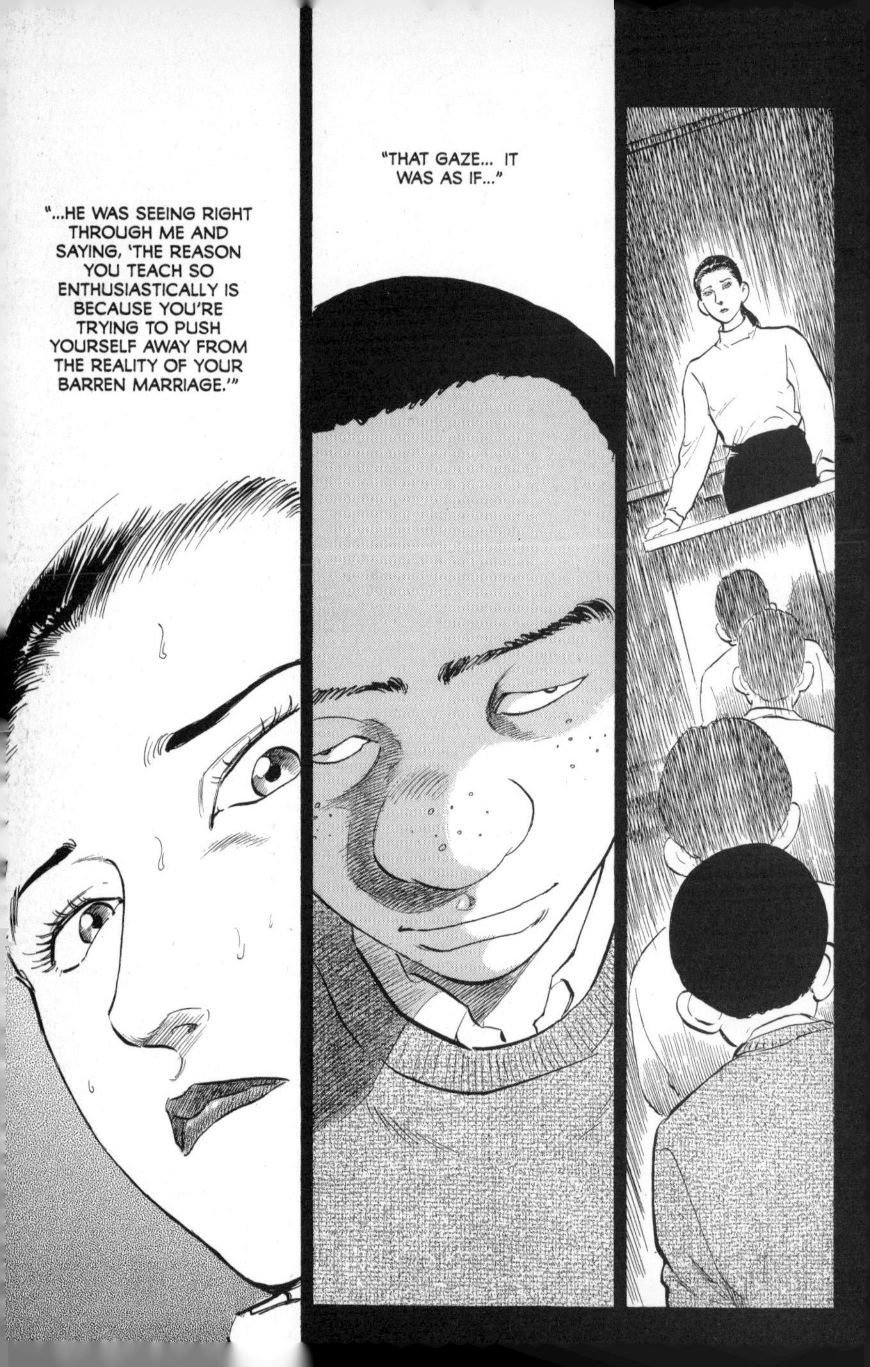
"THAT GAZE... IT WAS AS IF..."
"...HE WAS SEEING RIGHT THROUGH ME AND SAYING, 'THE REASON YOU TEACH SO ENTHUSIASTICALLY IS BECAUSE YOU'RE TRYING TO PUSH YOURSELF AWAY FROM THE REALITY OF YOUR BARREN MARRIAGE.'"

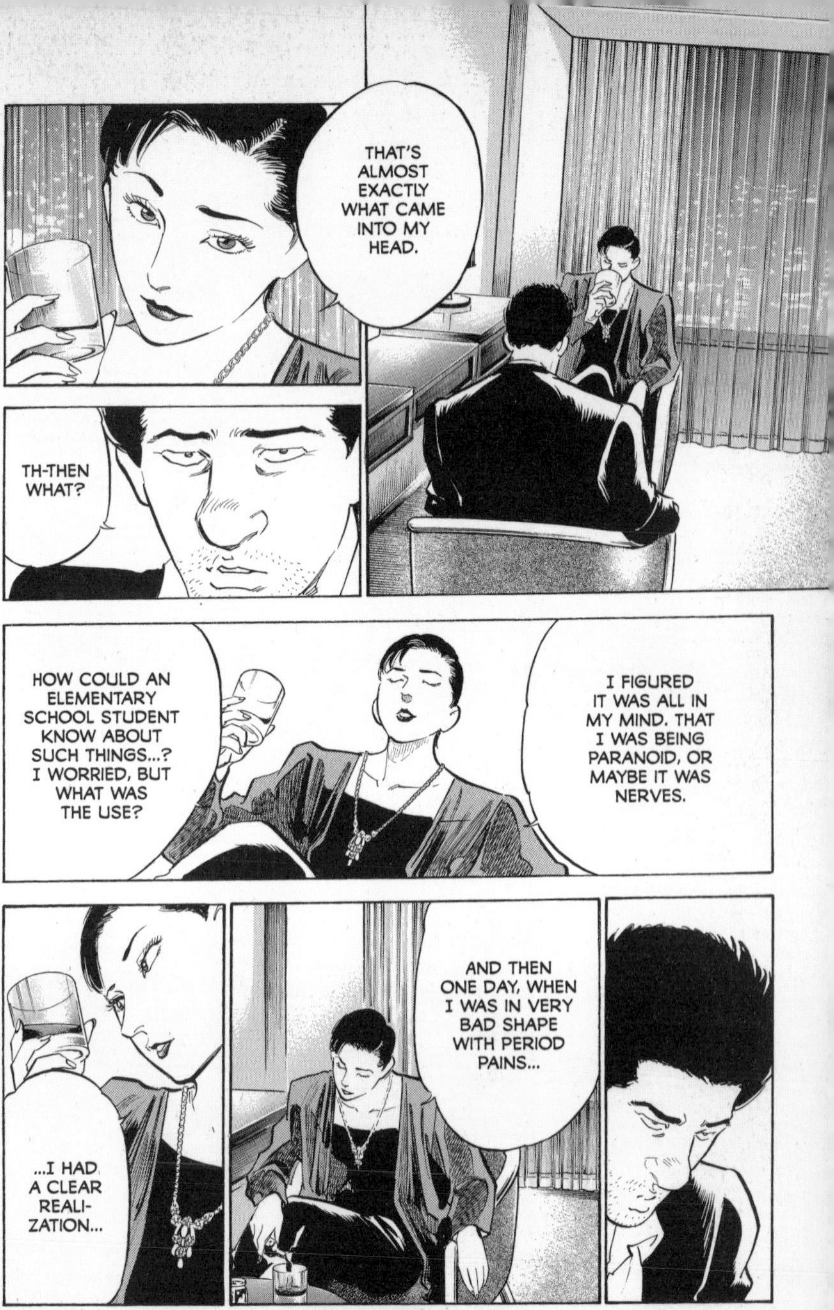
THAT'S ALMOST EXACTLY WHAT CAME INTO MY HEAD.
TH-THEN WHAT?
I FIGURED IT WAS ALL IN MY MIND. THAT I WAS BEING PARANOID, OR MAYBE IT WAS NERVES.
HOW COULD AN ELEMENTARY SCHOOL STUDENT KNOW ABOUT SUCH THINGS...? I WORRIED, BUT WHAT WAS THE USE?
AND THEN ONE DAY, WHEN I WAS IN VERY BAD SHAPE WITH PERIOD PAINS...
...I HAD A CLEAR REALI- ZATION...

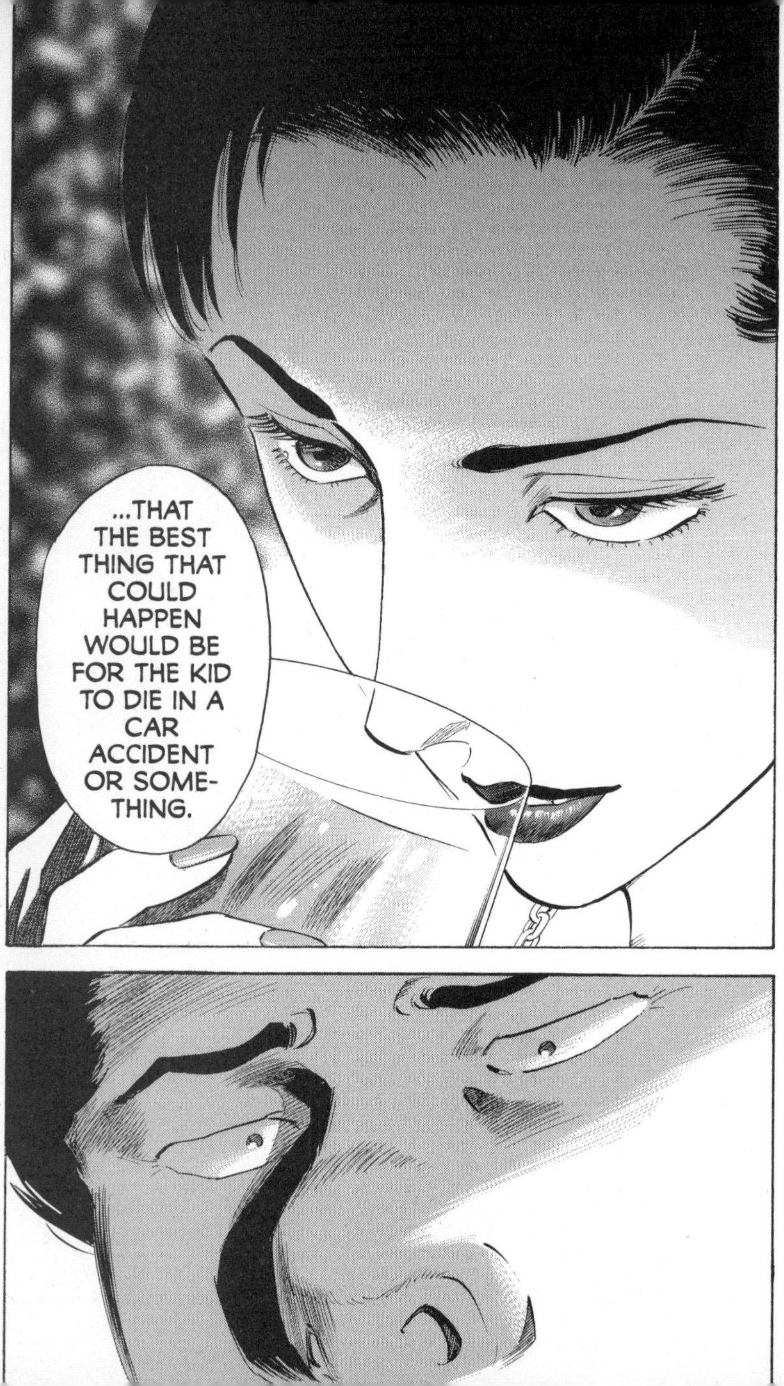
...THAT THE BEST THING THAT COULD HAPPEN WOULD BE FOR THE KID TO DIE IN A CAR ACCIDENT OR SOME-THING.

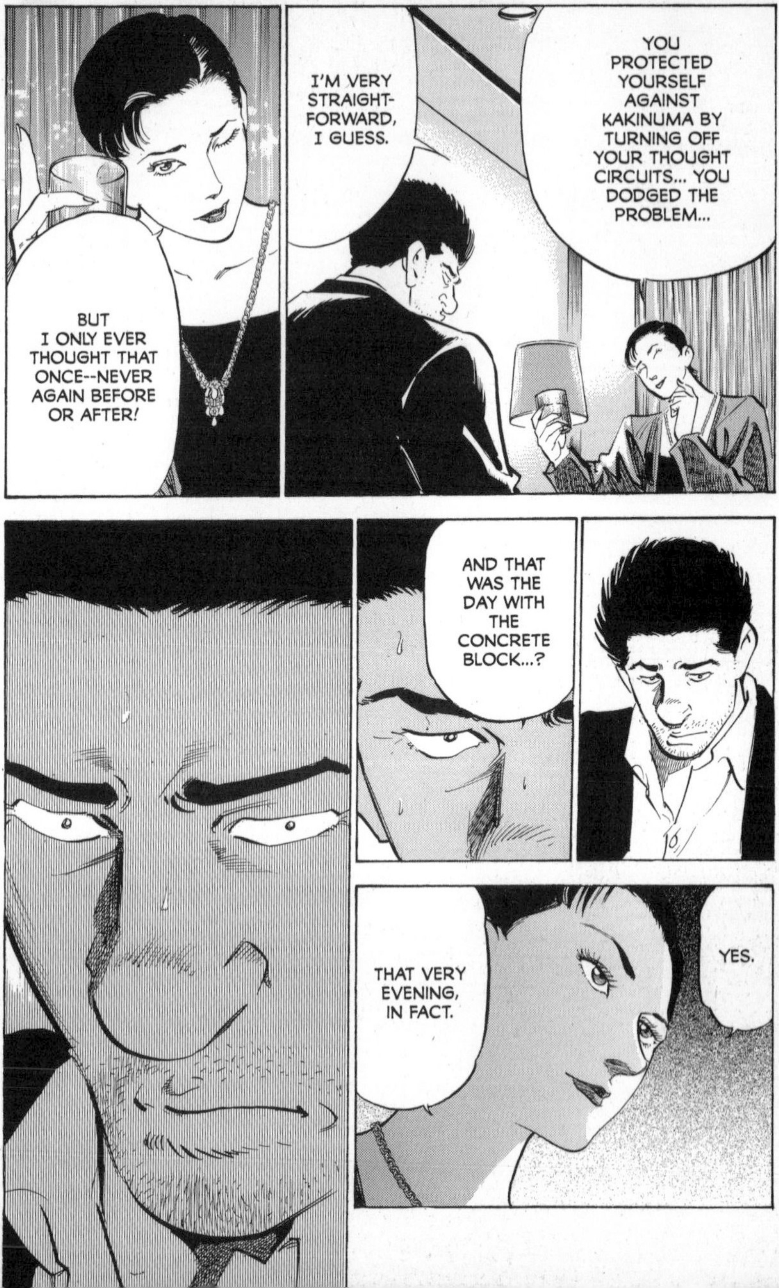
YOU PROTECTED YOURSELF AGAINST KAKINUMA BY TURNING OFF YOUR THOUGHT CIRCUITS... YOU DODGED THE PROBLEM...
I'M VERY STRAIGHT-FORWARD, I GUESS.
BUT I ONLY EVER THOUGHT THAT ONCE--NEVER AGAIN BEFORE OR AFTER!
AND THAT WAS THE DAY WITH THE CONCRETE BLOCK...?
YES.
THAT VERY EVENING, IN FACT.

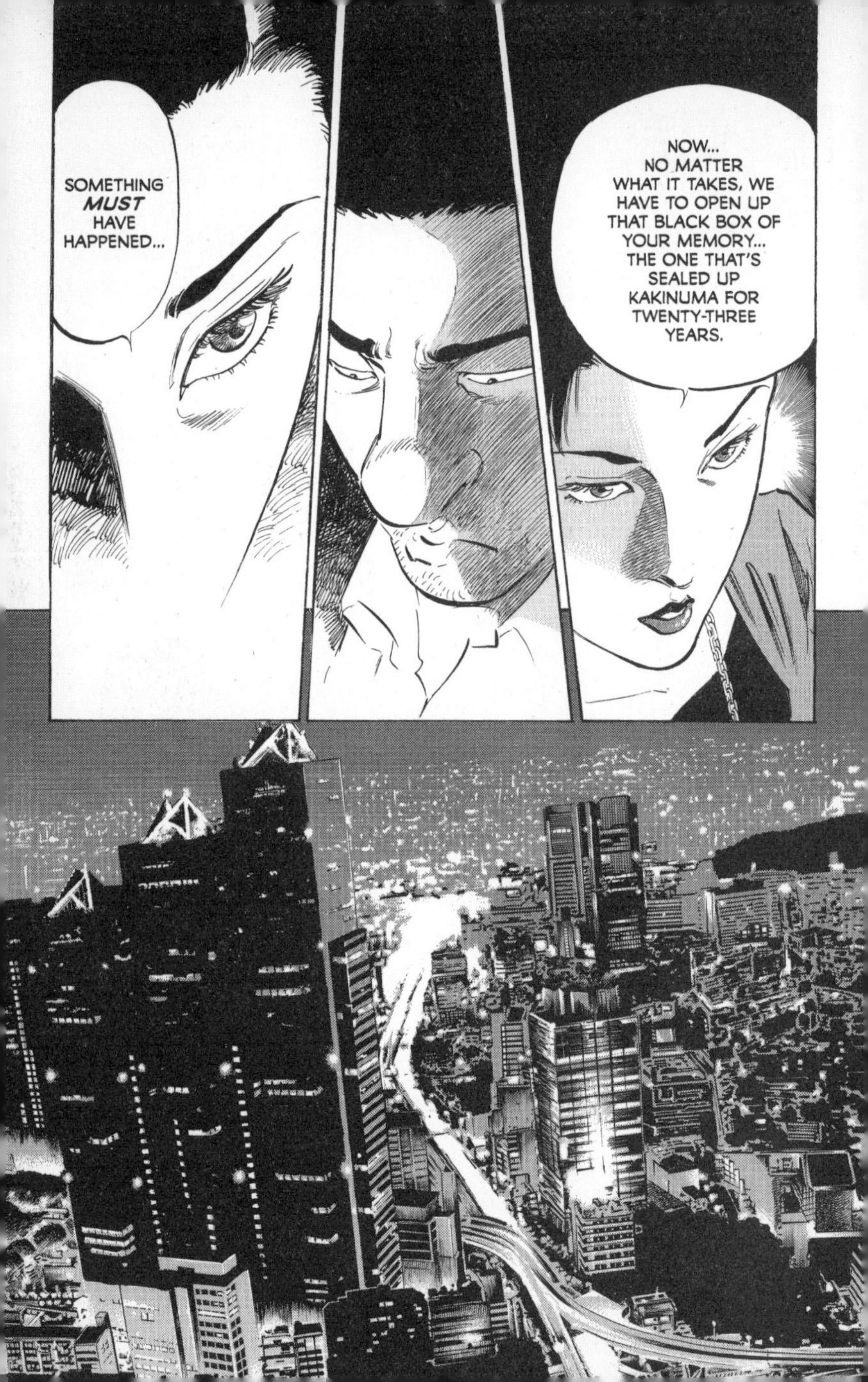
NOW... NO MATTER WHAT IT TAKES, WE HAVE TO OPEN UP THAT BLACK BOX OF YOUR MEMORY... THE ONE THAT'S SEALED UP KAKINUMA FOR TWENTY-THREE YEARS.
SOMETHING *MUST* HAVE HAPPENED...

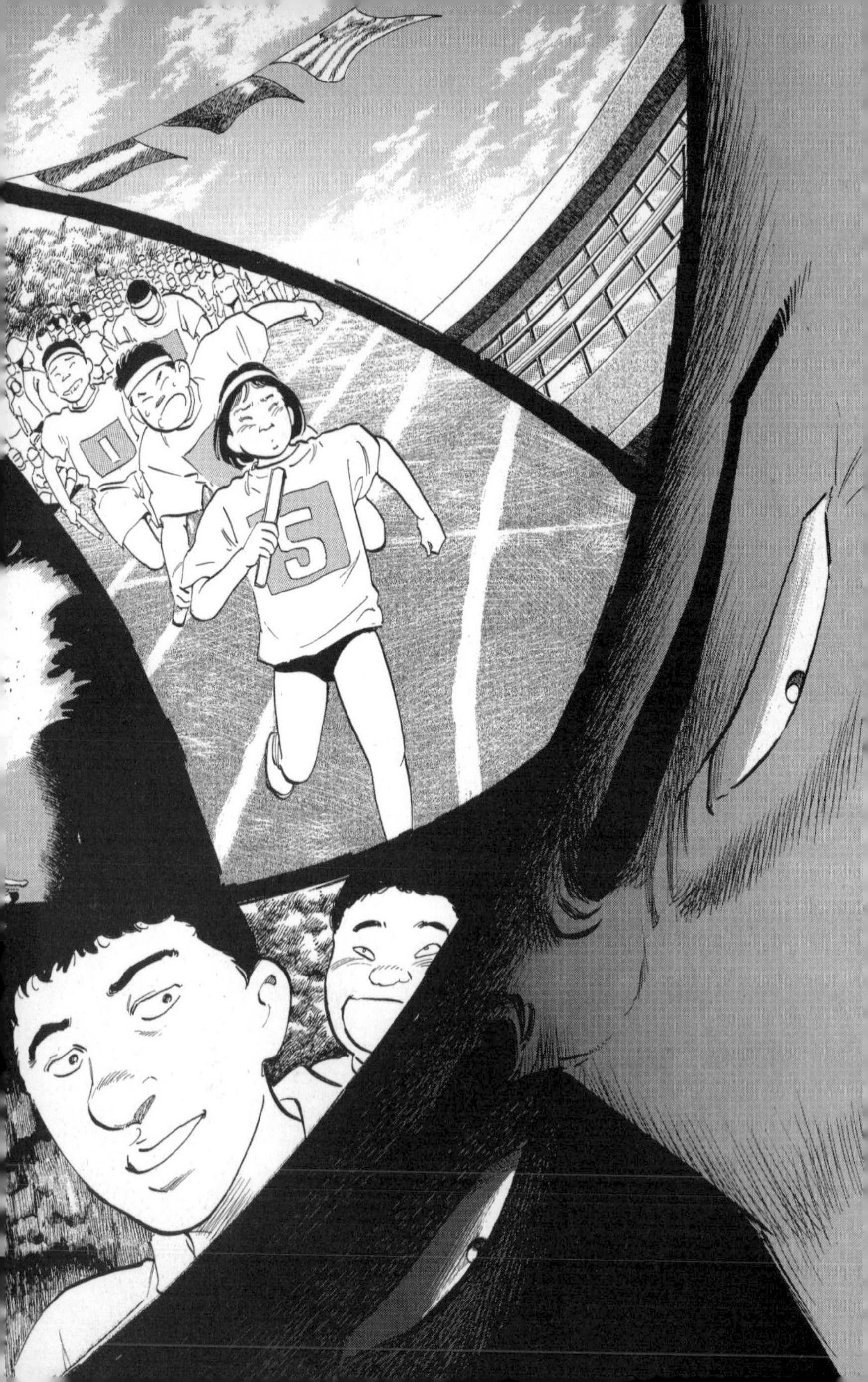

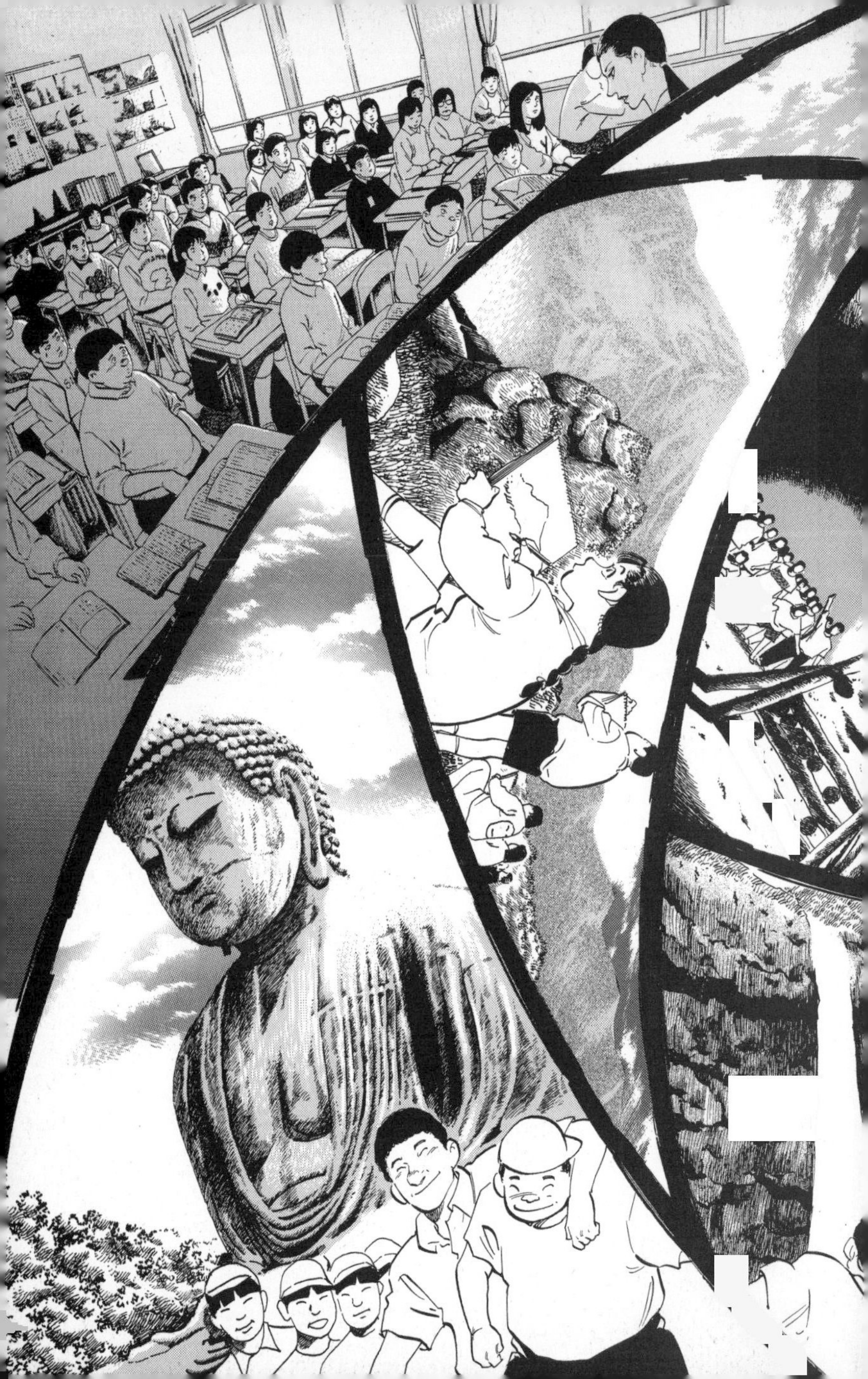

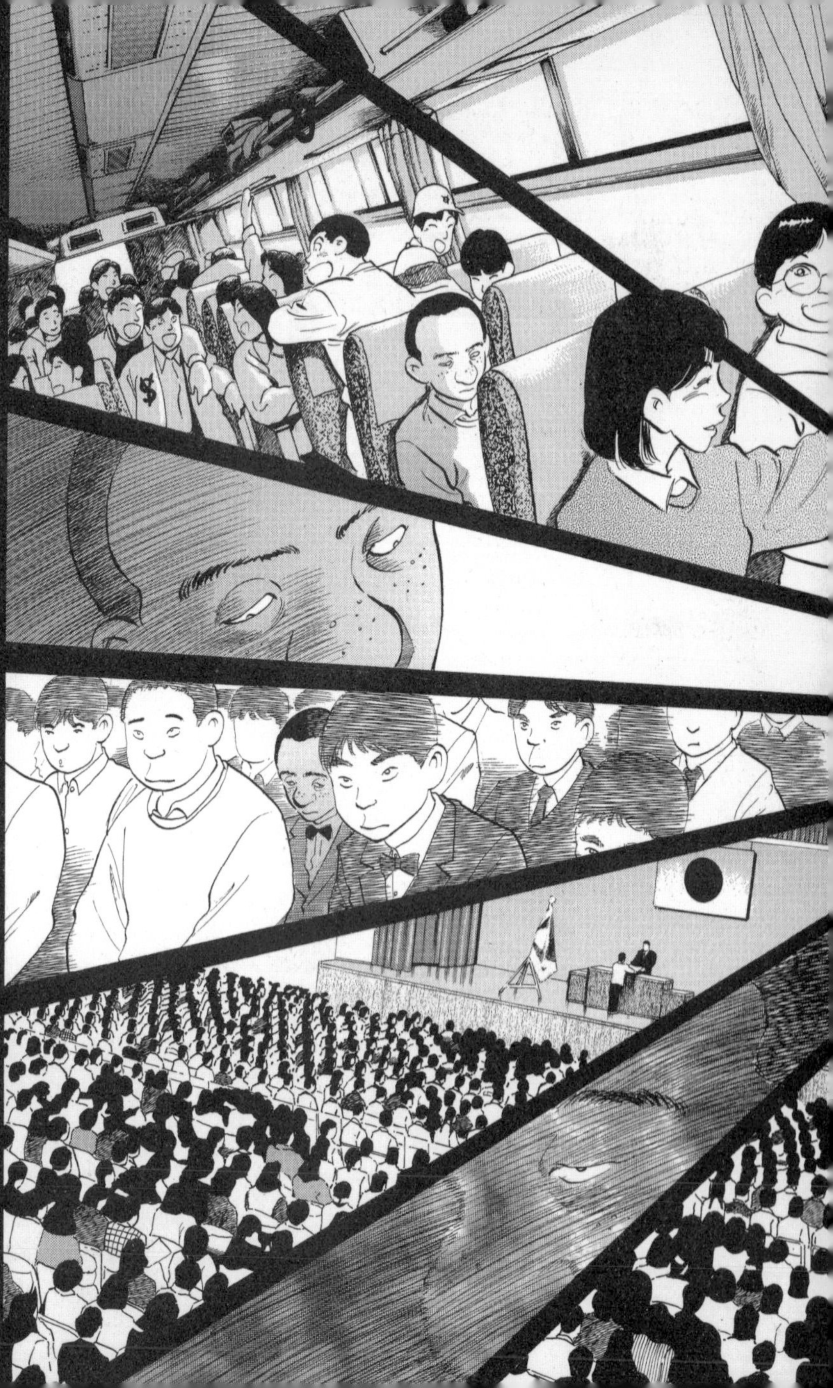

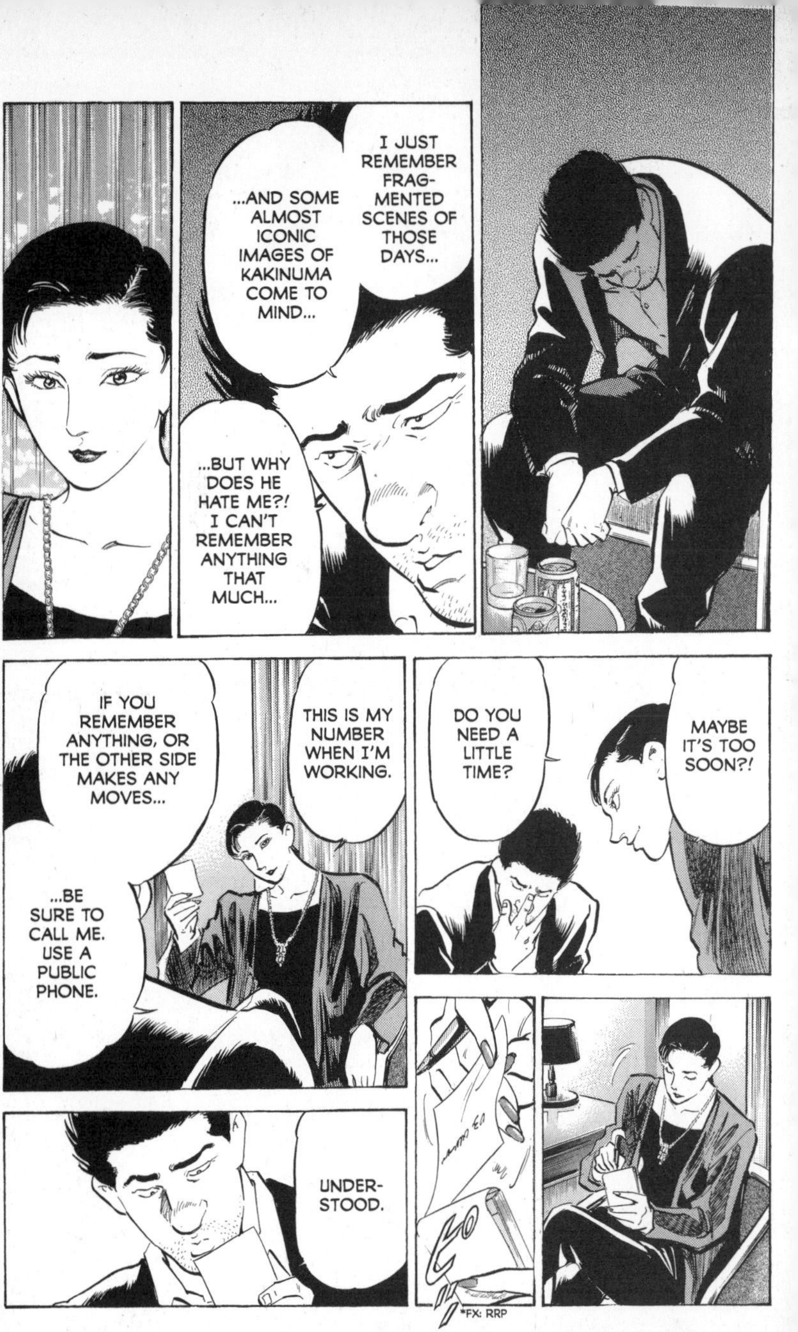
I JUST REMEMBER FRAG-MENTED SCENES OF THOSE DAYS...
...AND SOME ALMOST ICONIC IMAGES OF KAKINUMA COME TO MIND...
...BUT WHY DOES HE HATE ME?! I CAN'T REMEMBER ANYTHING THAT MUCH...
MAYBE IT'S TOO SOON?!
DO YOU NEED A LITTLE TIME?
THIS IS MY NUMBER WHEN I'M WORKING.
IF YOU REMEMBER ANYTHING, OR THE OTHER SIDE MAKES ANY MOVES...
...BE SURE TO CALL ME. USE A PUBLIC PHONE.
*FX: RRP
UNDER-STOOD.

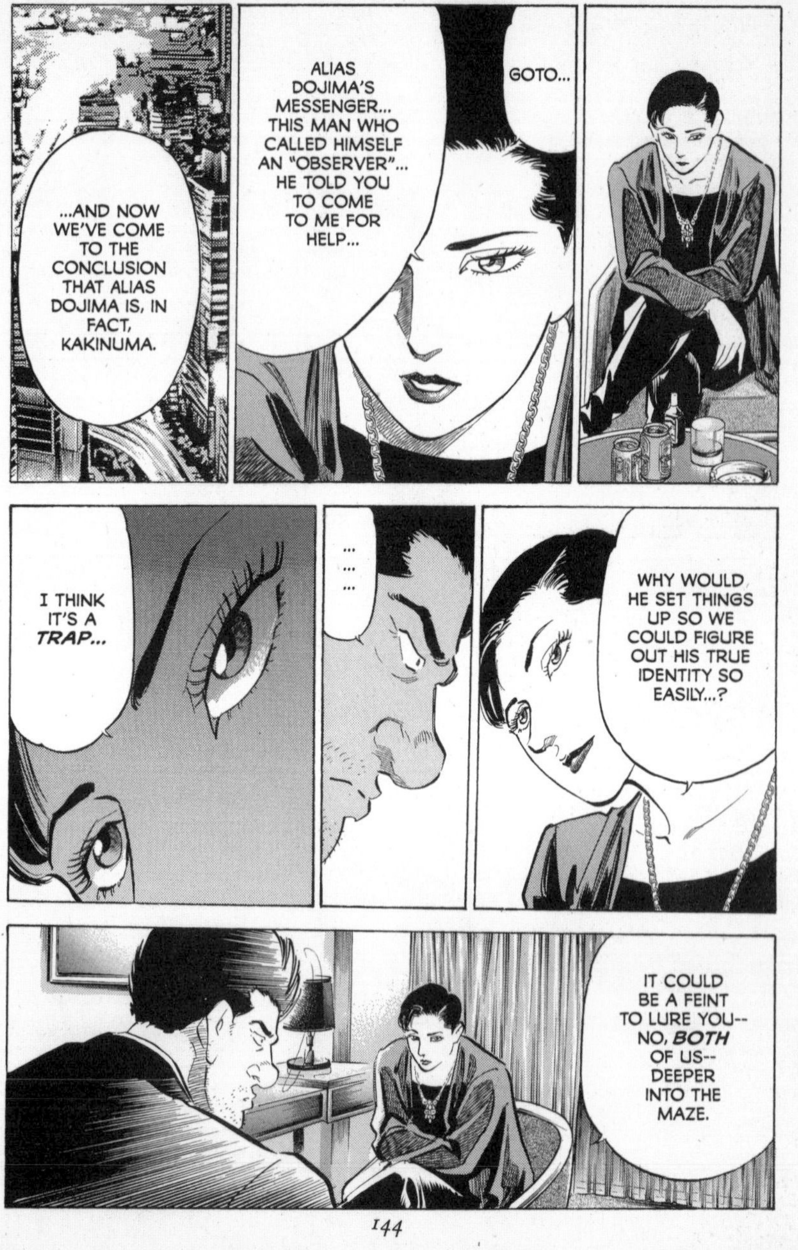
GOTO...
ALIAS DOJIMA'S MESSENGER... THIS MAN WHO CALLED HIMSELF AN "OBSERVER"... HE TOLD YOU TO COME TO ME FOR HELP...
...AND NOW WE'VE COME TO THE CONCLUSION THAT ALIAS DOJIMA IS, IN FACT, KAKINUMA.
WHY WOULD HE SET THINGS UP SO WE COULD FIGURE OUT HIS TRUE IDENTITY SO EASILY...?
... ...
I THINK IT'S A ***TRAP...***
IT COULD BE A FEINT TO LURE YOU-- NO, ***BOTH*** OF US-- DEEPER INTO THE MAZE.

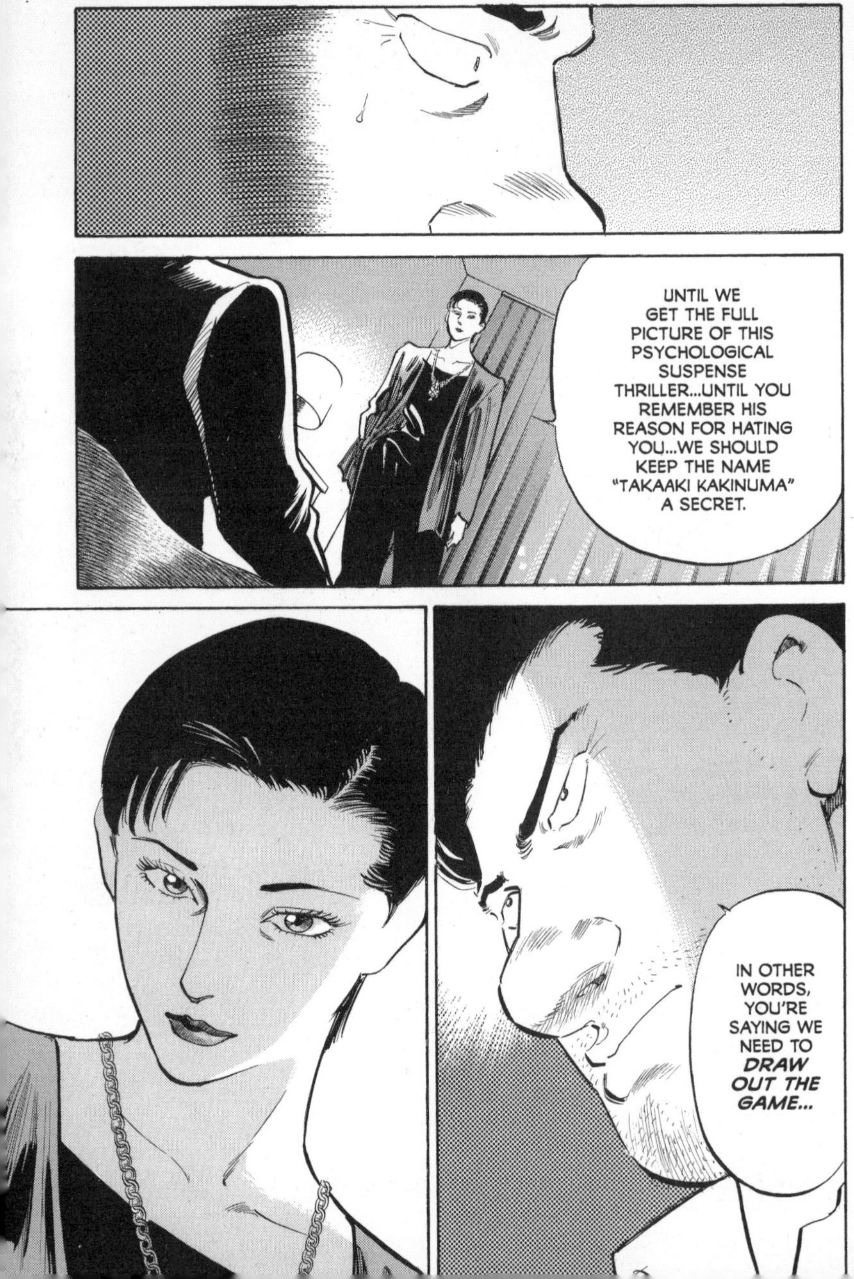
UNTIL WE GET THE FULL PICTURE OF THIS PSYCHOLOGICAL SUSPENSE THRILLER...UNTIL YOU REMEMBER HIS REASON FOR HATING YOU...WE SHOULD KEEP THE NAME "TAKAAKI KAKINUMA" A SECRET.
IN OTHER WORDS, YOU'RE SAYING WE NEED TO *DRAW OUT THE GAME...*

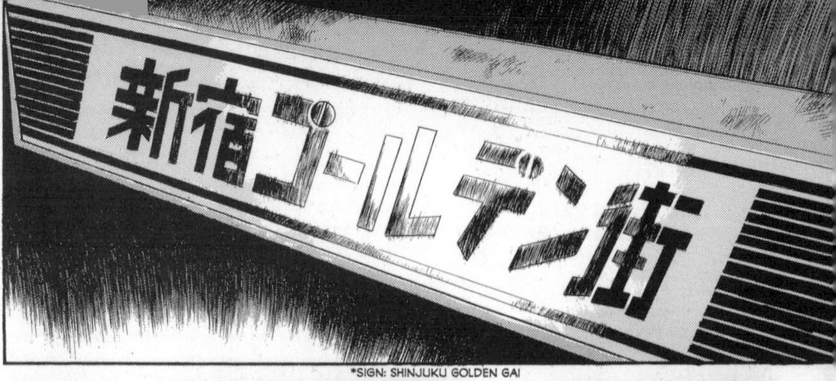
新宿ゴールデン街

*SIGN: SHINJUKU GOLDEN GAI

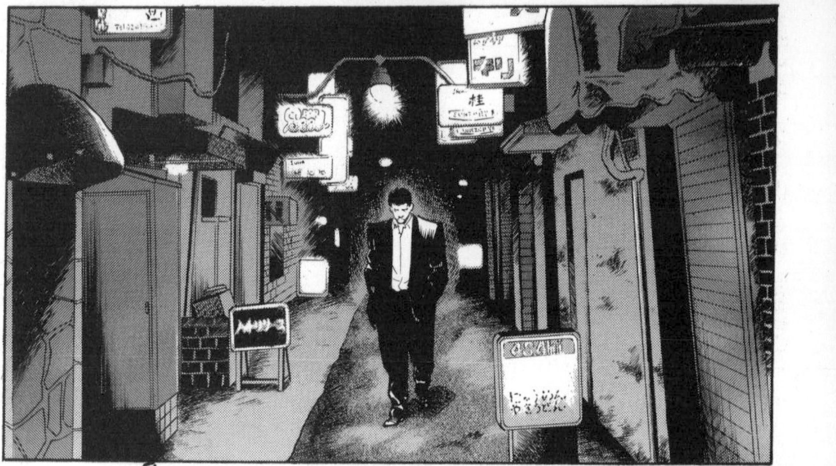

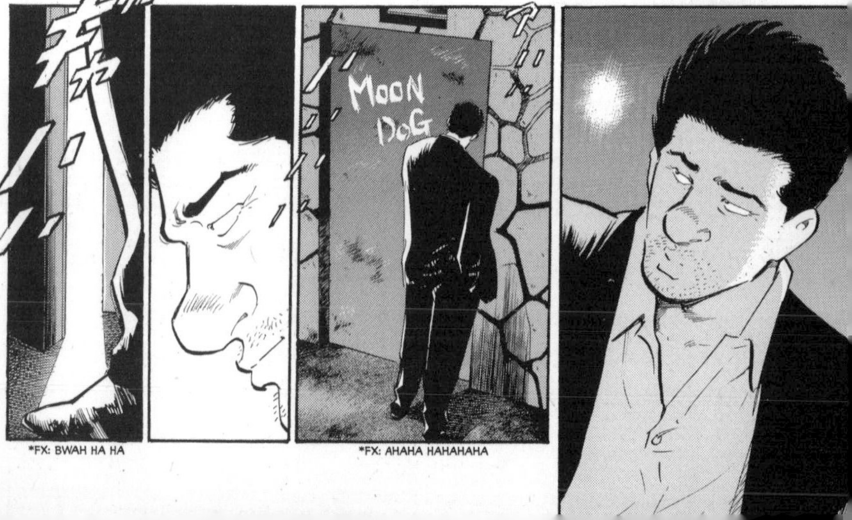
MOON DOG

*FX: AHAHA HAHAHAHA

*FX: BWAH HA HA

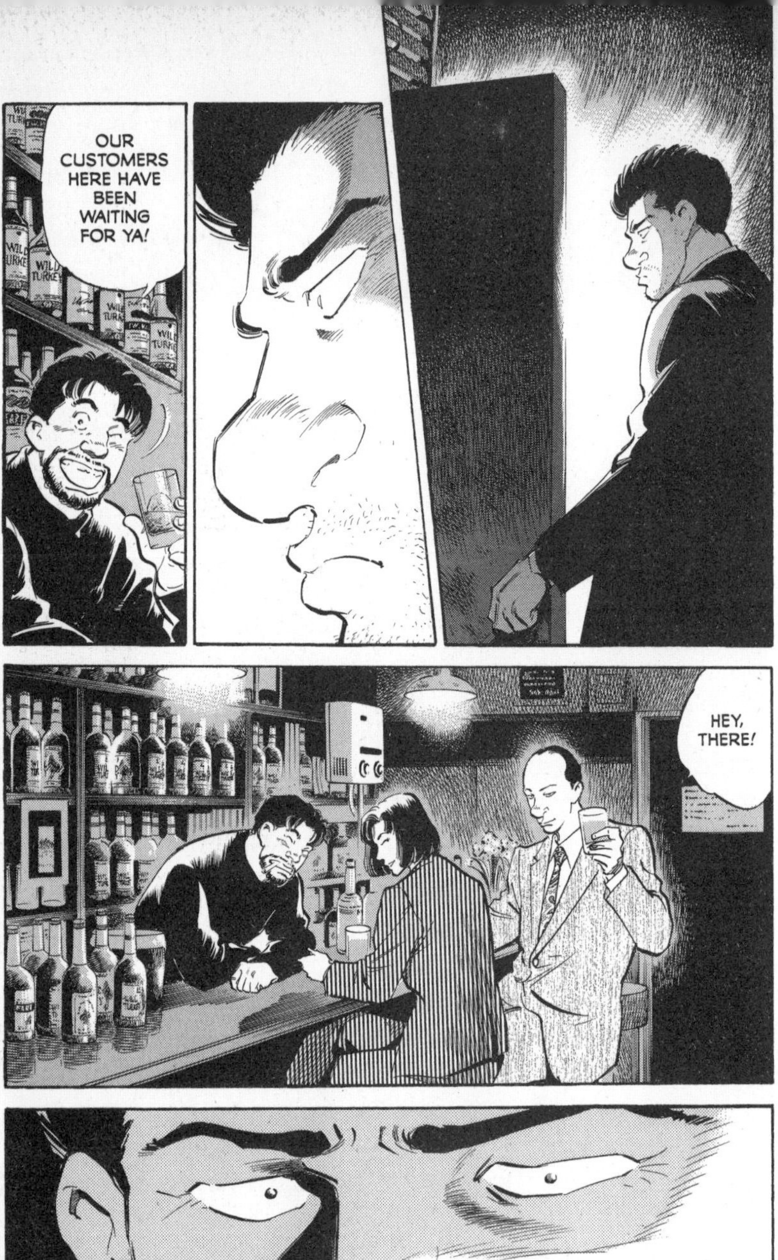
OUR CUSTOMERS HERE HAVE BEEN WAITING FOR YA!
HEY, THERE!

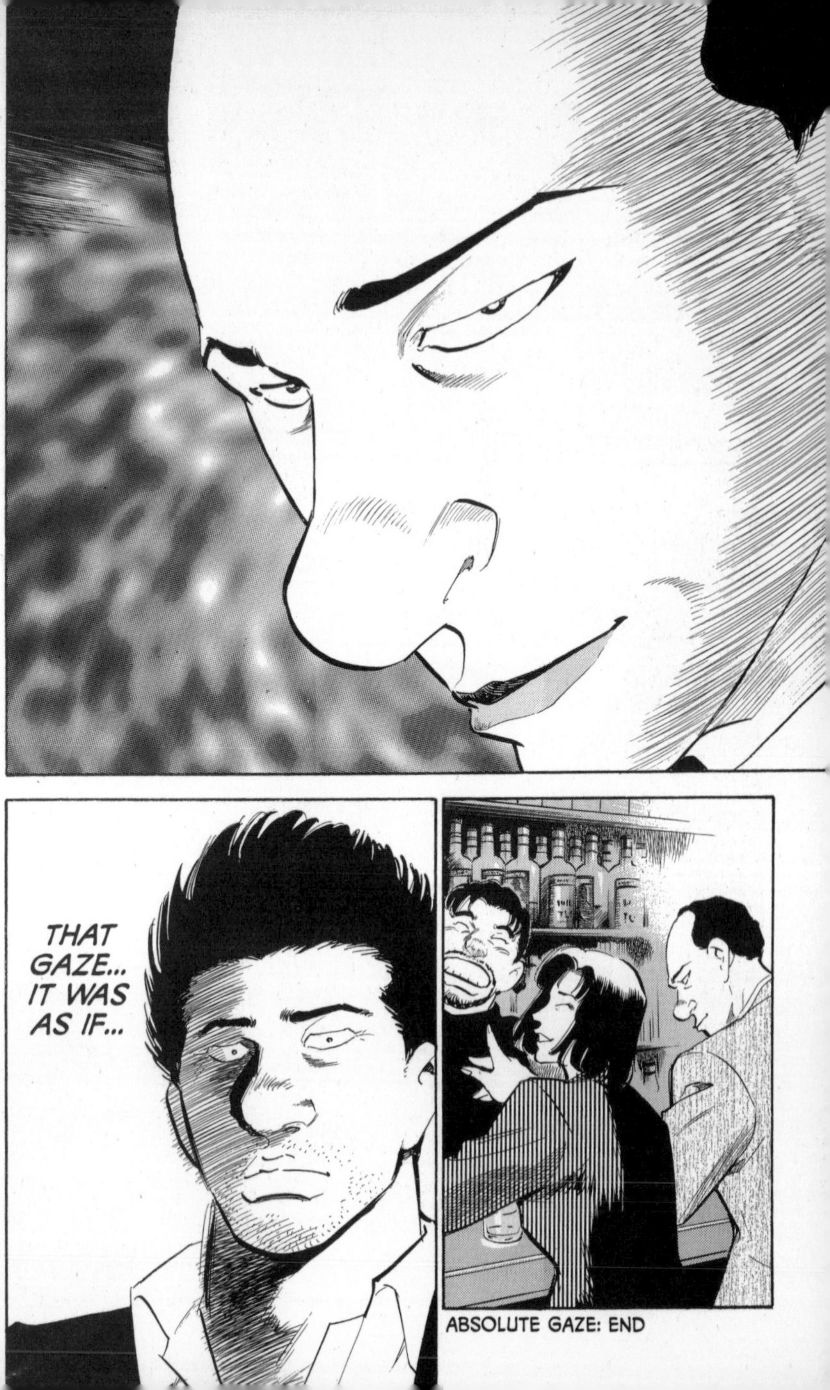
THAT GAZE... IT WAS AS IF...

ABSOLUTE GAZE: END

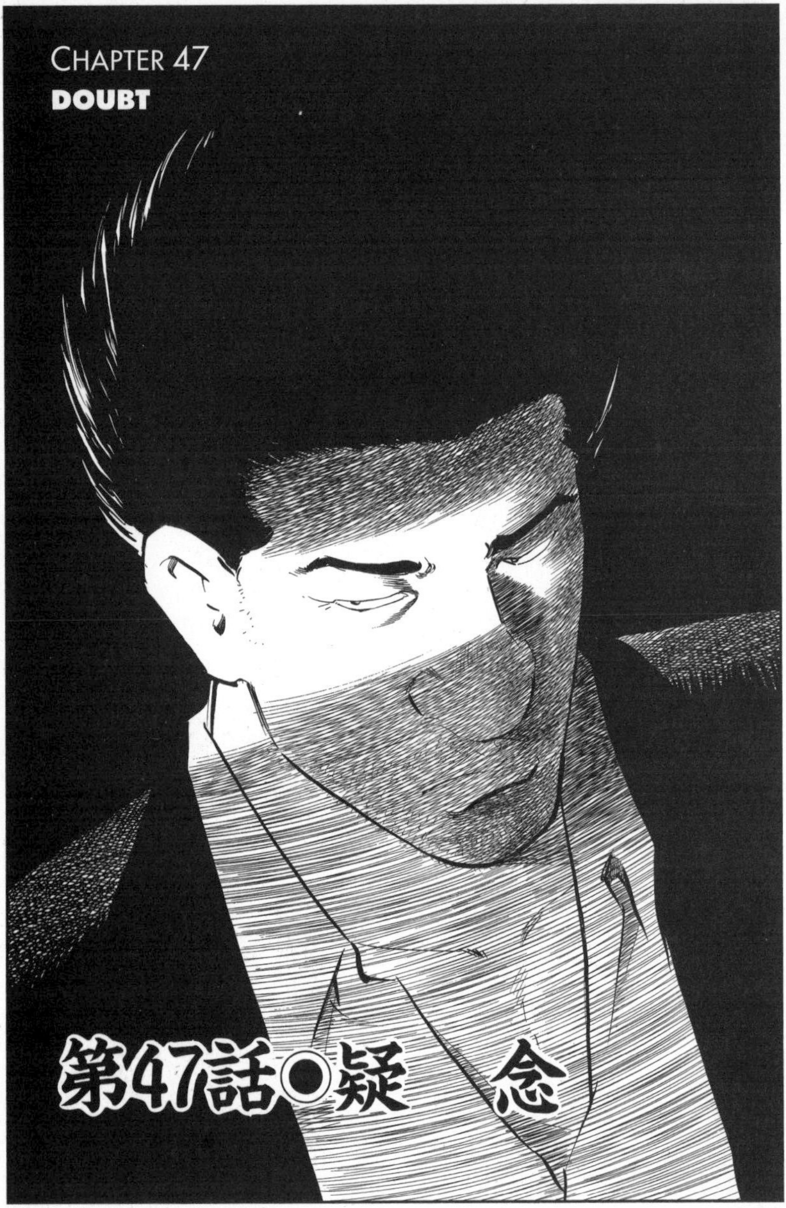
CHAPTER 47
DOUBT
第47話○疑　念

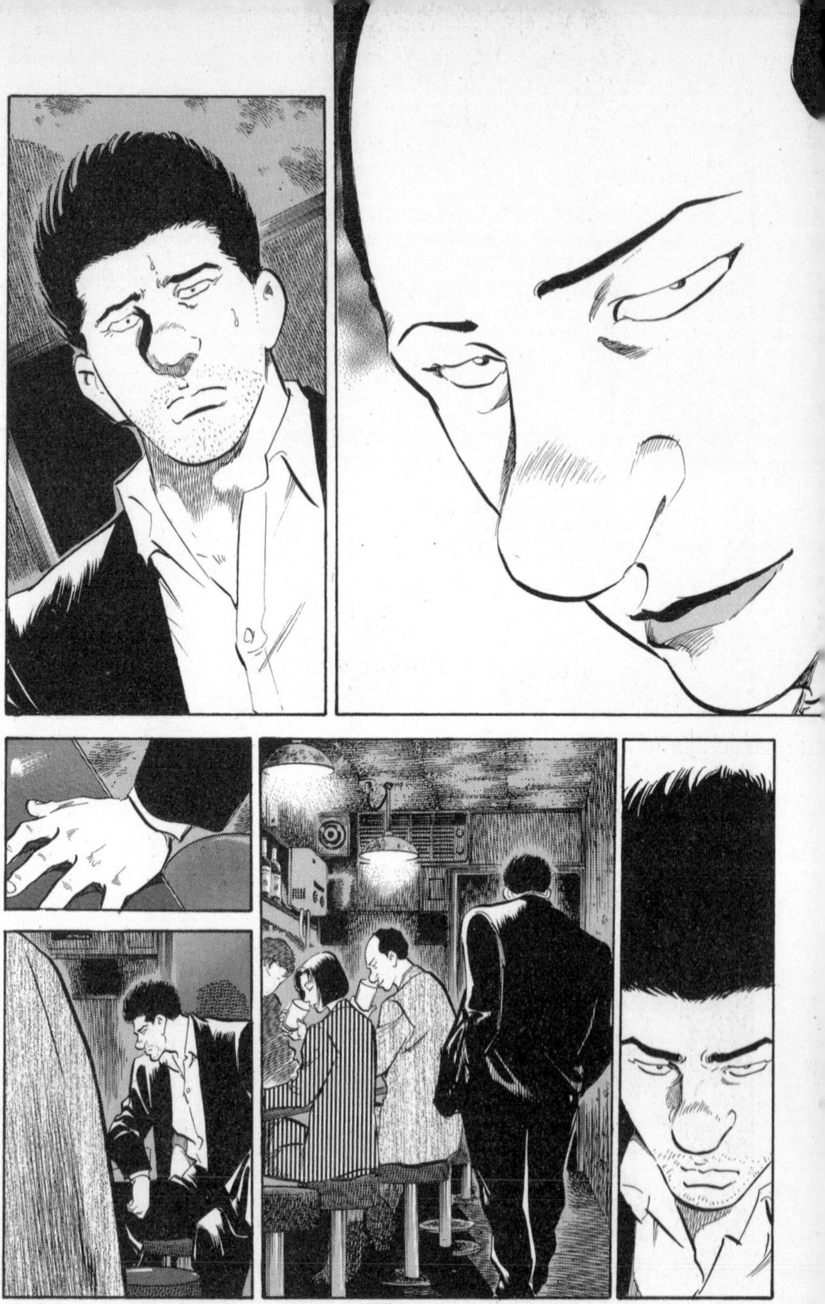

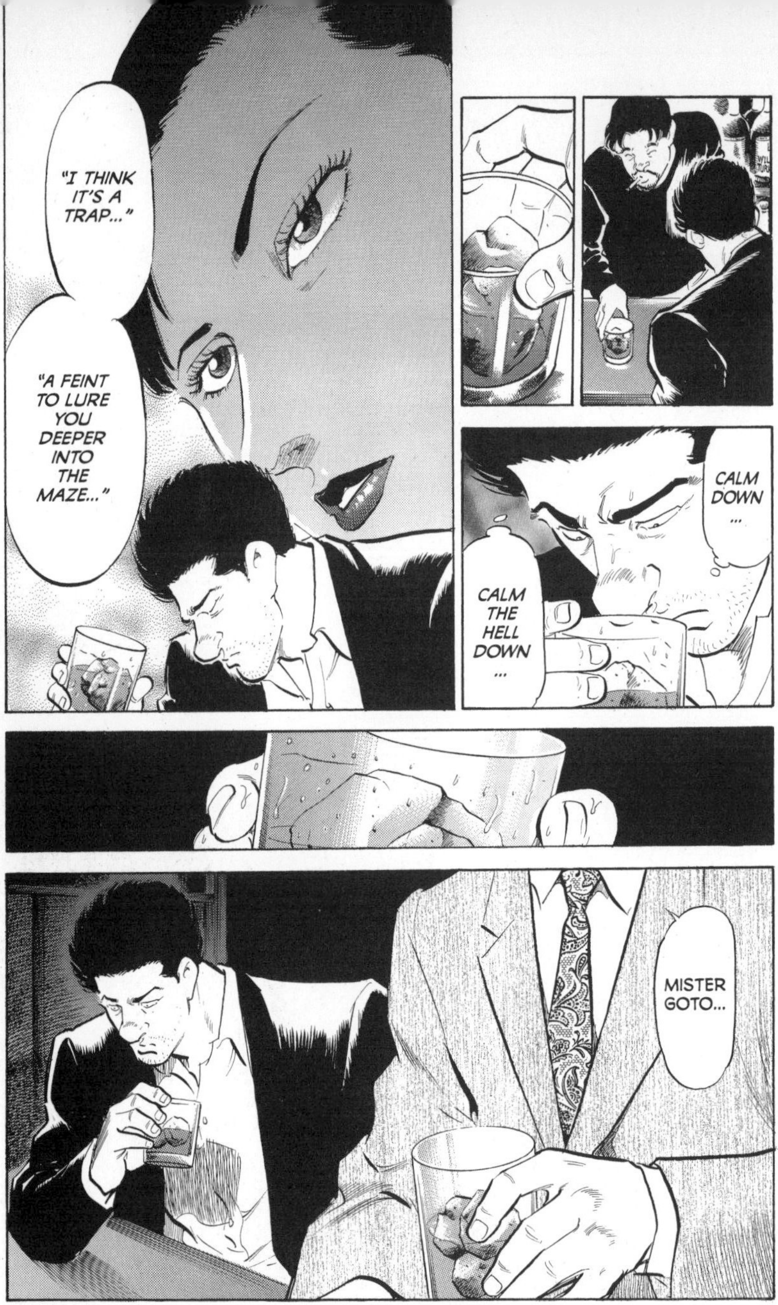
CALM DOWN ...
CALM THE HELL DOWN ...
"I THINK IT'S A TRAP..."
"A FEINT TO LURE YOU DEEPER INTO THE MAZE..."
MISTER GOTO...

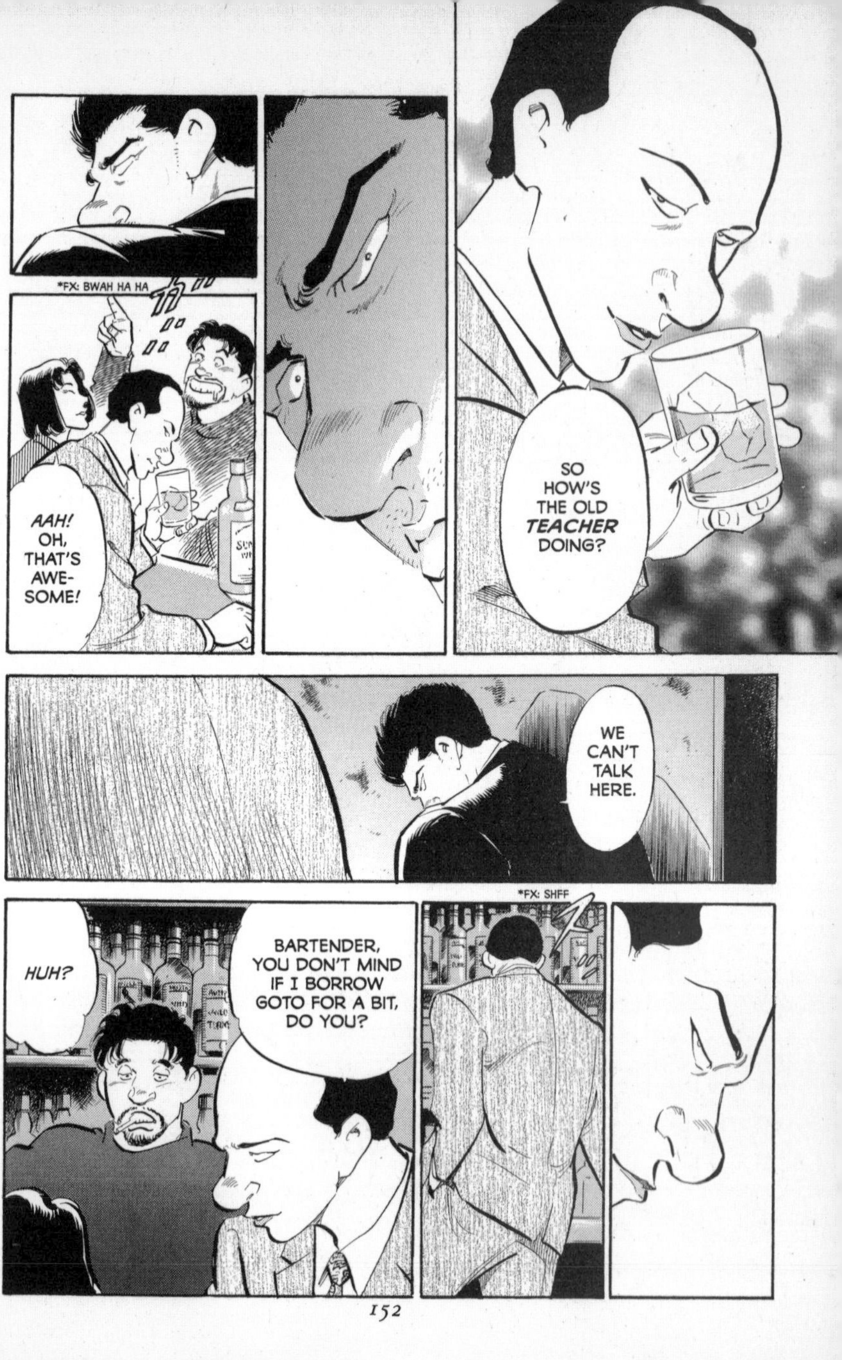
SO HOW'S THE OLD TEACHER DOING?
*FX: BWAH HA HA
AAH! OH, THAT'S AWESOME!
WE CAN'T TALK HERE.
*FX: SHFF
BARTENDER, YOU DON'T MIND IF I BORROW GOTO FOR A BIT, DO YOU?
HUH?

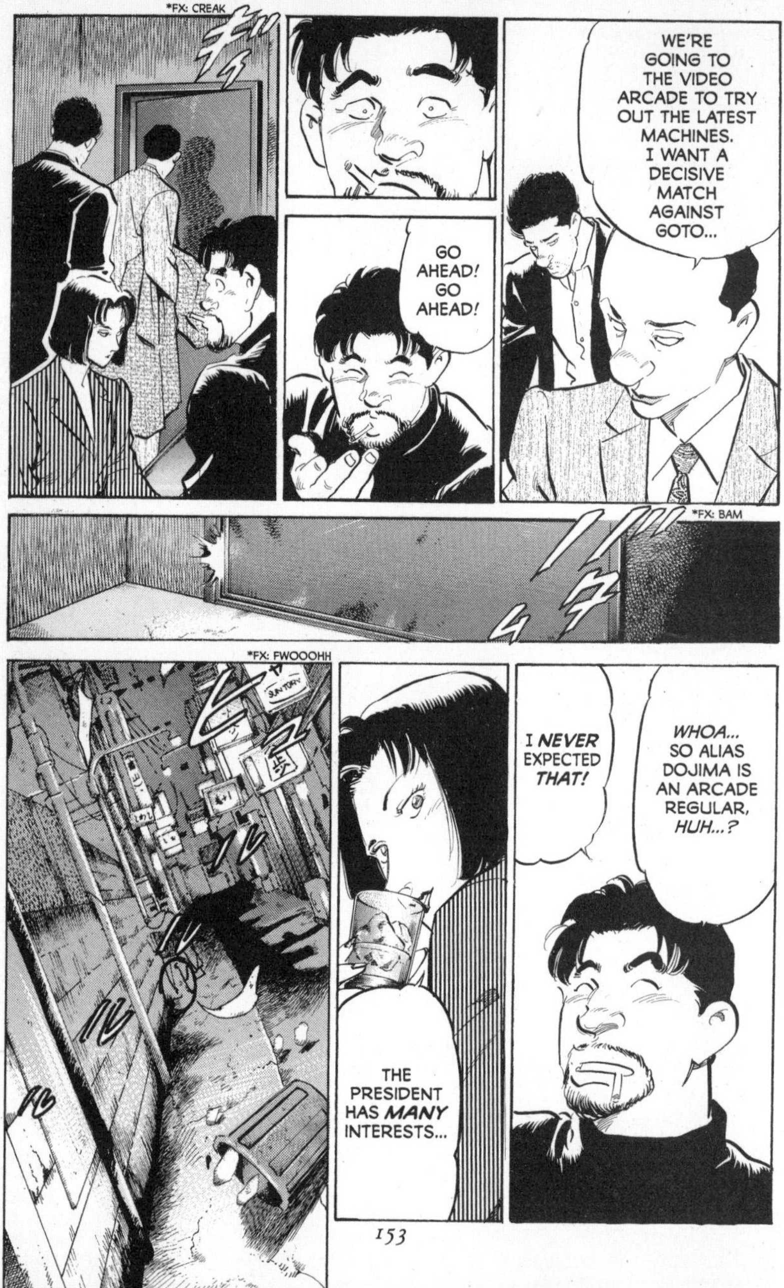
WE'RE GOING TO THE VIDEO ARCADE TO TRY OUT THE LATEST MACHINES. I WANT A DECISIVE MATCH AGAINST GOTO...
GO AHEAD! GO AHEAD!
*FX: CREAK
*FX: BAM
WHOA... SO ALIAS DOJIMA IS AN ARCADE REGULAR, HUH...?
I *NEVER* EXPECTED *THAT!*
THE PRESIDENT HAS *MANY* INTERESTS...
*FX: FWOOOHH

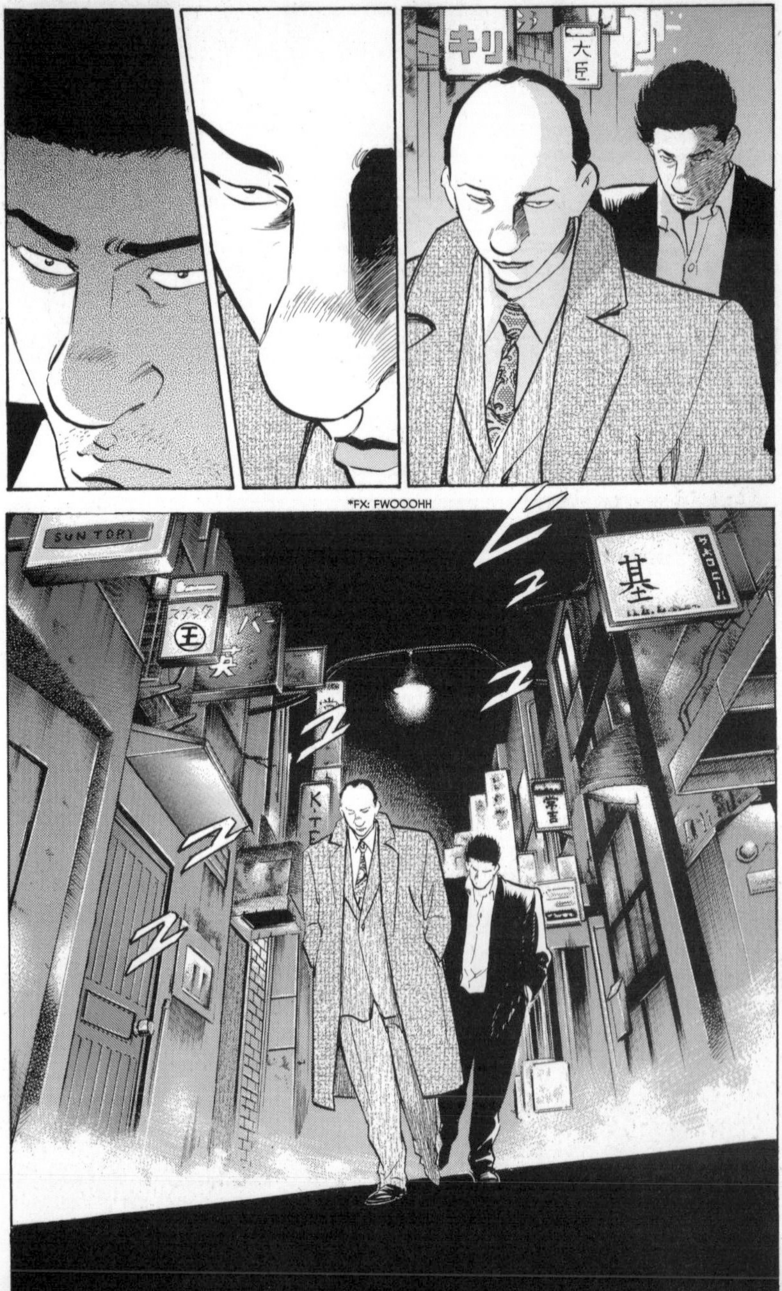
キリ
大臣
*FX: FWOOOHH
基
SUNTORY
バー
K-TE
常吉

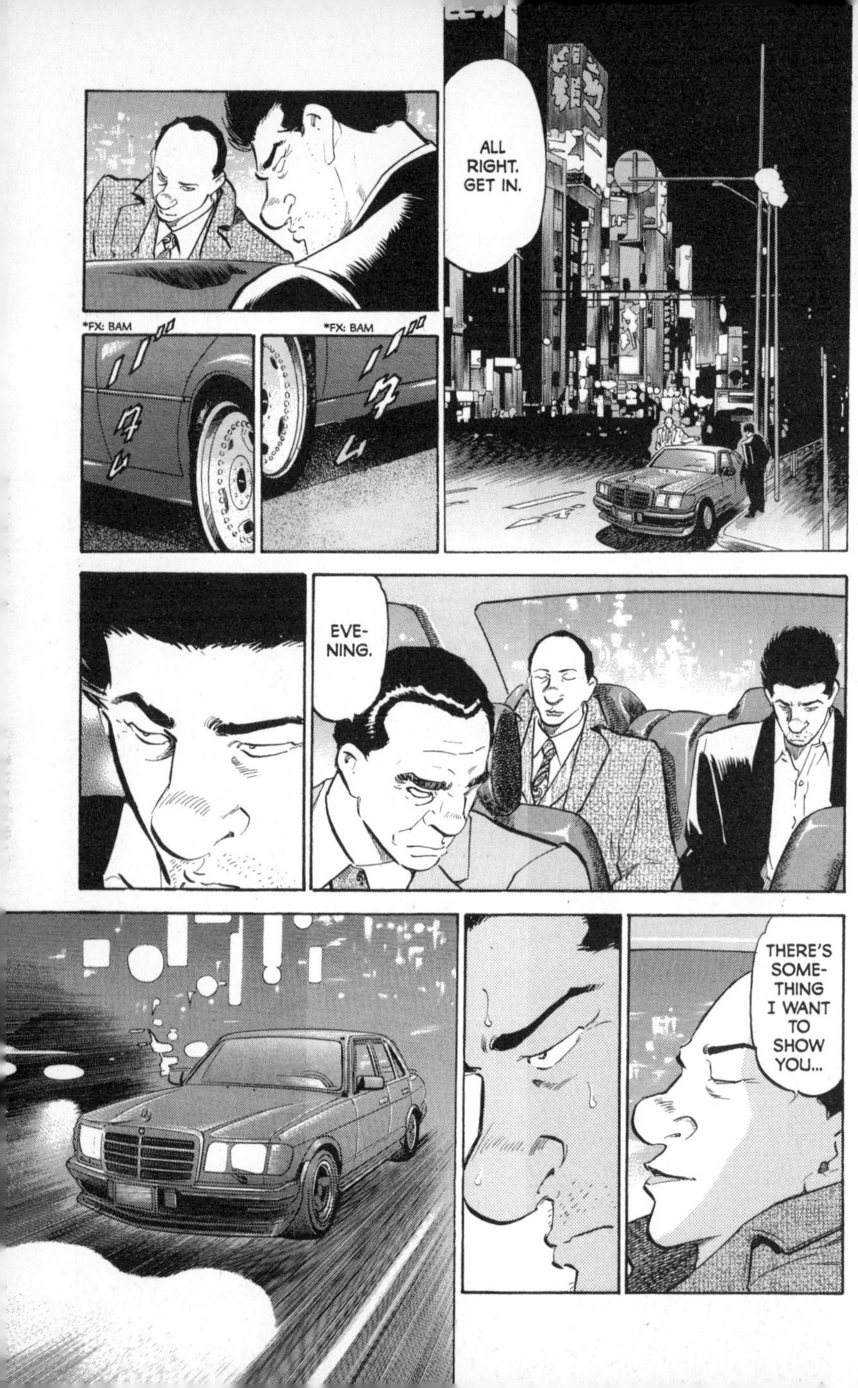
ALL RIGHT. GET IN.
*FX: BAM
*FX: BAM
EVE-NING.
THERE'S SOME-THING I WANT TO SHOW YOU...

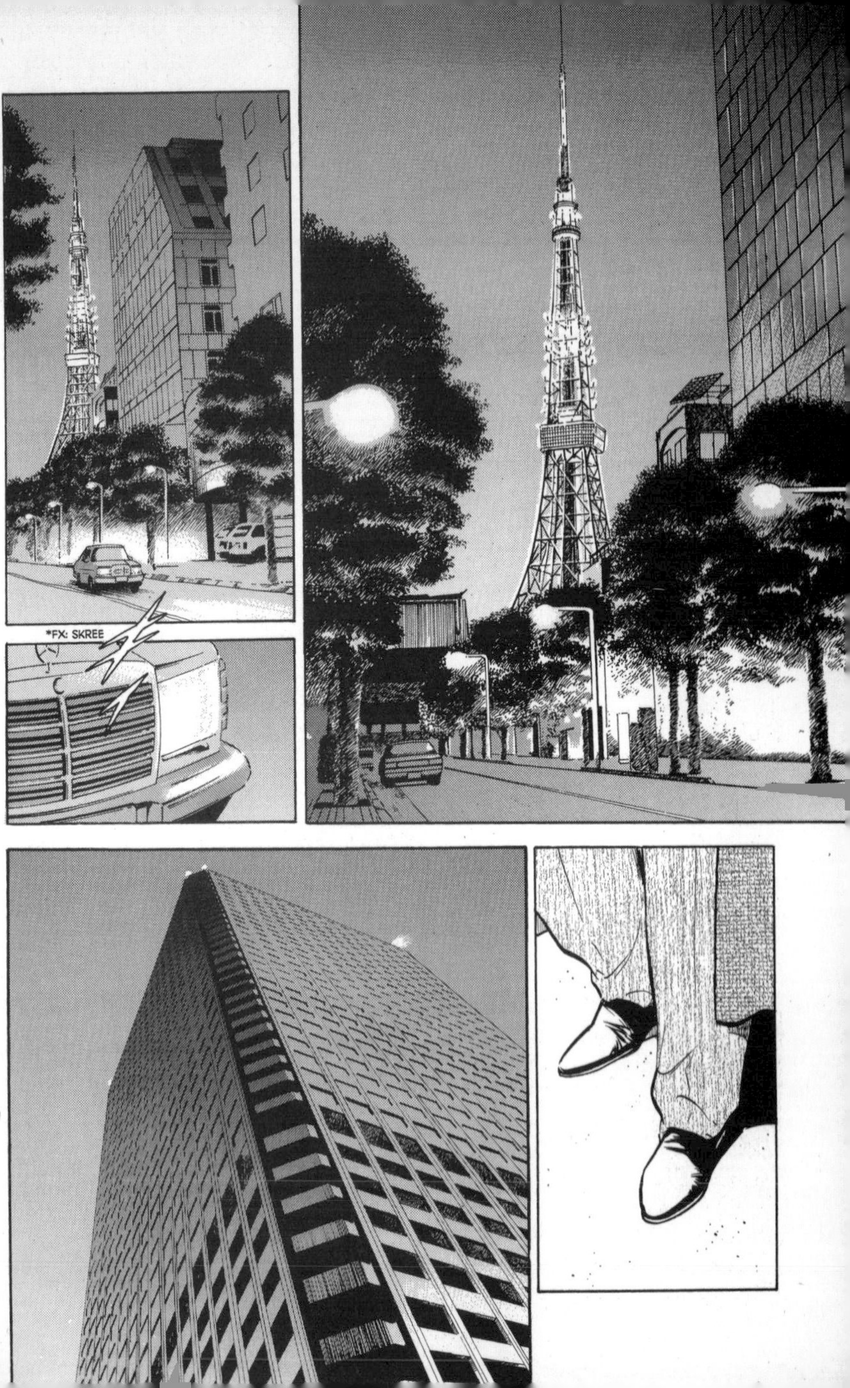
*FX: SKREE

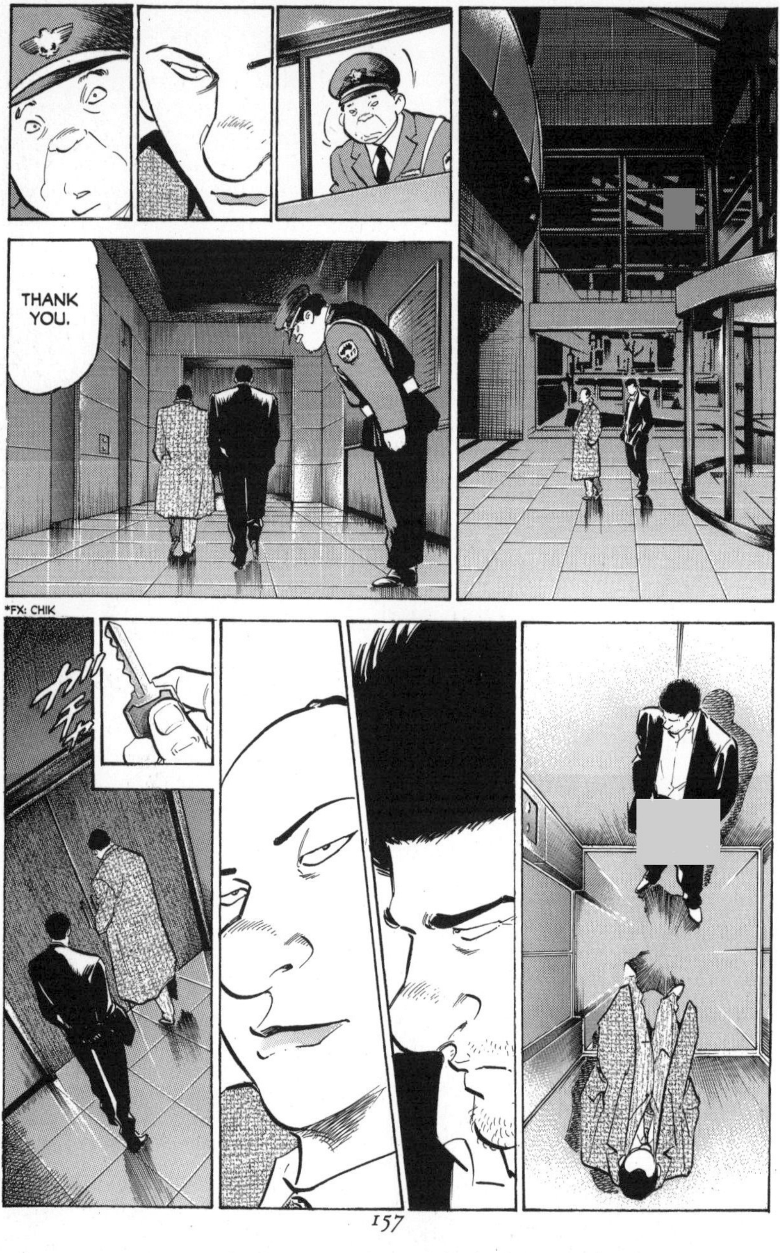
THANK YOU.
*FX: CHIK

THIS BUILDING BELONGS TO A CERTAIN CORPORATION I HAVE SOME CONNECTIONS WITH.

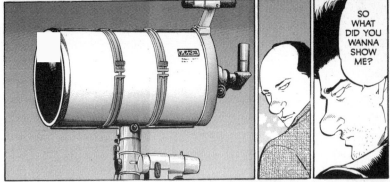

SO WHAT DID YOU WANNA SHOW ME?

GO AHEAD.

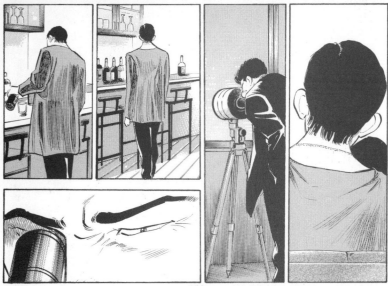

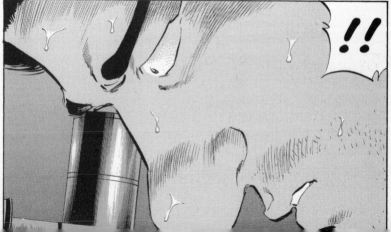

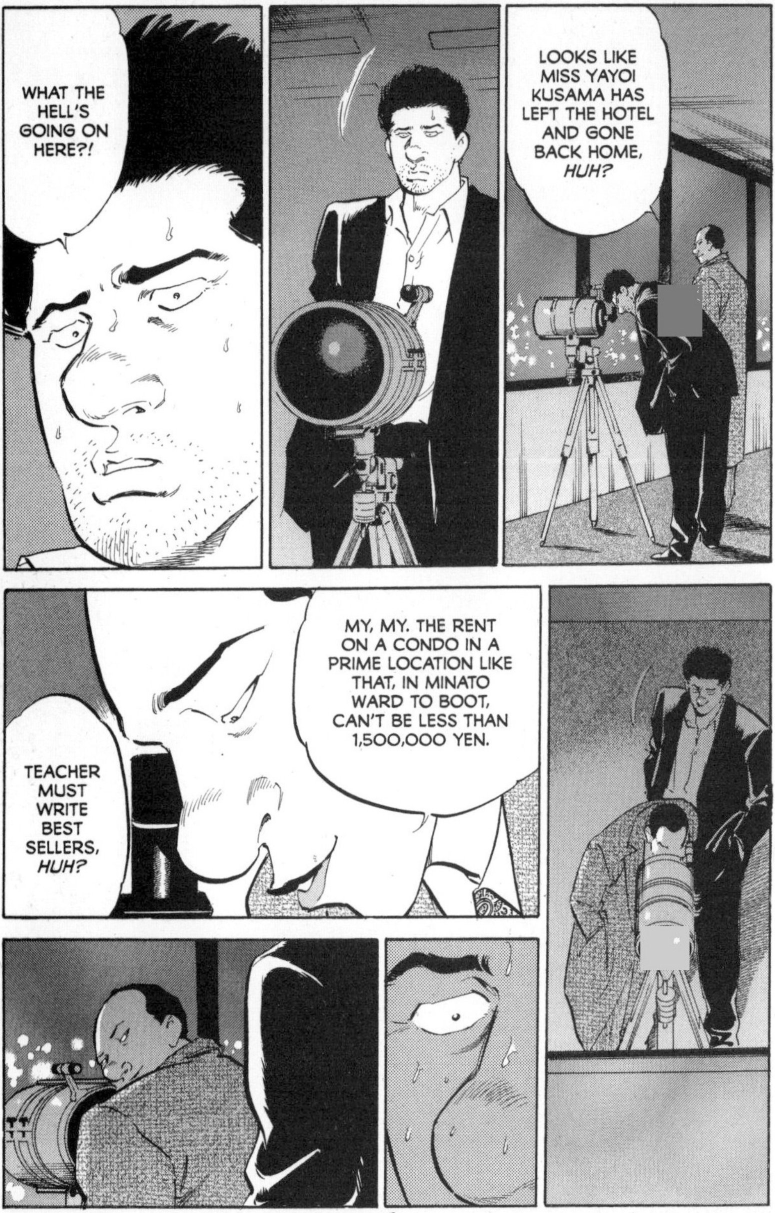
LOOKS LIKE MISS YAYOI KUSAMA HAS LEFT THE HOTEL AND GONE BACK HOME, *HUH?*
WHAT THE HELL'S GOING ON HERE?!
MY, MY. THE RENT ON A CONDO IN A PRIME LOCATION LIKE THAT, IN MINATO WARD TO BOOT, CAN'T BE LESS THAN 1,500,000 YEN.
TEACHER MUST WRITE BEST SELLERS, *HUH?*

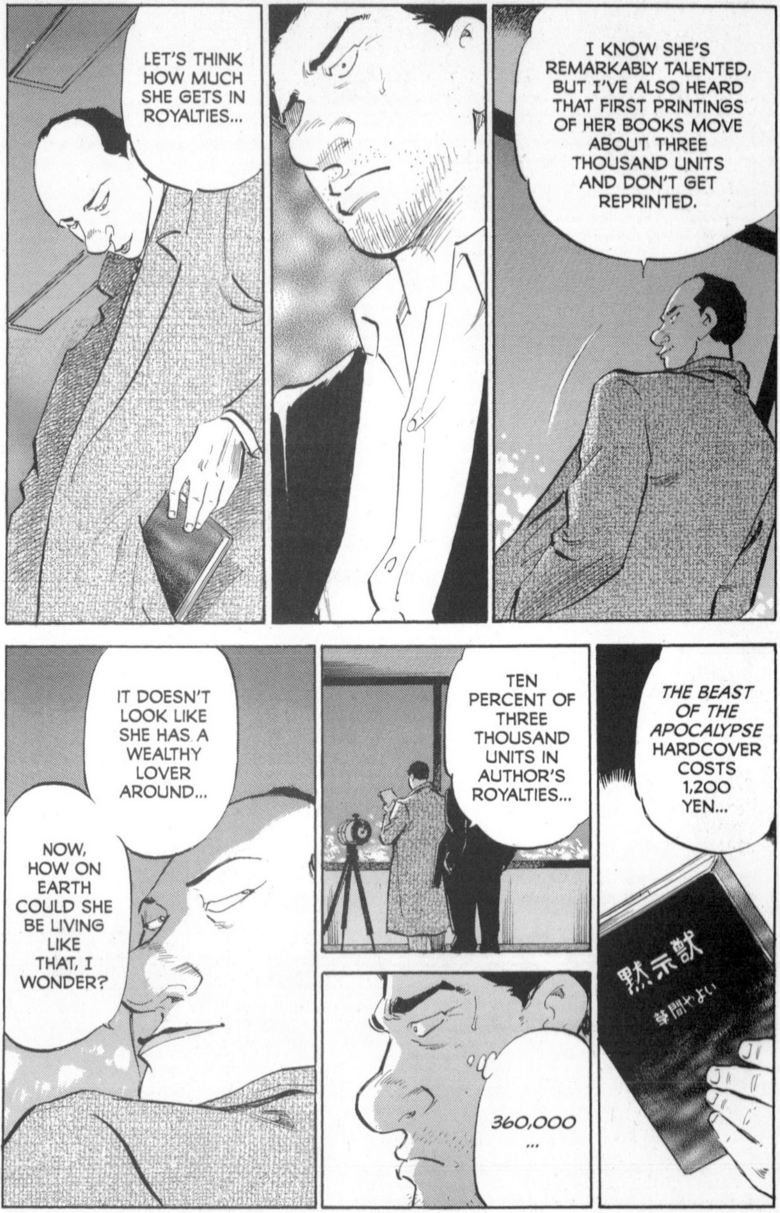
I KNOW SHE'S REMARKABLY TALENTED, BUT I'VE ALSO HEARD THAT FIRST PRINTINGS OF HER BOOKS MOVE ABOUT THREE THOUSAND UNITS AND DON'T GET REPRINTED.
LET'S THINK HOW MUCH SHE GETS IN ROYALTIES...
THE BEAST OF THE APOCALYPSE HARDCOVER COSTS 1,200 YEN...
黙示獣
草間やよい
TEN PERCENT OF THREE THOUSAND UNITS IN AUTHOR'S ROYALTIES...
360,000 ...
IT DOESN'T LOOK LIKE SHE HAS A WEALTHY LOVER AROUND...
NOW, HOW ON EARTH COULD SHE BE LIVING LIKE THAT, I WONDER?

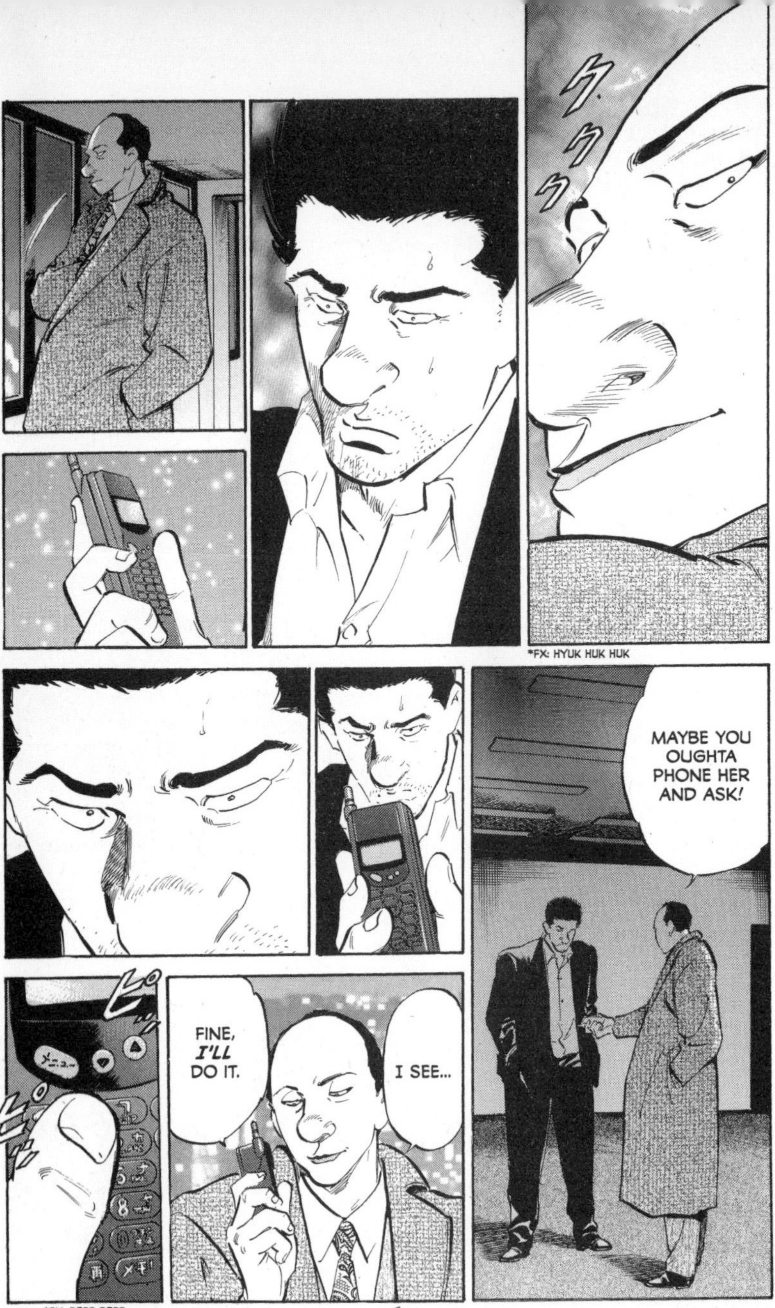
*FX: HYUK HUK HUK
MAYBE YOU OUGHTA PHONE HER AND ASK!
I SEE...
FINE, ***I'LL*** DO IT.
*FX: BEEP BEEP

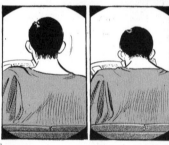

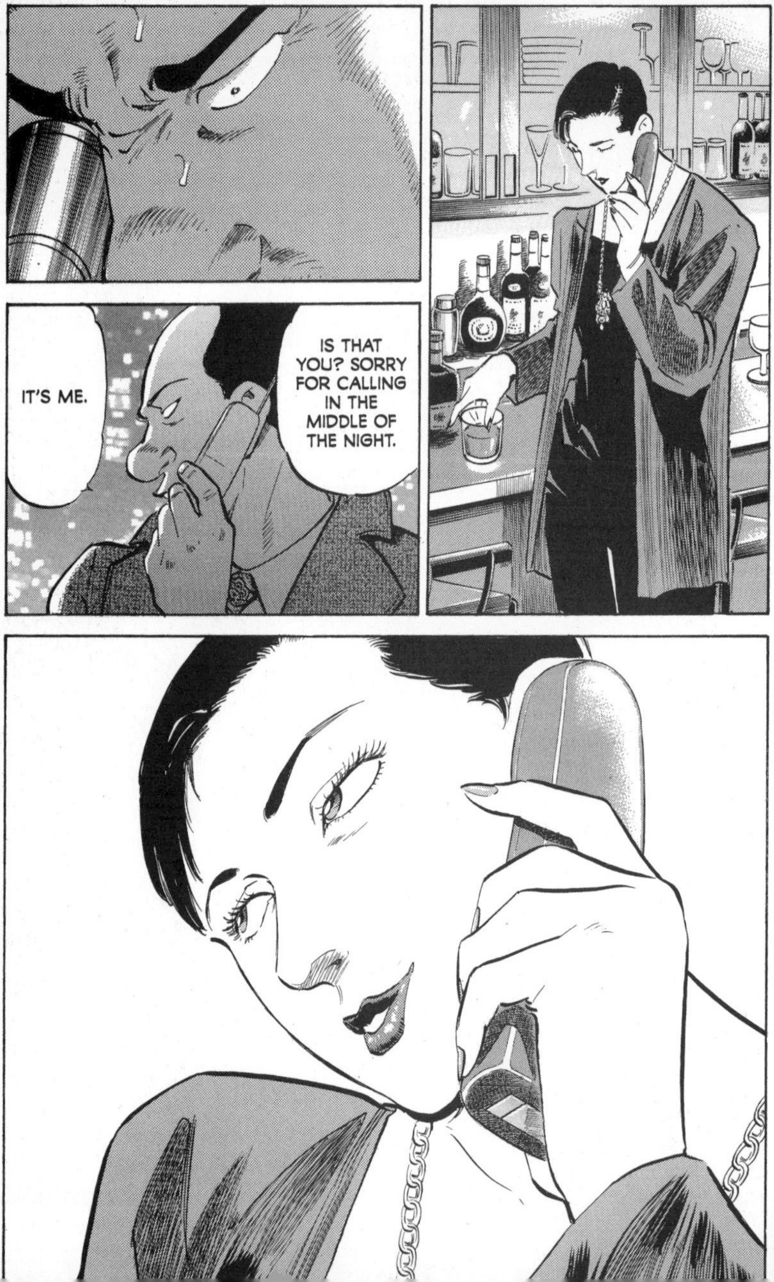
IS THAT YOU? SORRY FOR CALLING IN THE MIDDLE OF THE NIGHT.
IT'S ME.

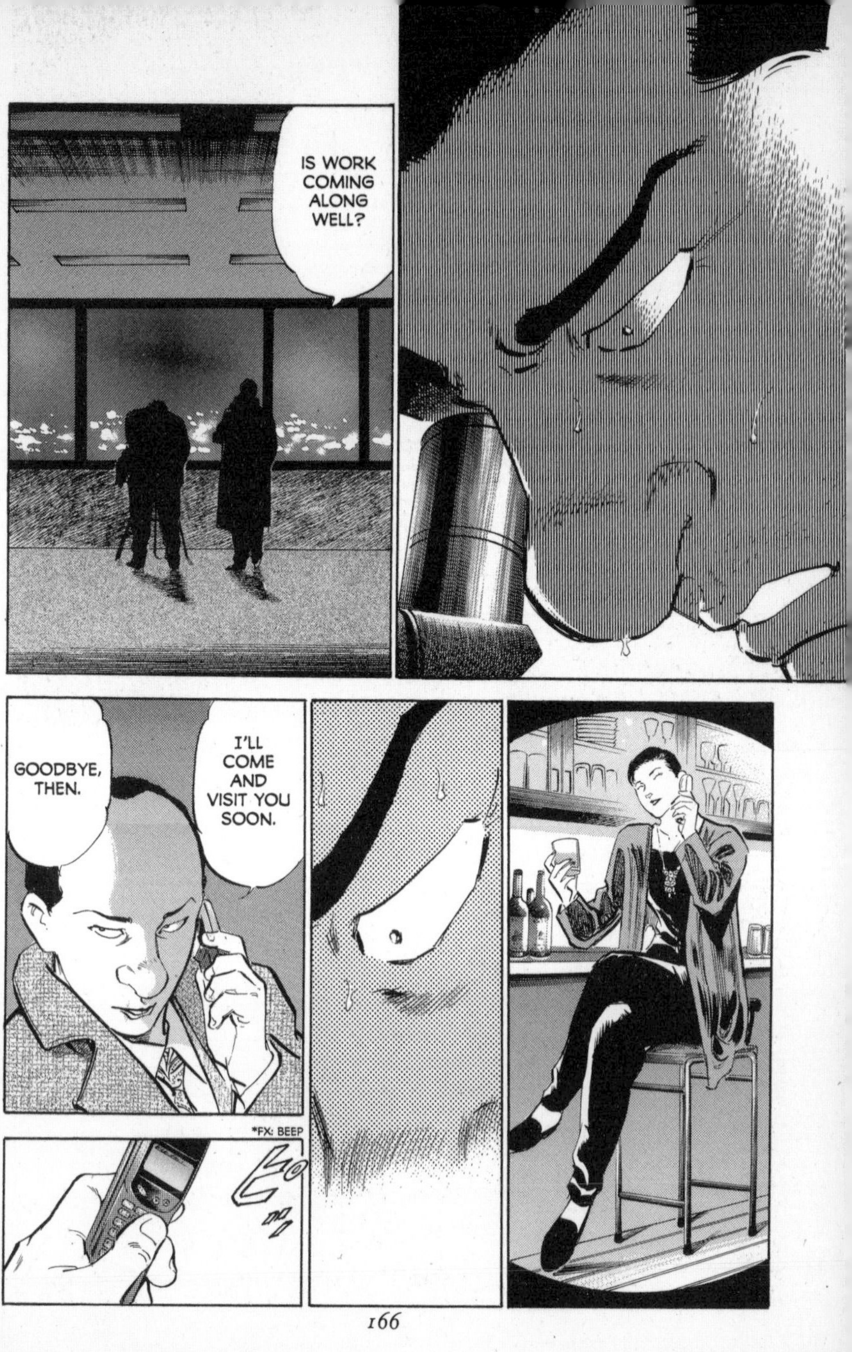
IS WORK COMING ALONG WELL?
I'LL COME AND VISIT YOU SOON.
GOODBYE, THEN.
*FX: BEEP

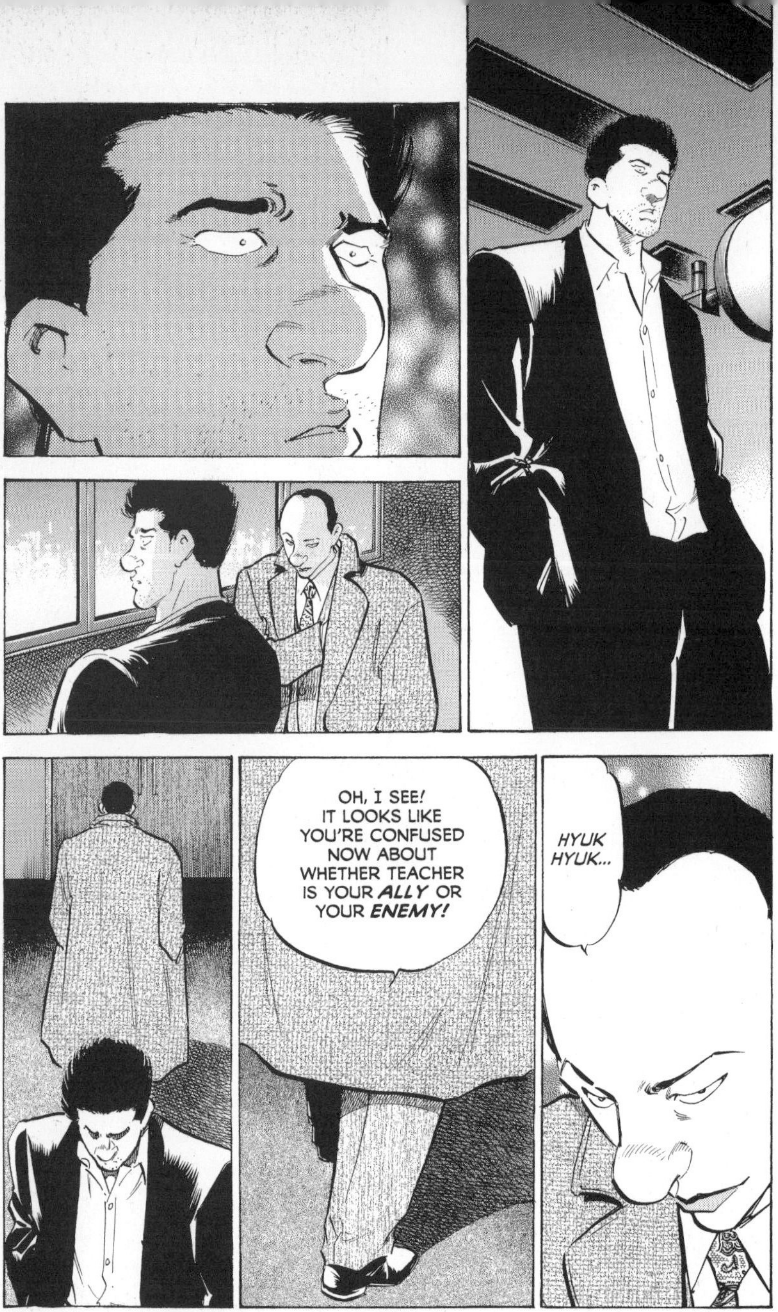
HYUK HYUK...
OH, I SEE! IT LOOKS LIKE YOU'RE CONFUSED NOW ABOUT WHETHER TEACHER IS YOUR ALLY OR YOUR ENEMY!

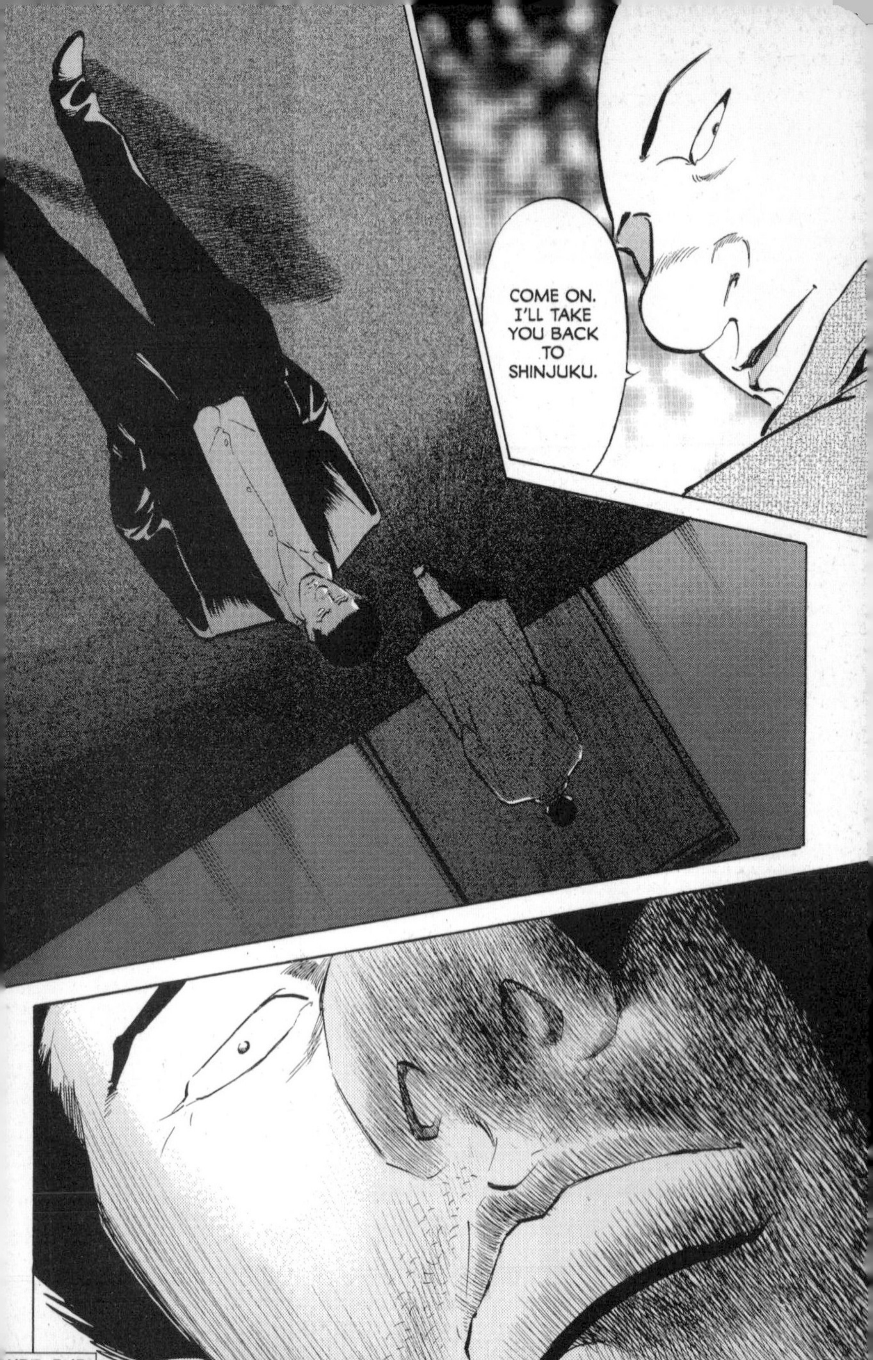
COME ON. I'LL TAKE YOU BACK TO SHINJUKU.

UBT: END

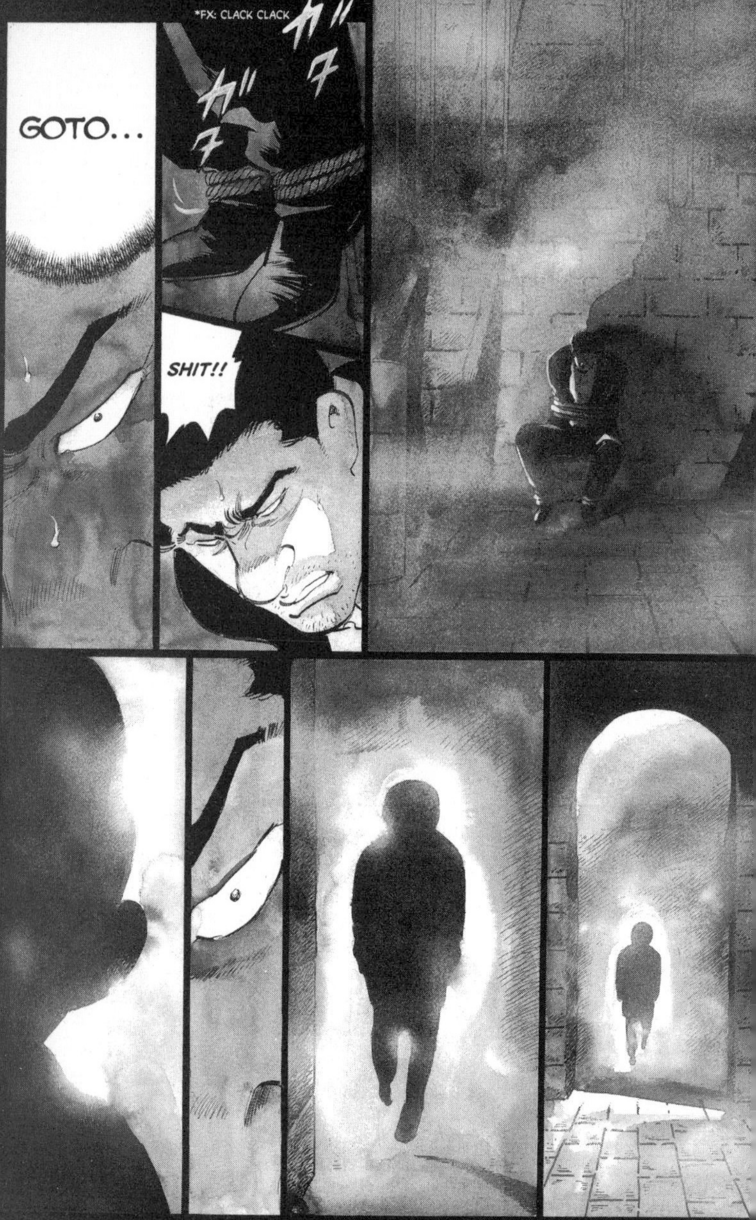
*FX: CLACK CLACK
SHIT!!
GOTO...

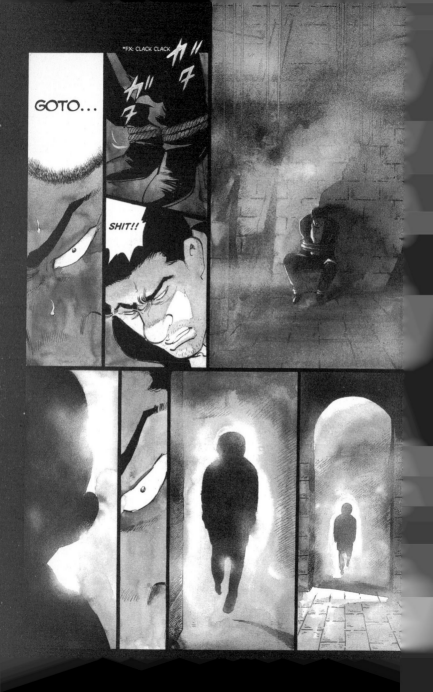

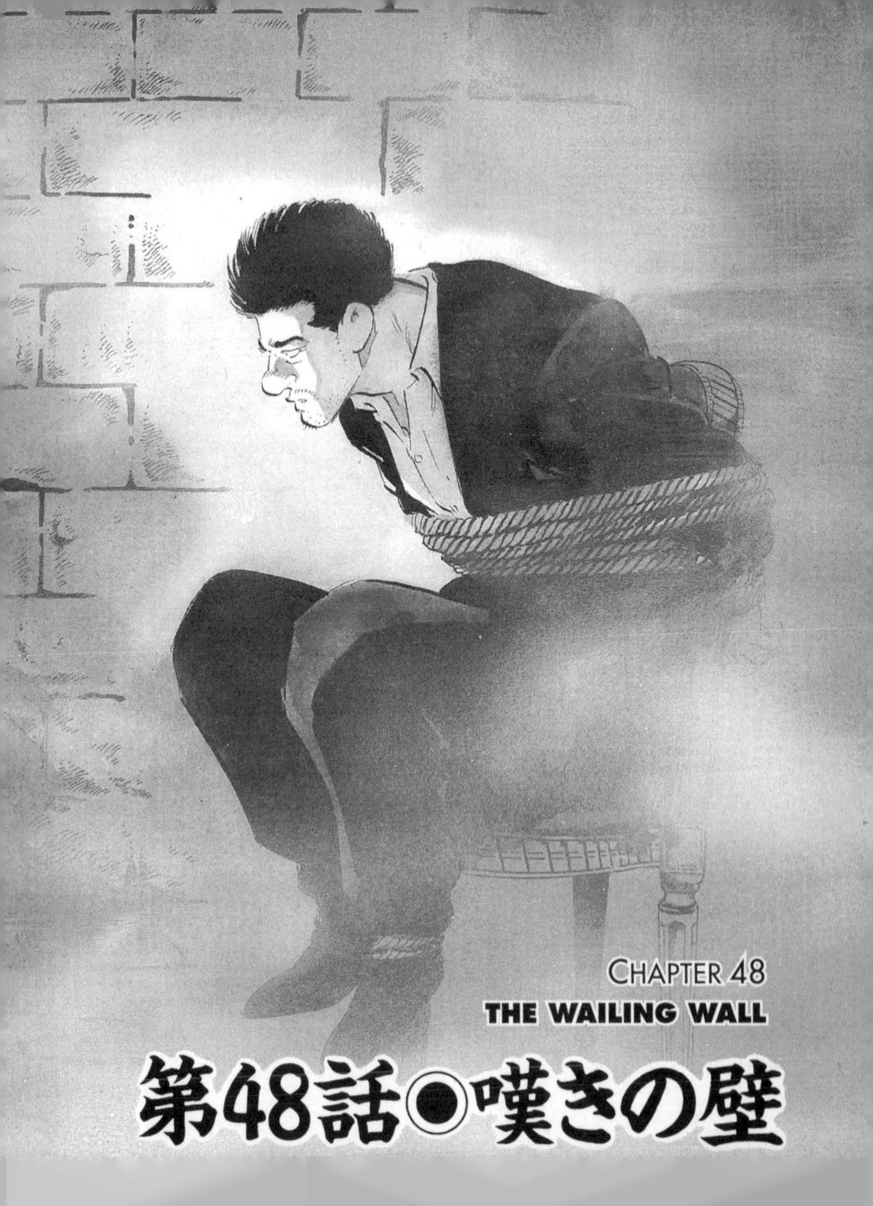
CHAPTER 48
THE WAILING WALL
第48話◎嘆きの壁

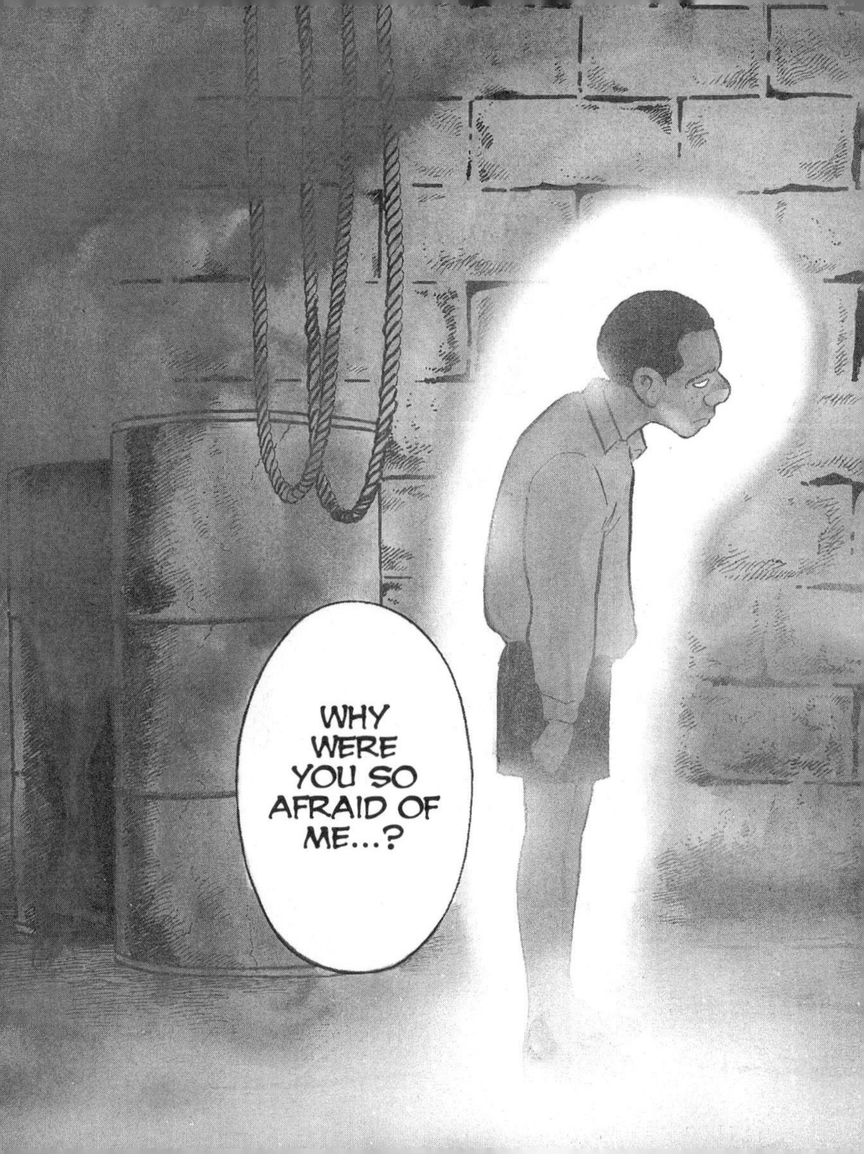
WHY WERE YOU SO AFRAID OF ME...?

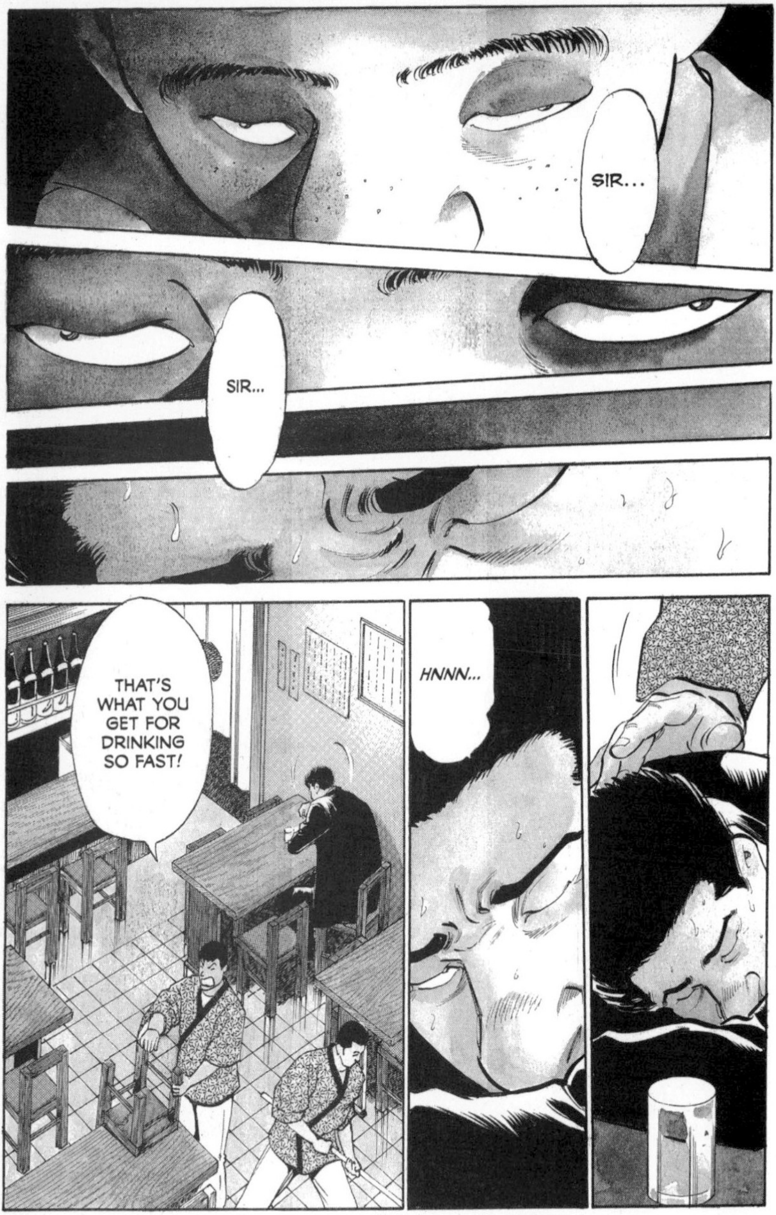
SIR...
SIR...
HNNN...
THAT'S WHAT YOU GET FOR DRINKING SO FAST!

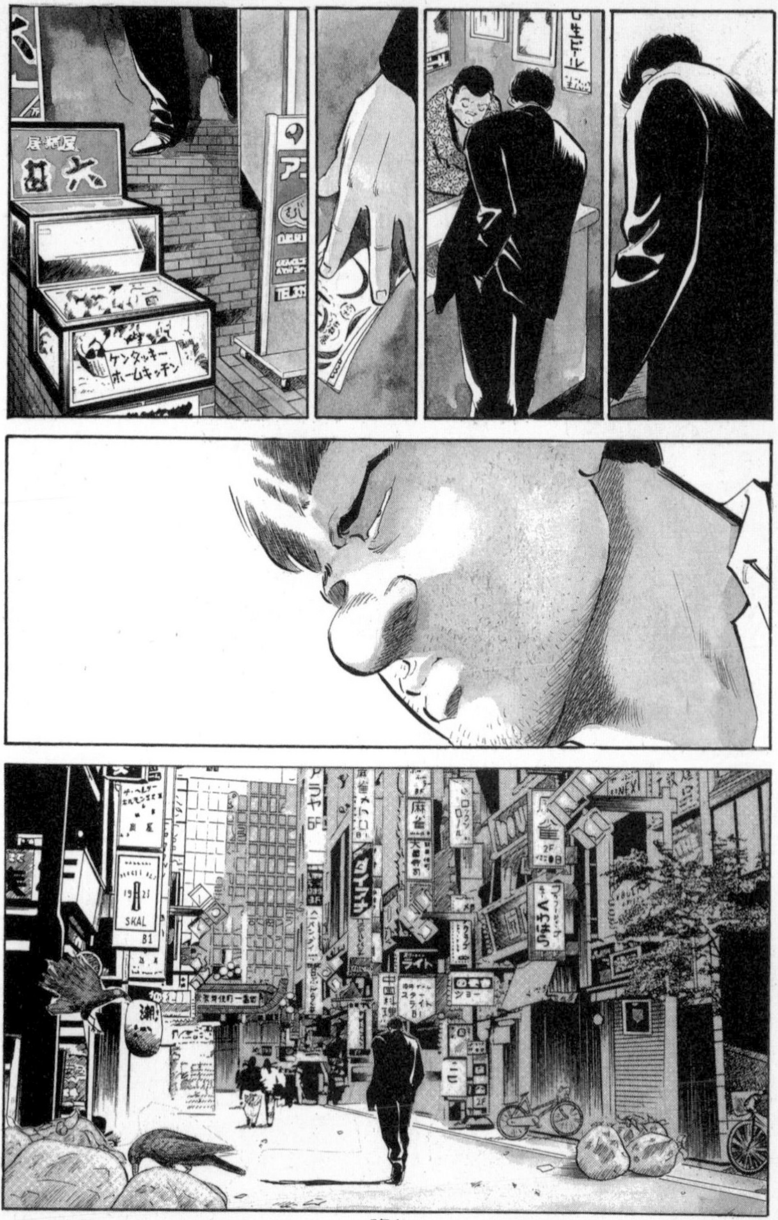
生ビール
ケンタッキー
ホームキッチン
麻雀
ショー
ライト
麻雀
SKAL
B1

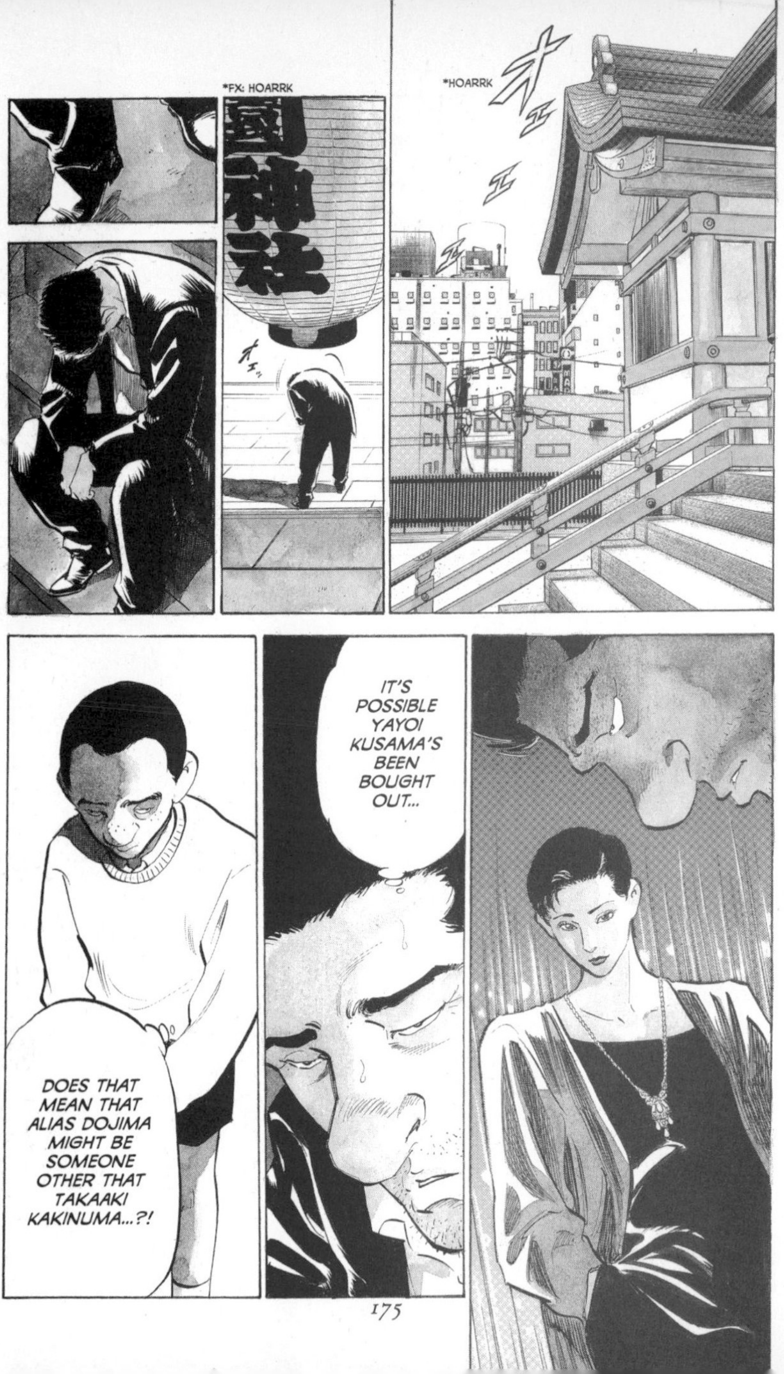
*HOARRK
*FX: HOARRK
國神社
IT'S POSSIBLE YAYOI KUSAMA'S BEEN BOUGHT OUT...
DOES THAT MEAN THAT ALIAS DOJIMA MIGHT BE SOMEONE OTHER THAT TAKAAKI KAKINUMA...?!

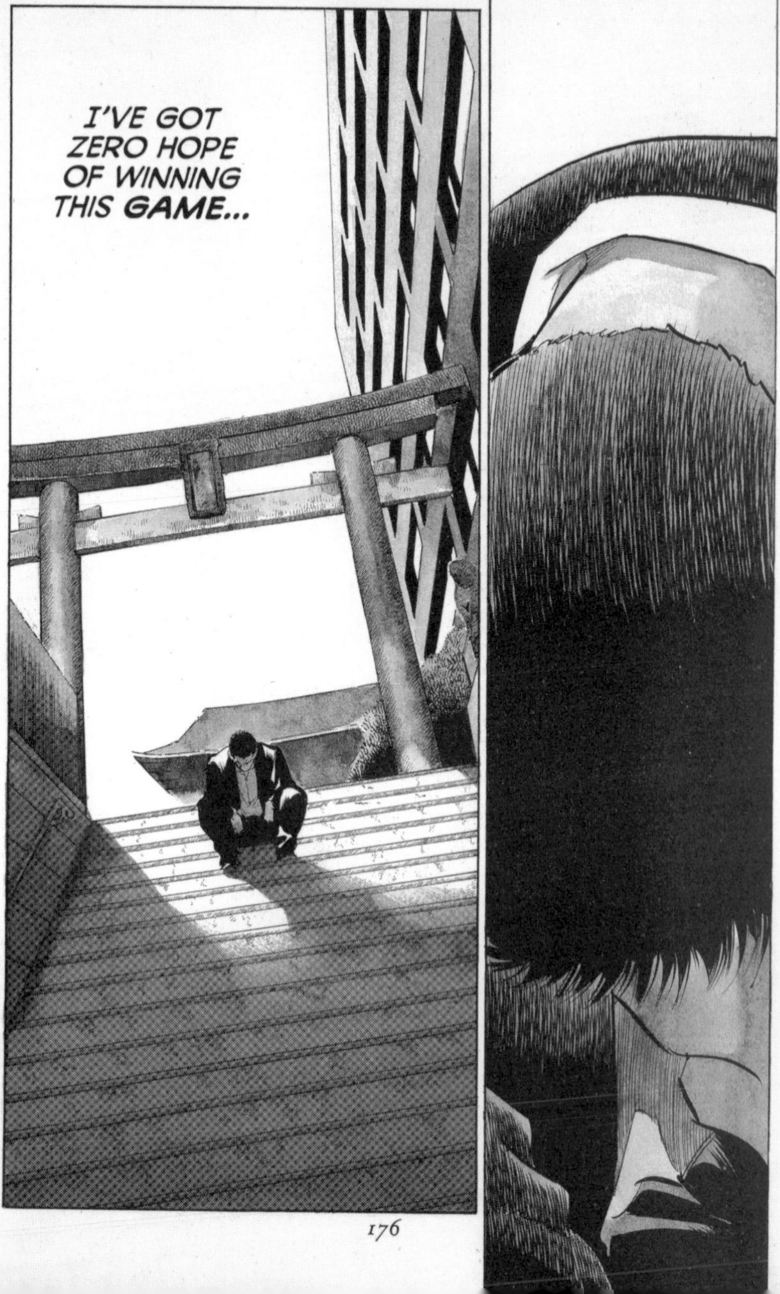
I'VE GOT ZERO HOPE OF WINNING THIS **GAME**...

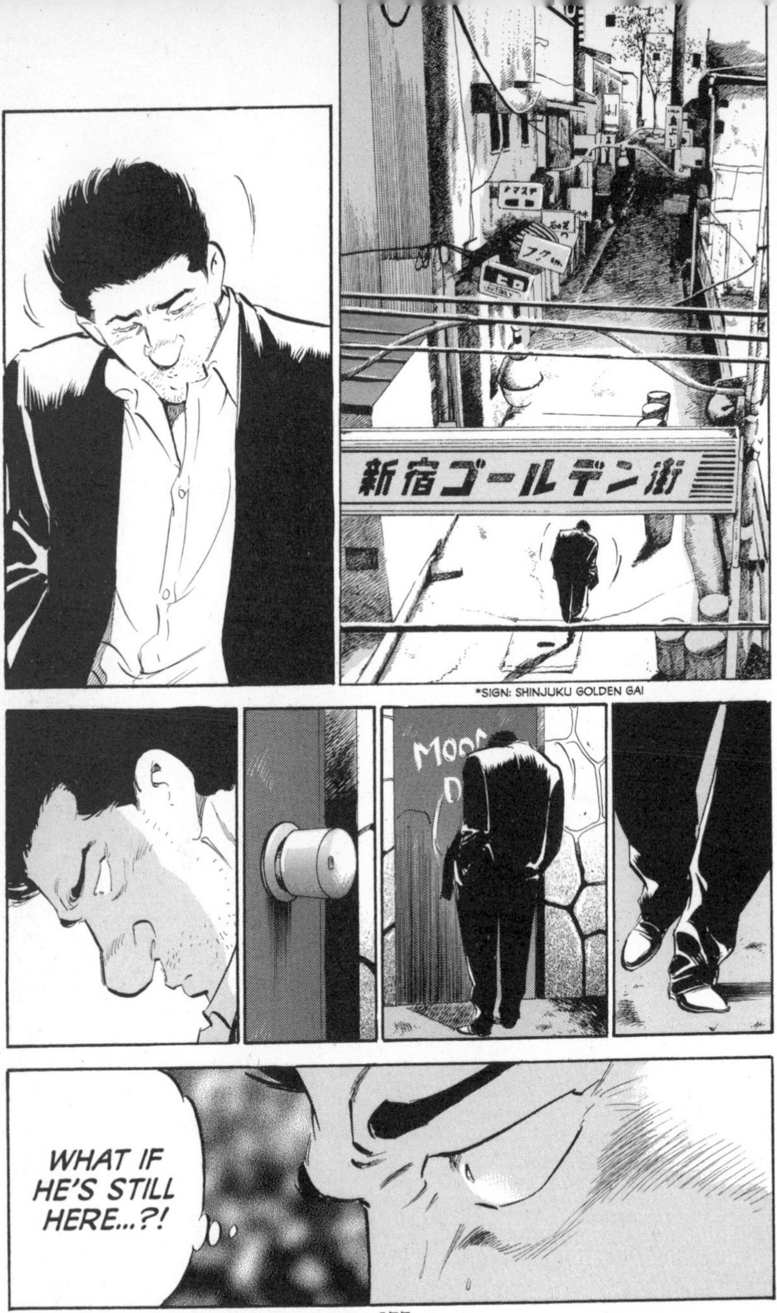
新宿ゴールデン街
*SIGN: SHINJUKU GOLDEN GAI
WHAT IF HE'S STILL HERE...?!

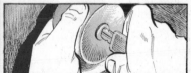

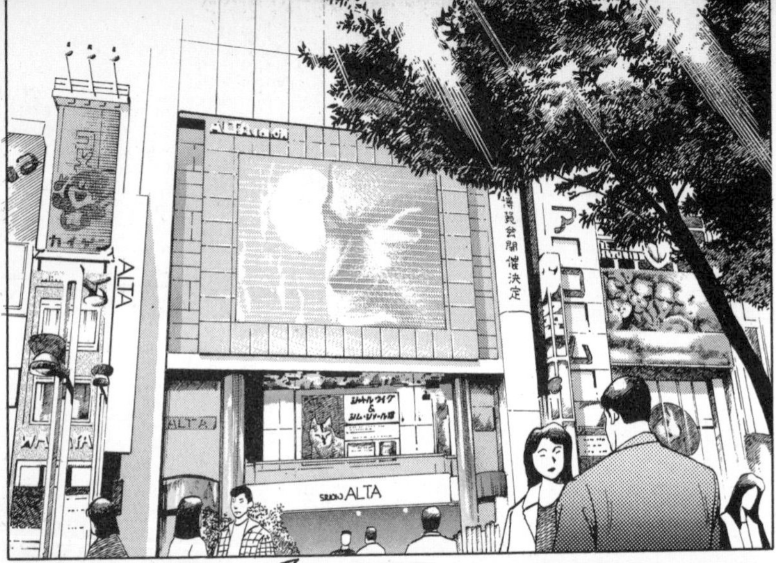
ALTA
カイゲン
ALTA

*FX: NZZZ NZZZ

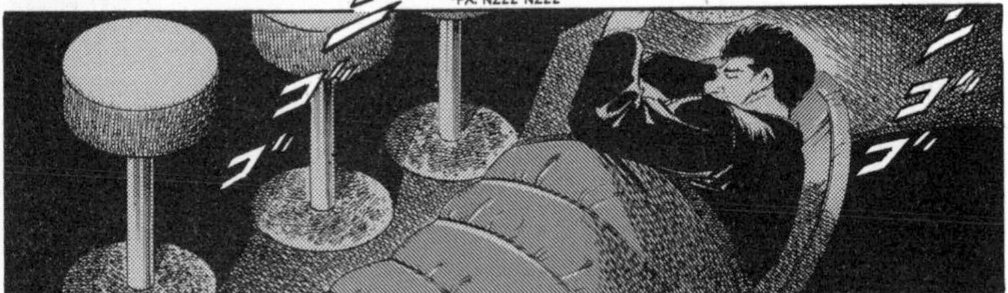

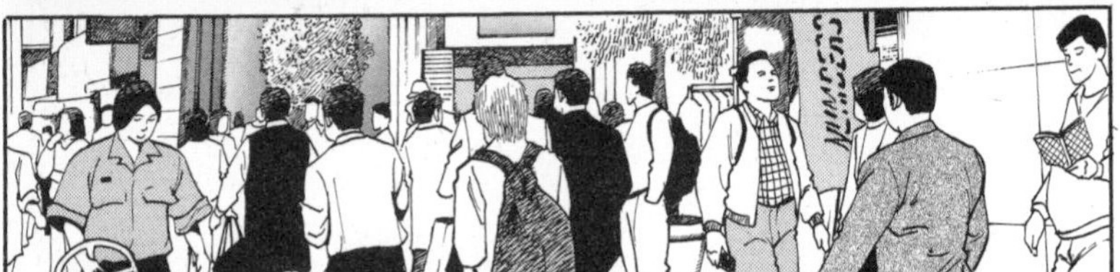

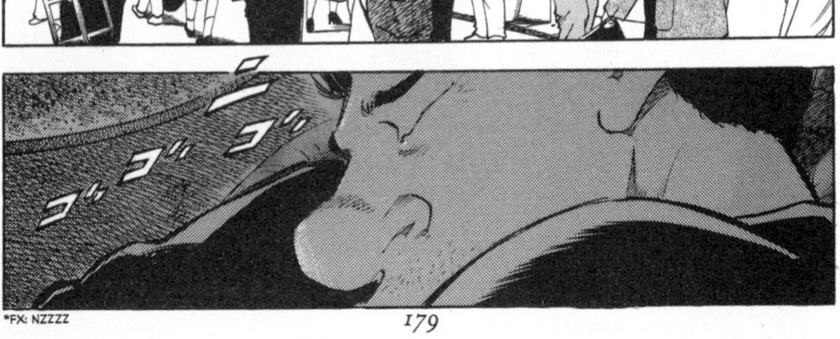

*FX: NZZZZ

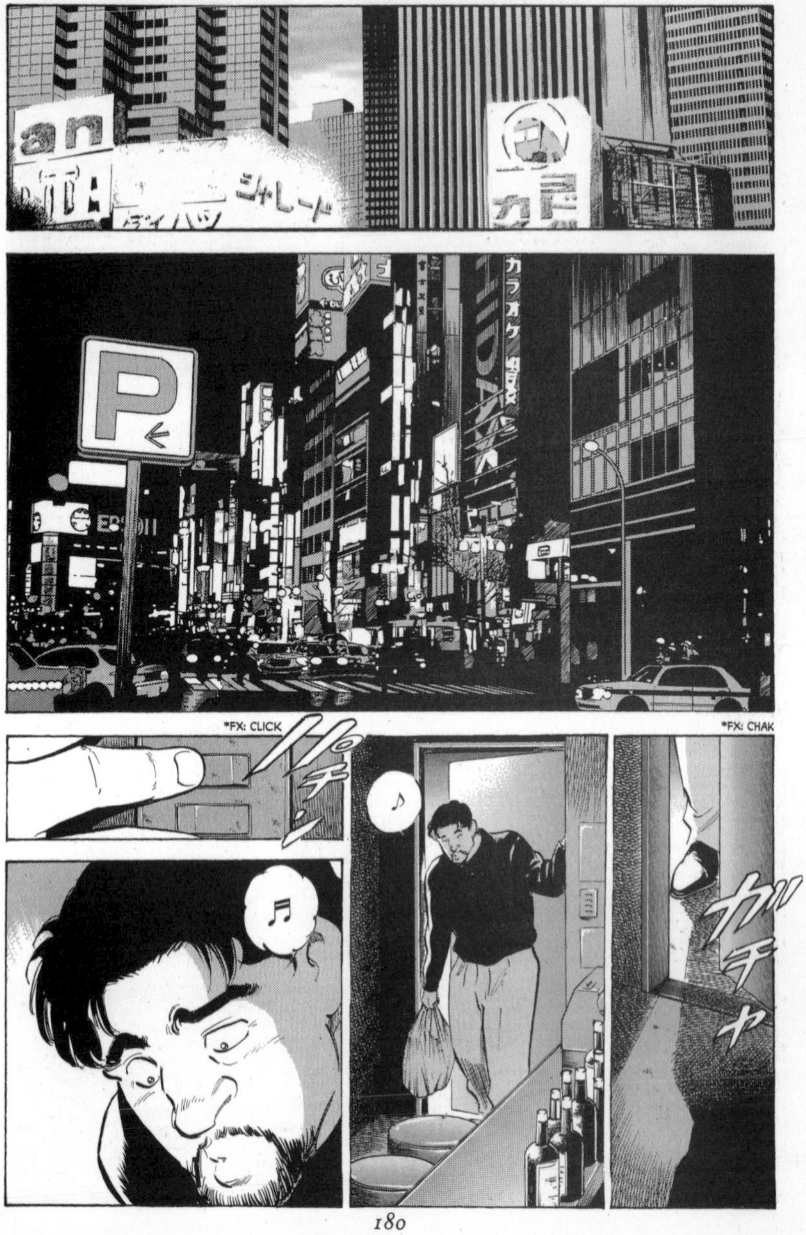
an
シャレード
カラオケ
*FX: CHAK
ガチャ
*FX: CLICK
パチン

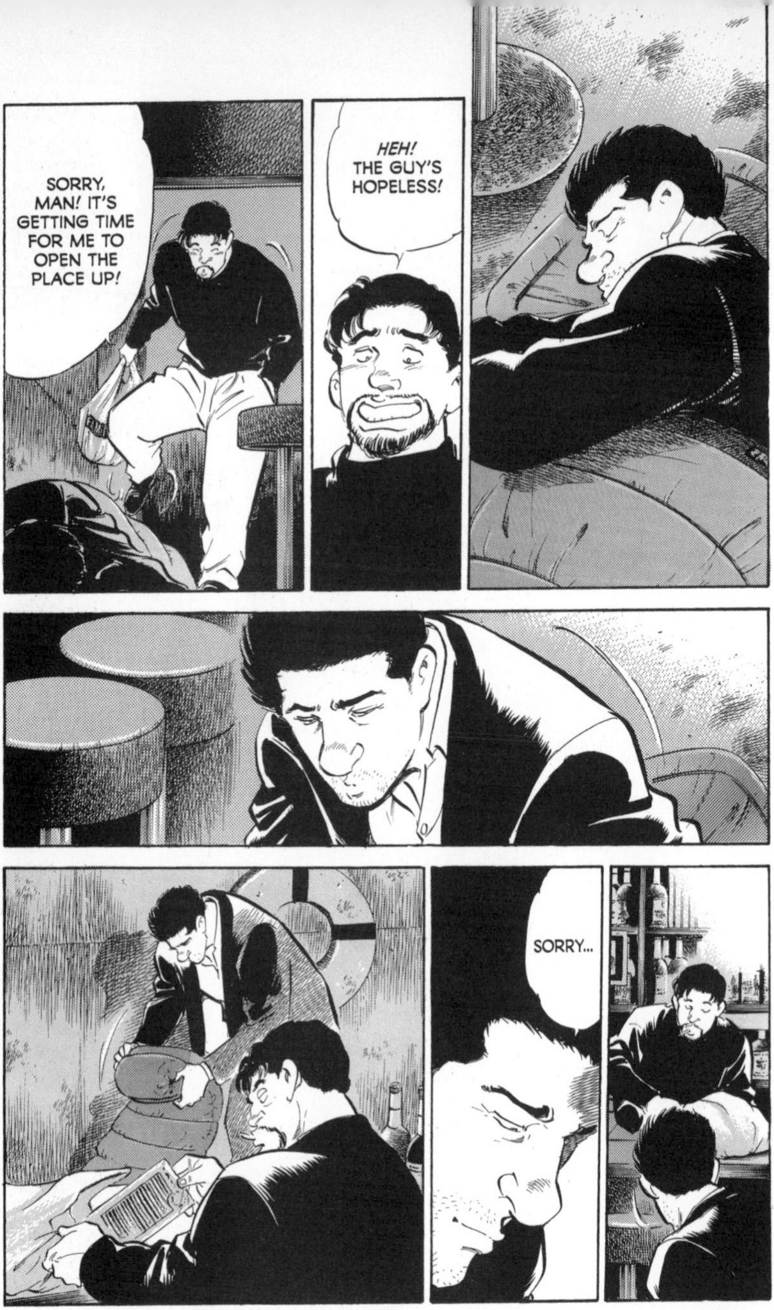
HEH! THE GUY'S HOPELESS!
SORRY, MAN! IT'S GETTING TIME FOR ME TO OPEN THE PLACE UP!
SORRY...

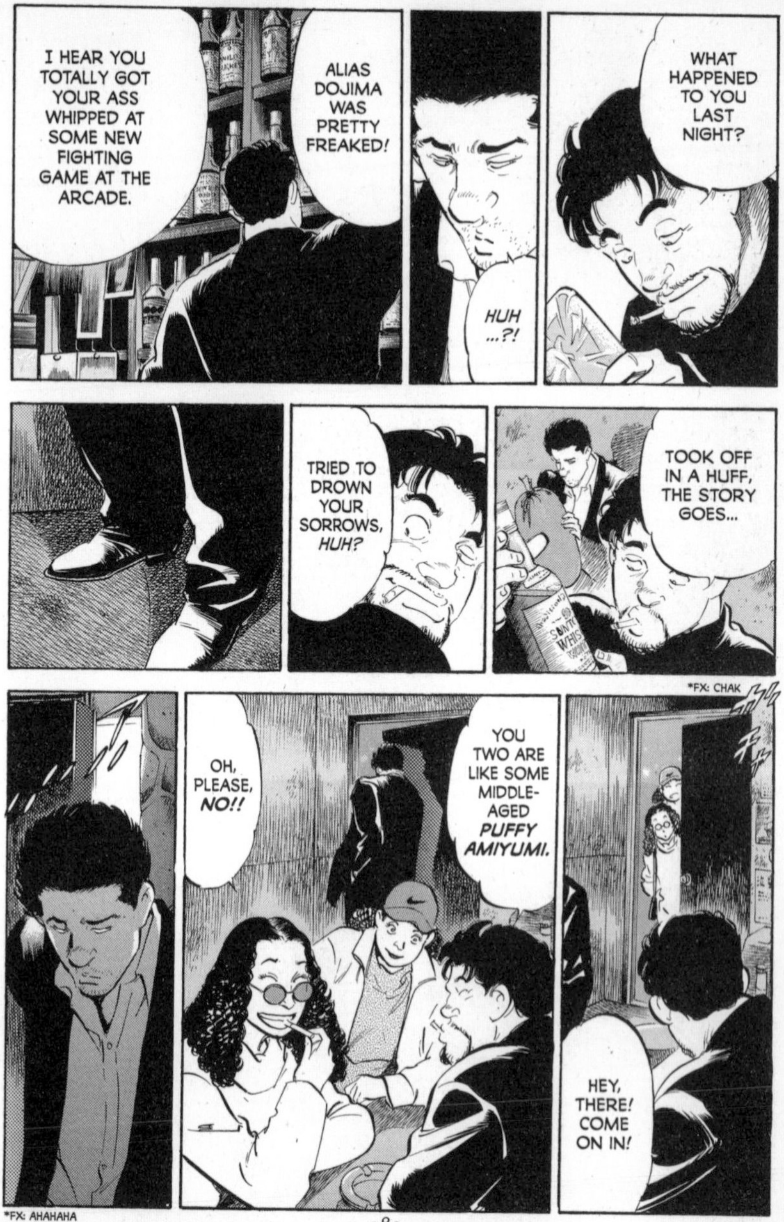
WHAT HAPPENED TO YOU LAST NIGHT?
HUH ...?!
ALIAS DOJIMA WAS PRETTY FREAKED!
I HEAR YOU TOTALLY GOT YOUR ASS WHIPPED AT SOME NEW FIGHTING GAME AT THE ARCADE.
TOOK OFF IN A HUFF, THE STORY GOES...
TRIED TO DROWN YOUR SORROWS, *HUH?*
HEY, THERE! COME ON IN!
YOU TWO ARE LIKE SOME MIDDLE-AGED **PUFFY AMIYUMI.**
OH, PLEASE, ***NO!!***

*FX: CHAK

*FX: AHAHAHA

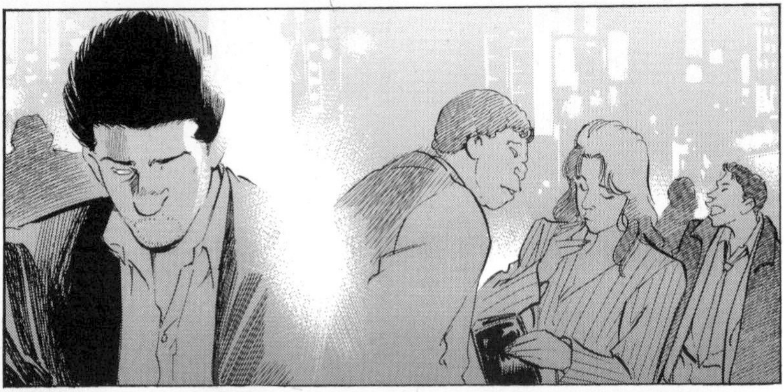

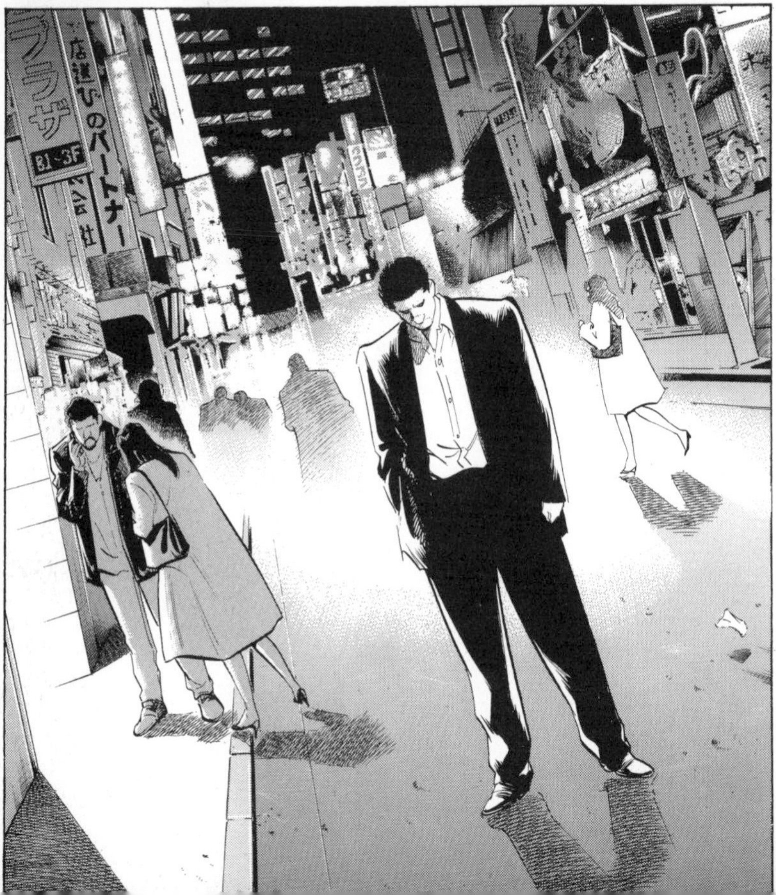
ラザ
B1-3F
店選びのパートナー
会社

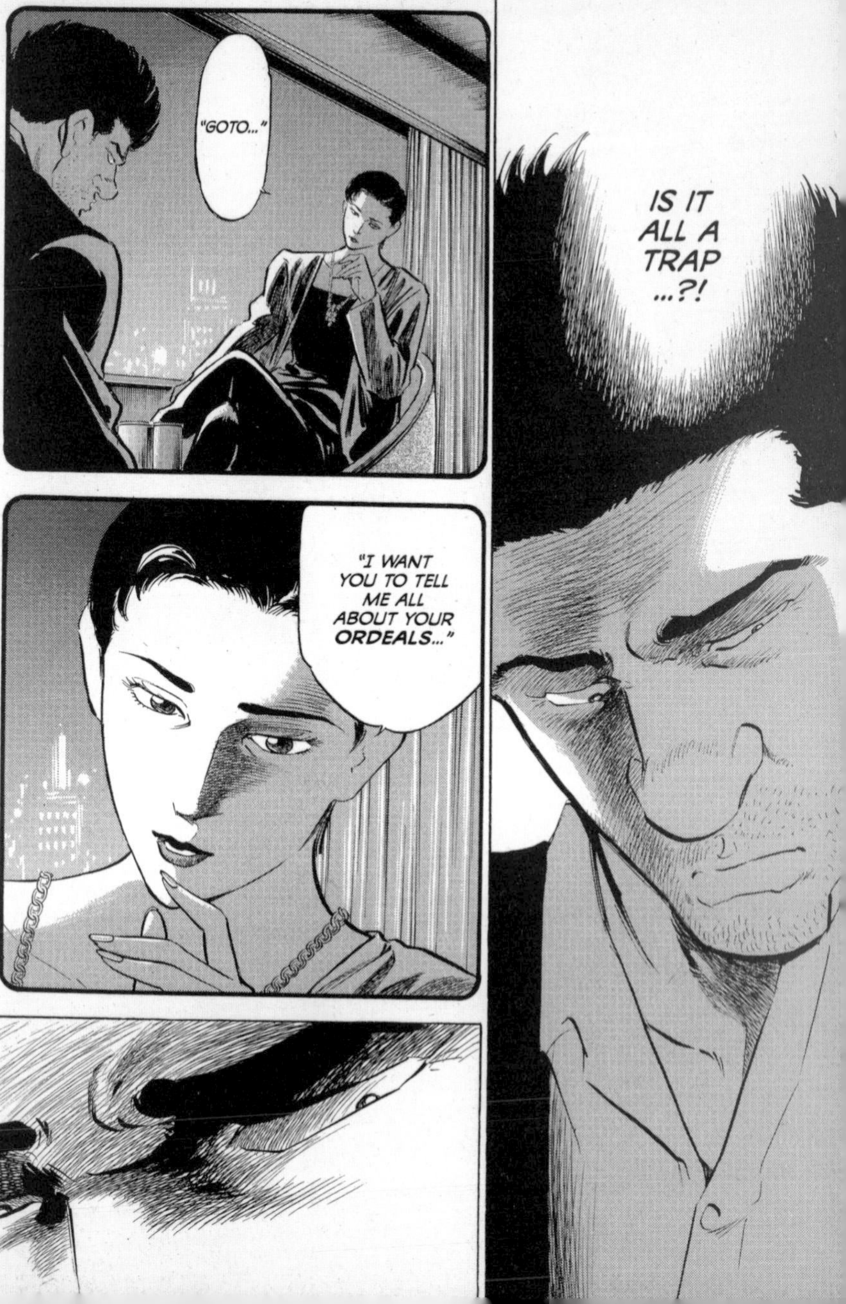
IS IT ALL A TRAP ...?!
"GOTO..."
"I WANT YOU TO TELL ME ALL ABOUT YOUR ORDEALS..."

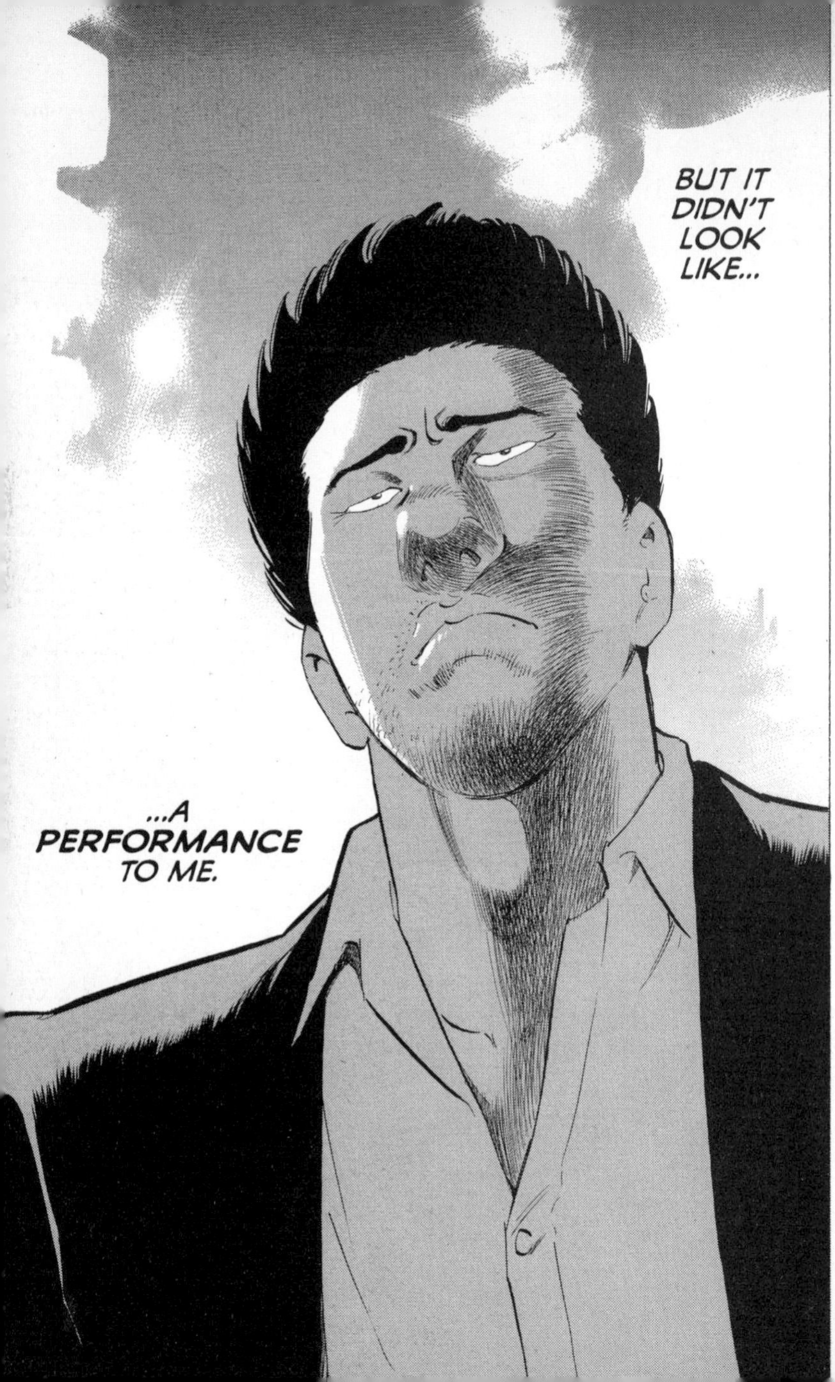
BUT IT DIDN'T LOOK LIKE...
...A PERFORMANCE TO ME.

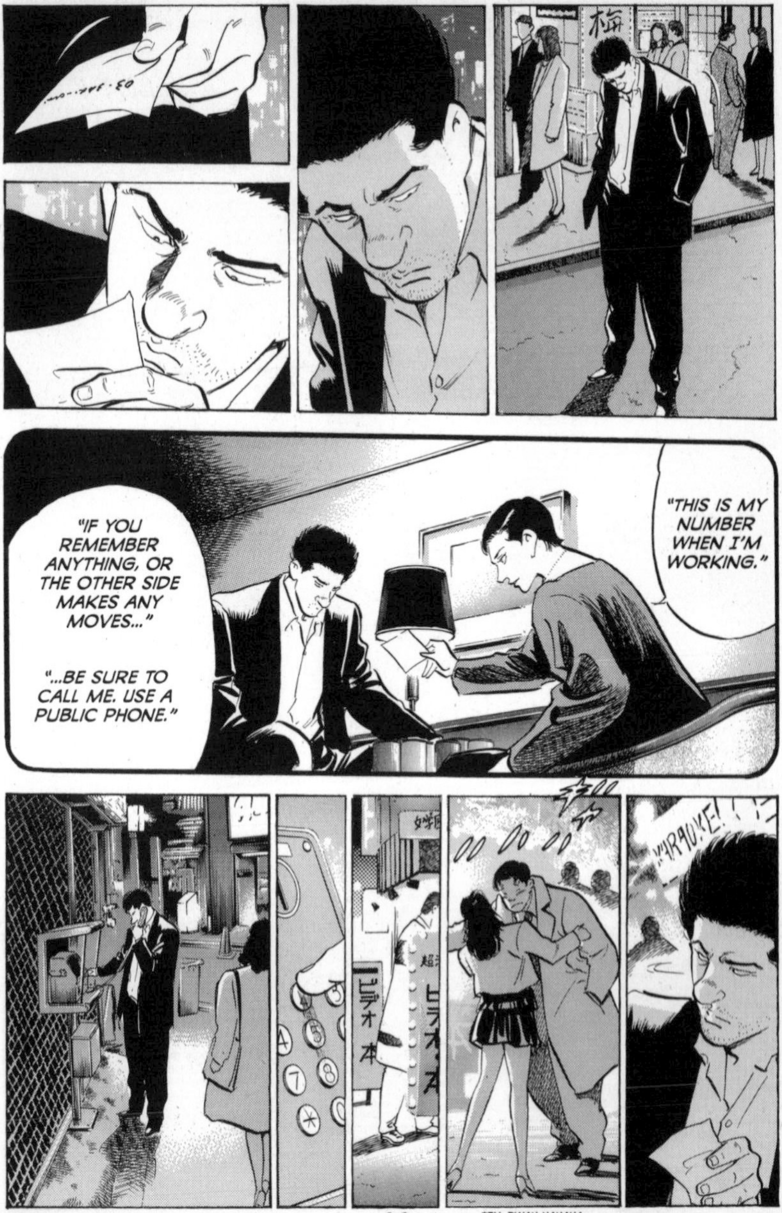
"THIS IS MY NUMBER WHEN I'M WORKING."
"IF YOU REMEMBER ANYTHING, OR THE OTHER SIDE MAKES ANY MOVES..."
"...BE SURE TO CALL ME. USE A PUBLIC PHONE."

*FX: BWAH HAHAHA

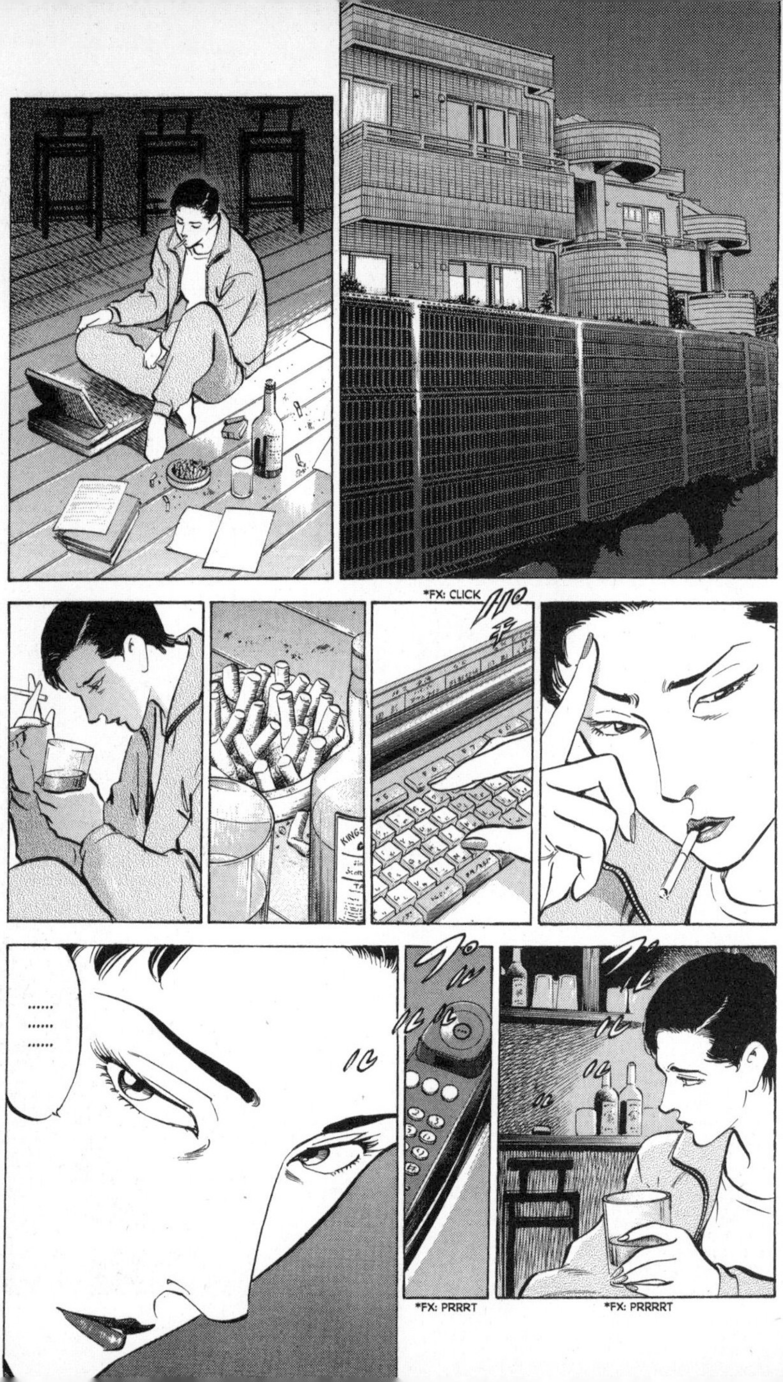
*FX: CLICK
*FX: PRRRRT
*FX: PRRRT
......
......
......

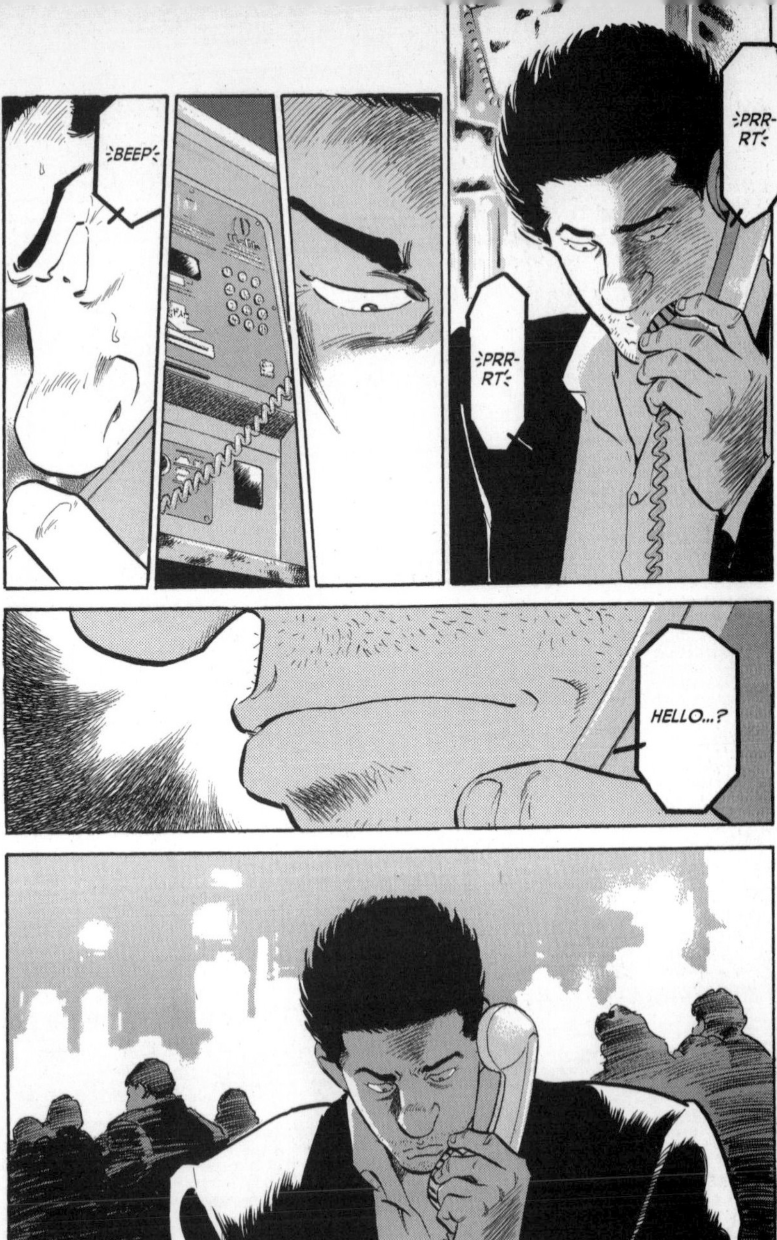
PRR-RT
PRR-RT
BEEP
HELLO...?

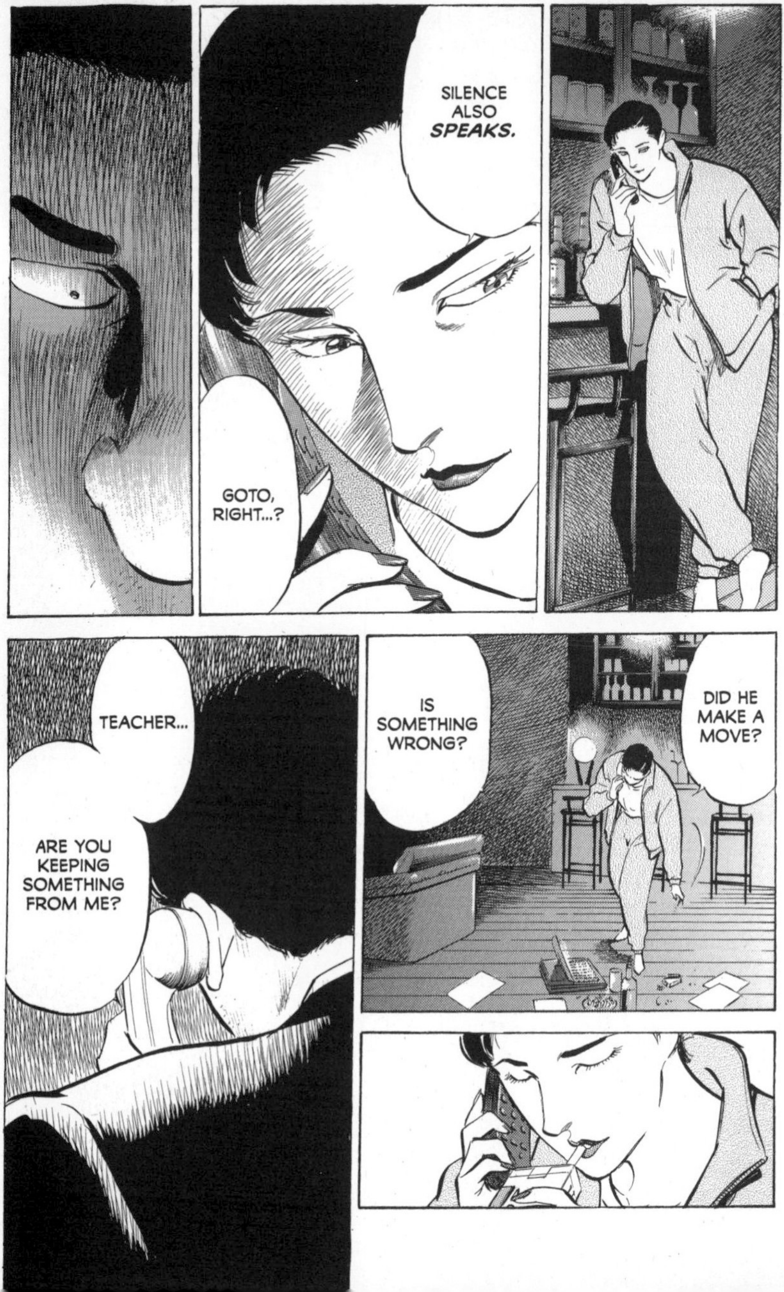
SILENCE ALSO *SPEAKS.*
GOTO, RIGHT...?
DID HE MAKE A MOVE?
IS SOMETHING WRONG?
TEACHER...
ARE YOU KEEPING SOMETHING FROM ME?

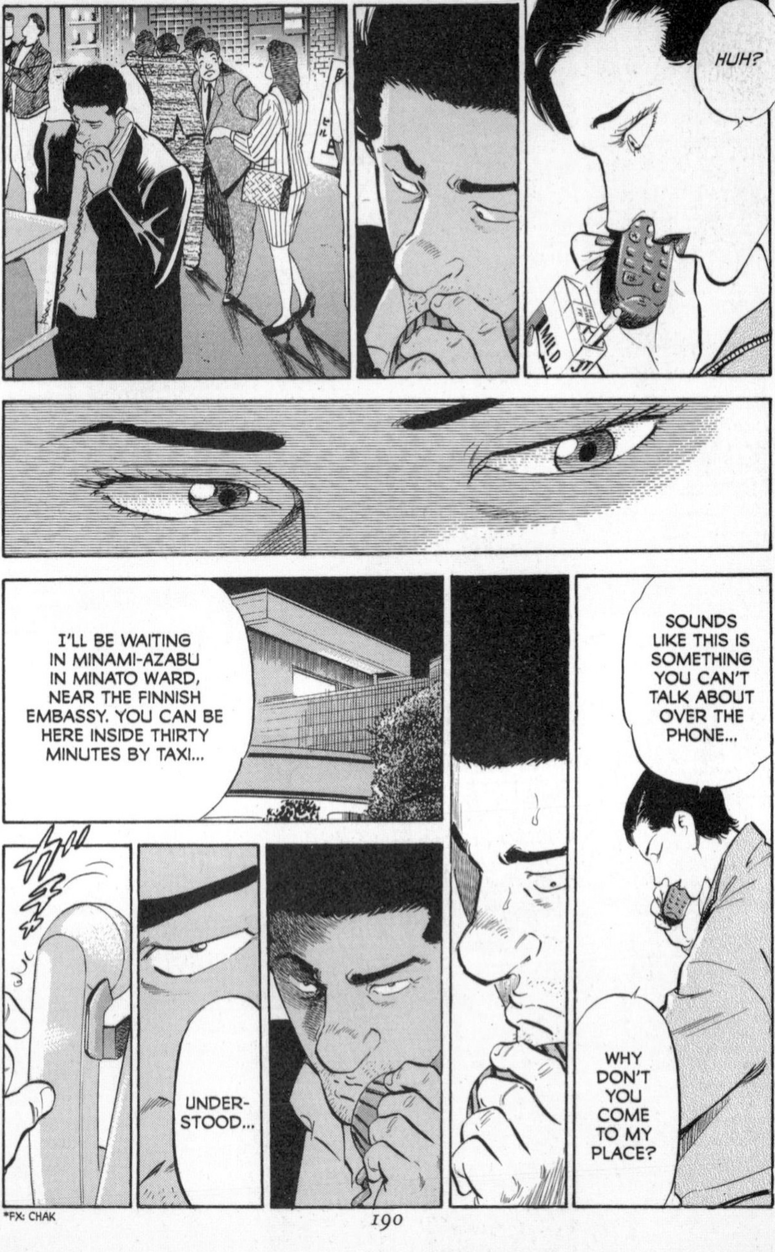
HUH?
SOUNDS LIKE THIS IS SOMETHING YOU CAN'T TALK ABOUT OVER THE PHONE...
WHY DON'T YOU COME TO MY PLACE?
I'LL BE WAITING IN MINAMI-AZABU IN MINATO WARD, NEAR THE FINNISH EMBASSY. YOU CAN BE HERE INSIDE THIRTY MINUTES BY TAXI...
UNDER-STOOD...

*FX: CHAK

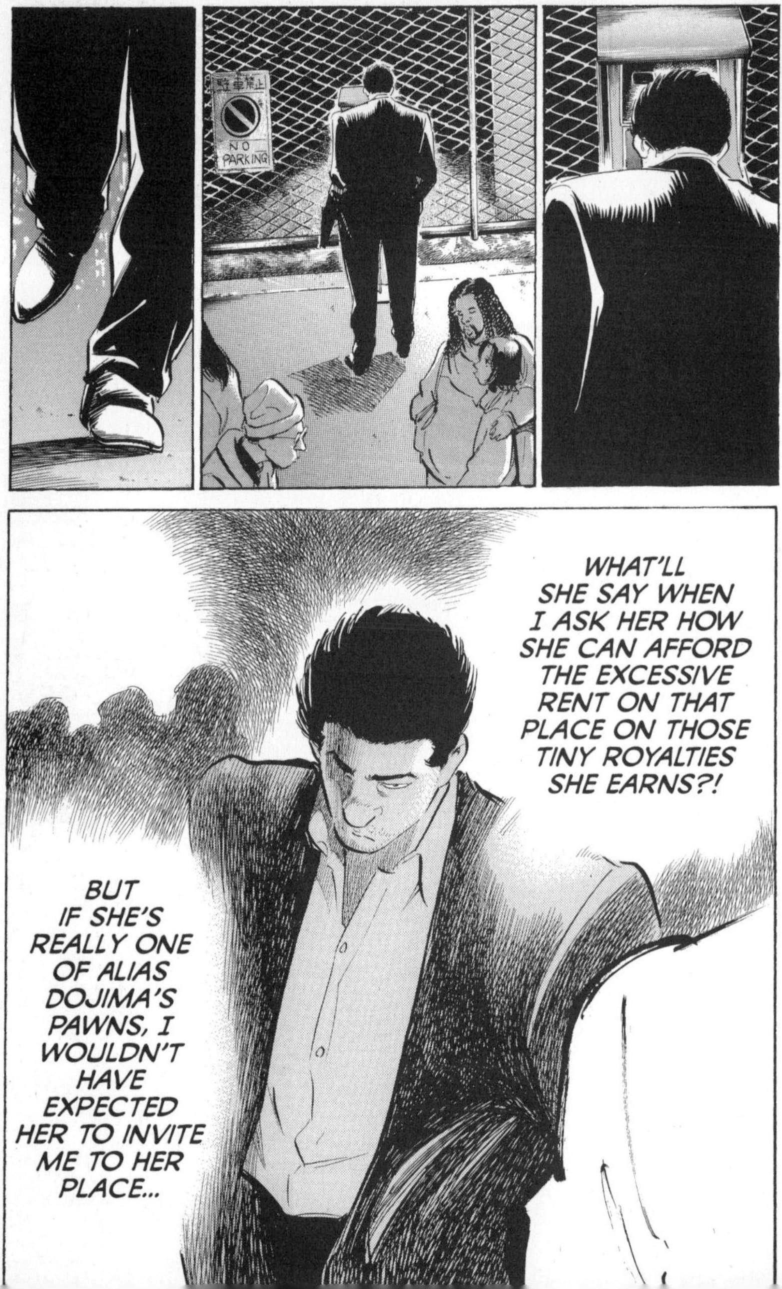
NO PARKING
WHAT'LL SHE SAY WHEN I ASK HER HOW SHE CAN AFFORD THE EXCESSIVE RENT ON THAT PLACE ON THOSE TINY ROYALTIES SHE EARNS?!
BUT IF SHE'S REALLY ONE OF ALIAS DOJIMA'S PAWNS, I WOULDN'T HAVE EXPECTED HER TO INVITE ME TO HER PLACE...

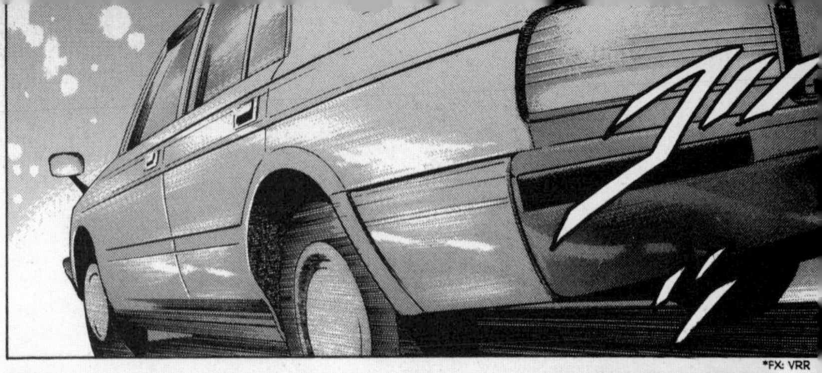

*FX: VRR

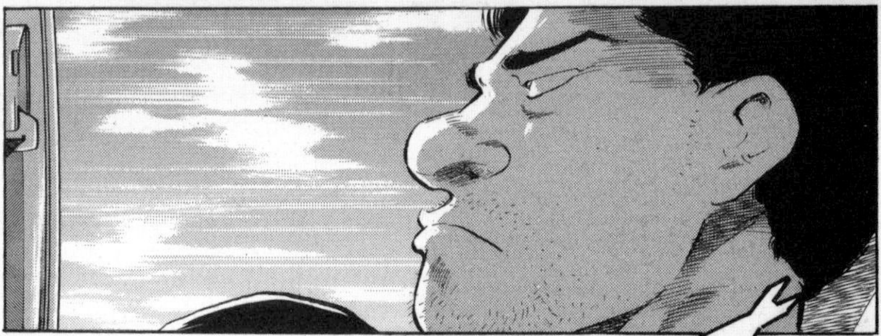

*FX: RRR RMM

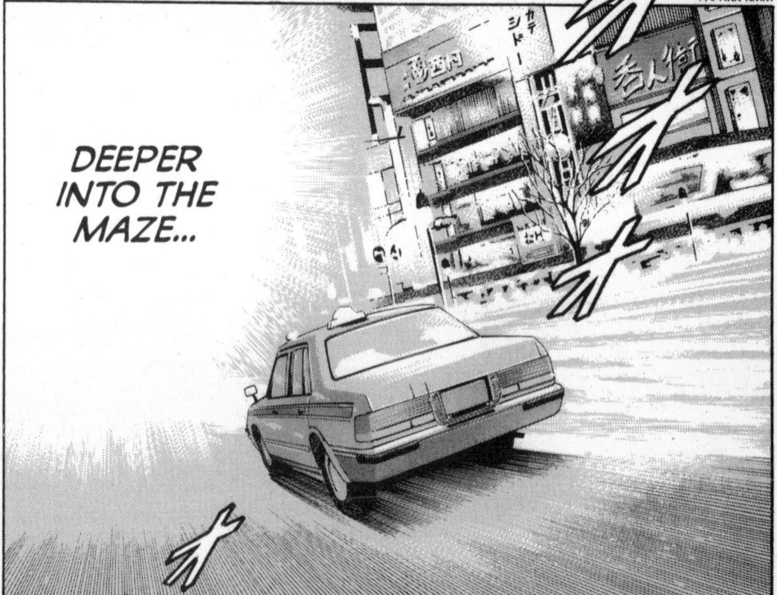
DEEPER INTO THE MAZE...

THE WAILING WALL: END

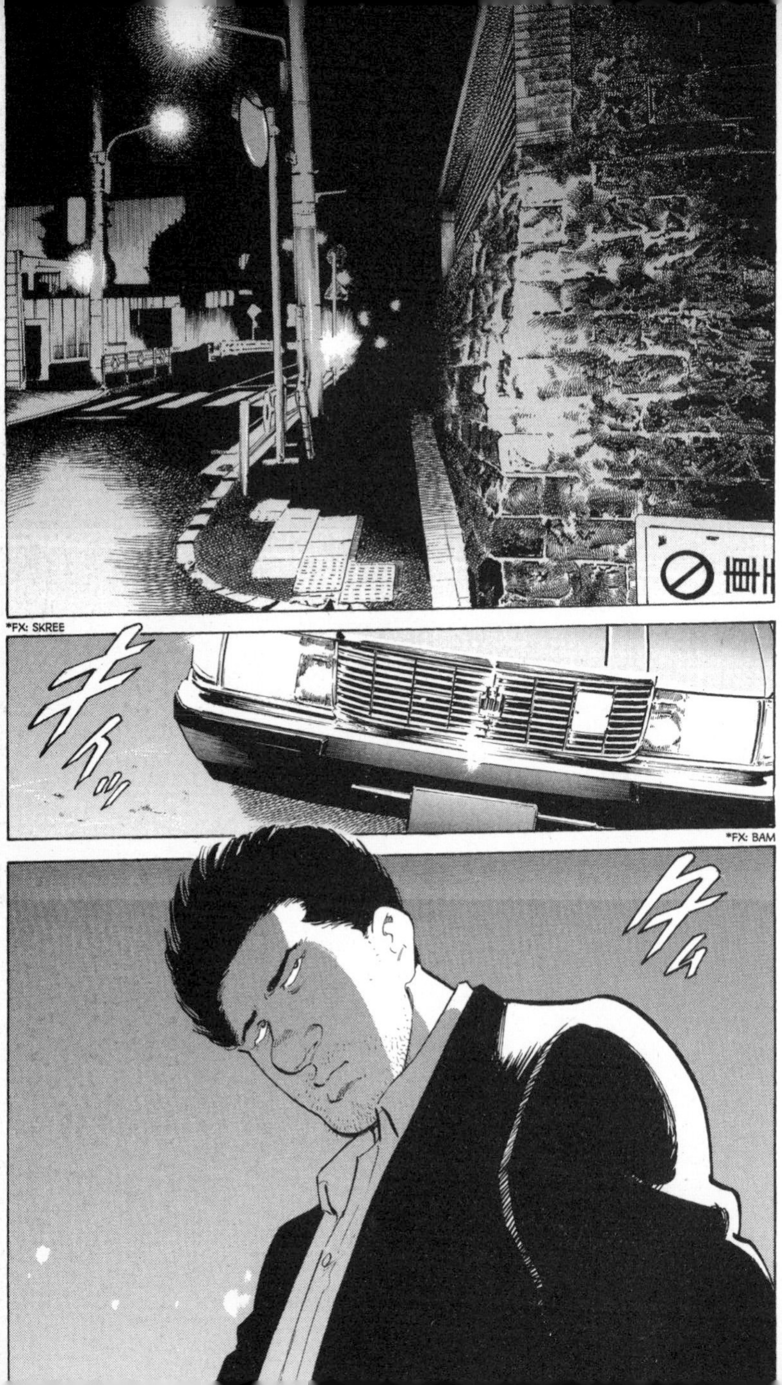
*FX: SKREE
キキッ
*FX: BAM

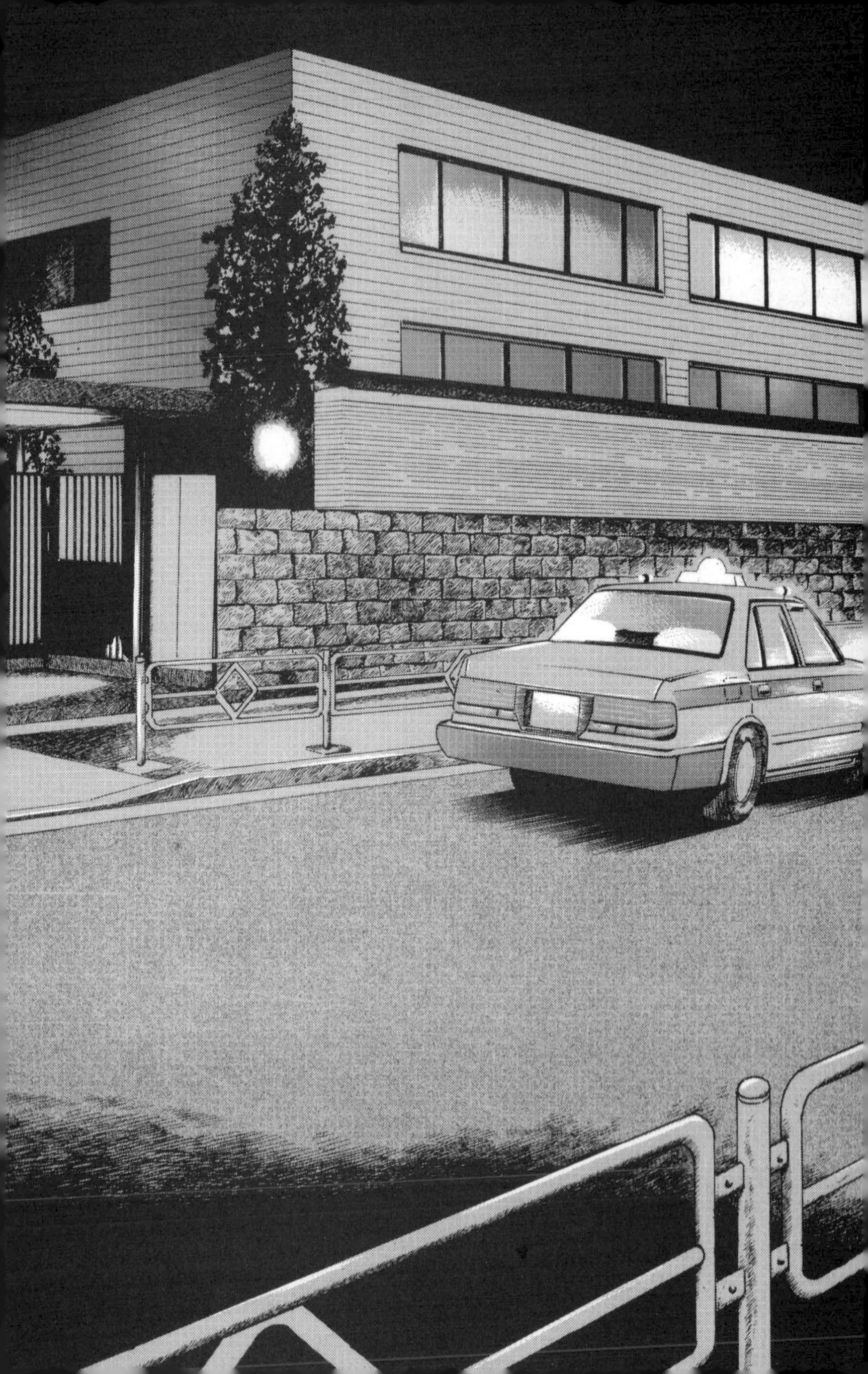

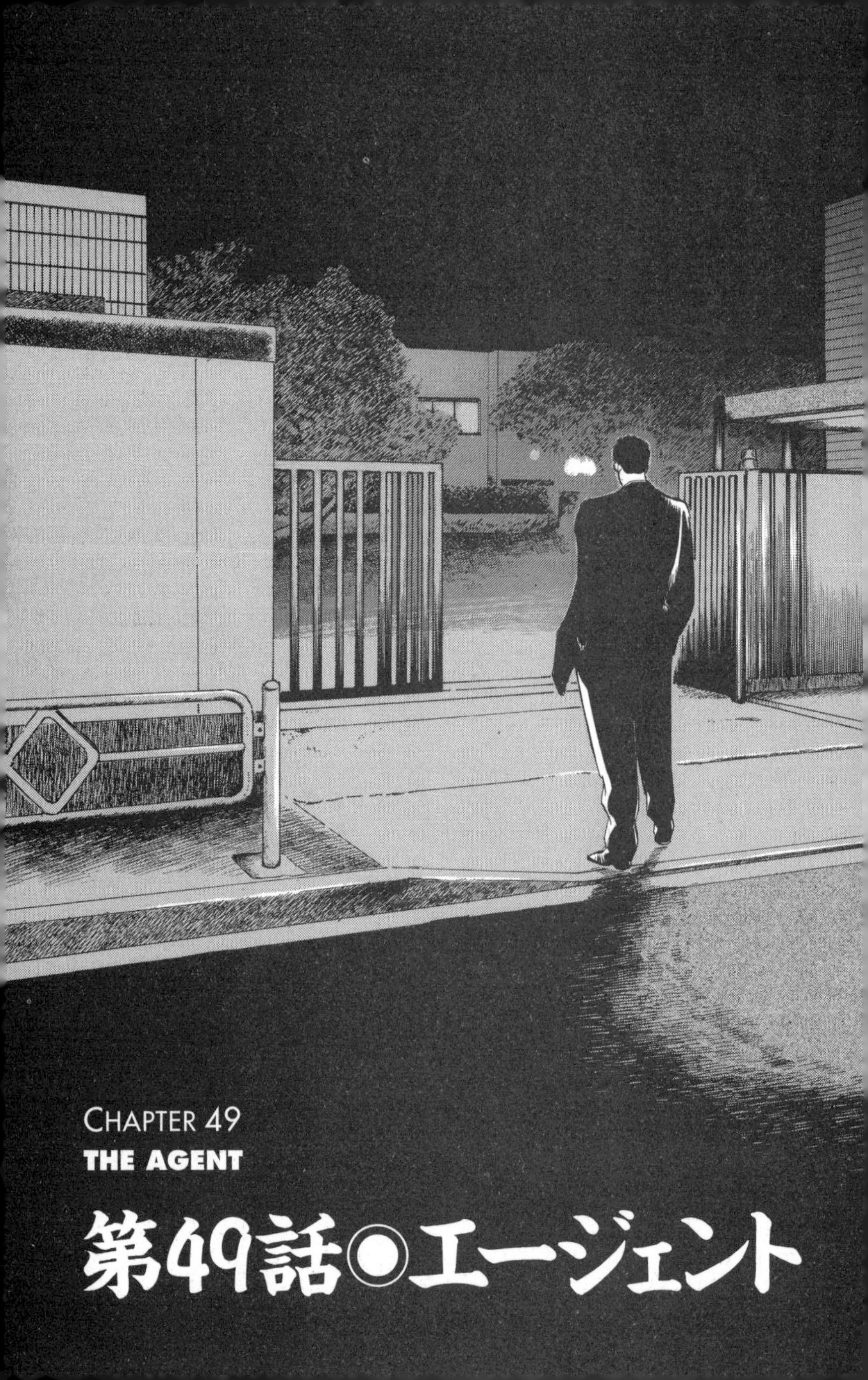
CHAPTER 49
THE AGENT
第49話◎エージェント

*FX: TAP TAP

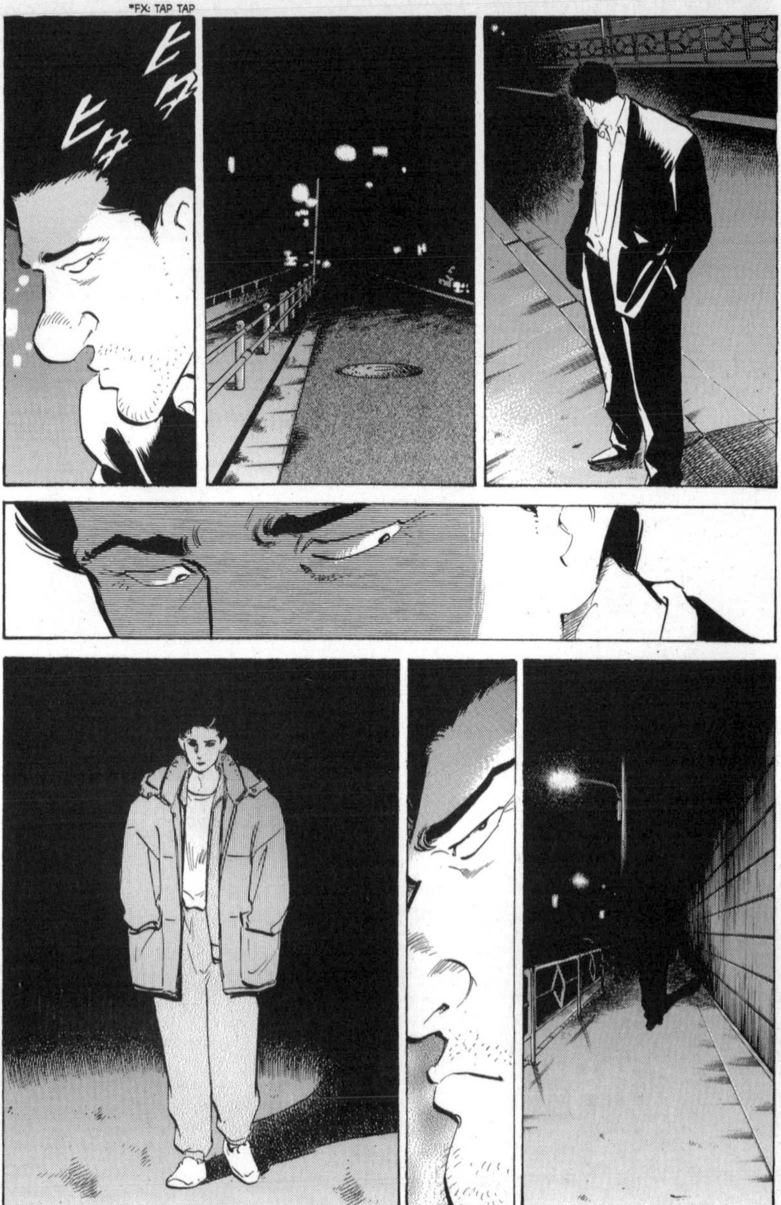
ヒタ
ヒタ

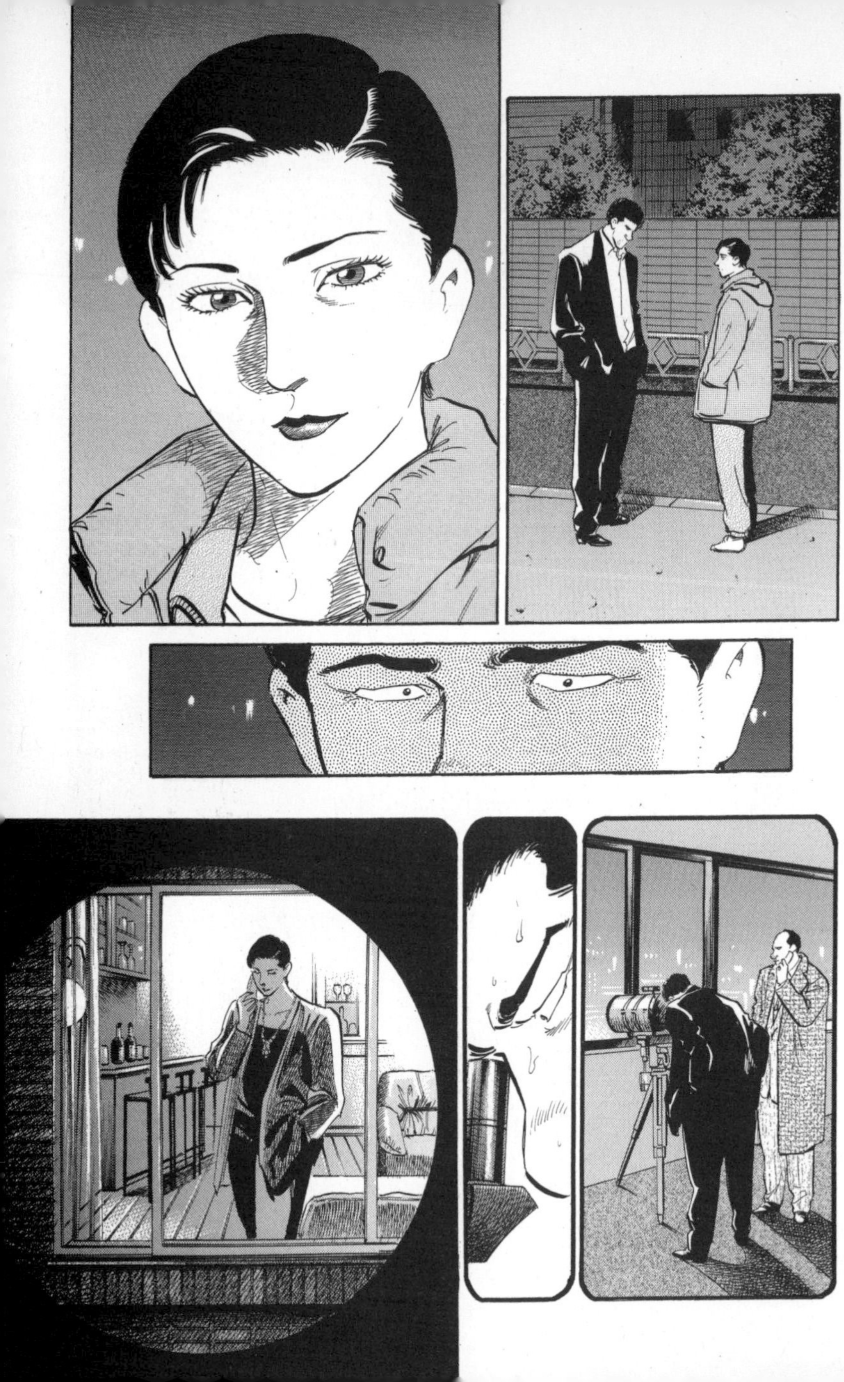

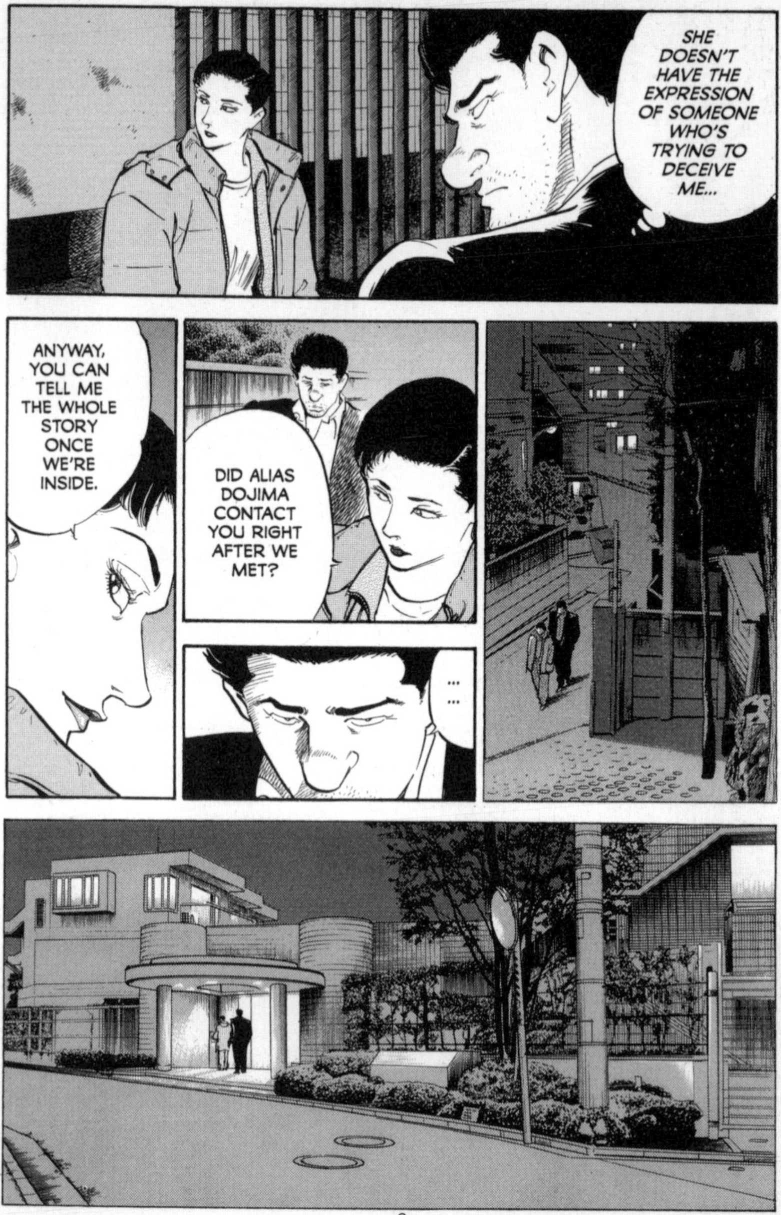
SHE DOESN'T HAVE THE EXPRESSION OF SOMEONE WHO'S TRYING TO DECEIVE ME...
DID ALIAS DOJIMA CONTACT YOU RIGHT AFTER WE MET?
... ...
ANYWAY, YOU CAN TELL ME THE WHOLE STORY ONCE WE'RE INSIDE.

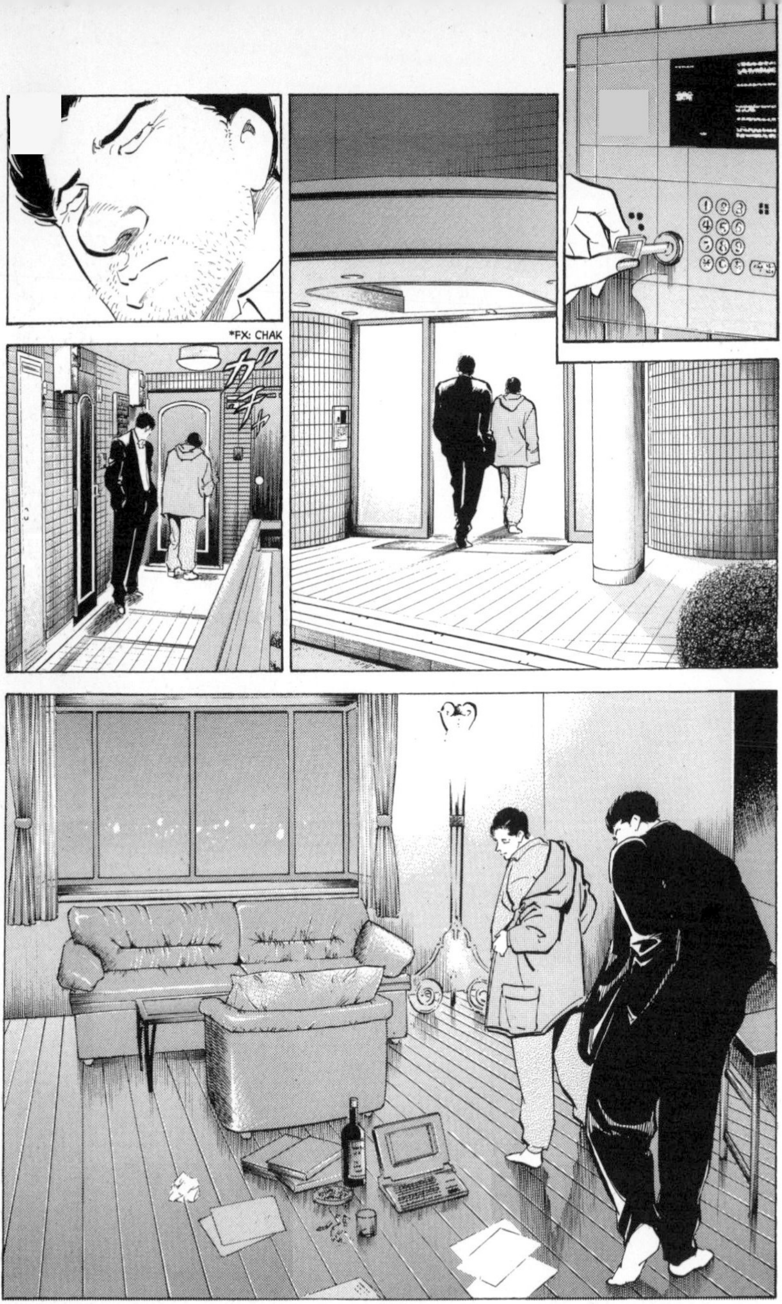
ガチャ
*FX: CHAK

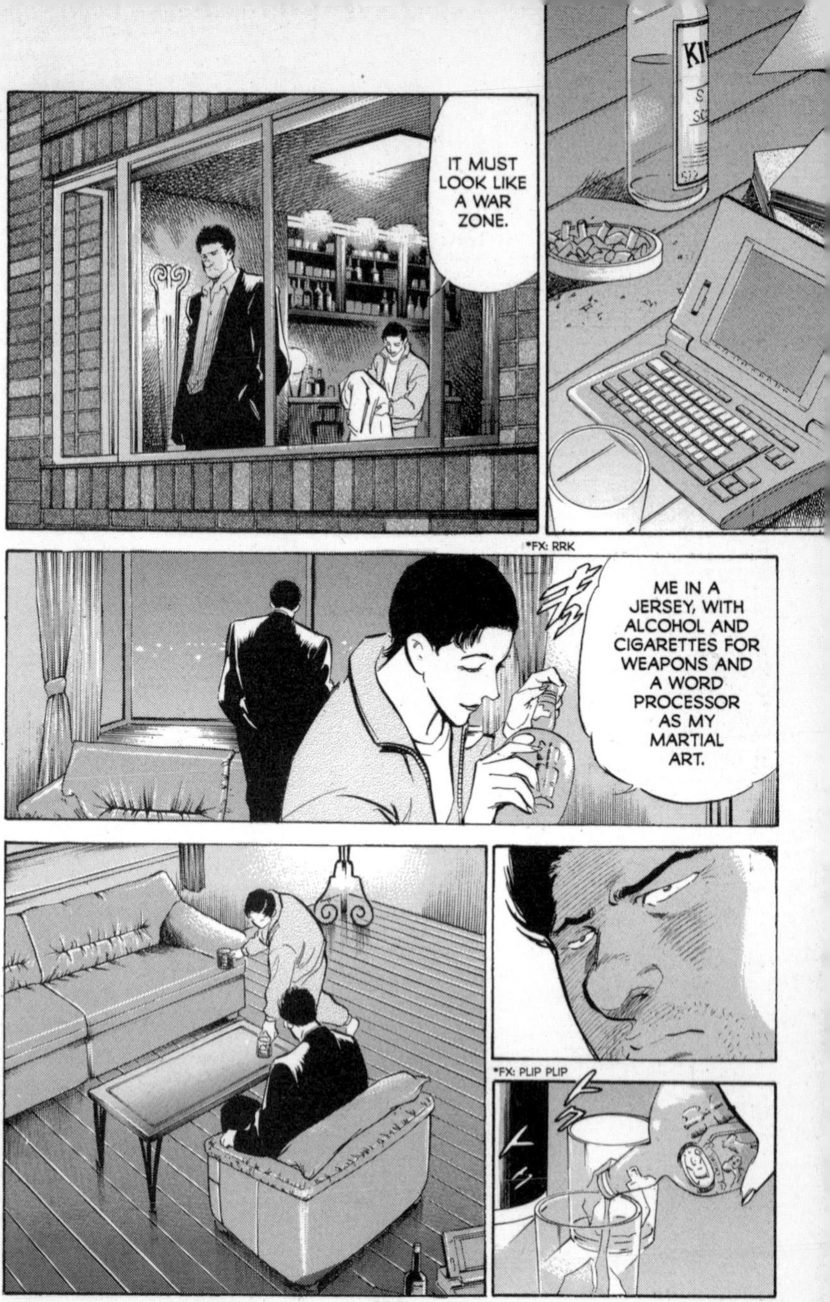
IT MUST LOOK LIKE A WAR ZONE.
*FX: RRK
ME IN A JERSEY, WITH ALCOHOL AND CIGARETTES FOR WEAPONS AND A WORD PROCESSOR AS MY MARTIAL ART.
*FX: PLIP PLIP

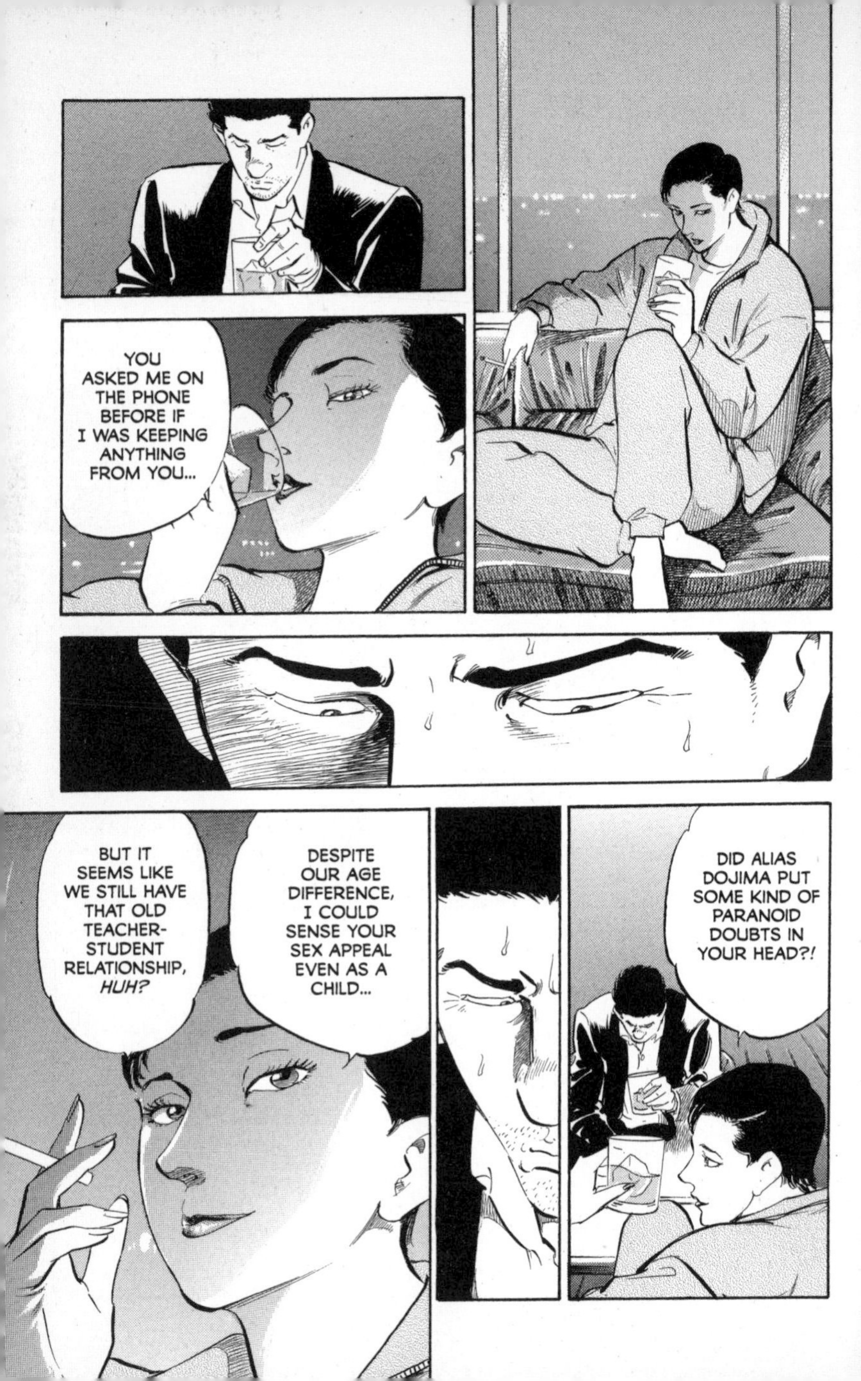
YOU ASKED ME ON THE PHONE BEFORE IF I WAS KEEPING ANYTHING FROM YOU...
DID ALIAS DOJIMA PUT SOME KIND OF PARANOID DOUBTS IN YOUR HEAD?!
DESPITE OUR AGE DIFFERENCE, I COULD SENSE YOUR SEX APPEAL EVEN AS A CHILD...
BUT IT SEEMS LIKE WE STILL HAVE THAT OLD TEACHER-STUDENT RELATIONSHIP, *HUH?*

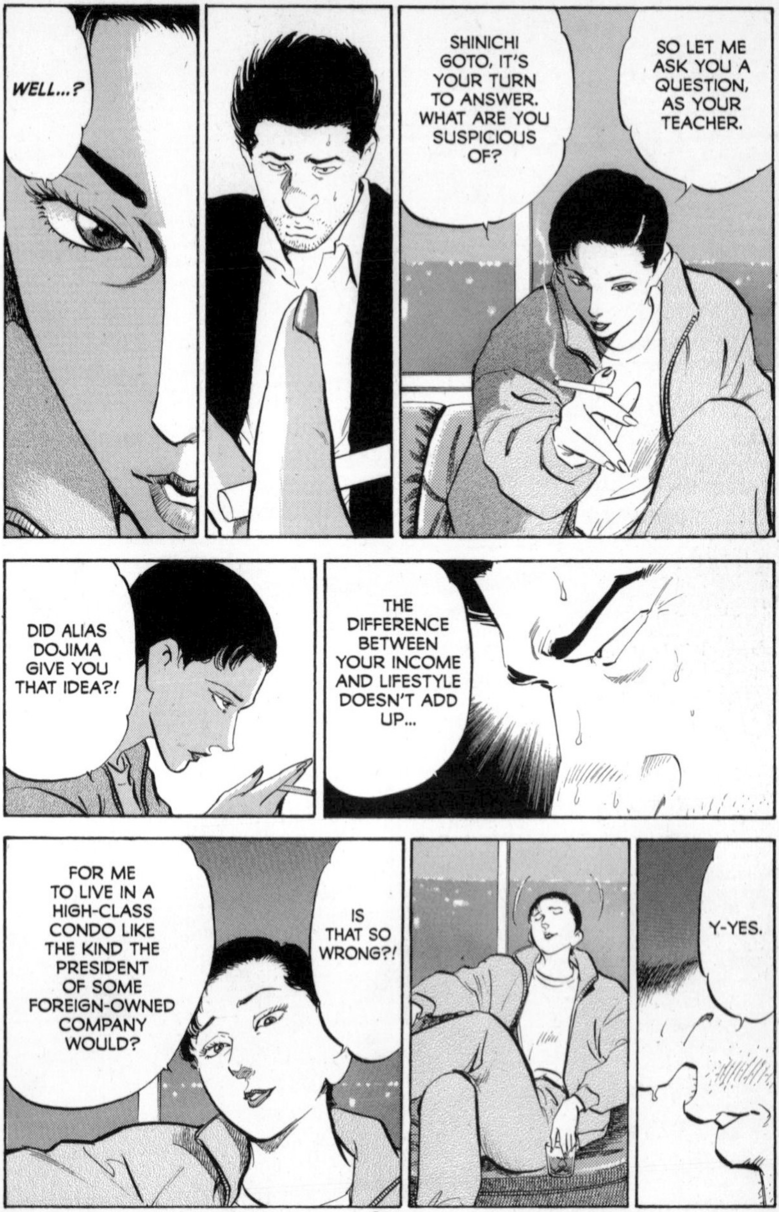
SO LET ME ASK YOU A QUESTION, AS YOUR TEACHER.
SHINICHI GOTO, IT'S YOUR TURN TO ANSWER. WHAT ARE YOU SUSPICIOUS OF?
WELL...?
THE DIFFERENCE BETWEEN YOUR INCOME AND LIFESTYLE DOESN'T ADD UP...
DID ALIAS DOJIMA GIVE YOU THAT IDEA?!
Y-YES.
FOR ME TO LIVE IN A HIGH-CLASS CONDO LIKE THE KIND THE PRESIDENT OF SOME FOREIGN-OWNED COMPANY WOULD?
IS THAT SO WRONG?!

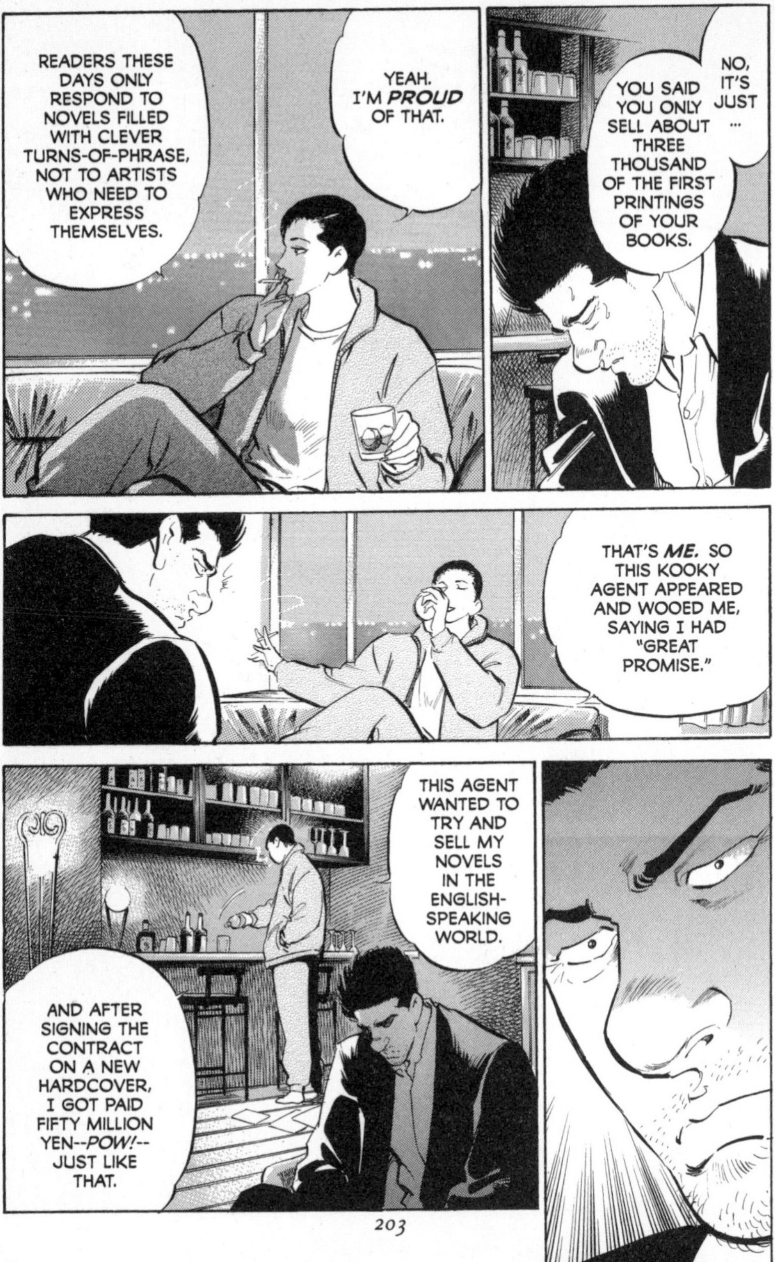
NO, IT'S JUST ...
YOU SAID YOU ONLY SELL ABOUT THREE THOUSAND OF THE FIRST PRINTINGS OF YOUR BOOKS.
YEAH. I'M *PROUD* OF THAT.
READERS THESE DAYS ONLY RESPOND TO NOVELS FILLED WITH CLEVER TURNS-OF-PHRASE, NOT TO ARTISTS WHO NEED TO EXPRESS THEMSELVES.
THAT'S *ME.* SO THIS KOOKY AGENT APPEARED AND WOOED ME, SAYING I HAD "GREAT PROMISE."
THIS AGENT WANTED TO TRY AND SELL MY NOVELS IN THE ENGLISH-SPEAKING WORLD.
AND AFTER SIGNING THE CONTRACT ON A NEW HARDCOVER, I GOT PAID FIFTY MILLION YEN--*POW!*--JUST LIKE THAT.

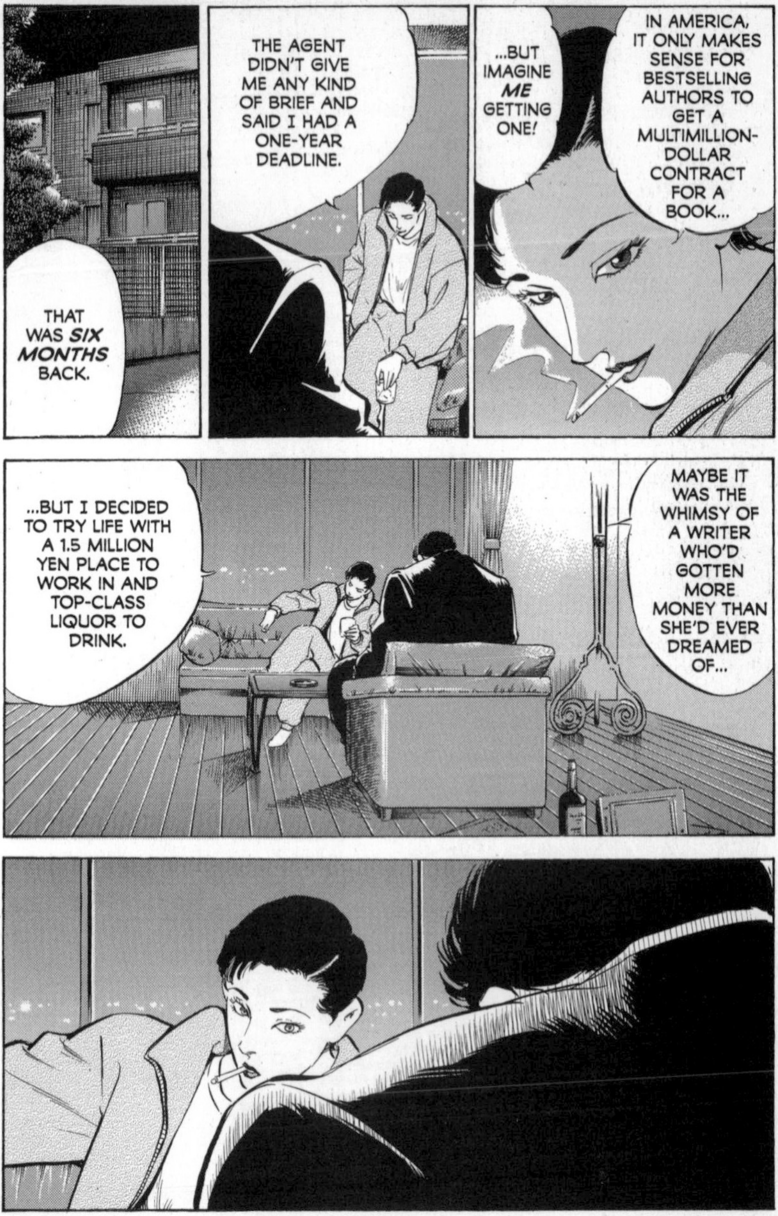
IN AMERICA, IT ONLY MAKES SENSE FOR BESTSELLING AUTHORS TO GET A MULTIMILLION-DOLLAR CONTRACT FOR A BOOK...
...BUT IMAGINE *ME* GETTING ONE!
THE AGENT DIDN'T GIVE ME ANY KIND OF BRIEF AND SAID I HAD A ONE-YEAR DEADLINE.
THAT WAS *SIX MONTHS* BACK.
MAYBE IT WAS THE WHIMSY OF A WRITER WHO'D GOTTEN MORE MONEY THAN SHE'D EVER DREAMED OF...
...BUT I DECIDED TO TRY LIFE WITH A 1.5 MILLION YEN PLACE TO WORK IN AND TOP-CLASS LIQUOR TO DRINK.

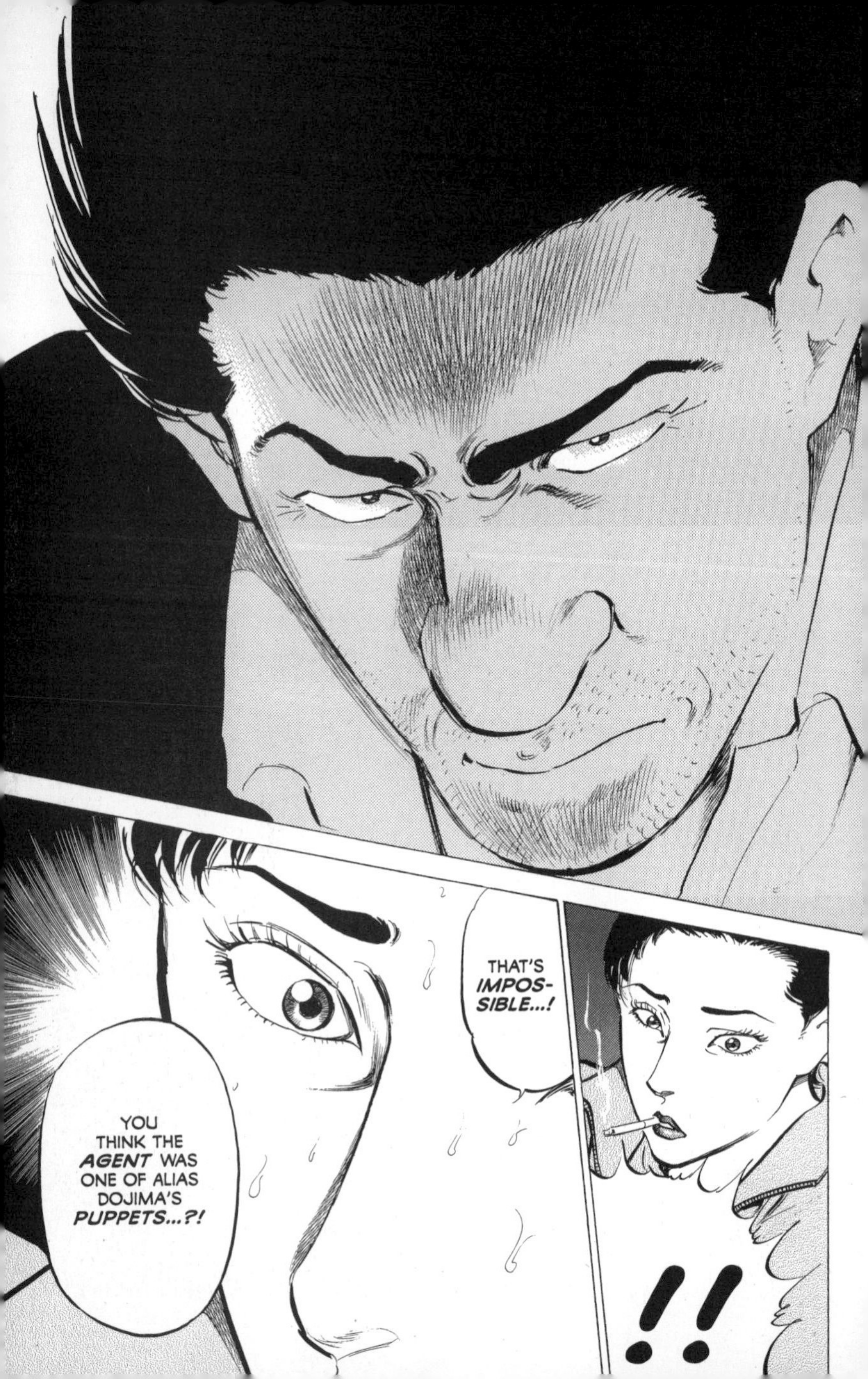
!!
THAT'S IMPOSSIBLE...!
YOU THINK THE AGENT WAS ONE OF ALIAS DOJIMA'S PUPPETS...?!

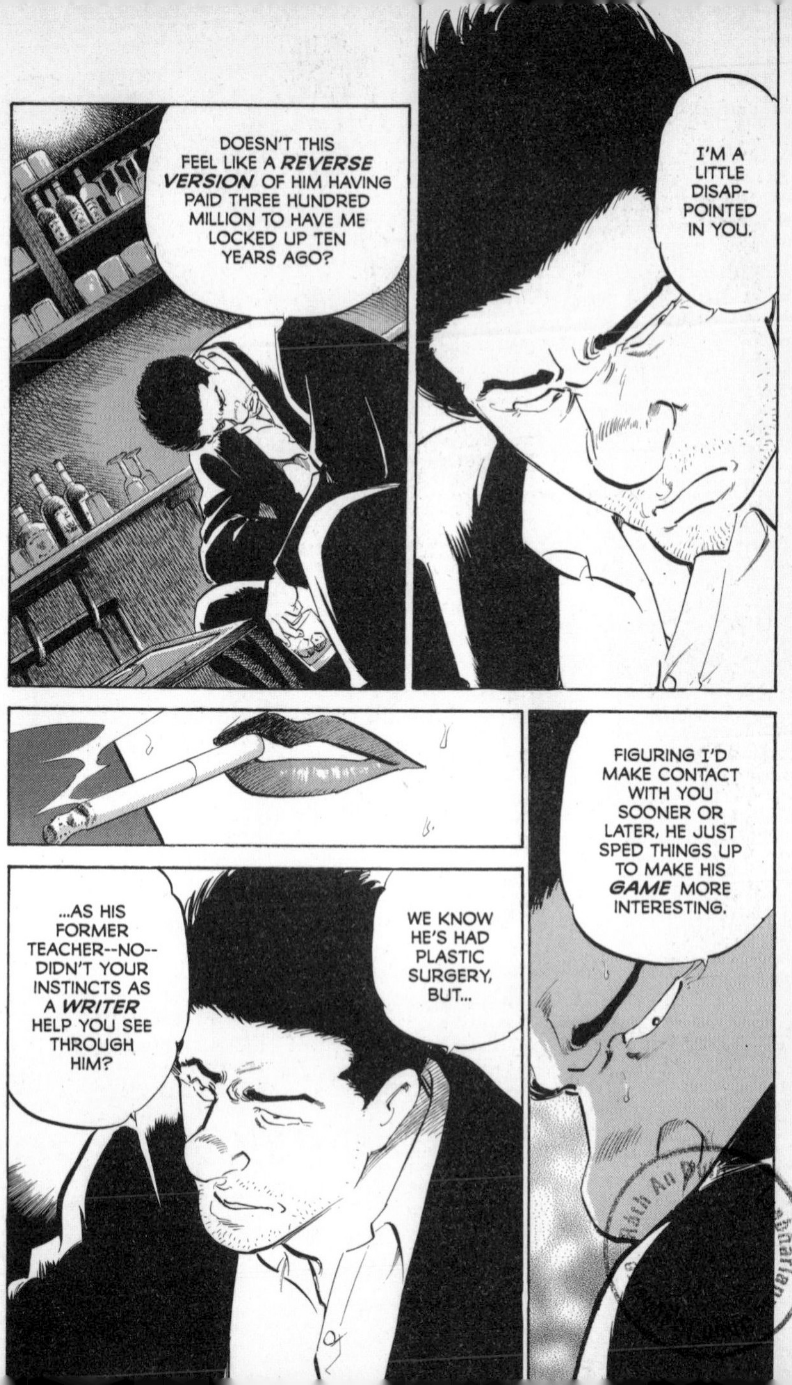
I'M A LITTLE DISAPPOINTED IN YOU.
DOESN'T THIS FEEL LIKE A *REVERSE VERSION* OF HIM HAVING PAID THREE HUNDRED MILLION TO HAVE ME LOCKED UP TEN YEARS AGO?
FIGURING I'D MAKE CONTACT WITH YOU SOONER OR LATER, HE JUST SPED THINGS UP TO MAKE HIS *GAME* MORE INTERESTING.
WE KNOW HE'S HAD PLASTIC SURGERY, BUT...
...AS HIS FORMER TEACHER--NO--DIDN'T YOUR INSTINCTS AS A *WRITER* HELP YOU SEE THROUGH HIM?

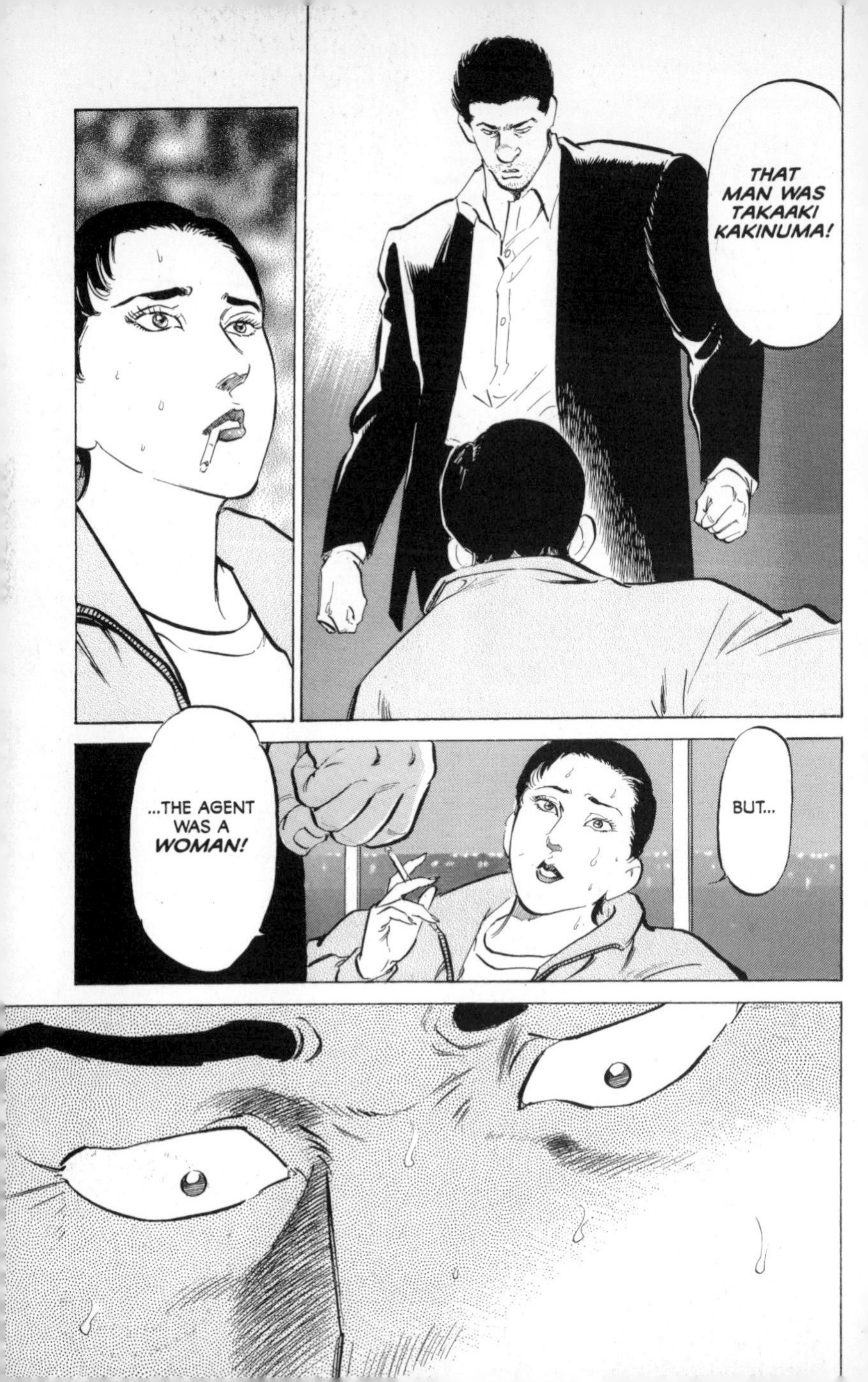
THAT MAN WAS TAKAAKI KAKINUMA!
BUT...
...THE AGENT WAS A WOMAN!

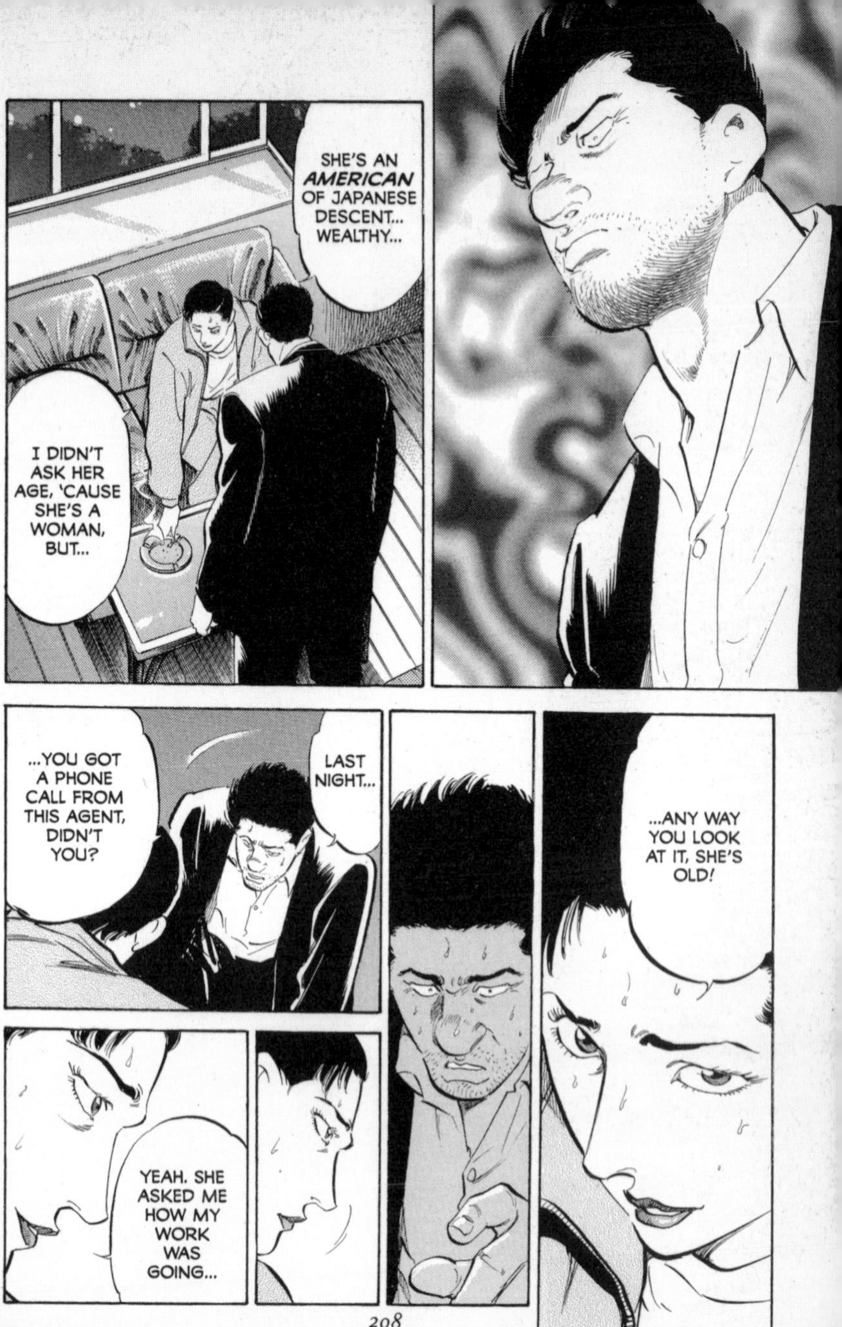
SHE'S AN *AMERICAN* OF JAPANESE DESCENT... WEALTHY...
I DIDN'T ASK HER AGE, 'CAUSE SHE'S A WOMAN, BUT...
...ANY WAY YOU LOOK AT IT, SHE'S OLD!
LAST NIGHT...
...YOU GOT A PHONE CALL FROM THIS AGENT, DIDN'T YOU?
YEAH. SHE ASKED ME HOW MY WORK WAS GOING...

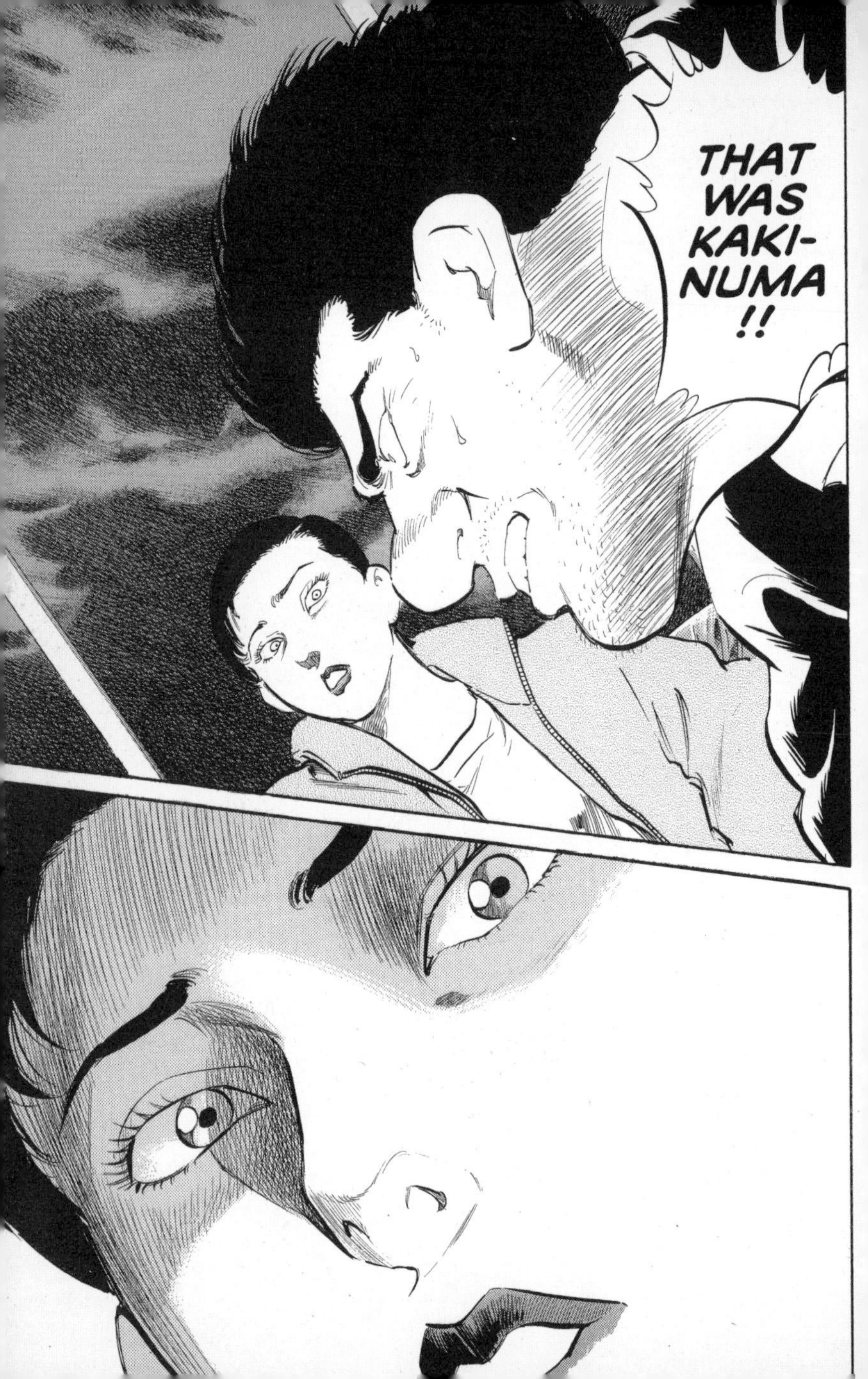
THAT WAS KAKI-NUMA !!

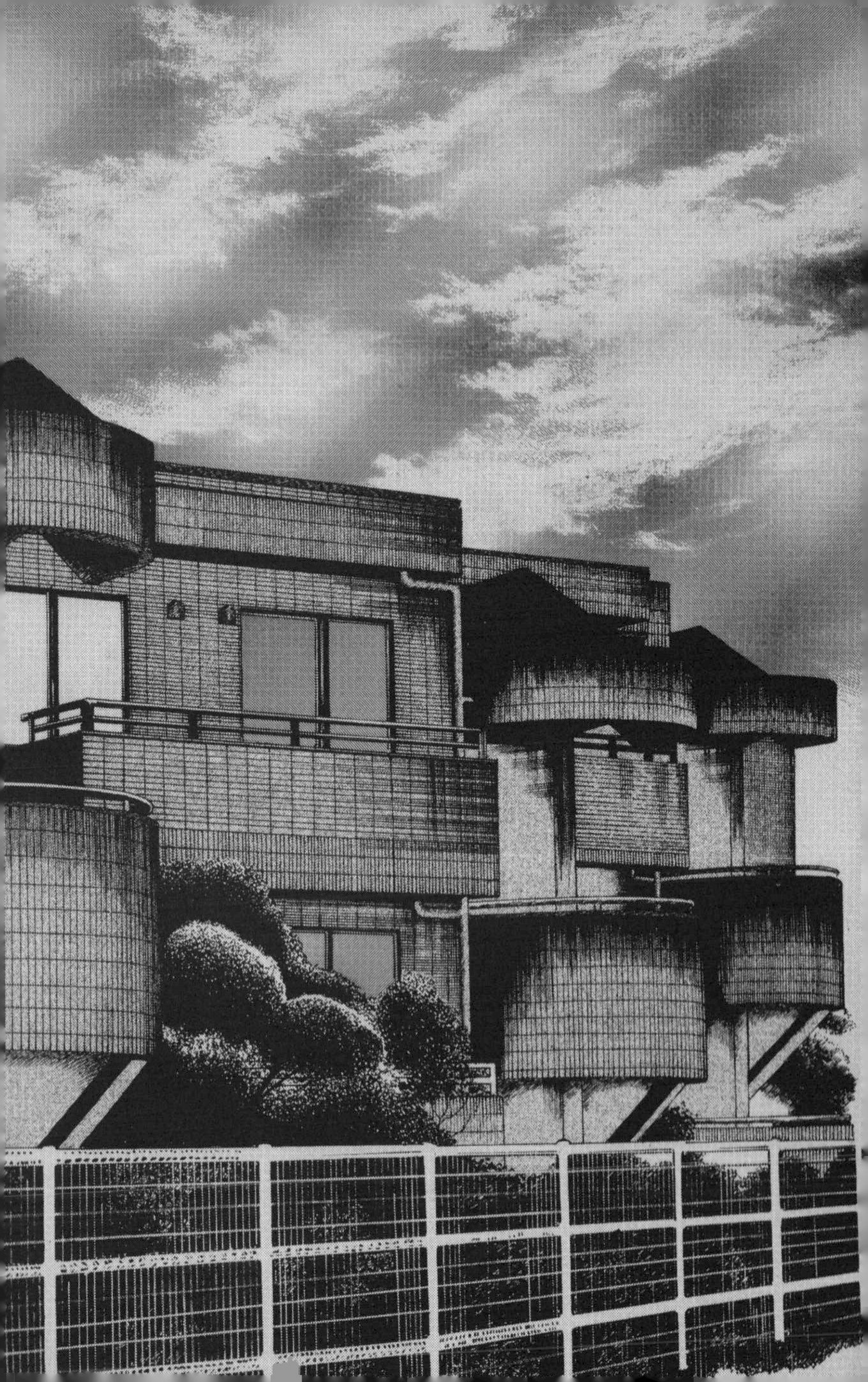

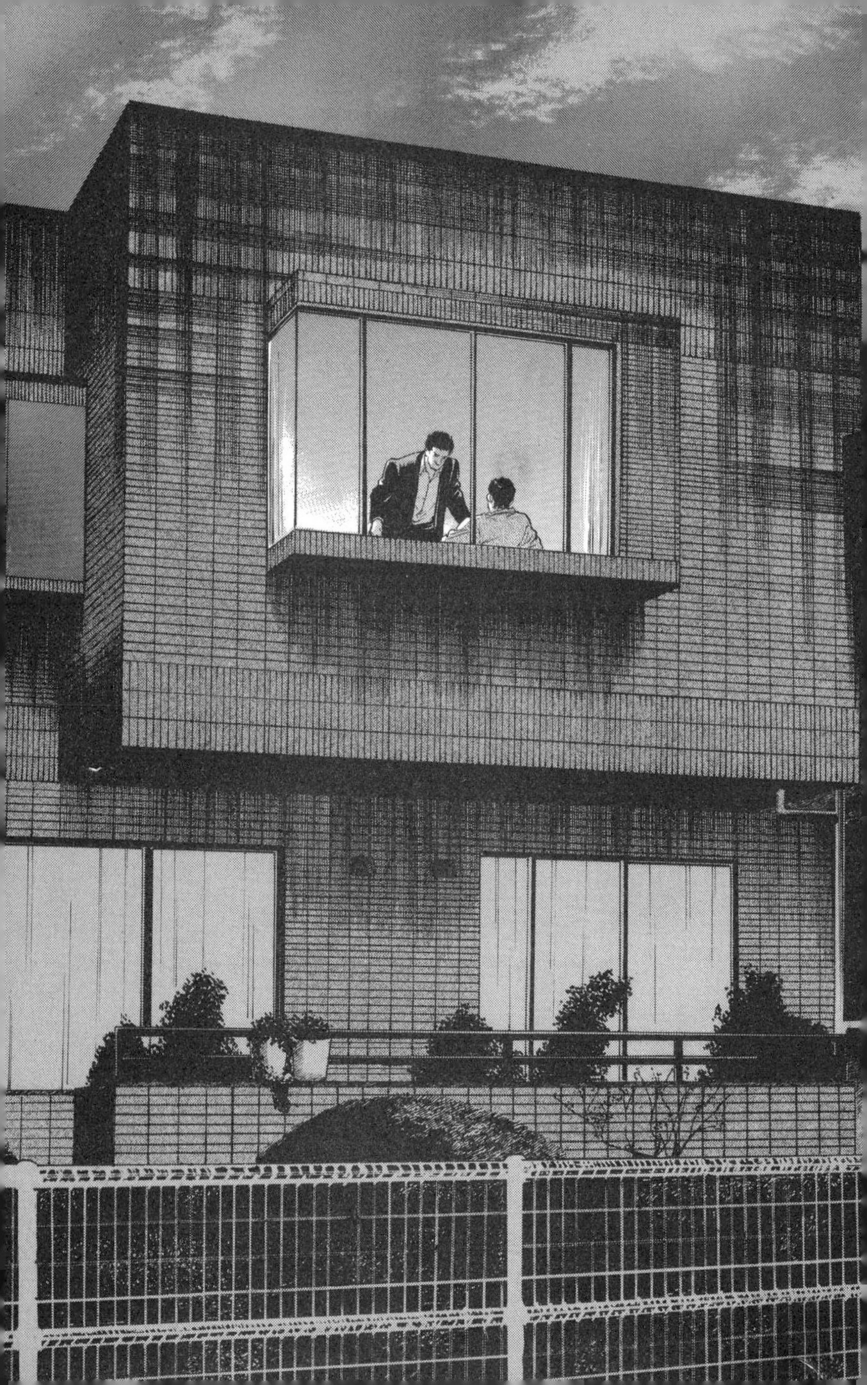

SHE HAS A LOW VOICE, FOR A WOMAN...

...BUT SHE SAID IT WAS AN AFTER-EFFECT OF *SURGERY* ON HER THROAT...

TAKAAKI KAKINUMA, DISGUISED AS AN OLD WOMAN...

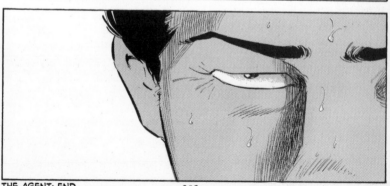

THE AGENT: END

OLDBOY

n years ago, he was abduct-
and confined to a private
ison. He was never told why
was there, or who put him
ere. Suddenly his incarcera-
n has ended, again without
planation. He is sedated,
uffed inside a trunk, and
mped in a park. When he
vakes, he is free to reclaim
nat's left of his life . . . and
nat's left is revenge.

is series is the inspiration
the *Oldboy* film directed
Chan-wook Park, which
is awarded the Grand Jury
ize at the 2004 Cannes
m Festival!

LUME 1:
N-10: 1-59307-568-5
N-13: 978-1-59307-568-2

LUME 2:
N-10: 1-59307-569-3
N-13: 978-1-59307-569-9

LUME 3:
N-10: 1-59307-570-7
N-13: 978-1-59307-570-5

LUME 4:
N-10: 1-59307-703-3
N-13: 978-1-59307-703-7

LUME 5:
N-10: 1-59307-714-9
N-13: 978-1-59307-714-3

LUME 6:
N-10: 1-59307-720-3
N-13: 978-1-59307-720-4
ning in June!

.95 EACH!

AVAILABLE AT YOUR LOCAL COMICS SHOP OR BOOKSTORE!
To find a comics shop in your area, call 1-888-266-4226.

For more information or to order direct visit darkhorse.com or call 1-800-862-0052
Mon.-Fri. 9 A.M. to 5 P.M. Pacific Time. Prices and availability subject to change without notice.

OLD BOY © 1997 by GARON TSUCHIYA & NOBUAKI MINEGISHI. Originally published in Japan in 1997 by
FUTABASHA PUBLISHERS CO., LTD. Tokyo. English translation rights arranged with FUTABASHA PUBLISH-
ERS CO., LTD. Tokyo, through TOHAN CORPORATION, Tokyo. All rights reserved. Dark Horse Manga™ is a
trademark of Dark Horse Comics, Inc. All rights reserved. (BL 7003)

STOP! THIS IS THE BACK OF THE BOOK!

This manga collection is translated into English, but arranged in right-to-left reading format to maintain the artwork's visual orientation as originally drawn and published in Japan. If you've never read comics this way before, take a look at the diagram below to give yourself an idea of how to go about it. Basically, you'll be starting in the upper right-hand corner, and will read each word balloon and panel moving right-to-left. It may take a little getting used to, but you should get the hang of it very quickly. Have fun!

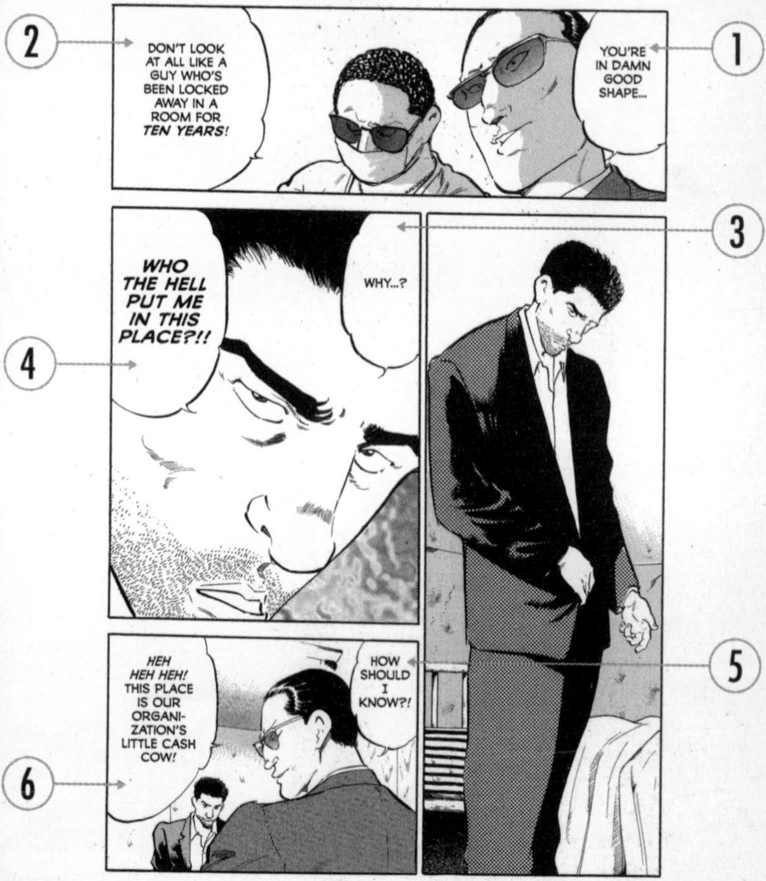
1
YOU'RE IN DAMN GOOD SHAPE...
2
DON'T LOOK AT ALL LIKE A GUY WHO'S BEEN LOCKED AWAY IN A ROOM FOR *TEN YEARS!*
3
WHY...?
4
WHO THE HELL PUT ME IN THIS PLACE?!!
5
HOW SHOULD I KNOW?!
6
HEH HEH HEH! THIS PLACE IS OUR ORGANI-ZATION'S LITTLE CASH COW!